Portraits in the Wild

Portraits in the Wild

Behavior Studies of East African Mammals

Second Edition

CYNTHIA MOSS

The University of Chicago Press

For Lynne, Keith, and Stefan

A portion of this book has appeared in
Smithsonian magazine.
The University of Chicago Press, Chicago 60637
© 1975, 1982 by Cynthia Moss
All rights reserved. Published 1975
Second edition 1982
Printed in the United States of America
00 99 98 97 96 95 94 93 92 91 90   10 9 8 7 6 5

Library of Congress Cataloging in Publication Data
Moss, Cynthia.
  Portraits in the wild.

  Bibliography: p. 336
  Includes index.
  1. Mammals — Behavior. 2. Mammals — Africa, East.
I. Title.
QL739.3.M67   1982   599.05′1   81-23092
ISBN 0-226-54232-7   AACR2
ISBN 0-226-54233-5 (pbk.)

Contents

Acknowledgments   vii

Introduction   ix

I.   The African Elephant   1

II.   The Giraffe   39

III.   The Black Rhinoceros   62

IV.   Zebras   88

V.   Antelopes   127
     The Dikdik   130
     The Gerenuk   142
     The Impala   150
     The Uganda Kob   160
     The Wildebeest   167
     The Eland   181

VI.   Baboons   193

VII.   The Big Cats   231
     The Lion   234
     The Cheetah   262
     The Leopard   284

VIII.   The Spotted Hyena   297

List of Support   331

Picture Credits   333

Bibliography   336

Index   357

Illustrations

Elephants
Giraffes
following page 46

Rhinoceroses
Zebras
following page 110

Antelopes
Baboons
following page 238

Cats
Hyenas
following page 302

Map of East Africa by Hugh Russell
page xii

Acknowledgments

THIS BOOK would simply not exist if it were not for the cooperation and advice of the wildlife scientists who have worked in East Africa. Without exception they have been tremendously helpful in reading chapters, providing pictures, allowing me to use unpublished material, correcting me on errors, and taking the time to talk with me or write to me. I want to thank in particular David Western and Harvey Croze for reading the entire manuscript and checking it for scientific accuracy. Individual chapters were read by the scientists concerned, and I am deeply grateful for their comments: Iain Douglas-Hamilton, Bristol Foster, Carlos Mejia, Hans and Ute Klingel, Walter and Barbara Leuthold, Peter and Mattie Jarman, Richard D. Estes, Patrick Duncan, Christopher Hillman, Stuart and Jeanne Altmann, Glenn Hausfater, Shirley Strum, George Schaller, Judith A. Rudnai, Brian Bertram, Patrick Hamilton, and Hans Kruuk. Any remaining errors are entirely my own.

The following people have generously allowed me to use their photographs: Harvey Croze, Iain and Oria Douglas-Hamilton, Richard D. Estes, Chris Hillman, William Holz, Peter and Mattie Jarman, Peter Jenkins, John King, Marion Kaplan, Hans Klingel, Hans Kruuk, Walter Leuthold, Ronald McLaughlin, L. J. Parker, Mark Stanley Price, Timothy W. Ransom, John Reader, Audrey Ross, Judith A. Rudnai, and David Western.

In particular I would like to thank Hugh Russell for the map of

East Africa, and Gloria and John Seneres for the time and effort they put into helping to choose the photographs and design the layout. I would also like to thank Barbara Leuthold and Nani Croze for their translations of the German scientific papers, Tricia Wright for typing part of the manuscript, and Photofinishers for their careful developing and printing.

Several people have helped in many ways with their encouragement, hospitality, suggestions, and patience: Mariana Gosnell, Sandra Price, Penelope Naylor, Marcia and Saul Gordon, Willa Beattie, Virginia Finch, Martha Moss, and Carolyn and Jan Long.

And finally I want to thank my agent and friend, Wendy Weil.

Introduction

AFRICA'S ANIMALS, particularly its large mammals, have long stimulated the imaginations of the inhabitants of other parts of the world, from the time of Pliny the Elder to the present. They have been put on display in Ancient Rome, described and marveled about in scores of books, captured for zoos, killed for museums, and hunted for food and sport, but oddly enough it was not until about twenty years ago that anyone thought seriously about watching these animals in the wild in order to try to understand their way of life — to see how lions behaved with each other, how so many species of antelopes could coexist, how the elephant made a living, and how they all related to each other and their environment.

By the beginning of this century most of the major African animals had been mounted and displayed in museums and had been more or less classified into orders, families, genera, and species, etc., but then two world wars intervened and temporarily halted scientific work on wildlife in Africa. In the meantime studies of animal behavior, with a few exceptions, concentrated on observing and experimenting with animals in captivity. It was generally agreed that an animal's behavior should be studied under completely controlled conditions.

Then in the 1950s a new interest arose in the conservation of wild areas and wild animals. At the same time the work of a few pioneering zoologists, notably Nobel Prize winners Konrad

Lorenz and Niko Tinbergen, began to influence trends in zoology. Tinbergen's brilliant studies of herring gulls showed that it is only by also observing an animal's way of life in its natural habitat that we can understand its total biology.

Although it was slow in coming, the era of "field studies" began, and scientists took to the woods, fields, and streams to study moles, field mice, robins, salmon, and sticklebacks. But the lure of Africa's big mammals was irresistible. Because of climatic conditions, Africa retained more of the vast numbers and diversity of Pleistocene animals than any other continent, and in East Africa in particular there is still an abundance of wildlife living in a rich natural tapestry. As the well-known ecologist A. Starker Leopold wrote in the introduction to one of the first studies conducted in East Africa: "The fascination of East Africa stems from its biological wealth . . . Nowhere on this earth are so many kinds of life found coexisting in one great ecosystem . . . Thus it is to Africa that the ecologist must go to see the end product of community evolution — the web of life in its most intricate design."

In this book I have brought together the results of some of the important studies carried out on Africa's mammals in the last fifteen years. Some animals, such as the elephant, have been studied by at least thirty scientists; others, such as the hyena, really intensively by only one. Though some wildlife scientists write popular accounts of their work, many do not; often their results appear only in scientific journals and monographs not easily accessible to the layman. I have attempted to synthesize the results of these studies and present a picture of the behavior of fifteen major species in light of the new scientific material. For the most part, I have restricted the descriptions to studies carried out in East Africa, but I have brought in studies in other parts of Africa that seemed particularly relevant or provided unique information.

The systematic scientific observations contradict many of the long-held myths and beliefs about African animals, but they present a new and much more realistic portrayal of the day-to-day existence of these animals. Far from making them seem dull compared to hunters' and explorers' tales, these scientific descriptions actually reveal the animals to be infinitely more complex and fascinating.

CYNTHIA MOSS

Nairobi
February 1975

Seven years after its completion, I have been asked to revise *Portraits in the Wild* for a new edition. After consulting wildlife researchers and reviewing the latest scientific papers, I am happy to find that the fifteen original animal "portraits" remain essentially up to date, with only two exceptions. The African elephant chapter has been revised to include important new data on the sexual behavior of the males, as well as on the elephant's current conservation status, which has changed as a result of the intensive poaching of the 1970s. The black rhinoceros chapter now describes the desperate plight of the rhino whose existence hangs by a thread with fewer than 25,000 remaining in the wild. The revisions also include the results of a recent study on the trade and uses of rhino horn.

The remaining thirteen portraits of East African mammals continue to reflect current knowledge and have not required revisions. Since the original publication, new scientific studies have come to light, and although most contribute details to the total behavioral and ecological picture of each species, none alters the accuracy of the original descriptions. For readers interested in pursuing the latest findings, I have expanded the Bibliography to include 143 additional references, most of which have been published since 1975.

CYNTHIA MOSS

Nairobi
January 1982

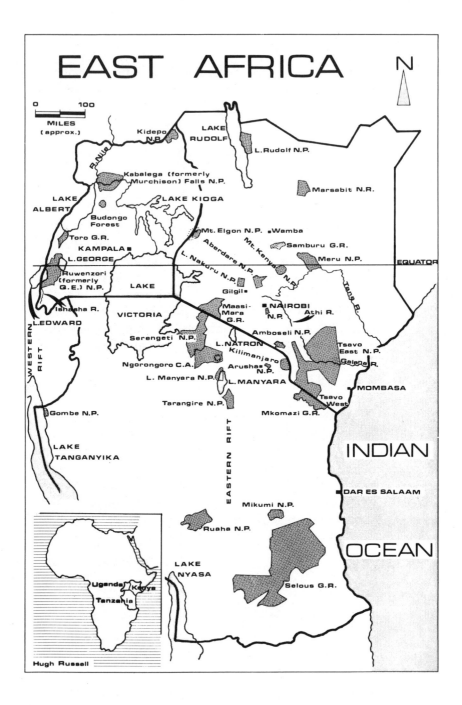

I

The African Elephant

THERE IS a majesty and mystery to the African elephant — that monumental beast that uses its nose as a hand. Its loose, wrinkled skin and huge ears make it an object of mirth in circuses and zoos, and yet the elephant is still loved and respected by people from all over the world. In Africa it is almost a mythical animal. The subject of countless legends, the elephant is said to have superintelligence and almost human feelings for its companions; it is also thought to understand the concept of death as it goes off to die in the elephants' graveyard. Certainly, there is something special about the elephant — not just its size, or its long life, or its ivory; there is something else, perhaps its intelligence, that somehow sets it apart from the other African animals.

Unfortunately, its specialness has not kept the elephant from being hunted and killed for its meat and ivory ever since man became a predator. Man learned where to find the elephant, how to track it, and where to hit it, whether with a poison arrow, or later with the Arab musket, or today with the high-powered, double-barreled rifle. The great elephant hunters have always been considered experts on their prey, but it is doubtful whether many of them ever simply watched a group of undisturbed elephants. With no one to contradict them, the myths multiplied as the hunters told tales of their own bravery in the face of an enraged bull defending his "harem" of elephant cows.

Even the books by the early explorer-naturalists are sadly lacking in accurate observations. The naturalists were busy shooting animals and sending their skeletons and hides back to natural history museums in Europe and America. There were a few exceptions: some of these men did take the time to sit and watch, to try to learn a little about the way of life of the African elephant. But usually the opinions of the more flamboyant hunters prevailed.

It was not until the creation of national parks and reserves in East Africa in the 1940s and 1950s, combined with the growing realization that elephants are capable of radically altering their own environment in a way second only to man, that scientists began to take a more active interest in the wild elephant. In Uganda, in particular, elephants were coming into conflict with man as human population rapidly grew and elephant ranges shrank. The Uganda Game Department began a program of "controlling" elephants, that is, shooting those who raided crops or lived near human settlements. Later, large numbers of elephants were killed in national parks that were considered "overcrowded." [1] The carcasses of these elephants were the subject of some of the first scientific studies of elephants in East Africa. As early as 1946 J. S. Perry was able to study the reproductive physiology of elephants by examining the organs of the dead animals.

In the 1950s and early 1960s more scientists came to Uganda and carried out pioneering work on the numbers, distribution, and movements of elephants; growth, weight, height, and age and their intercorrelations; diet and the interactions between elephants and their habitat; and population dynamics based on reproductive rates, mortality, and other factors, determining whether a given elephant population is increasing, declining, or stable, and what the future trends might be. This research was carried out by A. C. Brooks, I. O. Buss, H. K. Buechner, H. C. Dawkins, R.

[1] There are three terms commonly used for the killing of wild animals in contexts other than hunting or poaching. (Unfortunately, they are interchanged rather freely.) "Controlling" (or "shooting on control") usually means killing animals that are interfering with humans; "culling" is most often used to mean the killing of a certain percent of the population in order to reduce the numbers and/or change the age or sex structure of the population; "cropping" generally implies the systematic killing of animals for the utilization of meat, skins, and trophies.

M. Laws, I. S. C. Parker, S. K. Sikes, N. S. Smith, L. D. Wing, and others, and the results provide a vast amount of material on the biology of the elephant, making it one of the most extensively studied animals in East Africa.

However, a good deal of this work was carried out on dead elephants, and although Buss and later Laws and Parker described the basic social structure of elephants, there were still relatively few observations on elephant behavior. Finally, in 1965, a trained zoologist set out to study systematically the social organization, behavior, and ecology of African elephants; that is, to find out how elephants live naturally in the wild, how they relate and interact with each other and their environment. Iain Douglas-Hamilton, an enthusiastic young Scotsman from Oxford University, arrived in Lake Manyara National Park in Tanzania in December 1965 and began his pioneering 4½-year study of the Manyara elephants.

From general impressions and information attained from the dead animals, Buss and Laws and Parker had concluded that elephants are organized into "family units" of cows and calves, each led by an adult female — the matriarch — and not by a "herd bull" or "sire bull" as is still sometimes claimed. The bulls appeared to live independently of the females in loose, unstable groupings, only associating with the cows and calves from time to time, and particularly when there was a female in estrus. However, their studies had not involved collecting substantial and detailed data on individual elephants and their associations, so no one yet knew how stable these family units were, how they related to other family units, or how they might relate to particular bulls.

Douglas-Hamilton's methods for determining the social organization of elephants are almost as fascinating as his results. There is only one way to get the amount of data necessary to describe social organization and that is to be able to recognize individual animals. Douglas-Hamilton set out to do just that with the Manyara elephants. If he could recognize individual elephants, then he could collect data on each elephant's associations and interactions with other known elephants. From aerial counts he knew that there were approximately 420 elephants in the Park's 33 square miles. He bought a good camera and several lenses, and went about photographing every elephant he could find. This was somewhat hazardous work, as each elephant had to be photographed with its ears spread out, facing the camera. Generally the only time an elephant takes this position is when it is alarmed and about to charge.

There were many charges and many close calls, but gradually the elephants got to know Douglas-Hamilton and his Land-Rover, and they began to tolerate his presence. At the same time he got to know what disturbed them; he learned how to approach them in the Land-Rover without scaring them, simply by driving slowly and approaching them at an angle rather than straight on. By the end of one year many of the elephants in the Park almost ignored him. He could sit in his car with the engine off, surrounded by twenty or thirty elephants, some only a few yards away, who peacefully went on eating, resting, or playing with no apparent concern over his intrusion. This kind of situation was ideal for studying behavior, because he could observe elephants behaving naturally.

The photographs made it possible for Douglas-Hamilton to identify individual elephants. An elephant's ears are not usually smooth along the outer edge but are almost always tattered in a unique way with U-shaped or V-shaped notches, holes or slits, or combinations of them all. The veins in the ears are prominent and also form unique patterns. Each elephant's ears are different and can be used for identification in much the same way as are human fingerprints. A further recognition aid are the tusks: some tusks converge, some cross over each other, some splay out, some curve upward, some are straight; also, some elephants have only one tusk or a broken tusk, and a few have no tusks at all.

The combination of ear patterns, veins, and tusks shown in the photographs was more than enough to guarantee accurate identification. No two elephants are alike. There was never any need to capture and mark elephants by putting bright-colored tags in their ears or painting numbers on them, as some other researchers had tried to do. To Douglas-Hamilton each elephant was an individual, and once known, not easily forgotten.

He devised a filing system for his photographs and carried it with him in the Land-Rover. He could then note down every time he saw an individual, where it was, and what other elephants it was with. At first he coldly and scientifically numbered each elephant, but then he found that numbers were difficult to remember, and so he began naming them. Some were named after friends, others for literary and historical figures, and others for their physical characteristics: Queen Victoria, Oedipus, Clytemnestra, Cyclops, Sarah, Slender Tusks, and Jagged Ears were just a few. By the time Douglas-Hamilton finished his field work in 1970, he knew, and had named or numbered, over four hundred elephants.

As his study progressed, it became apparent that if he saw the large female, Victoria, she would invariably be with her own calves and the same adult females — Mary, Kali Ears, Innominate, Guenevere, and Short Assym Tusks — and their calves. There were twenty-one animals in Victoria's group, and whenever Douglas-Hamilton saw the group he would find the same twenty-one animals. It was the same with other cow/calf groups. If he saw Leonora, she would be with Slender Tusks, Deep Cup, and V-Nick, and their calves. Except for births, deaths, and the departure of the young males, the groups were consistent in composition over the 4½-year study period. Douglas-Hamilton saw only one exception, and that was when a young female, named Phoebe, was separated from her group (probably accidentally) and wandered around alone, or at the edge of other groups, for two months until she was reunited with her own family unit. After fifteen thousand independent observations of known individuals and their associations, Douglas-Hamilton was able to conclude without a doubt that the basic social structure of the Manyara elephants is the stable cow-calf family unit.

The family unit consists of the matriarch or leader (usually the oldest cow), her male and female calves ranging in age from newborn to about twelve to fifteen years old, her mature daughters, and their calves. The unit may also include one or two sisters, or even cousins, of the matriarch and their various offspring. In Manyara the mean size of a family unit is nine to ten members, and the range is from two to twenty-four. A typical family unit might consist of a matriarch with three calves aged nine, five, and one, another female with two calves aged six and two, and a young female, probably the matriarch's daughter, with a calf under a year old.

In the normal course of a day, the members of a family unit act as a coordinated body. While eating, drinking, and moving from place to place, the cows and calves will almost always be within fifty yards of the matriarch, and most of the time much closer than that. If they are in thick bush, they keep in contact with each other by their acute sense of smell and by a strange, rumbling noise with which they call to one another. (For years people called this noise "tummy rumbles," mistaking it for the workings of the elephant's digestive system. Elephants do make quite a bit of noise while digesting vegetation and are certainly not discreet when expelling gas, but the growling contact noise is distinct and has been shown by I. O. Buss to be made in the throat by the vocal cords.) If the group becomes alarmed, the members quickly bunch together and present a united front to the danger, the matriarch usually taking the most prominent position, while the calves squeeze in behind and underneath the big females. Then they all stand with heads up, ears spread out, and trunks up in the air smelling the wind. If the danger warrants it, one cow may charge or the whole group may come — a huge, gray mass of anger, even the littlest calves shaking their heads and trumpeting. It is a formidable sight and a very effective way of seeing off an enemy.

By the end of his study, Douglas-Hamilton had recorded forty-eight separate family units using the Park. In his observations of these groups he discovered a higher level of social organization above the family unit. The data on group associations showed that certain family units were found moving, resting, or feeding with certain other family units significantly more often than with other groups in the Park. Douglas-Hamilton concluded that two or more family units often had a special bond with one another and that the members were probably related; he called this relationship a "kin group." For example, in Manyara, at the time of the study, there was a kin group consisting of three separate family units: Boadicea's group of twenty-four, Jezebel's group of thirteen, and Leonora's group of twelve. Most of the time these three groups would be seen in close association with each other, although each group clearly maintained its own identity. Sometimes Jezebel's group would be seen ten miles from Boadicea's and Leonora's groups. Sometimes all three groups would be separated for a few days, or even a week or more, but this was rare, and they always joined up again. While moving about their range they were usually not more than 100 to 200 yards apart. Statistical analysis showed that the meetings of these three groups were not random but indicated a strongly significant association.

In the course of four and a half years it became evident how these kin groups might come about. There is a hierarchy within each family unit based on age and size, with the largest and oldest females as the highest-ranking and the youngest and smallest females the lowest-ranking adults. This rank order is not clearly seen except at a limited resource, such as a water hole, a mud wallow, or a single fallen branch, but in these cases the bigger females have priority and the smaller females are pushed aside until the larger females finish. In some of the groups, particularly those with the largest matriarchs, subgroups led by younger females sometimes form. While still maintaining a close association with the family unit, the subgroup gradually begins to feed and move at a slight distance from the main group, and eventually over a period of several years the distance increases and the group becomes an independent family unit within the kin group.

In Boadicea's group of twenty-four, which was the largest family unit in the Park, led by a very large female, it was apparent that a young female, named Isabelle, was becoming more and more independent. She had two young calves of her own and a

teenage daughter with a first-year calf. These five animals gradually spent increasingly more time on the periphery of Boadicea's
group and at times were found almost a mile away from her.

Douglas-Hamilton has an interesting theory about the forces at
work in the social organization of elephants. He speculates that
elephants partly evolved the family unit and kin group as an antipredator adaptation in response to the threats of larger carnivores
and early man. In the face of a predator the members of a family
unit immediately act cooperatively as a means of defense, and
what is more, other family units in the area will join the group in
danger and form an even larger defensive unit. However, competition within a family unit tends to promote subgroups, thus spacing elephants out in the normal course of the day. Douglas-
Hamilton suggests that "the young matriarchs, in splitting from
the old, choose distances from the group that reduce the amount of
competition and the likelihood of intolerant attacks from a dominant cow, while not being so far away that they cannot benefit
from the antipredator protection of larger groups. Thus the
young matriarch and her group should be able to get their water,
wallowing and feed without impediment and still be within ear-
shot, i.e., trumpet range of the others, should they run into
trouble."

One might well ask what the males were doing while the females were fighting off scimitar-tooth cats and defending their
calves from the crude weapons of early man. Although the bulls
are often twice the size of the cows, it appears that their presence,
for all their strength, is not necessary in the family unit as a further antipredator defense. In the elephant social system that has
evolved, the bulls live independently of the cows and calves for
much of the time. A bull joins cow-calf groups only if he happens to be feeding near them or there is a cow in estrus, and during the seasonal migrations. Douglas-Hamilton never saw a bull
with the same family unit for more than four consecutive days,
and there were no significant associations between a particular
bull and any cow-calf groups, disproving in Manyara the theory
of the "sire bull." Most often a bull will meet with a family unit,
greet the members, test the females to see if they are in estrus,

and then go his way. If there is a cow in estrus, then he may stay with the group for a few days.

At other times an adult bull spends his days alone or with a few male companions, eating, drinking, bathing, dusting, wallowing, resting, and playing. In fact, within the parks and reserves, where elephants are protected from hunters (and usually from poachers), the adult bull's life appears very pleasant by human standards. Bulls do not have to worry about any of the nonhuman predators, and they are not restricted in their day-to-day movements, as are cows, by the distance the small calves can travel.

The all-bull herds that form are loose and temporary groupings with weak social bonds. In Manyara the mean group size for bulls is 2.1, and very rarely were more than 15 males seen together. The Tsavo area seems to be an exception in this respect, as large groups of bulls are fairly often seen there. R. M. Laws once saw a herd of 35 bulls, and Ian Parker saw a herd of 144 bulls in the Galana area east of Tsavo.

The composition of these bull groups varies from day to day. For example, one day Douglas-Hamilton might see Oedipus, Cyclops, and Titan together; the next day he might find Titan ten miles from there, and Cyclops and Oedipus might be a mile away and joined by two new bulls. There are no indications that bulls form any lasting companionships with each other, although all the bulls in a park the size of Manyara would certainly know one another.

Adult bulls are exceptionally easygoing animals. In the first weeks that Douglas-Hamilton was working in Manyara, he was on the way to an appointment with the warden and came across two bulls seriously fighting. He was impressed with their tremendous power but said to himself, "I'll see this many times while I'm here." He took one picture, watched briefly, and then went on to his meeting. He never saw a serious fight again. He later realized that the lack of aggression among the adult bulls is due to the fact that there is a definite hierarchy among them, which is established in adolescence.

A bull calf stays with his mother's group until he reaches pu-

berty, around twelve to fourteen years, after which he is gradually but forcibly ejected from the family unit by the matriarch
and other adult females, including his own mother. Although
both male and female calves have mock fights, the males become
rougher and more serious in their sparring as they approach puberty. They fight with other calves in the family unit and with
the young males from any nearby family unit. It is possible that
the sparring irritates the adult females, and that is why the young
males are chased away. At first the young bull follows along
behind his group, staying as close as he is allowed. When he gets
too close, one or more adult cows threaten him, and often one
may viciously chase him away, prodding him in the backside with
her tusks, even inflicting wounds. Eventually he leaves the family
unit altogether and joins other bulls.

In the bull groups he meets more young males, and they play
and fight together in order to test each other's strength. By the
time they are adults, each bull knows the strength of the others
and will give way to any who is stronger. Bulls have been killed
in fights, but serious fighting is rare. It may occur over a cow in
estrus but is more likely to be the result of disruption in the elephant population caused by drought or intensive immigration
brought on by human population pressure. When a bull enters a
new area and meets bulls he has never seen before, he may have to
establish his place in the hierarchy. After the 1970–71 drought in
Tsavo (an area which also has considerable immigration of elephants), Simon Trevor, the naturalist and filmmaker, found, in
only a few months, six bulls who had died as a result of fighting.

In undisturbed areas, however, most adult bull interactions are
conducted on a "polite and gentlemanly" basis. This attitude is
clearly seen at water holes, where the hierarchical system comes
into play. If a bull is drinking and a dominant bull approaches
and wants to drink from the same hole, the subordinate bull will
quietly move away and wait for the other to finish. The communication between the two bulls in a situation like this is very
subtle indeed, consisting almost entirely of postural signals. Contrary to most film sequences on elephants, they do not run around

trumpeting all the time; in fact, adults trumpet only when they are highly disturbed or excited. When two elephants are within sight of each other, they communicate their intentions by slight differences in the positions of the head, ears, trunk, and tail, and sometimes by a movement of the feet. For instance, the slight raising of the head and spreading of the ears on the part of a dominant animal is usually enough to turn a subordinate one away; or one animal on meeting another might approach with extended trunk and place it in the other's mouth, which is a common "friendly" greeting ceremony, usually initiated by a subordinate animal.

It has been suggested that elephants are territorial; that is, that the elephants in one area, particularly the bulls, defend that area against the intrusions of strange elephants. Douglas-Hamilton found no evidence for this theory in Manyara. There the groups had definite home ranges — the area in which they moved and lived — but these overlapped extensively or entirely with those of other groups, and there were rarely any signs of aggression between groups and certainly nothing that could be construed as territorial behavior. This was true for both males and females. Most of the cow-calf groups were resident in the park year round; the bulls apparently had larger ranges which took them out of the Park. At times, though, strange bulls who had never been seen in the Park before, and unknown "wild" cow-calf groups would appear in the Park and spend time there before passing on, perhaps still following an age-old migration route. While these strangers were there, there was no display of territoriality on the part of the resident population, and in fact the strangers ate and drank peacefully side by side with the residents. One of the strange cow-calf groups even stayed and became residents of the Park.

There are still many aspects of elephant social organization and behavior that have barely been touched. We know little about leadership, communication, the behavior during migrations, and the massing of large numbers of elephants. It has been suggested that above the kin group there may be yet a higher level of organization that might be considered a "clan." Some social processes

are very slow; others may only be evident after very long-term observations. As an elephant's life span is close to that of a human,
ideally a population of elephants should be studied for the scientist's whole life.

But even if this were possible in a place like Manyara, it is only
one area, and a unique one at that. It has the highest known elephant density in Africa, with fourteen elephants per square mile,
and it seems to be a particularly favorable habitat for elephants in
terms of vegetation and rainfall. Elephants are remarkably adaptable animals — they can live in environments varying from lush
rain forest to near desert — and it is probable that their social behavior differs to some extent from area to area. Aside from a two-
year study of the bulls in Serengeti, carried out by Hubert Hendrichs of the Max-Planck-Institute, the only other long-term study of
the social organization and behavior of elephants in East Africa is the
Amboseli Elephant Research Project started by the author in 1972.

Since 1965, when Douglas-Hamilton began his study, there
have been several excellent studies carried out on other aspects of
elephant biology, concentrating particularly on elephant ecology
and population dynamics in an effort to try to predict the effects
of the interactions between elephants and their environment.
Douglas-Hamilton himself devoted half his study to the problem
of elephant destruction of the *Acacia tortilis* woodlands in Manyara. Harvey Croze carried out a three-year study of the ecology
of the Serengeti elephants with particular emphasis on tree destruction. R. M. Laws moved from Uganda to Tsavo National
Park in Kenya to study population dynamics there and in the adjoining Mkomazi Reserve in Tanzania. Further work on elephant
movements, habitat use, and mortality have been carried out in
Tsavo by Walter Leuthold, J. B. Sale, and Timothy Corfield. Additional elephant ecology studies have been carried out in Uganda by
Robert Malpas and Keith Eltringham, in Ruaha National Park,
Tanzania, by Richard Barnes, in the Tana River area of Kenya by
James Allaway, and in Zambia by John Hanks.

Thus, there seems to be no lack of elephant studies, and yet one
feels that the surface has only been scratched. Still, there is cer-

tainly enough information available now to give a picture of the elephant's way of life, to answer many of the old questions, and to clear up some of the myths. Given the elephant's long life span, it seems best to present this picture within the framework of the elephant's life cycle.

Contrary to popular belief, elephants do not give birth in secret breeding places or only at night. The elephant gives birth wherever she may be when she goes into labor. In 1969 Douglas-Hamilton reported that a calf was born right on the main road just outside the Park in broad daylight. However, this was a rare case; few people have actually witnessed the birth of an elephant, mainly because most cow-calf groups will not let anyone get close enough at such a time. Now that elephants are becoming habituated to cars in the national parks, there are more eyewitness accounts of births.

The baby elephant is born after a gestation period of around 660 days, or nearly 22 months — the longest for any mammal. When a cow is ready to give birth she stays with the family unit, or not far from it. She is usually accompanied by her own calves and sometimes by another female or two. It is not known what the average length of labor is, but it is thought to be relatively short. An African elephant that gave birth in the Basel Zoo was in labor for forty minutes. Ordinarily, the mother remains standing and the calf drops down hind feet first. The fall usually breaks the umbilical cord, but if not, the mother breaks it with her trunk. The cow then frees the calf of any remaining membrane either by eating it or tossing it aside; another cow may help her. The mother may or may not help the calf to its feet. If she does, she gently puts her foot under it and lifts it up, steadying it with her trunk. She then usually assumes the typical mothering attitude, pulling the calf toward her with her trunk and tusks until it is under her chin; there she fondles it and touches it with her trunk. It appears that young calves need the reassurance of being touched as often as possible. David Sheldrick, former warden of Tsavo National Park, and his wife, Daphne, successfully raised several orphaned elephant calves. They discovered that the calves were much "happier" and progressed much faster if someone stayed with them and frequently touched them. Fortunately for them and their staff, one of the female calves, Eleanor, took over the job of "mothering" the younger calves when she became a teenager.

The average weight at birth of an elephant calf is about 260 pounds, and the height is just under 3 feet at the shoulder. Male calves weigh more than female calves. Twin fetuses have been recorded in Africa by Laws, but he estimates the incidence of twinning to be less than 1 percent. Twins were born to a young female in Manyara in 1976, but one died when they were five months old. I recorded the birth of twins in Amboseli in 1980, and both calves, a male and female, have reached their first birthday.

Douglas-Hamilton observed a baby elephant known to be less than a day old (the mother had been seen the day before without a young calf). The calf was pinkish in color, and a coat of sparse hair covered its body. It appeared unable to see and kept in close contact with its mother by constantly reaching out its trunk and feeling and smelling her. Every few minutes it sank to the ground and seemed to want to sleep, but the mother kept gently nudging it to its feet. All this time the rest of the group was moving at a particularly slow pace, occasionally stopping to wait for the mother and calf to catch up. The calf appeared to be looking for its mother's teats but had difficulty finding them. The elephant has two teats behind the front legs, positioned in much the same way as and resembling human breasts. The calf finally found a teat and began to suckle, putting its trunk back over its head and sucking with its mouth. The next morning Douglas-Hamilton found the mother and calf about ¾ of a mile from where he had seen them the night before. The following day they had moved another 7 miles. By the end of the third day the calf was strong enough to keep up with the group, which was then moving at its normal pace.

For the first few months of its life the baby elephant stays very close to its mother, rarely venturing more than 5 yards away, and is in frequent contact with her, either leaning or rubbing against her, suckling, or being touched with her trunk. It is often seen under its mother's stomach and in between her front legs. It seems remarkable that the tiny calves do not get stepped on, as the big females cannot actually see the calves when they are underneath them, but even when the group panics and stampedes, the calves somehow avoid getting crushed. If a calf does get stepped on or hurt in any way, it lets out a tremendous bellow of pain, or perhaps protest.

The young calf is in very little danger from predators, aside from man, because a cow-calf group is a successful defensive unit against any number of lions or hyenas. If a calf is separated from the family unit, which is a rare occurrence but can happen in the confusion of a stampede, then it is bound to be taken by a predator, as it is defenseless on its own.

When it is a few months old, the baby elephant becomes more adventurous and starts wandering away from its mother, usually panicking at the slightest noise or movement and racing back to her, squealing with fright. It is at this age that the calves' individual personalities start to show. Some are placid and stay near their mothers, following behind and not getting into any mischief. Others are aggressive from the beginning, wandering away to play with other calves their own age, or chasing egrets and pelicans, shaking their heads, flapping their ears, and trumpeting. Some will race around, suckling from any available teat. Rather than stay with its own mother, one first-year calf in a well-known Manyara group that Douglas-Hamilton watched carefully preferred to stay with another cow who had a calf around its own age. It went back to its own mother only to take a drink from time to time and then immediately returned to the other cow and calf. Another calf with tremendous energy and spirit would constantly break away from its own family unit to visit other groups. There it would vigorously attack the other calves its own age. When baby elephants play, they back off and face each other and then rush together, knocking their heads, which is the closest they can come, not having tusks, to copying adult elephants. Calves also attempt to simulate the sex act, and this may end with as many as five calves in a heap on the ground.

Elephants are reputed to be extremely attentive mothers. Many people have observed cows helping their calves over rough ground. It is also said that cows will "spank" their calves with their trunks when the calves have misbehaved. There is no doubt that elephant mothers are very protective of their calves and will defend them to the death, but the amount of care that they give to their young has been exaggerated to a certain extent. One gets a picture of the mother elephant constantly watching and fussing over her baby. For the first six months this is more or less true, but after that, the young elephant takes on the responsibility of following its mother. Douglas-Hamilton made some detailed observations on cow-calf bonds and found that for the first six months if the cow and calf are separated by more than about 20 yards, the cow will more often approach the calf than vice versa, but after six months, it will almost always be the calf who returns to the mother.

For much of the day the mother elephant goes about the business of trying to find food for herself, and the calf must just follow along. This involves going over rough and hazardous ground, up and down almost vertical escarpments, into swamps and lakes, and across deep rivers. The calf must learn to swim at a very early age: it gets on the upstream side of its mother or an older calf, keeping as close as possible, and then swims along in a remarkable fashion, alternately submerging and then bobbing back up, looking something like a porpoise.

Nevertheless, the cow-calf bond is extremely strong and the mother will go to her calf's rescue (and to other calves' as well) at any sign of trouble, and she will not abandon her calf under even the most trying circumstances. Timothy Corfield speculates that in the 1970–71 drought in Tsavo many cows died because they would not abandon their weak and dying calves to seek food for themselves, and by the time the calves died, the mothers were irretrievably weakened. In Manyara there is a young female with a badly crippled hind leg, broken when she was a small calf. This animal could not possibly have survived had her mother and other members of her group not made allowances for her, such as avoiding difficult terrain and always waiting for her to catch up. Rennie Bere, Chief Park Warden in Uganda for many years, came across a female actually carrying a dead calf, which he judged by its smell to have been dead for three or four days. He relates, "She placed this gruesome little object on the ground beside her whenever she wanted to feed or drink and did this several times while I was watching; although this made her travel very slowly, the rest of the herd invariably waited for her."

The relationship between a first-year calf and its older brothers and sisters is also close. The older female calves often "mother" the babies, standing over them in a protective way and fondling them with their trunks. They also act as "baby sitters." Douglas-Hamilton once saw a female calf about eight years old standing over a sleeping first-year calf. The other members of the family unit had finished their siesta and had moved on. The young female waited there with the calf and after a while nudged it with her foot. It went on sleeping and she nudged it a few more times to no avail. Finally she gave it a solid kick, which got it quickly to its feet, and they went off together to catch up with the rest of the group.

If the mother of a young calf dies, it is thought that the calf may, under favorable conditions, be adopted by another member of the family unit. No one has authenticated a case of adoption within the family, but Michael Woodford, a veteranarian, and Simon Trevor, the filmmaker, actually witnessed the apparent adoption of a one-week-old calf by a family unit that was not its own. The mother of the calf had been killed outside of the Queen Elizabeth National Park (now Ruwenzori National Park), and the calf was found by Park rangers. As it is almost impossible to hand-raise a calf this young, Trevor suggested trying to introduce it to the first cow-calf group they could find. They found a group with other calves around the same age in it, and Woodford and Trevor took the calf and walked with it toward the group. The calf did not see the other elephants and kept following the men, but they finally got away from it by pushing it head first into a bush, whereupon it got very upset and trumpeted. The wild elephants immediately answered, and it raced to the nearest elephant, unfortunately a bull, who sent it flying through the air with one sweep of his trunk. The calf got up, shook itself, and hurried to the next adult, a big female, who reached out her trunk and gently pulled the calf right to her teat and let it drink. The next day the herd was found again, and the calf was apparently an accepted member of the family unit.

During its first year the calf's diet consists almost entirely of its mother's milk, but it will start eating small bits of vegetation at an early age. It is comical watching a tiny calf try to hold on to one piece of grass with its trunk and then get that piece of grass to its mouth. It may take as long as three minutes. The calf is fairly inept with its trunk for the first few months of its life; it sometimes appears not to know what to do with its trunk at all. Calves have even been seen stepping on their trunks as they walked along. They also suck their trunks, much as human babies suck their thumbs.

Toward the end of its first year the calf will begin to eat food in earnest along with the rest of the group, but it will go on drinking milk for another three or four years at least. The calf will also drink water from an early age, but it cannot suck the water up into its trunk and then blow it into its mouth as adults do; it has to drink with its mouth right in the water. If the group is drinking from a very shallow stream only a few inches deep, then the small calves have to kneel down or even lie down on their sides in the water in order to drink.

The calf will probably grow a foot or more in its first year. Size varies considerably, not only between males and females, but also among members of the same sex. The accepted field method for determining whether or not a calf is still in its first year is to see if it can pass under its mother. If it is too large, then it is into its second year.

For the next several years the calf is involved in the process of growing up. The years between two and twelve are mainly spent learning and developing. Zoologists sometimes argue about which aspects of an animal's behavior are "innate" and which are "learned." It would appear that a good deal of elephant behavior is learned or acquired. The long childhood of the elephant is comparable only to that of man. An elephant calf develops in the company of other elephants of varying ages, and from its interactions with them it learns a whole repertoire of behavior, from greeting gestures to reactions to danger. Very small elephants are rarely afraid of man and vehicles; they tame down immediately when caught and I have frequently had them come up and touch my car. The older calves have learned to be more suspicious.

At the same time the calf must learn how to make a living in its environment. The variety of food an elephant eats is vast, and a young calf must learn which types are palatable and which parts of the plant to eat. The calf watches its mother and other members of its group and follows their example. One often sees a calf taking food from its mother's mouth and then eating it, thus learning what plant she is eating. As the calf is growing up and moving with the group, it also acquires knowledge about its range: where there is water, where the best mud wallows are, where various plants can be found, where to go for shade in the heat of the day. In some areas it learns the seasonal migration routes.

When the calf is about four and a half years old, its mother will probably give birth to a new calf, and then it will no longer be allowed to suckle. If another calf is not born, it may go on suckling until its tusks get too long and the mother will no longer tolerate it. The tusks erupt at about sixteen months, but they do not show externally until about thirty months. The tusks of a five-to-six-year-old calf are about 5 inches long, just long enough to poke the mother's side while the calf is trying to suckle.

R. M. Laws's results on mortality rates show that once a calf reaches the age of six its chances of survival are good. For calves younger than this, the mortality rate differs according to the area. He suggests that where the habitat has been degraded, the mortality rate will be high. In Kabalega (Murchison) Falls National Park South, where woodland has been reduced to open grassland with very few shade trees, the calf mortality up to two to three years of age was estimated at 20 percent in 1945, 24 percent in 1953, and 38 percent in 1965. Laws speculates that heat stress and poor nutrition are responsible for the increase in calf mortality. Lack of shade seems to be an important factor, as calves are prone to heat stroke. Where the habitat allows, the cows take their calves to shady areas during the heat of the day, coming out in the open to eat in the late afternoon, at night, and early in the morning. In Manyara, where conditions are favorable, the mortality for first-year calves is 10 percent and thereafter it is the same as for adults, 3–4 percent.

The young females reach puberty a year or so earlier than the males — in Manyara at about eleven years of age. Douglas-Hamilton noted a definite change in behavior between males and females as they neared puberty. Beginning at around nine years of age the young females tend to take a great interest in the younger calves in the family unit, standing near them, touching them frequently, and generally mothering them. At the same time the young females remain in close association with their own mothers.

The young males, on the other hand, begin to show different behavior. Their play is much rougher and they frequently show sexual behavior, mounting other calves — something female calves are never seen to do. As we have noted, it is probable that the young males' behavior eventually leads to their expulsion from the family unit and the breaking of the mother-calf bond.

Laws's results from the elephants killed in Uganda and Tsavo indicate that the age at which an elephant reaches puberty may also be affected by the habitat in which it lives. Under optimal conditions a female reaches puberty at around eleven years of age. In an overcrowded and/or degraded habitat the age of puberty seems to be delayed. In effect, this acts as a system of birth control, but over a long period of time. For instance, in the Budongo Central Forest Reserve in Uganda, where the average density is 11.5 elephants per square mile, the mean age at puberty for females is twenty years. In the Mkomasi Game Reserve in Tanzania, where there are fewer than 3 elephants per square mile, the age of puberty for females is eleven years.

Douglas-Hamilton, however, would argue with Laws on the point that density is the prime factor in delaying puberty. In Manyara there are at least fourteen elephants per square mile, and the age of puberty is only eleven years. There are apparently other factors, such as adequate food and shade, that are more important in maintaining a healthy population. Density alone, with its suggested social stress, was not shown to have any effect on reducing reproductive rates in Manyara; on the contrary, the frequent interactions between groups in Manyara were not seen to cause any noticeable disturbance to the population as a whole.

Once an elephant reaches puberty it is by no means full-grown. During his study, Laws took measurements of hundreds of carcasses and, correlating these with age, was able to determine the growth rate of elephants. He concluded that elephants keep on growing for at least three quarters of their life span. The growth rate for females slows down after puberty but continues until it levels off in their forties. Laws's figures show that the mean maximum weight for females fifty years old is about 6100 pounds, and the mean maximum height at the shoulder is just under 9 feet. The growth rate for males also slows down after puberty, but then they have a second spurt of rapid growth in their twenties, after which their growth rate slows down again, leveling off in their forties. The mean maximum weight for males at fifty years old is 12,000 pounds, and the mean maximum height is 10½ feet. The heaviest elephant ever weighed was 14,500 pounds, and the tallest recorded was 13 feet 2 inches after mounting.

Although the males may reach puberty at twelve to thirteen years and are physically capable of mating with and fertilizing a female, they are not yet "socially mature" and do not compete with older males for estrous females until they are in their mid-twenties. The young females apparently mate during their first estrous cycles and usually get pregnant immediately; most of the young females in Manyara have their first calves when they are thirteen years old.

The reproductive behavior of male African elephants has been the focus of controversy for a long time. In the Asian elephant it has long been recognized that the male goes through a period each year called "musth" during which the animal becomes markedly aggressive,

secretes a thick substance from his temporal gland (an opening located midway between the eye and ear), and continuously
dribbles urine. Recent studies have shown that musth is a period
of heightened sexual activity similar to rutting in deer during
which testosterone levels in the blood are extremely high. There
has been much speculation on whether musth occurs in the African
elephant.

In Amboseli, Joyce Poole, who has been studying the bulls,
and I have been able to clear up this controversy. Musth definitely
occurs in the African elephant. We first discovered it by noting
the continuous dribbling of urine in the large adult males from
time to time. This dribbling caused the penis and sheath to turn
a greenish color, and at first we thought it was a disease and called
it the "green penis disease," or "GP." We also noticed that GP
was accompanied by secretions from the temporal glands and a
definite increase in aggressive behavior towards other bulls and
sometimes most disconcertingly towards us. Only bulls over thirty
come into musth and only for two to three months each year.
Interestingly, they do not all come into musth at once, but musth
periods are spread throughout the year. Bulls who are not in musth
and younger bulls who have not yet started to come into musth also
mate with females, but musth bulls are apparently preferred by
females in estrus.

One of the reasons that musth was overlooked in the African
elephant for so long is the fact that only Asian males secrete from
the temporal glands only during musth, whereas males, females, and
juvenile African elephants secrete frequently. This short-term secretion of "temporin" remains something of a mystery. Douglas-
Hamilton speculates that temporin may aid in individual recognition
among members of families and kin groups.

The female African elephant comes into season with a regular
estrous cycle. In Amboseli, I found that estrus lasts about four days
during which the female will usually mate with several bulls, but
in the middle of the cycle she is likely to go into consort with
the most dominant male in attendance. In most cases this bull will
be in musth.

There does not seem to be any definite mating season, although there are indications that there is a higher conception rate during the rainy season. Certain years show higher conception rates than others, probably due to nutritional factors. In Kabalega Falls, Laws and Parker found that three times as many cows conceived in 1963–64 as did in 1964–65.

Some of the more incredible stories told about elephants are concerned with mating behavior. Perhaps the most fantastic tale was described to "Elephant Bill" in John Williams' well-known book about Asian elephants: "The female elephant turns to thoughts of love in the spring-time, and prepares for her honeymoon by digging a deep pit, round which she stacks a month's supply of fruit and fodder for herself and her young bridegroom. When she has completed these preparations she lies down in the nuptial pit and trumpets a love-call to her mate. After his arrival they live in one unending embrace for the whole month, and do not separate until they have shared their last pineapple or banana!" Williams dismisses this story, but his own account of elephant mating behavior is just as unbelievable. He claims that elephants become attracted to each other and fall in love. Weeks of courtship may take place and then the elephants go off to the forest, where they stay together for ten months making love. This belief in the elephant honeymoon has extended to Africa as well. Elephants appear to be very affectionate — they often stand facing each other with trunks entwined — and this has probably led people to romanticize.

When the female comes into estrus, she does not go off with a male but remains with her family unit. Bulls may be attracted to the female by picking up a particular odor in the urine, but usually when a bull is in the vicinity of a cow-calf group he will test the females anyway. When a bull approaches a family unit, he goes up to each of the females, reaches down between her hind legs with his trunk, and gently touches her vulva. He then puts his trunk tip in his mouth, presumably testing the taste and smell for hormone content.

It is not at all common to see elephants mating, but it is not

nearly as rare as seeing a birth. There are a number of good scientific eyewitness accounts of mating. Behavior seems to vary —
sometimes there is courtship and sometimes there are no preliminaries at all. I. O. Buss and N. S. Smith came to the conclusion
that "cows have multiple mates, there is no prolonged male-female
relationship, and frequently there is no fighting by bulls over
females."

Buss and Smith observed elephants copulating on eleven different occasions. On one occasion they saw a cow with four
bulls. One of the bulls was slightly larger than the others and apparently dominant, and he remained with the cow, occasionally
chasing away one of the subordinate bulls. At one point, when
the dominant bull tried to mount the female, one of the subordinate bulls rolled on the ground. When the dominant bull did
succeed in mounting her, he held his trunk and tusks lengthwise
on her back. No form of courtship behavior was observed during
the two hours the group was watched. On another occasion when
Buss and Smith watched a female and a bull copulating, not only
was there no courtship behavior, but during intercourse, which
lasted one minute, the cow continued to feed. On a third occasion they saw two adult males and one adult female all fighting.
The bulls appeared to be equal in size, but one bull seemed dominant. The cow occasionally butted one bull or the other. At one
point, while the bulls were fighting, the cow approached them
and the dominant bull mounted her but was promply "unseated"
by the other bull. The bulls then fought again and the subordinate bull was driven away. The remaining bull and the female
faced each other, butting heads and entwining trunks. After a
short time the bull successfully mounted her.

Once a cow reaches maturity and produces her first calf, she is
capable of producing a calf every three or four years (under the
best of circumstances) for nearly the rest of her life. After the age
of thirteen, unless she loses her first calf, she will almost surely be
accompanied by at least one offspring until she dies. Most cows
are followed by two or three calves, and older cows are still accompanied by their mature daughters as well. Usually when the
cow's youngest calf is about two years old, she will come into

estrus again and become pregnant. At this time she will still be suckling her two-year-old calf and she will continue to do so while she is pregnant; thus a cow is generally lactating continuously during her reproductive years. However, this is only the case in a healthy population. Laws found that the calving interval — that is, the time between the birth of one calf and the birth of the next — is lengthened in certain areas, and he speculates that this is due again to high density and poor nutrition. The shortest recorded calving interval is two and three-quarter years, which means that the cow came into estrus only ten to eleven months after the birth of her calf. The maximum individual calving interval may be as much as thirteen years, which means that the cow does not come into estrus until eleven years after the birth of her calf. Thus, if a female does not reach puberty until she is twenty years old and her calving interval is thirteen years, she is only going to produce three or four calves in her lifetime. On the other hand, if a female reaches puberty at eleven and has a calf every three or four years, then she could possibly have fifteen calves in her lifetime.

Some scientists have concluded that a cow can go on having calves for the rest of her life; that is, until she is around sixty-five years old. Perry examined the carcass of one very old female and found milk in her teats. Although she was not pregnant, nothing in her reproductive tract suggested that she could not have become pregnant. However, Laws has reason to believe that females experience menopause at around fifty-five years of age. The females that have stopped breeding constitute the "grandmother class" and are often matriarchs of family units. With their accumulated experience, they undoubtedly provide important leadership for the group, and in times of drought and danger their knowledge may be a key to survival.

As there were very few males over the age of fifty in Laws's samples, it is difficult to determine whether or not old males are sexually active. With his larger size and bigger tusks, an old male would almost certainly be dominant over the younger ones in the area and probably would not be challenged if he wanted to mate with a female. However, there are some indications that older males might retire from the competition. Ahmed, the famous old bull of Marsabit Mountain, only rarely associated with females in the last years of his life.

On a day-to-day basis, however, sexual activities do not take up very much of an elephant's time; of more immediate importance are the activities that go into making a living. Elephants have a daily rhythm that varies little from day to day, and usually only slightly from season to season. Differences do occur according to habitat: for instance, elephants living in a high-altitude forest will not follow the same daily pattern as those living in lowland savannah.

The best way to follow elephants' seasonal movements and daily activity patterns is by radio-tracking, a method introduced relatively recently in East Africa. Wildlife scientists in North America have been following radio-collared grizzly bears, wolves, and many other animals for several years now and have helped to perfect the technique. The introduction to East Africa of a highly potent drug called M99 (it is ten thousand times stronger than morphine) made it possible to immobilize full-grown elephants. The drug is shot into the elephant by means of an ingenious dart syringe, which is fired from a special gun and on impact releases the drug into the animal. Within fifteen minutes the elephant is usually down and the scientist can fit a strong collar, made of machine belting, around its neck. Attached to the collar is a radio transmitter and aerial. An antidote is then injected into a vein in the ear and within a few minutes the elephant gets up and walks away.

Douglas-Hamilton immobilized and put a radio collar on an immature male member of Boadicea's large family unit, and by following the one elephant, he was able to follow the whole group. The radio collar sends out beeping noises that can be picked up by a receiver and directional aerial attached to a vehicle or to a light airplane. Every morning Douglas-Hamilton could fly over the Park, pick up the elephant, who was called Radio Robert, on the receiver, spot him, return to the airstrip, and go to the elephant in his Land-Rover. Radio Robert and the whole group were followed in this way every day for four months.

He found that the elephants in Boadicea's group rarely left the Park and that they followed the same routes within their range, spending a few days in one area and then moving on to another, gradually circling around. Some days they would move 20 miles, other days only 5.

From Douglas-Hamilton's data and the observations of other scientists and naturalists, it is possible to give a general outline of the day in the life of elephants living in typical African bush country. Their day starts sometime in the early hours of the morning, probably around three or four o'clock, when the herd begins feeding after their night's sleep. At daybreak they will slowly start moving toward a shady area, feeding as they move and stopping to drink along the way. If there is a forest or thick riverine vegetation in the area, they will head for that and spend the hottest hours of the day in the shade, resting, dusting, and eating small amounts from time to time. In the late afternoon the herd will return to open country and eat until around midnight, when they will go to sleep for a few hours.

The most time-consuming and ultimately most important daily activity of the elephant is eating. As the elephant digests only 40 percent of what it eats, it needs to consume a tremendous amount of food to keep it going. Each day an adult elephant must eat approximately 300 pounds of food and may drink as much as 30 to 50 gallons of water. It is estimated that the elephant spends sixteen hours out of the day eating — no wonder it is said that the elephant's life is virtually one long meal.

One might think that the elephant would indiscriminately stuff down anything and everything in reach, but the elephant is a selective feeder and its diet is extremely varied, including such exotic foods as desert dates, wild celery, black plums, wild ginger, the Shea butternut, wild olives and figs, wild coffee berries, and wild raspberries. There are some foods that elephants will not eat at all and others that they will eat only during certain times of the year or at certain growth stages.

Out of 650 species of plants in Manyara, the elephants eat at least 134. One day's diet of a tame elephant at Tsavo consisted of 64 species from 28 botanical families. Among the foods commonly eaten are herbs, creepers, leaves, twigs, bark, roots, reeds, flowers, and fruits, but the greatest proportion of the diet consists of grass.

I. O. Buss did a study of the food habits of elephants by examining the stomach contents of seventy-one elephants shot on control in Uganda. He discovered that grass made up 88 percent of the total contents of the stomachs. Even in Manyara, where there is an abundance of woody vegetation, or browse, the elephants' diet still contained a high proportion of grass.

It has long been thought that elephants become intoxicated by feeding on the fermented fruits of various trees. In Kruger National Park in South Africa elephants eat the fruits of the marula tree, which are said to ferment in their stomachs, making them drunk. In Tsavo National Park they supposedly eat doom palm fruits with the same effect. There are accounts of elephants staggering around and acting in drunken manner, but so far there are no scientific data to substantiate the theory.

When there is water readily available, elephants drink at least once a day; but they go without water for several days if they have access to plants with a high moisture content, such as sansevieria. They chew this plant, swallow the moisture, and then spit out the fiber. However, they could not live very long on the water content from these plants alone.

In many African rivers the water ceases to flow above the ground during the dry season but remains flowing under the sand. When this happens, the elephants dig down in the sand, making very neat holes, and then wait for the water to seep in and the sand to settle. They show great patience in waiting for the water to clear; in the dry season they have probably come many miles to drink and are undoubtedly very thirsty when they arrive. Sometimes the calves try to drink before the sand settles, but the cows force them to wait also. Finally they all drink in order of seniority. When the elephants are finished, other animals drink from the holes. The presence of elephants can sometimes mean the difference between life and death to the animals that are not capable of digging holes themselves.

Elephants bathe in fresh water or mud at least once a day if they can. Bathing can consist of simply spraying water or mud over their bodies or actually lying right down and submerging themselves. The mud or water cools the elephants and may help protect them from parasites such as ticks. Elephants appear to enjoy mud-wallowing more than anything else they do. Often the whole family unit will get down in the mud; even the usually regal females completely abandon themselves in obvious delight. They lie down first on one side, then on the other; even their ears, eyes, and tusks get covered with mud. The calves frolic and play, butting and stepping on each other. Once the wallowing is over, each elephant finds a convenient tree (if there is only one tree, they line up and take turns) and scratches all the places where ticks lodge. The mud that remains on the body also helps to protect the skin from the sun.

Elephants then usually take dust into their trunks and blow it over themselves—the dust acts as a sun reflector and as an abrasive to help dislodge ticks. Dusting, which is done frequently during the day, makes the elephant take on the color of the earth in that area. The elephants in Tsavo are not actually red as some people believe. It is simply that the soil in Tsavo is deep red in color.

Resting occurs during the hottest hours of the day. The herd will find a convenient tree, and one by one all the members will congregate there and settle down. Soon their eyes will partially close and their ears will flap slowly and rhythmically. The youngest babies, and sometimes calves up to eight or ten years old, will lie down to sleep. Adult females rarely, if ever, lie down in the daytime, but there have been reports of adult males lying down during the day. The cows remain standing and appear to be sleeping lightly, with their trunks hanging down limply. A dozing elephant often drapes its trunk over one tusk — they seem to avoid letting their trunks touch the ground, probably because of snakes and ants. They have even been seen to rest with their trunks lying in the crooks of trees.

The siesta usually lasts no more than forty minutes, and then the herd moves on, perhaps eating a little and dusting and then stopping at another tree to rest some more. If it is a hot, sunny day, they will rest off and on in this way until late afternoon, when they come out into the open and begin feeding vigorously.

An adult elephant probably sleeps only three to five hours out of every twenty-four. As far as can be ascertained, deep sleep occurs after midnight. Douglas-Hamilton radio-tracked another young bull and his companions throughout a day and night. They ate until around midnight and then went to sleep. He could not see whether or not they were lying down, but he could clearly hear them snoring!

Professor Hediger of the Zurich Zoo studied the sleep patterns of elephants in zoos, circuses, and in the elephant training station in the Belgian Congo (now Zaïre). He could not catch the zoo elephants lying down, because they always got up when they heard him approach, but he found that the circus and Congo elephants lay down for an average of two hours every night after midnight. He claims that the circus elephants made pillows for their heads from straw and that the Congo elephants used pillows of grass, papyrus, and branches. So far there is no evidence that this occurs in the wild, but elephants have been seen resting their heads on the slopes of anthills.

In some parts of East Africa the area an elephant population uses may change fairly drastically from one season to the next. In Manyara the elephants would probably move farther afield than they do, but now their range has been reduced by human population encroachment. In fact, Douglas-Hamilton estimates that the range of the Manyara elephants has decreased by 75 percent in less than fifty years. The largest home range for a group in Manyara is only 20 square miles and the smallest is 5½. In most other parks in East Africa the ranges of elephant groups are much larger, and the movements within these ranges depend on the season.

During the dry season elephants tend to stay near permanent water, usually foraging within a 30-mile radius of the water source, but in the wet season, with temporary water holes well distributed throughout their range, elephants can move over a larger area and usually abandon their dry-season range altogether. For instance, in the dry season in Amboseli, the elephants concentrate around the permanent swamps in the Park, which are fed by underground streams from Kilimanjaro, but almost immediately after the rains begin they move out of the Park into the surrounding bushland, following well-worn migration routes. In Tsavo, where John Sale and Walter Leuthold radio-tracked elephants, the movements after the rains begin are sometimes spectacular. One female in Tsavo East was seen in her dry-season range on November 3 and on November 11 was found 50 miles away in an area that had recently received heavy rain. The mean home range size for the radio-tracked elephants in Tsavo East is 609 square miles.

Where they are not excessively harassed by man, elephants follow the same daily patterns and seasonal movements throughout their lifetimes, and if they are fortunate they may live out their natural life spans.

In 1938 an article appeared in an Australian newspaper stating that Alice, the famous African elephant who had lived in the London Zoo in the nineteenth century, was alive and living in Australia at the age of 149. A picture of "Alice" that accompanied the article unmistakably showed an Asian elephant! This is only one of the many tales told of elephants living to phenomenal ages. It is generally accepted that the maximum age for elephants living in captivity or in the wild is around seventy years.

Old females stay with their family units until they die (although Laws "collected" six old females — average age, fifty-five — who were on their own but were obviously sick or senile). Elephants are subject to very few diseases, and the main cause of death among old females is the loss of grinding area in their final set of molars. The elephant grows six sets of molars during its lifetime, each comprising four teeth, one on each side of the upper and lower jaws. There are never more than two sets of molars in use at any one time. Each subsequent tooth is larger and grows forward, pushing out the previous tooth. The sixth molar appears at thirty years of age and the fifth molar is finally pushed out at around forty to forty-five years of age. When the sixth set of molars is worn down or falls out, the elephant weakens from malnutrition, because it can no longer chew properly, and then usually dies of infection or disease.

Bulls would also die in this way if they had a chance to grow old, but they are mercilessly hunted for their tusks, and now there are thought to be very few bulls over the age of fifty. Until recently it was believed that big tusks are caused solely by genetic factors. Laws showed that the tusks in both male and female elephants grow throughout their lifetime and that the older the animal is, the larger its tusks. Furthermore, he found that as the male elephant grows older, his tusks grow faster. He suggests that exceptionally large tusks (the record pair of bull tusks is 226 and 214 pounds, a combined weight of 440 pounds) are due to a combination of unusually rapid growth and extreme longevity. In the last decade of the natural life span of a bull, the potential annual production of ivory exceeds 6 pounds per year.

The females' tusks appear to stop growing after around thirty years of age. Actually the tusks keep growing, but breakage and wear keep them at about the same length. The record female tusks weigh only 56 pounds each.

If a bull is lucky or smart enough to escape the hunters, he might settle down to live his last years in one of the national parks, and there is no doubt that elephants know they are safe in parks and are aware of the boundaries. One hunter was tracking a big bull, with tusks each weighing over 100 pounds, in northern Tanzania. When the bull realized he was being followed, he started walking rapidly to the northeast. The hunter followed him for the rest of that day, picked up his tracks the next morning, and followed him all the rest of that day and into the next, when the hunter was stopped short at the border of Tsavo National Park in Kenya. The bull had walked over 100 miles in an almost straight line to safety.

The old bulls usually stay near water, preferably in swampy areas, where the food is easier to chew. An old male is often accompanied by one or two younger bulls, who are said to act as his guards, but studies of bull groups have shown that the companions of a given bull may change from day to day, and there is little evidence to suggest that there is any planned protection of the older bull. However, there are many well-authenticated accounts of bulls aiding wounded companions. Two bulls have been seen to get on either side of the wounded animal and between them lift and carry him off. If one bull in the group is killed, the other bulls often refuse to leave the body and will even threaten and charge the hunter. Such incidents have given rise to the belief that old bulls have "loyal retainers."

Many uncanny tales are told concerning elephants and death that even scientists cannot explain. Elephants often bury the dead, including dead elephants, other dead animals they find, and even dead humans they have killed. They cover the bodies with earth and vegetation. A group of scientists and parks officials working on a cropping scheme in Uganda collected the ears and feet of the dead elephants to sell later for making handbags and umbrella stands, and put them in a shed. One night a group of elephants broke into the shed and buried the ears and feet. The people involved still feel uncomfortable about the incident.

Another strange and unexplained thing that elephants do is to fondle and examine the bones and tusks of a dead elephant. They often carry bones and tusks away, sometimes a mile or more from the rest of the carcass. This happens frequently in Tsavo, where there is heavy poaching by tribesmen using poison arrows. The elephants are shot and left to die; the hunters come back a few days later to pull the tusks from the already rotting carcasses. It has seriously been considered that the elephants know their companions are being killed for their tusks and that they carry the tusks away to hide them. What is more, tusks have been found smashed against rocks.

The myth of the elephant graveyard has survived right up to the present. It probably arose when large numbers of elephant skeletons (but not ivory) were found in certain areas. This is one phenomenon that can be explained. Certain African tribes hunted elephants by building a ring of fire around a group or several groups of elephants. Once the elephants were trapped, the hunters could kill them with spears or let them burn or suffocate to death. In 1921, two hundred elephants were killed in a ring fire in South Africa. Also, as was mentioned, old elephants tend to stay near water and soft vegetation and often die in these areas, and thus many skeletons are found near rivers and swamps.

It has been claimed that elephants who die natural deaths are never found, and therefore they must go off to some secret place to die. This is not true. Dead elephants are found in the national parks all the time. In Rennie Bere's last year as Chief Park Warden in Uganda he found 188 carcasses of elephants who had died of natural causes. After the 1970–71 drought in Tsavo nearly 3000 carcasses (out of an estimated 6000 mortalities) were found after a thorough search. The reason that many carcasses are not usually found is that they disappear very rapidly once the hyenas, lions, vultures, and ants get to them. The bones soon disintegrate and the tusks sink into the ground after a few rainstorms.

Elephants may be aware of death, but they definitely do not go away to die. Harvey Croze once witnessed the death of a matriarch. He came across an old cow who was obviously sick: her head fell forward, she swayed back and forth, and then fell to the ground. The rest of the group quickly gathered around her, trumpeting and rumbling. One young bull tried repeatedly to lift her by putting his tusks under her and straining with all his might. When he could not do that, he tried stuffing vegetation in her mouth, and finally tried sexually mounting her. According to Croze, the bull went through his whole behavior repertoire trying to arouse her. The others stood around, obviously disturbed, touching her and caressing her with their trunks. One calf got down and tried to suckle. Eventually the group started moving away, until only one female and her calf were left with the dead matriarch. The cow did not face the dead animal, but stood and reached back from time to time and touched the carcass with one hind foot. Finally, as the other elephants called, very slowly and apparently reluctantly, she left the dead animal and began walking up the hill to join the others.

This cow died a "natural" death in the relative security of Serengeti National Park. However, the existence of national parks does not necessarily assure the future of elephants. Recent events have shown that the animals within national parks are vulnerable in countries where, for a variety of reasons, poaching is uncontrollable. And even in those countries where strict law enforcement is maintained, elephants face the equally difficult problem of overcrowded protected areas.

While the overall number of elephants in Africa declined over the past fifty years because of both human encroachment and poaching, the number and density in some national parks and reserves increased through immigration and compression. For example, in Uganda, A. C. Brooks and I. O. Buss showed that in 1929 elephants occupied approximately 70 percent of all the land in that country; in 1959 they occupied only 17 percent of the land. The human population rose from 3.5 to 5.5 million in that same period and is continuing to rise steadily. With this human increase elephants were compressed into parks and reserves, and in many of these areas they had a marked effect on the woody vegetation, killing mature trees by either stripping off the bark or pushing them over to get at the foliage that is normally out of reach. Elephants (with the important aid of fire, which kills young trees that would normally replace the older ones) converted vast areas from woodland to open grassland, the prime examples being Kabalega (Murchison) Falls National Park in Uganda and Tsavo (East) National Park in Kenya.

It is speculated that elephants have always killed trees and have always changed areas from one vegetation type to another in a natural succession or cycle of which they are only an agent. It was thought that once an area became unfavorable to elephants they moved on, but now that elephants are being restricted to certain areas they can no longer move out, and their effect on the habitats to which they are confined is devastating. Even this theory is not agreed upon by everyone. It is possible that before man's recent heavy intervention an elephant population stayed in one area, killed trees, and declined in numbers (through natural regulatory processes triggered by the degraded habitat) until the vegetation recovered, woodland returned, and elephant numbers increased again, the whole process taking place over a very long period, probably at least a century.

Whatever happened in the past, the problem today revolves around the question of whether to allow these long-term cycles to occur in national parks and reserves. Left to their own devices, elephants would probably come into equilibrium with their environment, but at what cost? In the short term, if woodland is allowed to become grassland, the area will certainly lose some diversity in both plant and animal life; and in many cases the aesthetic appeal will also be reduced, an important consideration for tourism. On the other hand, if the parks decide to step in and cull elephants, there is the danger of freezing the environment in one particular stage of a cycle. Further, the idea of killing large numbers of elephants is abhorrent to most people and seems to go against the purpose of a national park, which is to maintain an environment in as natural a state as possible. The problem is complicated by the fact that we do not yet know what is "natural" and we are only beginning to understand short-term cycles, much less long-term ones. Scientists are trying to provide answers to help parks administrators make decisions, but the problems are very complex indeed, and it is no wonder that definite policies have not yet been set down in most cases.

However, scientists have been able to make suggestions for some areas. For instance, in Manyara the elephants are gradually destroying the *Acacia tortilis* woodlands by stripping the bark from the trees. There is some regeneration, but not enough to compensate for the dead trees. At the completion of his study, Douglas-Hamilton did not altogether rule out culling in order to reduce the elephant population but suggested instead that the Park be enlarged to the south where there were then foreign-owned farms and to the southwest to include the Marang Forest on the escarpment above the Park. Both these areas were part of the former range of the Manyara elephants. Today the Park has already been extended to the south and the inclusion of the Marang Forest is in the final stage of negotiations. These changes in the Park boundaries should greatly relieve the pressure on the *Acacia tortilis* woodlands.

In Serengeti National Park, where there are relatively few elephants, groups of bulls move into the Seronera area every dry season and push down the yellow-barked *Acacia xanthophloea* trees along the river. As this is the prime tourist viewing area in the Park, the bulls are looked on with disfavor. Although Harvey Croze's three-year study on the Serengeti elephants has shown that there are enough younger trees coming up to replace the mature ones being killed, there still remains the aesthetic consideration. In this case the Park's administrators have come to a definite decision: the current presence of trees is more important than the presence of elephants, and they have taken measures to keep the bulls out of the area — chasing them, using thunder flashes, even killing some.

Tsavo National Park in Kenya has been the focus of much heated debate about the problem of elephant destruction. In the Tsavo ecosystem of approximately 17,000 square miles, compression and immigration had brought the numbers of elephants up to over forty thousand, a high density for a semiarid area. By 1970 the elephants had turned vast areas of woodland into open grassland. Culling had been recommended, but the Park's authorities decided on a policy of noninterference. There were dire predictions that Tsavo would turn into a desert, but today Tsavo is covered in grasses and regenerating trees. Both natural and man-made events had intervened. In 1970–71 there was a severe drought in Tsavo, and approximately six thousand elephants died during that period. Then poaching intensified in the mid-seventies, and in the space of a few years the whole population was reduced to an estimated ten thousand elephants, and thus the pressure on the habitat has been greatly reduced.

It may seem ironic that conservationists who are greatly disturbed by the changes in habitat they are witnessing because of "too many" elephants should be equally worried about the present high rate of poaching of elephants for ivory. Unfortunately, uncontrolled and illegal hunting of elephants is not the answer to overcrowding in the parks and in fact only aggravates the problem in most areas. Although there is considerable poaching in the parks, most of it takes place outside, and the result is only to drive more elephants into the protected areas.

The rate of elephant poaching has increased alarmingly in the last decade as the price of ivory leapt from about $3 per pound in the sixties to an all-time high of over $50 per pound in the mid-seventies. In Kenya alone ivory exports rose by 86 percent from 1970 to 1971. Kenya's elephant population of 170,000 was rapidly reduced to 65,000 in a few years. This bleak picture was similar in almost all the other African countries. In 1976 Iain Douglas-Hamilton was commissioned by the IUCN to do a three-year study to assess the status and future prospects of the African elephant. He estimated that there were 1.3 million elephants in Africa, and while the elephant was not in immediate danger of extinction, individual populations were, for example, those in Kabalega Falls (South) in Uganda, where 8000 elephants have been reduced to a tightly clumped, terrified herd of 160.

However, international pressure and the signing of the Convention on International Trade in Endangered Species of Wild Fauna and Flora (CITES) by many of the ivory dealing countries have gone a long way to alleviate the situation. Nevertheless, as a result of poaching and rapidly expanding human populations, it is more than likely that there will be no elephants left outside national parks and reserves in the near future. Therefore, the future of elephants must lie in the protected areas. First and foremost, poaching and illegal ivory trading must be stopped, and secondly, studies must be continued on elephants and their interactions with their environment.

Admittedly, there is a lot of work involved and good deal of money will have to be spent, but elephants are indeed very special animals and they are worth saving. It would be a great loss if such an intelligent, complex, and splendid creature became extinct or had to be relegated to zoos. In the seventeenth century, the poet John Donne described the species as:

> Natures great master-peece, an Elephant
> The onely harmlesse great thing . . .

Whether man and these great things can live together is still open to question.

II

The Giraffe

AN IMMENSE, STRANGE, AND WONDERFUL CREATURE arrived in Paris in 1827, causing an unprecedented reaction in that sophisticated city. Ten thousand people flocked to gaze in awe at the animal called Camelopardalis by the Greeks, who thought it was a cross between a camel and a leopard. This marvelous beast was not a hoax or a side-show freak, but simply a young female giraffe. Since all but a few explorers in Paris had never seen a giraffe before, no wonder the graceful, long-necked creature was received with such enthusiasm.

The tallest animal in the world had stirred the imagination of man from the earliest times. It was painted on rocks by the bushmen, immortalized on tomb walls by ancient Egyptians, and paraded by the Romans. For the Arabs it played an important role in maintaining stability in Middle Eastern politics. The rarity, gentleness, and beauty of the giraffe made it a perfect gift as a token of goodwill and peace. Arab potentates had young giraffes captured in the Sudan and Ethiopia, and then sent them as symbols of friendship to other Arab rulers and to kings and emperors in Europe, India, and as far as China.

When the first giraffe reached the Emperor's court in China in 1414, it was believed to be a mythical Confucian beast called the Kilin and was met with unparalleled excitement. For a time the giraffe was practically deified, representing to the Chinese the emblem of Perfect Virtue, Perfect Government, and Perfect Harmony.

Europeans were not convinced that the giraffe even existed until the eighteenth century, when explorers' reports reached Europe from South Africa. Then in 1826 the Pasha of Egypt, continuing the Arab tradition, presented the King of France with a giraffe (which was to reach Paris the next year) and sent another to the Emperor of Austria and a third to the King of England. With the arrival and display of these three animals in Europe, the existence of the giraffe was no longer in doubt.

Scientific study of the giraffe had begun as soon as information, skins, and skeletons were sent to Europe from Africa. There was a certain amount of confusion as to how to classify the giraffe. For a while it was placed in the same genus as the deer, and later it was included with the antelopes. In 1756, it was finally recognized as unique, placed in its own genus, *Giraffa,* and given the scientific name *Giraffa camelopardalis.*

For the next two centuries work on the giraffe concentrated on studying its anatomy, maintaining and breeding it in zoos, and classifying the various giraffes by skin patterns and horns. At one time, fifteen different subspecies or races of giraffe were recorded, some from the evidence of only a patch of skin or a single skull. Today it is generally agreed that there is only one species of giraffe — *Giraffa camelopardalis* — but the number of subspecies has not yet been decided upon. Until recently, the reticulated giraffe (*G. c. reticulata*) from northern Kenya, Somalia, and southern Ethiopia was thought to be a separate species, and it is still recorded as such in many books. As the reticulated giraffe will readily interbreed with *G. camelopardalis* in zoos, it is not thought to be a separate species. There are seven other subspecies of *G. camelopardalis* currently recognized: the Nubian; the Maasai of East Africa; Rothschild's, or Baringo, from western Kenya and Uganda; the West African; Thornicroft's from Zambia; the Angola; and the Cape giraffe from South Africa.

While classification was going on in Europe, travelers were watching and appreciating giraffes in their natural habitat in

Africa. The explorer Sir Samuel Baker wrote the following account of his first encounter with them in 1871: "These were my first giraffe, and I admired them as they lay before me with a hunter's pride and satisfaction, but mingled with a feeling of pity for such beautiful and utterly helpless creatures. The giraffe, although from 16 to 20 feet in height, is perfectly defenceless and can only trust to the swiftness of its pace, and the extraordinary power of vision, for its means of protection. The eye of this animal is the most beautiful exaggeration of that of the gazelle, while the colour of the reddish hide, mottled with darker spots, changes the tint of the skin with the differing rays of light, according to the muscular movement of the body. No one who has merely seen the giraffe in a cold climate can form the least idea of its beauty in its native land."

The giraffe was, and still is, a very popular animal, but like the elephant, its behavior and way of life in the wild were not really closely observed in any systematic way until fairly recently. In 1956–57 Anne Innis, now Anne I. Dagg, carried out the first systematic scientific study of giraffes on a farm in South Africa. There, wild giraffes were allowed to come and go as they pleased, and she was able to make detailed observations on feeding, movements, and social behavior. A few years later Deiter Backhaus did a short study of the giraffe in Garamba National Park in Zaïre and combined it with a study of captive giraffes.

The first extensive East African study of the giraffe was begun in 1965 by J. Bristol Foster, a Canadian, who was then teaching zoology at the University of Nairobi. For three years Foster visited Nairobi National Park at least once a week to observe the giraffe population. He was the first scientist to know every individual giraffe in a given population. Neither Innis nor Backhaus could recognize all their giraffes. Innis knew some of them by their patterns, and Backhaus tried to recognize individuals by their horns and scars but was only partially successful.

At first glance all giraffes seem very much alike, but actually the giraffe is one of the easiest animals to recognize, since each giraffe's coat has a remarkably individual pattern. In fact, on the

Maasai giraffes that Foster studied, the markings look very much like Rorschach inkblots. A group of these markings always seems to stand out and can be easily memorized. Once Foster realized how unique each giraffe is, he decided to photograph each one from the left side and to learn the pattern of its neck. Each animal was assigned a number and its picture was glued onto a file card. Foster then carried these cards in the field with him and entered data on the appropriate card each time he found a known giraffe. By the end of his study he knew and had on record 250 giraffes.

Another study was carried out on the Maasai giraffe from 1969 to 1971 by Carlos Mejia, a Colombian from the Max-Planck-Institut in Germany. Mejia did his work at the Serengeti Research Institute in Tanzania. His results corroborate many of Foster's findings, but the giraffe refuses to be a simple animal, and Foster and Mejia found some fascinating differences between their populations.

A third East African study, still in progress, is being carried out by Barbara Leuthold in Tsavo (East) National Park. Her work on the feeding ecology of giraffes is now available, and her behavior work is awaited with much interest, because she is studying yet another population of giraffes living in conditions quite different from those in either Nairobi or the Serengeti.

In the Serengeti Mejia worked in an area of approximately 100 square miles in the middle of the Park. There he recorded and knew nearly 350 giraffes. Like Foster, Mejia photographed his giraffes, but he photographed both sides of the neck and shoulder and then taped the two photographs together.

Mejia used various methods for collecting data on his giraffes. At first it was necessary to find them, photograph them, and learn to recognize them. Once this was done, he could begin to gather data on social organization. Two or three times a week he took the same route through the study area and noted which giraffes he saw, the size and composition of the group, and the location. On other days he would follow an individual giraffe or a whole group for twelve-, twenty-four-, or thirty-six-hour periods. (He made the night observations whenever there was a full moon.) During these periods he would record at three-minute intervals what the animal or group was doing, thus providing data on daily activity patterns.

Although there are always problems in any study of wild animals, Mejia did not encounter the usual ones. It was not difficult to find his animals or to photograph and recognize them. Many of the giraffes were already used to cars and the others tamed down fairly easily. In fact, he could usually watch a giraffe from 15 to 20 yards away in his Land-Rover. The problem that he did come across was inherent in giraffe behavior itself: giraffes rarely interact and have at best a loose social structure. For a behaviorist this is both puzzling and frustrating. As Mejia says, with much consternation, "They are gregarious but they don't interact." He found it difficult to understand why they come together at all.

Giraffes are found singly, in two and threes, and in herds of up to fifty. Most often they seem to form small groups, but it is often difficult to determine where a herd begins and ends. Giraffes are sometimes spread over a large area, and as they have excellent eyesight coupled with a clear view from their height, it is possible that giraffes a mile apart could be part of the same group. As Foster posed the question: "Could a herd be a mile long yet made up of only twelve individuals?" For the purposes of his study Foster decided to consider all giraffes as being in the same herd if they were less than 1 kilometer (.621 miles) apart and moving in the same general direction.

Foster and Mejia both found that giraffes come together in groups, but that these groups are loose and open, with giraffes coming and going as they please. The groups may consist of males, females, and young, all males or all females, or any combination of sexes and ages. There is no consistency in the male/female ratio of a group or in the size of the groups. There are no obvious leaders in any case, and the group does not act as a coordinated unit. Generally the composition of the groups changes from day to day. A herd rarely comprises the same individuals for more than a few consecutive days. Apparently adult giraffes do not form bonds with one another. A giraffe may feed with three or four individuals one day and then be seen with five entirely different ones the next.

While Mejia found that the giraffes in his study area are usually in mixed herds (males and females), the sexes in Nairobi Park show distinct preferences for different areas. The females and young stay on the plains, whereas the males tend to stay in the forested area. Females associate with large numbers of other females, sometimes with particular individuals for long periods. They associate with far fewer males and rarely with one male for very long. The same is true for the males. They associate with other males more than with females. Lone males come from the forest to meet with the females on the plains, eventually returning to the forest. Foster records that lone males are almost always walking rather than feeding.

The data on individual associations puzzled Mejia, who was trying to work out the function of a giraffe group, since they did not explain why giraffes come together. It has been suggested that the giraffe group is a mutually protective arrangement — seven or eight giraffes all watching for predators is better than one. However, Mejia does not think that this is so. For one thing, if there is danger, the giraffe that notices it may or may not give a warning snort. And even more odd, but very giraffelike, if the giraffe does give a snort, the other giraffes may not respond at all. Even when one or some of the giraffes snort and run away, others quite nearby will calmly go on feeding. If it is not for protection that giraffes form groups, then Mejia is not sure what the reason is. He can only speculate that it may simply be natural gregariousness — members of the same species are attracted to one another.

Giraffes do not hold a territory in the sense of a defended area, but they do move in a limited home range. Foster put a radio collar on a young female giraffe and followed her every day for a month. From this data, combined with other observations, he was able to establish that the home range for females in the Nairobi study area is about 25 square miles. The home range for males appears to be much larger.

Within their home range giraffes know one another. Whereas there appears to be no hierarchy among females, there is a very definite rank order among males. If one male is feeding at a tree, a dominant male needs only to walk toward him and the subordinate male will move away. When the dominant male is threatening another male, he holds his head in a characteristic manner, head and chin high, and neck straight and slightly back. Threat behavior is shown only when the other male does not leave immediately. Mejia once watched two males coming toward each other, each with his head up in the typical threat behavior posture. They walked closer and closer until one put his head down, let his ears fall forward, and jumped aside, thus acknowledging the other's dominance.

When there is a female in estrus, the dominant male in the group will sometimes show aggression. Foster reports that occasionally a bull will maintain a temporary "harem," keeping all other adult males away. In one case, whenever the attending bull saw a male coming toward his harem, the bull would go out to meet the other male when he was still more than 200 yards away. The intruding male always turned away when the threatening bull came within 50 yards of him and would then sometimes circle around to try to get to the group from the other side.

Foster never saw this behavior lead to a fight. As with elephants, the hierarchy among the males, according to which each male knows his dominance relation with every other male, prevents serious fights. The rank order is determined in adolescence and early adulthood by frequent sparring, although it is probably never rigidly fixed, as even adult males continue to spar. The way in which giraffes spar, a behavior called "necking," has always fascinated people. Necking has sometimes mistakenly been reported as love play between a male and female, but in the wild it is performed only by males.

A necking match is a lovely sight. The two giraffes usually stand shoulder to shoulder, facing in the same direction. Then in graceful slow motion their long, sinuous necks appear to wrap and unwrap around each other. With typical giraffe aloofness they sometimes stop and gaze into the distance for a while, or stop and eat or ruminate, and then start necking again. Sometimes this gentle sparring builds to a higher intensity. The males may then stand head to tail and make passes with their heads, trying to hit each other. Matches can last for more than a half-hour. Often the bout ends with one of the males, with a full erection, mounting the other. Sometimes a third male will come and mount both the contestants.

This mounting behavior has led many people to speculate on the role of homosexuality in giraffe social behavior. Innis found that sexual activity among males (who outnumbered females in her study area) was the most common interaction in the giraffes she observed: "Homosexual behaviour is much more in evidence than heterosexual behaviour. Even when females are present in a herd, the males often gather together apart from them and neck and mount each other."

It would appear then that, sexually, males are more interested in other males than in females. Mejia does not believe that this is so and feels that the so-called sexual activity among the males has been overemphasized and misinterpreted. Erections and mountings during sparring matches are common to many animals and seem to be more closely related to dominance than to sex. The animal that is mounted is usually thought to be the subordinate animal. In conjunction with sparring, mounting may be a non-violent way of expressing dominance. Mejia suggests that rather than engaging in serious fights that could lead to injuries, giraffes determine rank order with relatively gentle necking and mounting.

From all reports, a serious fight between two adult bulls is quite a spectacle. Standing together, usually shoulder to shoulder, with legs spread apart for better support, they swing their massive heads at each other, wielding them like sledgehammers, aiming their blows at the body, neck, and legs of their opponent. Each tries to avoid or counteract the other's blows. When one is hit, the sound of the impact can be heard from more than 100 yards away. The horns are used in these fights, but as they are blunt and the skin of the giraffe is exceptionally thick, there is seldom

Identification photographs of four different elephants in Lake Manyara National Park.

Iain Douglas-Hamilton with Virgo, an adult female who became exceptionally tolerant of his presence on foot.

First-year calves playing: the
sequence, with the same gestures,
will be used in adult life.

A calf plays on a sleeping older member of its family unit and is completely tolerated.

A family unit drinking: the first-year calf is still inept with its trunk and has to bend down and drink with its mouth.

Ahmed, the magnificent bull of Marsabit Mountain in Kenya: for the last years of his life he was protected by Presidential Decree. His tusks were just under 10 feet long and weighed 147 pounds apiece.

A calf taking vegetation from its mother's mouth, thus learning what plants she eats.

One of the things elephants learn to eat in some areas are baobab trees: this bull gouges out the pulp of a baobab that had been knocked over the night before.

Some common elephant interactions:

Young bulls sparring;

Adults greeting;

A bull testing
a young female for
estrus.

A newborn giraffe
still with its
umbilical cord.

A giraffe feeding on an
acacia tree using its
18-inch-long tongue.

Carlos Mejia with an
identification photo of the
giraffe in the distance.

Giraffe drinking.

A male closely following a female just prior to mating. A second female apparently takes interest.

An acacia tree with an hourglass browse line caused by giraffes feeding.

serious damage. The horns of the giraffe are not, in fact, true horns, but bones covered with skin and hair. As the bull grows older, layers of bone are deposited on the head and knobs of bone protrude from the forehead and behind the horns. This adds extra weight and bulk to the head, making it an even more formidable weapon. Bernhard Grzimek of the Frankfurt Zoo reports that the force of a blow by a giraffe is "almost unimaginable." Their bull giraffe, Otto, became annoyed with a big bull eland one day and took a swing at him. "The eland, a massive animal weighing more than half a ton, was propelled through the air with such force that it broke a shoulder and had to be destroyed." Innis relates an incident in Kruger National Park, when one bull was knocked unconscious in a fight and lay on the ground for twenty minutes before coming to and getting to its feet. It is probably rare, but certainly possible, for a bull to be killed in a fight. Dead giraffes have been found with no obvious sign of predation or disease.

Mejia was able to witness a few serious fights. These could be distinguished from necking by the circumstances and the intensity. In all cases there was a estrous female present, and the fight was short and fierce, with the opponents fighting for less than a minute before jumping apart. In a true fight of this nature there is no mounting afterward. The fight usually occurs between a dominant bull and a newcomer, and the winner gains the right to the estrous female. Thus, in a fight the motivation stems from attempting to attain an immediate goal — the female in heat. Necking, on the other hand, is a means of slowly establishing the dominance hierarchy in a population.

Like the males of other species, the giraffe bull's main goal is to pass on his genetic material. In order to fulfill this goal he must work his way up through the rank order until he is in a position to court and mate with a female without undue interference from other males. Fights are rare, because there is usually one dominant male around whom the other males will not challenge.

Giraffe bulls wander from group to group, testing the females to see if they are in estrus. The particular behavior associated with the testing, called *Flehmen*, is common to most ungulates. The bull approaches a female and either gently nudges or licks her tail, which induces the female to urinate. The male collects some of the urine in his mouth, raises his head, and curls back his lips or "flehmens." He may then eject the urine from his mouth in a thin stream. It is thought that the action of lifting the head and curling the lip facilitates the analysis (by smell and taste) of the urine's hormone content, thus making it possible for the bull to determine whether the female is in estrus. Flehmen occurs frequently and there seems to be no aggression among the bulls at this point; Innis has seen as many as three bulls all testing the same female at one time.

If the female is not in estrus (as is usually the case), the bull will move on to the other females in the group, testing each one in turn. If he finds an estrous female, he will begin to follow her persistently, coming up to her from behind, leaning his chest against her rump, and nosing the base of her neck. In the beginning of courtship the female invariably moves or runs away when the bull touches her. During this early period the female continues feeding, while the male does not eat but constantly pursues the female. As courtship progresses, the female stops running away and allows the bull to mount. Coitus is brief, lasting only a few seconds. There is generally a series of mountings.

Innis gave a detailed account of the one mating she saw. She watched a known bull, whom she had named Star, mount a female three times while a medium-sized bull looked on: "Star walked behind the female in an open area about 20 yards across surrounded by low bushes. Every time she came to the edge of the clearing Star hurried up beside her to head her back again into the clearing. This happened at least twice between each mounting. Star sometimes walked beside her and put his head down besides hers but she would move away from him. He followed her until she stood still facing downhill, and then stood behind her for a minute or so without either of them moving. He may have lightly kicked her hindlegs once with his forelegs. Then he mounted her by sliding his forelegs loosely onto her flanks and after a second or two she ran forward and he followed with his penis still erected for a short while. Then they walked around in a circle again until she stood still facing downhill. The medium-sized bull always stood to the front and the side of them and watched the mounting." After the third mounting the smaller bull tried to approach the female but Star always chased him away. The three giraffes all ended up running at full speed, with Star trying to keep the other male away by heading him off. At about that point they all disappeared into the bush.

Mejia has seen mating behavior at least twenty times in the Serengeti, and he has concluded that there is pair bonding during estrus. Mejia followed one estrous female for three days and the same male stayed close to her all of that time. On another occasion he watched a courting pair who had apparently formed a bond. The male wandered off at one point, and another male immediately came up to the female, but she would not let him mount. The original male then returned and the female immediately allowed him to mount her.

The gestation period for the giraffe is fourteen to fifteen months. Calves are born throughout the year, although there are peak calving times in some areas. In Nairobi National Park more calves are born in the dry seasons, the peaks being in January and July and August. In the Serengeti the peak calving period is from May to August.

When it is time to give birth, the mother giraffe leaves the company of the herd and goes to a secluded spot to have her calf. Both Mejia and Foster always spotted females with very newborn calves in places away from other giraffes. In addition, Mejia found all the mothers with newborn giraffes in one particular part of his study area. He never saw a newborn calf anywhere else.

During birth the mother remains standing; the calf is dropped head first 5½ feet to the ground and, from all reports, lands with a thud. Obviously, it survives its rather precipitous descent into life, for it is soon on its feet, standing close to 6 feet and weighing about 150 pounds.

None of the scientists working on giraffes has seen a birth in the wild, but some tourists in Kruger National Park in South Africa watched a birth from only 20 yards away. When they arrived, the neck and head of the calf were already visible. The mother continued to have contractions and gradually the shoulders appeared, followed by the rest of the body, which fell to the ground, breaking the umbilical cord. The calf managed to stand up after fifteen minutes without the help of the mother, who was feeding on nearby trees.

There is a certain amount of controversy over the female giraffe's maternal role. It has been claimed that giraffes are indifferent mothers and that the cow-calf bond is very weak. Innis' study points to this weakness and so does Foster's for Nairobi Park, but the latest data from Mejia reveal new information about mother/infant relations in the giraffe, at least in the Serengeti. (It is always dangerous to say that one scientist has discovered something new or disproved someone else, when the scientists have worked in different places, since habitat plays an extremely important role in behavior; it is possible that the giraffes in the Serengeti simply behave in a way peculiar to that particular environment.)

Innis concluded that there was "a rather weak maternal instinct." She mentions one incident in which a female giraffe jumped a fence on the farm and her calf was unable to follow. The mother and calf paced along the fence, but the calf did not know how to get over and the mother would not cross back. Eventually the mother left the calf, who wandered off and presumably died. In two cases Innis saw the calves in a group being rounded up and herded away by a bull while the mothers paid no attention to the proceedings.

Foster also found the maternal bond to be weak in the Nairobi population. He saw groups of up to five young giraffes together, sometimes with a female and sometimes on their own. Month-old calves were seen more than a mile from their mothers and had apparently been separated from them for days. He rarely saw a calf suckle after it was a month old. One two-month-old calf disappeared, presumably out of the Park, and was not seen again for twenty-nine months, while the mother was frequently seen in the Park without the calf.

Mejia's particular interest was in the mother-calf relationship and its changes with age. He devoted a large part of his study time to the daily activity patterns of the calves, watching each calf for twelve- and twenty-four-hour periods several times a month. The results are fascinating: The first few days after the birth the mother stays secluded with her calf in the same area where it was born. In fact, the female may be quite adamant about staying on her own at this point. Mejia saw a female with a newborn calf attacking any other females who tried to come near, and another one who attacked any calves who came close. In these early days the mother spends a good deal of time nosing and licking the calf. There is a special ritual in which the mother bends down and licks the calf and the calf then licks the mother. While the newborn calf is suckling, the female bends and licks its rump.

The seclusion and close contact of the mother and calf both help to imprint one on the other. In this way, when they are later in a herd, they can recognize each other by sight, smell, and perhaps by sounds. The imprinting process may take a few days, and during this time it is essential to keep other giraffes away so that the calf does not confuse them with its mother.

Mejia thinks that the nosing is an invitation to suckle and that it also plays a role in keeping the calf close to the mother when there is danger. He once saw a hyena stalking a calf; the mother bent and nosed the calf, who immediately moved in close beside her.

After three or four days the mother and calf join other females with newborn calves. As all the females have given birth in approximately the same area, the mother does not have to go far to find the other mothers. When the females and calves come together, a remarkable phenomenon occurs — a kindergarten is formed. The calves actually form bonds with one another that are much stronger than any bonds between the adult females. In fact, Mejia feels that the females have come together only because of the calves. In a group of females and calves there is actually less distance between the calves than between mother and calf.

When the newborn calves meet, they frequently perform a nosing ceremony that apparently creates and then cements bonds among them. Nosing consists of the two calves coming together and touching noses, sometimes tongues and nostrils. With noses together, they simultaneously put their heads down and then jump apart.

During the first few weeks, the baby giraffes play with each other in the early morning and late afternoon. They run together, kicking up their legs, but playing stops completely after they are about a month old, and like adults, they take on an air of quiet self-possession. A giraffe calf is certainly one of the most charming of the baby animals in Africa. It is nearly a perfect miniature of its parents, except that on the tips of its horns it has delightful tassels of dark hair. A baby giraffe appears to be very curious and unafraid; while adults often run away from a stopped car, the calves sometimes come nearer to investigate. They then stand and watch with what looks like a slight air of superiority.

The kindergarten was first mentioned by Backhaus, who studied giraffes in Zaïre. He described it as a group of giraffe calves that is left in the care of one female. Mejia found something more unusual: in the Serengeti, once the subgroup is formed by individual bonding, the calves are left alone all day, with *no* female to look after them. The mothers spend the night with the calves, but then in the morning, at around nine o'clock, they leave the calves and go off to browse. The area they inhabit at this time is one of wooded hills and gullies; the calves stay on the top of a hill all day while the females go down to the gullies to feed, usually going ½ to 1 mile away. The mothers give no obvious signals as they are leaving. The calves simply watch them leave and remain on the hill, spending their time standing around, lying down, and eating a little. (Giraffe calves begin nibbling at food within a few days of birth.) The mothers return at around five o'clock, immediately go to their calves, nose them, and then suckle them.

Most observers have concluded that baby giraffes stop suckling at a very early age and that this is one of the reasons for their early independence. Mejia's data show that the calves in his study area suckle until they are over one year old. Mejia records that except for the first few days of life baby giraffes suckle twice a day, once in the morning before their mothers leave and again in the evening when they return.

Mejia followed up the suckling behavior of a number of calves month by month. The following are the data for one calf: when it was very newborn it suckled six times during a twenty-four-hour period, and each time it suckled for over a minute. Three months later it suckled twice during twenty-four hours, one time for fifty-six seconds, the other for fifty-five seconds. One year later the same calf still suckled twice in twenty-four hours, once for thirty-six seconds and again for thirty-five seconds.

Whether or not the kindergarten has a survival value for the calves is not known. Mejia found a mortality rate of 50 percent for calves up to three months old. Foster found a mortality rate of 73 percent for the first year of life in the Nairobi giraffe population. Most of the calves are probably killed by predators. Mejia thinks that it may be to the calves' advantage to stay on the tops of hills; visibility is better there than it is down in the gullies where the females are feeding. Also, the time of day when the mothers are gone is usually when the predators are less active. The only time Mejia saw a calf being attacked by a lion, its mother was only 3 yards away. The lion pounced on the calf and brought it down. The mother immediately came to the rescue by kicking the lion off with her front legs. The calf then got up, and mother and calf ran off with the lion in hot pursuit, but the lion was unable to catch them once the giraffes began to run.

The kindergarten stays on the tops of hills for three to four months, and then the calves gradually begin to move down the slopes. They follow their mothers down to the edges of gullies, feed for a while, then return to a hilltop, where they may lie down for a time. The calves may go up and down several times in a day.

At five to six months, the Serengeti calves begin to follow the adults all the time. This allows the females to range farther for feeding. Normally a calf follows its own mother, although not always. It may go off with another female and calf. However, it usually finds its own mother sometime during the day, as it is still suckling at this age. The calf will remain with its mother until it is sixteen to eighteen months old, when it becomes independent. Mejia found that both males and females leave the mother at about this age. Backhaus thought that the female calf stayed with the mother, but Mejia did not find this. The newly independent females join up with other females, maintaining no permanent associations with them either. The young males spend more of their time with other bulls. It is at this stage that the males have frequent necking matches.

Giraffes become sexually mature at four years, but are not their full size at that age. According to Foster, females reach their full height — about 15 feet — at five years, and males reach their full height — 15 to 17 feet — at seven. Only 6 feet at birth, giraffes have a lot of growing to do, so it is not surprising that their growth rate is impressive. In just their first year giraffes grow 4 feet, and it has been reported that they can grow as much as 9 inches in a single week.

Once a female reaches maturity, she will produce a calf about every two years. She usually gives birth again six months after her former calf becomes independent, which means that she gets pregnant when it is seven to nine months old. However, if her calf dies within a few months of birth, she will come into estrus soon after losing the calf and produce another calf as soon as seventeen months after the former birth.

In general, life for the adult giraffe appears to be peaceful and, by human standards, slightly dull compared to that of some other African animals. To begin with, giraffes spend sixteen to twenty hours a day feeding. They are browsers, feeding mainly on trees and shrubs and on a few creepers and vines. Barbara Leuthold found that the giraffes in Tsavo (East) National Park ate at least sixty-six plant species, usually choosing the leaves and small twigs of the plant but sometimes eating the bark, fruits, and flowers of certain plants. She also found that their diet changes from season to season: in the wet season they feed on deciduous plants; in the dry season, on evergreen plants.

An odd fact about the diet of the giraffe has emerged recently. Giraffes have sometimes been seen chewing on the bones of carcasses. Three different scientists have recorded giraffes with bones in their mouths in different parts of Kenya. In Amboseli, David Western found giraffes chewing on the bones of a Grant's gazelle carcass, actually breaking bits of bones into splinters. The only explanation put forward for this behavior is that these giraffes may have been deficient in phosphorus or some other mineral and were chewing bones to supplement their normal diet.

Chewing on bones is a rare occurrence. Generally, giraffes eat only leaves and twigs. In many areas giraffes prefer various species of acacia trees, which often stay green throughout both the wet and dry seasons. Although acacias are guarded by long, wicked-looking thorns, these apparently cause no trouble to the giraffe. It simply eats the tender tips of the thorns and carefully rakes the leaves off the branches with its lower incisors. The upper lip is prehensile; the giraffe uses it to grab bunches of leaves. The 18-inch-long tongue is also used in securing vegetation. With head raised and tongue fully extended, a big giraffe can reach as high as 20 feet from the ground; no other animals, except for the largest elephants, can feed at this height.

The impact of giraffe feeding can easily be seen in the form of a "browse line" on many trees. On tall trees the giraffes cut the foliage at an even height from the ground (the height the tallest giraffes can reach), giving them a flat bottom. There are also large bushes with an hourglass shape, the result of giraffes feeding at about 15 feet and below. The lower part of the tree is rounded and looks almost as if it had been manicured by a gardener; above 15 feet, the branches are able to grow and spread out. Small trees like the whistling thorn, or *Acacia drepanolobium* (which is a favorite food of the giraffes in Nairobi National Park), have what Foster has called an "inverse browse line"; that is, the giraffes feed on these small trees from the top, keeping them from growing taller. The whistling thorn trees in the Park rarely grow over 6 feet tall, while trees outside of the Park, where giraffes do not feed, grow 3 or 4 feet higher.

Foster noted a peculiar and very interesting adaptation that may serve to protect the *Acacia drepanolobium* from extensive over-browsing. The tree harbors colonies of ants, which live in the black, hollow galls that cover the branches. Each leaf stem has a nectar outlet that apparently serves no other purpose than that of feeding the ants. When a giraffe comes to browse on the tree, it disturbs the ants, which scurry all over the branches and onto the animal. These particular ants, of the *Crematogaster* species, have a very painful sting; therefore, the giraffe does not spend very long at one tree, but goes from tree to tree. Although this mechanism does not stop the giraffe from browsing on this type of acacia, it apparently insures that the damage is distributed throughout the tree population.

It is estimated that a large bull giraffe (3000 pounds) consumes some 75 pounds of food a day. The giraffe is a ruminant, which means that all this vegetation has to be swallowed and then re-chewed. Like other ruminants, the giraffe has a four-chambered stomach; the barely chewed food first goes into the reticulum, where the vegetation is formed into fist-sized balls, which are later regurgitated, chewed thoroughly, swallowed again, and passed into the rumen, and later into the omasum and abomasum, where final digestion takes place.

The giraffe spends three to five hours a day ruminating, or "chewing the cud," as it is commonly called. Innis recorded data on ruminating that almost sound like a take-off on scientific endeavors: "Giraffe chew their cud at any time throughout the day, when walking, standing or lying down and between spells of browsing. Often all the giraffe in a herd will stand or lie in one place for hours, patiently chewing. A female giraffe was timed while she chewed seven cuds. The highest number of chews per cud was forty-nine, the lowest twenty-nine and the average forty-four chews per cud. Each chewing motion took an average of 0.94 seconds. A chew per second seems to be about normal, as two other giraffe took 0.98 and 1.0 seconds per chew respectively."

Another two to three hours are spent lying down. Male giraffes sometimes lie down in the daytime. They do not lie flat out on their sides — they lie on the brisket, with legs curled under them and neck and head held upright. Deep sleep, with the head resting on the flank, lasts only about one minute, and no more than five to thirty minutes are spent sleeping throughout a twenty-four-hour period. Females rarely, if ever, lie down in the daytime but do so at night. When giraffes do lie down, they sometimes form a star pattern, each facing in a different direction; it has been suggested that this may be an antipredator device.

A typical day for giraffes in the Serengeti would be as follows: Early in the morning the giraffes would be found eating in the area where the group had spent the night. Soon afterward they begin to move toward the stream beds, where they feed for most of the day. At midday they stop and rest for an hour or two, ruminating or just standing around. After their rest period they begin to feed again, and then late in the afternoon they move toward the place where they will spend the night, usually an open grassy area where visibility is good. Some time after midnight they stop feeding and lie down and ruminate for two to three hours. It is at this time that they sleep for very short intervals.

One might well ask when giraffes drink in this schedule. It appears that the giraffe's drinking habits are as unpredictable as its other behavior. There have been various estimates of how much water a giraffe needs, but no one has been able to arrive at a definite figure because there are many factors involved. In zoos giraffes have been known to drink as much as 10 gallons of water on a hot day and around 2 gallons in cool weather.

In the wild, of course, it is even more difficult to determine how much they drink. On the South African farm where Innis worked, the giraffes drank frequently from the cattle troughs, actually mixing with the cattle to do so. Foster concluded that giraffes do not need to drink water if their food has a high moisture content, which it does at most times of the year, except perhaps at the height of the dry season. Mejia saw giraffes drinking only about twenty times during his whole two-year study, and he often followed giraffes for up to thirty-six hours at a time.

Permanent water was available to them in the Serengeti, but they did not seek it out. The vegetation that the giraffes feed on collects a surprising amount of dew during the night. Giraffes browsing in the early morning probably take in much of this moisture. That, and the natural moisture content of the vegetation (the tender twigs of *Acacia drepanolobium* contain 74 percent water), seems to supply the giraffe with adequate water.

When the giraffe does drink, it is quite a feat, as its head and neck are not long enough to reach ground level unless the giraffe spreads its front legs out sideways and also usually bends its knees. Giraffes lose some of their great dignity and self-possession at watering places. They become shy and cautious — and with good reason, as this is where the predators lurk. The whole process of getting to the water is most ungainly. When they spread their legs out sideways, they do so in a series of jerks, drink briefly, and then snap their heads back up and their legs back together. They may have to repeat this procedure as many as six times before getting enough to drink.

For a long time it was a great mystery to scientists how the giraffe could lift its head up so quickly without all the blood draining from its brain, causing it to faint. Studies were carried out on the giraffe's blood pressure and circulation. The results revealed that the giraffe has an intricate system of valves in its arteries and veins and highly elastic and absorbent blood vessels in its brain. These devices prevent the blood from flowing too quickly away from or to the brain.

One myth about the giraffe that should be clarified is that of its voice. The giraffe does have vocal cords and a larynx, but the muscles attached to the larynx are exceptionally small compared to those of other animals. Both these muscles and the inner ear are more pronounced in the young giraffe, but do not grow in proportion to size in the adult. However, the giraffe is able to make various noises. Zoos have reported that giraffe calves bleat and make a half-mewing, half-mooing call, and Mejia has heard calves calling on two occasions. Adults also occasionally moo, grunt, or bleat. In the wild they can be heard to snort, which is a noise but not one made by the vocal cords.

The snort seems to be the only sound made by giraffes that could be construed as an alarm signal. Giraffes will snort when they see something that disturbs them — a lion or a man on foot — but, as we have seen, other giraffes do not necessarily respond by looking or running away. Giraffes in national parks seem very blasé about possible predation but, in fact, they only seem to lack caution. The giraffe's long neck provides a watch-tower for its sharp eyes, and it is constantly aware of movement. One often sees a giraffe staring into the distance, and when one looks in the same direction, a tiny speck can usually be seen (sometimes only with binoculars) moving on the horizon. Rather than running away, the giraffe keeps the predator in sight and may even move closer. If the predator gets too close, then the giraffe might run or simply walk away. The giraffe can gallop at almost 35 miles per hour and can maintain this speed for a considerable distance; so an alert, healthy adult giraffe has little to fear from predators.

However, lions sometimes do kill adult giraffes. A lion can overcome a giraffe if it can get hold of the head when the giraffe has bent down at a watering place or salt lick. The lion is then able to get a grip on the giraffe's nose and mouth and suffocate it. Even then the lion may not succeed, however, for giraffes can deliver powerful kicks with both back and front legs, and they have been known to kill lions in this way. Also, a lion may jump onto a giraffe's back and bite into its neck, injuring the spinal cord. During Mejia's time in the Serengeti he knew of four giraffes definitely killed by lions: two adult males, one calf, and one very old female.

Foster found the overall mortality rate of giraffes to be 13 percent in Nairobi Park, making the average life span of the giraffe ten years. It is rare for a giraffe to die of old age; when it becomes very old and weak, it is usually taken by a predator. Foster was able to establish the minimum ages of some of the giraffes in Nairobi National Park through a fortuitous set of circumstances. People have been photographing giraffes in the Nairobi area for many years, and Foster was able to collect old photographs and compare them to those he had on file. One photograph taken in 1948 was of a male that he knew. In 1948 the giraffe was seen to be an adult and thus at least seven years old, so in 1968 that giraffe was at least twenty-seven years old. With this system Foster found two more males at least twenty-six and twenty-five, two females at least twenty-five, and two more females at least twenty-four and twenty-three. The oldest age to which a giraffe has lived in captivity is twenty-eight; presumably, a giraffe in the wild could not live much longer than this.

The giraffe does not seem to spend its old age any differently than it does its prime. The only noticeable difference in appearance is the darker shade of both ground and pattern colors in old giraffes. It is not known whether or not females stop breeding at a certain age. Supposedly, the older the bull, the higher his rank, although very old bulls may give up sexual pursuits. In a herd of eighteen captive giraffes that Innis studied in Australia, the one very old male was a complete dropout from the social scene, not interacting in any way with males or females, whereas the other giraffes engaged in sparring, fighting, and mating. It is possible that old males in the wild also retire in this way. Old bulls are sometimes called "stink bulls" because they give off a powerful odor; but its cause is not known and it is not thought to have any social significance.

While adult giraffes may not be heavily preyed upon by lions and hyenas, man is another matter. Giraffes have been hunted by man from the earliest times, as has been depicted in the beautiful bushman rock paintings. In South Africa the Boers used the tough giraffe hide to make bullwhips and almost succeeded in wiping out every giraffe in the country. African hunters killed the giraffe for its long leg sinews, which they used as strings for their hunting bows. Today there is still some poaching of giraffes for meat and tail hairs (used for making bracelets and other ornaments).

For many years the giraffe was designated "Royal Game" and no one was allowed to hunt it in Kenya. The giraffe was not rare; it simply seemed like such a peaceful, gentle creature, putting up no defense against the hunter, that shooting it seemed unfair.

Now the giraffe can be hunted in Kenya with a special license that costs a little more than $100, plus another $200 if one is killed. With all the sport hunting that goes on in Kenya, there were only ten giraffes shot by licensed hunters in the last year (1974).

There used to be a stuffed head and neck of a giraffe in one of the curio shops in Nairobi. It was extremely distasteful and elicited comments from residents and tourists alike. Why people should take offense at a stuffed giraffe and not a stuffed lion or leopard says something about the aura of the giraffe — that dignity, aloofness, and overwhelming gentleness. Perhaps Karen Blixen described that quality best in her book *Out of Africa:* "I had time after time watched the progression across the plain of the giraffe, in their queer, inimitable, vegetative gracefulness, as if it were not a herd of animals but a family of rare, long-stemmed, speckled gigantic flowers slowly advancing."

III

The Black Rhinoceros

WHEN JOHN GODDARD DIED in July 1971 in Zambia at the age of thirty-five, the scientific community of East Africa lost one of its most respected members and the rhinoceros lost a very good friend, for Goddard devoted seven years of his life to the black rhinoceros, and he probably knew more about that animal than anyone else in the world.[1]

The rhinoceros does not have many friends in this world. It is considered a stupid, ill-tempered brute that attacks at the slightest provocation. This is not altogether untrue, but the rhino has not had an easy time of it, to say the least. It has been mercilessly pursued by hunters for its horns, which are sold in various forms in the Middle and Far East. The rhino is very nearsighted and cannot even see his enemy until it is too late. Most hunters agree that it is the easiest of all the big game animals to kill. But on more than one occasion, conservationists have rallied round the black rhino and come to its aid. The first time was in 1960 when it was estimated that there were only twenty-five hundred rhinos left in all of Kenya, and in a 6000-square-mile area that included most of the Serengeti National Park and the Ngorongoro Crater in Tanzania, a census produced only fifty-five rhinos.

But what did this actually mean in terms of the rhino's future?

---

[1] Five species of rhinoceros exist today: two in Africa — the black rhinoceros, *Diceros bicornis,* and the less numerous square-lipped or white rhinoceros, *Ceratotherium simum;* three in Asia — the Sumatran rhinoceros, *Dicerorhinus sumatrensis*, the Javan rhinoceros, *Rhinoceros sondaicus,* and the Indian Rhinoceros, *Rhinoceros unicornis.*

Were there really so few and were they going to die out? As is usual in cases of panic like this, no thorough census of the existing rhino populations had been made and little was known about the rhino itself.

An intensive and systematic study of the rhino was needed, and this is exactly what John Goddard was asked to carry out by the Tanzanian government. Goddard came out to Tanzania in 1964 from Canada, with his wife and small daughter, to take up the position of Game Biologist for the Ngorongoro Conservation Area. There he studied two distinct rhino populations: the one in the Ngorongoro Crater and the one in Olduvai Gorge, the famous site where Louis and Mary Leakey found the tools, homes, and eventually the skulls of early man. Goddard was able to continue his studies and gather valuable comparative data, when, after three years in Tanzania, he went on to study the rhino population in Tsavo National Park in Kenya. `(This Park, believed to have the largest population of black rhinos remaining in Africa, has steadily been undergoing severe damage from elephants and fire, which together are radically changing the habitat from woodland to open grassland.) In the 1960–61 drought in Tsavo at least 282 rhinos had died from malnutrition. No one knew how many remained or whether those that did could survive the change in habitat. The rhino is a browser, and the parks authorities feared there would not be enough woody vegetation in the new habitat to support the large rhino population.

The main purpose of Goddard's work was to determine the state of the black rhinoceros populations in each of his three study areas; that is, to see how many rhinos there were and whether the populations were stable, increasing, or decreasing. In order to answer these questions it was necessary to make an accurate census of the populations and to collect data on birth rates, mortality, life span, calving intervals, age at maturity, etc. It was also important to understand the social structure, to find out the average range of an animal, and to study its feeding behavior. In other words, Goddard had to find out just about everything there was to know about the rhinoceros.

Since the rhino populations in Ngorongoro and Olduvai are relatively small, Goddard decided to use the method of individual recognition in his study. While observing the plains zebra in Ngorongoro Crater from 1962 to 1965, Hans and Ute Klingel (see chapter IV) had photographed all the rhinos they encountered and found that they were able to identify individuals by differences in horns, ears, and by scars on the body, combined with sex and age. Altogether they recorded sixty-one different rhinos in the crater, thirty-four of which used the crater most of the time and twenty-seven of which appeared to be temporary visitors.

When Goddard arrived in 1964, the Klingels gave him a duplicate set of their photographs. Goddard added to their records and made a new set of files for Olduvai. He also improved on their technique by photographing each rhino from the front in order to use the wrinkle contours on the snout as a further aid to identification. In some cases he found that horns alone could be misleading, especially if the horns were small. Also rhino horns have a tendency to break, which could cause confusion. Snout wrinkles apparently remain constant.

In the open area of the Ngorongoro Crater Goddard could do most of his observing from his Land-Rover, but in the bushier areas of Olduvai and Tsavo he had to work on foot, and to his wife's great consternation he refused to take a gun with him, relying on the rhino's myopia. He tried to keep upwind of the rhino, making his observations from the tops of rocks, anthills, or trees whenever possible. However, he did comment rather wryly that while watching one rhino "the possibility of encountering another rhinoceros concealed from view should also not be overlooked."

By his identification technique Goddard eventually recognized 108 rhinos on the floor of Ngorongoro Crater, which is 102 square miles, and 70 in Olduvai Gorge, in an area of 170 square miles. These figures indicated a larger population than was thought to exist, which was a welcome relief to conservationists. In Tsavo, by combining ground observations and extensive aerial counts, Goddard estimated the population to be over 7000, which came as a surprise to almost everyone. (Before Goddard's study, most estimates had been based on the numbers of rhino seen while driving or walking through an area. Rhinos are difficult to see in thick bush, and without the aid of aerial counts, underestimates were invariably made.) He found that the density of rhinos in Tsavo (8034 square miles) ranged from 4 rhinos per square mile to 1 rhino per 10 square miles, depending on the habitat. Although the area was huge, he did get to know individual rhinos — he catalogued 700 rhinos, or approximately 10 percent of the population, by his photographic method.

However, these revelations about the number of rhinos did not necessarily mean that the rhino was no longer in danger. The rhino's behavior and ecology in each of these areas had to be examined before a statement could be made about its future.

While Goddard was studying the rhino in Tanzania, two Swiss zoologists, Rudolf Schenkel and his wife, Lotte Schenkel-Hullinger, who were staff members of the University of Nairobi, also carried out a part-time study of the rhinos in Amboseli Game Reserve and in one area of Tsavo (East) National Park from January 1963 to October 1966. They visited these areas for periods of up to three months whenever they could get away from their duties at the university. Their work on the ecology and behavior of the black rhinoceros was published in a 101-page monograph. Their results complement Goddard's, and the combined studies now provide a fairly thorough picture of the way of life of the rhinoceros.

It is not easy to put the rhinoceros into a definite category in terms of social structure. It is not a herding animal or a pairing animal. The rhino is essentially solitary but not exclusively so. The most common sightings are of single animals or a mother and calf, but groups of three, four, and five rhinos have also been seen; Goddard once saw a group of thirteen. Every possible combination of sexes and ages has been seen. Two adult males have been seen feeding and lying together. Groups of three often consist of an adult female, her calf, and an immature rhino that may or may not be her previous offspring. Some of these group associations may last a few hours (as did, for instance, the group of thirteen rhinos that Goddard saw); others may last for months. The Klingels recorded two adult cows remaining with each other for thirteen months; and a bull, a cow and calf, and an immature bull were seen together for four months.

It had been assumed by some observers that the rhinoceros is territorial; that is, that a bull will defend a given area from intrusion by other males of his species and that he specifically marks out his territory by strategically placing dung heaps and spraying bushes with urine. Observations by both Goddard and the Schenkels indicate that the rhino is not territorial, but that each rhino does have a well-defined home range. Rhinos will tolerate the presence of other rhinos in their home range and will even keep company with other rhinos for a while, but they are not basically gregarious and apparently prefer being on their own. In fact, Schenkel reports that if two rhinos are walking along or feeding along the same path, moving toward each other, one will often avoid the other by making a large detour off the track. The only strong bond is that between mother and calf, which lasts for two to four years.

Goddard plotted the home ranges of most of his known animals and discovered that the home ranges overlapped considerably; each range overlapped with one or more other ranges by a mean of 35 percent. One adult bull shared 40 percent of his home range with another adult bull. Obviously, rhinos whose home ranges overlap will frequently meet and thus know each other.

The size of the home range differs according to sex, age, and habitat. On the floor of Ngorongoro the mean home range for an adult male is 6.1 square miles, for an adult female 5.8, for an immature male 13.9, and for an immature female 10.7. In the arid, bushier area of Olduvai the mean home range for an adult male is 8.5 square miles, for an adult female 13.7, for an immature male 14.5, and for an immature female 8.4. In the wet season the home range is considerably larger, as there is a greater variety of palatable plants available throughout the area during this time. In the dry season the rhinos tend to stay near water and marshes and do not range so far.

Serious fighting is not a major factor in rhino interactions. Within a community such as the one on the floor of the Ngorongoro Crater, an individual usually knows the other rhinos that it encounters. However, when a stranger enters a new area, there may be a violent reaction, especially if the newcomer is a male and has been seen by another bull. Goddard reported that strangers sometimes came down into the crater to obtain salt. Whenever they were seen, there was a fierce reaction. "The resident rhinoceros invariably attacks and is extremely vocal. The head is lowered, eyes rolled, ears flattened, tail raised, and the animal curls its upper lip, emitting a screaming groan. The stranger is invariably silent and on the defensive, but repels the vicious charges of its opponent. The anterior horns are used for goring, or for clubbing the other animal on the sides of the head. If the intruder retreats, he is pursued, sometimes for up to a mile." In nearly all the incidents of this type that Goddard witnessed, the stranger was driven out; in one case, however, the intruder forced out the resident, who eventually had to occupy an adjoining home range.

When rhinos who know each other meet, they react in different ways according to the sexes involved. A. T. A. Ritchie, former Chief Game Warden of Kenya and a long-time rhino observer, described the general pattern of rhino meetings quite succinctly: "At normal times two rhinos on meeting regard each other at first with suspicion, then incipient defiance and potential resentment, but these soon pass and leave the tolerance of indifference."

The Schenkels reported that a mother rhino and calf on meeting another female rhino with calf have a special greeting ceremony. If within hearing or smell, they will actually change directions in order to meet one another. The mothers approach each other and touch noses, then the calves touch noses, and sometimes each mother will greet the other's calf. After greeting, they remain together for a few seconds and then go their separate ways.

When rhinos meet at a wallow, the rhino or rhinos in possession of the wallow may very well show aggression to any newcomers. According to Schenkel this is usually accomplished by symbolized

horning, in which the animal jerks its head and horn up in the air.
The rhino might not even bother to stand up in order to do this,
but simply lift its head while lying down. If the newcomer is de-
terred, it will wait nearby or lie down a few yards from the others
just outside the wallow.

When a male and female meet and the female is not in estrus,
another sequence of events occurs. On seeing each other, they
each emit a puffing snort; then the bull approaches the female,
usually with short mincing steps, sometimes swishing his head
from side to side or jerking his horn into the air. If the female
responds, either by approaching or attacking, the male turns and
runs away, making a circle, and then returns to the female with
the same short steps. This behavior may go on for hours until
one of the animals decides to leave.

Meetings between bulls vary greatly. They may simply try to
avoid each other and walk away, or they may show some type of
testing behavior, which can range from lifting the head in a threatening manner and staring at each other to rushing forward with
lowered heads and shrill screams. In the latter case, the bulls
make a number of these rushes and finally stop nose to nose,
without quite touching. One may end up chasing the other. On
one occasion the Schenkels saw a bull fall down while it was being
chased by another. The other bull stopped next to the fallen one
and then walked away. He did not take advantage of the situation
by horning the other animal, which indicates something about the
quality of the aggression in encounters of this sort. More serious
and violent fights might occur when there is a female in estrus or
when a stranger appears.

If, as indicated, the rhino is not territorial, there remains the
mystery of the rhino's dung deposits. There have been many
theories put forth about the dung heaps, but the scientists are still
not altogether sure of the function of the behavior. Instead of
simply dropping its dung anywhere, the rhino has a number of
places throughout its home range where it deposits dung. While
still defecating or immediately afterward, the rhino scrapes its
back feet through the dung (in an action like that of a domestic

dog), breaking up the dung and spreading it around. The rhino may also sniff at the dung and root in the deposit with its horn. Several rhinos — including males, females, and even very young calves — may use the same dung heap. This communal use tends to contradict the theory that the dung heaps mark a territory held by an individual, and the possibility of a territory held by a group of rhinos seems unlikely but deserves further investigation. Whatever the case, the dung heaps are thought to convey information to other rhinos.

Goddard tried some experiments with rhino dung in order to see if rhinos could distinguish dung of different rhinos and to see what their reactions would be to the various samples of dung. Dung was collected from the rhino being tested, other rhinos in overlapping home ranges, and rhinos in far distant home ranges. These samples were put in a net bag and towed near the experimental animal. Artificial deposits of the three kinds of dung were also made and the reactions of ten rhinos were recorded. Some of the results follow: "60% followed the scent of their own dung, and 50% defecated on an artificial deposit of their own faeces; 70% followed scent trails of dung from animals with which they shared a home range, but only 20% defecated on artificial deposits of these animals. Only 30% followed scent trails of dung taken from animals several miles distant and 30% defecated on deposits from these animals . . . On one occasion a dung sample was collected from a rhinoceros and introduced to the same animal 48 hours later; the sample was then towed for a distance of just over two miles. The trail was zig-zagged to determine if the animal actually followed the set trail, which it did exactly, and 38 minutes later it was alongside the Land-Rover still sniffing the trail laid by the sample."

Goddard thought that the kicking and scraping action causes the dung to adhere to the hind feet, so that the rhino leaves a scent trail as it walks. During his studies Goddard immobilized forty rhinos, and while working on the drugged animals he noted that they all had characteristically smelly feet. Goddard suggested that with its very poor eyesight the rhino may need these scent trails in order to orient itself in its home range and also to keep in contact with other animals. Although the results are not conclusive, the experiments indicate that the rhino can recognize dung deposits and scent trails of the rhinos with which it shares its home range. As it moves about in its world of smells, the rhino can tell which rhinos have been through its home range and which way they are going. If it wants to follow another rhino for any reason, it will have no trouble doing so.

Urination does not take place at the same time as defecation, but it also appears to play a definite role for the rhino. The Schenkels reported that bulls perform nonritualized and ritualized urination: in the nonritualized type, the bull simply releases urine downward and backward between his hind legs onto the ground; in ritualized urination, the bull ejects a fine shower of urine in bursts, usually onto a shrub or bush. These bursts are aimed horizontally and backward and can reach distances of three to four yards.

Sometimes the ritualized urination is part of a more complex series of actions, which involves attacking a bush, horning and trampling it, then urinating on it, followed by walking over it and then scraping the area. This may be done with other bulls or cows around or when the bull is completely on its own. Schenkel believes that it is a way of scent-marking, which announces the presence of a bull. When there are other rhinos around, it is a way of "showing off"; when the rhino is alone, it functions as an indirect communication to other rhinos. The sense of smell plays an extremely important part in the life of the rhino, and many of its actions that probably once were direct contacts have now become symbolic and indirect.

Life begins for the black rhinoceros after a gestation period varying from fifteen to eighteen months. Most of the gestation records are from zoos, but Goddard was able to get two records from Ngorongoro Crater when he saw a cow mating and months later saw the newborn calf whose birth date could be estimated to within five days. The two gestation periods he recorded were approximately 446 and 478 days (about fifteen and sixteen months).

There have been no scientific observations of births in the wild, but births have been seen in zoos. The calf weighs about 85 pounds at birth and can walk within three hours. A rhino calf born in the Frankfurt Zoo stood up less than ten minutes after birth, only to fall down almost immediately, but it was back up again shortly after, and although very wobbly, it managed to stay on its feet and even walked around a bit. It found the teats and suckled approximately three hours after birth.

No detailed studies of cow-calf relations in the rhino have been carried out to date. Apparently it is difficult to observe very young rhino babies, as the mothers keep to thick bush when their calves are small, and even when they are older, both mothers and calves are wary. Perhaps as rhinos become tamer in the national parks, a study of this sort can be undertaken. However, both Goddard and the Schenkels have made interesting and valuable observations of rhino calves.

For the first few days after birth in the wild, the mother walks very slowly on her accustomed paths, and after that, the calf is able to keep up at the regular pace, which in any case is still rather slow. The calf keeps very close to the mother, either at her side or behind her. In the first weeks of life the calf suckles often for short periods.

When the calf is still only a few weeks old, it begins to feed on small twigs. It soon leaves its mother's side for short periods, sometimes venturing as far as 25 yards away. A rhino calf appears to be more alert than an adult and also seems to have better eyesight. During the cooler hours of the day it may become playful, running around the mother and even butting her. But as long as the calf remains with the mother, it is totally oriented to her and the two of them form a coordinated unit.

When it is still small, the calf suckles by standing up at right angles to the mother. The female has two teats, situated between the hind legs. As the calf gets older and larger, it has to lie down in order to reach the teats. The mother remains standing. The Schenkels report that a calf suckles for about four minutes each time, but they do not know how often it will do so during a day.

The calf suckles for over one year and may not be totally weaned until it is two years old.

If a cow and calf become separated, the cow emits a high-pitched mew and the calf reacts immediately by going directly to her. Hunters and scientists have used this mewing sound to call a rhino out of the bush. Goddard used the call when he could not see an individual and needed to recognize it. When a calf is in distress, it emits a bellowing squeal. The calves that Goddard immobilized squealed in this way and inevitably brought all the rhinos within hearing distance to their aid, not just their mothers. This must have been somewhat disconcerting for Goddard as he tried to work on the immobilized animal.

As long as the mother and calf are together, the mother will vigorously defend her calf against predators. Goddard related one incident in which a lion tried to kill an eleven-month-old calf: "At 1030 hours three sub-adult male lions were seen watching a rhinoceros with her calf. One lion got up and approached them. As he neared the animals he broke into a run. The calf snuggled against its mother, who moved toward the approaching lion. The calf retreated and the lion pursued it, separating it from the female. The mother followed the pursuing lion at a steady trot, and the calf doubled back to the female. The adult immediately engaged the lion, who diverted his attention to her. He bit her just above the hock, attempting to hang on, and clawed her thigh. The female wheeled around with incredible speed and gored him twice in the centre of the ribs, using the anterior horns with quick stabbing thrusts. The lion rolled over, completely winded. The rhinoceros then gored the lion once in the centre of the neck, followed by another thrust through the base of the mandible, killing him instantly. The other two lions had not moved during the entire proceedings."

The rhino calf stays with its mother until she has another calf, which could be as long as four or five years. If for some reason the female does not have another calf, her present calf may stay on with her, but in the normal course of events the calf is rejected when it is between two and four years old. It tries to stay with the mother but is actively chased away — viciously so, once the new calf is born. The older calf finds itself on its own and usually tries to join another youngster, or another female with or without a calf, or sometimes even a bull. Adult females, other than its mother, are more tolerant of the newly independent calf. When people report seeing a female rhino with two calves of different ages, the older calf is more likely the offspring of a cow from a nearby home range.

Goddard's figures show that the home ranges for immature animals are usually larger than those for adults and he speculated about the function of this phenomenon. When the rejected calf joins up with another rhino, then the young animal wanders not only in its mother's home range, but also in the home range of its new companion. Goddard concluded that "these factors (the larger home range of the immature animal, and the intolerance of the mother for her offspring) may serve an evolutionary function, assuring population dispersal in a species which is very sedentary and therefore susceptible to the effect of inbreeding."

When the young rhino becomes independent of its mother, it is not yet fully grown. Both males and females may continue growing until they are seven or eight years old. An adult rhino weighs between 2000 and 4000 pounds, and its shoulder height is 5 feet 6 inches to 5 feet 8 inches.

Records from zoos indicate that mating takes place around the sixth year for both the male and female rhinoceros. In the Hanover Zoo the female of a pair of rhinos began having estrous periods every month during her sixth year. The male showed no interest until he turned six years, and then copulated with the female, who produced a calf the following year. However, Goddard found that four known-age rhinos in Ngorongoro reached sexual maturity at an earlier age. One male was seen mating at four years and three months, and three females got pregnant at approximately four and a half years of age.

Courtship and mating behavior in the black rhinoceros is complex and fascinating. Mating apparently takes place at any time of the year and at any time of the day, although evidence in the

Schenkels' study area indicated possible rutting periods, one in March and April and another in July. In the July period they observed that almost overnight a large proportion of bulls and cows began sexual activities.

Precopulatory or courtship behavior involves complex encounters between the bull and cow. When the female comes into estrus, she walks about, squirting small amounts of urine on the ground. The bull comes along, sniffs the urine, and performs Flehmen.

During the early stages of courtship the male approaches the female with great caution. The female may walk a considerable distance with the male following behind. When she stops, the male approaches with a short, stiff-legged gait, dragging his rigid hind legs along the ground, but if she turns toward him or approaches, he may run off in a circle and then hesitantly come back to her again. Eventually they may stand facing each other, jousting gently with their horns. The approaching, circling, and jousting phase may go on for several hours.

Observers have reported that the male and female fight seriously and viciously during courtship, but both Goddard and the Schenkels deny this. In their observations these encounters never involved truly serious fights. On one occasion Goddard saw a female fiercely attack a bull, emitting the characteristic puffing snort. The bull turned and ran off in a circle, then approached her again with the stiff-legged gait. He eventually mounted her and she did not attack him again. Another female allowed a bull to mount her, but each time he dismounted she viciously attacked him. On all the other occasions when Goddard witnessed mating behavior, he saw nothing more serious than the jousting; the female did not attack the bull. Sometimes the bull would swing his head from side to side, sweeping his horn along the ground. The bull also frequently horns the female between the legs or under the stomach, but in a relatively harmless manner.

After the walking and jousting phase the female relaxes and accepts the male. The bull rests his head on the female's back and, using his neck as a lever, rises up and moves forward until his forefeet are behind the female's shoulders. Once in this position he may stay up for ten minutes before being dislodged by the female. No attempt at copulation occurs. He may mount the female in this way as many as twenty times over a period of several hours. In between mountings the pair usually feeds and walks.

True copulation occurs after the long period of mountings. Then the male moves forward still further, and either with upper body held high or with his chin right down on the shoulders of the female, he achieves coitus. The rhino is a remarkable animal in that copulation lasts for quite a long time compared to the few seconds most animals take. Rhinos copulate for thirty minutes or even longer — there is one record of thirty-six minutes. Goddard reported that the male remained silent but that "the female periodically emitted a low pitched squeal during coitus." He also observed that the calf of the female paid no attention to the proceedings once the female obviously accepted the male, but that other animals in the area, such as wildebeests and spotted hyenas, took "an intense interest in the courtship activities." Goddard thought that the lengthy copulation might be one reason behind the belief that the rhino's horn is an aphrodisiac. The shape of the horn is considered phallic and must also be an important element behind the myth. Scientists have proved that there is no truth in the belief, at least not from a chemical or hormonal point of view; the psychological effect is something else again.

It has been suggested that the male and female remain closely associated after mating. Goddard's records indicate that this varies widely, depending largely on whether or not the female normally uses the home range of the male with whom she has mated. One pair remained together for four months after mating, while the male of another pair left the day after he was seen mating with the female. Nor is the female necessarily faithful to one male. Goddard saw one female mounted by two different bulls in a six-hour period.

Violent, aggressive behavior can be displayed when more than one bull is in the vicinity of an estrous female. Goddard watched one female who was being closely followed by a bull. A second bull arrived and the first bull immediately "charged the second male viciously, his ears flattened, upper lip contorted, and emitting a ghastly puffing shriek. The second male was silent, but retreated in the face of the charge." In the meantime a third male approached, and he too was charged in the same way by the first male. The first and third males proceeded to fight, jousting with their horns and trying to hit each other on the sides of the head. As the fight continued, the female and the second male went off together, and he mounted her after a period of jousting and running about, but they did not copulate.

There does not appear to be a rank order among the bulls of a rhino community as there is with elephants and giraffes. The female apparently goes off with whoever happens to be around. Further studies may reveal subtle differences in positions among bulls and subsequent differences in reaction by females, but for now it looks as though there is no well-defined hierarchy.

Goddard estimated that once a female reaches maturity, she can produce a calf every twenty-seven months. When her calf is about a year old and still suckling, she comes into estrus and mates. However, evidence from zoos and from the wild suggests that the female comes into estrus within a few weeks after giving birth, but that conception does not take place until a year after parturition, even though she may mate with bulls before this. Although twenty-seven months is the estimated minimal calving interval, Goddard found that the average calving interval based on the existing population in Olduvai and Ngorongoro was one calf per female every four years. He suggested that there are self-regulatory mechanisms at work reducing the fertility rate.

Goddard was happy to report that, according to these results, the populations in Ngorongoro, Olduvai, and Tsavo were stable; that is, the birth rate was keeping pace with the mortality rate. The recruitment rates (the number of young added to a population per year), in Ngorongoro and Olduvai were both about 7 percent, while in Tsavo it was 10 percent.

Once a rhinoceros is an adult, it becomes more and more sedentary, and it may remain in the same home range for the rest of its life. As an adult, its home range becomes smaller and its daily activity patterns become fairly predictable. Some people have said that the adult rhino does exactly the same thing every day, following exactly the same paths, drinking, resting, and eating at exactly the same times every day. This is certainly an exaggeration, but the rhino does settle down to a somewhat routine way of life.

The rhino's day depends largely on whether it is going to walk to water. In the Schenkels' study area in Tsavo East, the rhinos do not drink every day but at intervals of several days, so that some days are spent moving toward water, others moving away from it, and others not moving at all, but remaining in the feeding area.

In Ngorongoro, where water is readily available, each day takes on something of a routine as follows: Early in the morning the rhino feeds and walks about. As the day gets hotter, usually by about nine o'clock, the rhino finds a place in which to lie down and rest. Oddly, rhinos do not seem to seek shade during the heat of the day. They have been seen at noontime lying in the hot sun, when an acacia tree provided shade less than 20 yards away. The rhino prefers sleeping in a dusty or sandy depression. What advantage this might have is not clearly understood.

Goddard watched a resting rhino for ten hours and discovered that it stood up for ten to fifteen minutes every ninety minutes or so. Resting or sleeping rhinos usually lie with their legs curled under them; thus they may get stiff and need to stand up from time to time. Calves are sometimes seen lying flat out on their sides, but adults are rarely seen in this position.

In the afternoon rhinos become active again, walking and feeding. It is at this time that they wallow if there is mud around. More than 90 percent of Goddard's observations of wallowing occurred between four and six o'clock in the afternoon. Wallowing is important to the rhino as a cooling mechanism. It has been variously claimed that rhinos have no sweat glands and that they have more per square inch than most animals. Whatever the case is, wallowing would still cool the animal after a day's accumulation of heat. In order to wallow, the rhino lies down and covers itself with mud, wallowing first on one side and then on the other, sometimes actually rolling right over on its back. The mud also helps to rid the rhino of ticks and flies, and the mud and dust adhering to the skin act as camouflage. Like the elephant, the rhino takes on the color of the soil in its habitat. Without mud, the black rhino is actually a grayish color.

In Ngorongoro the rhinos go to water in the evening and may stay there for several hours. They often meet other rhinos at the water holes and this is the time when rhinos interact. It has been reported that they run about, squealing and snorting. Many a camper has spent a sleepless night when camped near a favorite rhino watering place.

After drinking, the rhino returns to its normal feeding area, sometimes stopping and feeding along the way. The rhinos that live on the walls of the crater come down to the crater floor at night to get water and then return to the walls before daybreak. From night observations, Goddard concluded that rhinos are usually active most of the night, but he also saw individuals sleeping.

Goddard suspected that in the more arid region of Olduvai Gorge (where annual rainfall is 16 inches, compared to 26 inches at Ngorongoro), some rhinos did not drink at all during the dry season. There they feed on succulent plants such as the finger euphorbia, which contains a white latex fluid. In the dry season they also chew on plants with a high moisture content, such as *Sansevieria ehrenbergii* and *Cissus quadrangularis*. Evidence showed that the rhinos stuck to their small home ranges, even after all the water holes had dried up. There was no indication that they walked long distances to the nearest available water. Goddard postulated that the rhinos could live on the water from the moisture-rich plants alone. The finger euphorbia, which in Olduvai makes up 70 percent of the rhino's diet during the dry season, is not indigenous to Africa but was introduced from India and has spread. Goddard said, "It is interesting to speculate on the influence that the colonization and spread of this plant has had on the utilization of arid habitats by this animal."

In most parts of East Africa the rhino is not alone during these daily activities but is accompanied by another species of animal — either the red-billed or the yellow-billed oxpecker, both commonly called tick birds. These gregarious, noisy birds play an important role for the rhino. In Swahili they are called *askari wa kifaru* ("the rhino's policemen," or guards), and they are just that. When they hear or see anything alarming, especially man, they chatter and call, stimulating the rhino to react. While asleep, the rhino relies on these birds to act as its sight and hearing. The rhino's reactions will vary, depending on its individual disposition and the particular behavior of the tick birds. If the rhino is lying down and the tick birds have raised the alarm, it may simply lift its head or move its ears about, it may get up and smell the air, or it may get up and run, either toward or away from the object of alarm.

The tick birds benefit from their association with the rhino by finding food on the rhino's body. While it was always assumed that the tick birds' major food consisted of ticks and flies, Goddard thought that they mainly ate the blood from the open sores that all black rhinos seem to have. The source of these sores, or skin lesions, has been something of a mystery to scientists.

P. M. Hitchins, working on rhinos in the Natal Parks of South Africa, used the skin lesions as a field method for aging rhinos, since the lesions appear at regular intervals in different parts of the body as the rhino grows. All adult black rhinos in Natal have skin lesions situated behind the shoulders and on the chest, neck, and forelegs. A calf is born without them, but between the ages of six months and one year they begin to appear on the chest as bare pink patches. By three years, they are found on the chest and sides, but not behind the shoulders, as in adults. By four and a half to five and a half years, they are found in all the usual areas of the adult. The skin lesions appear as black, blood-encrusted areas that ulcerate and hemorrhage from time to time.

Upon further investigation scientists found the filaria parasite,

Stephanofilaria dinniki, in every skin lesion examined. It is known that parasites of this type require blood-sucking flies or ticks to complete their life cycle. There are many of these kinds of ticks and flies associated with the rhino. Hitchins and M. E. Keep, a veterinarian who also worked on the problem, concluded that the filaria are introduced to the animal by a blood-sucking insect, and the filaria then cause the skin lesions, although it is not known why they prefer specific sites. The skin lesions along with the resultant hemorrhages attract more blood-sucking flies and ticks; thus the life cycle is able to continue. On top of this, the ox-peckers keep the sores open and festering, and secondary bacterial infections aggravate the situation.

It had been suggested that the skin lesions were found only on debilitated rhinos, but since every rhino in the Hluhluwe Game Reserve in Natal had them and was apparently healthy in every other way, this could not be the case. In Kenya every rhino captured by the Game Capture Unit for translocation had skin lesions, and these rhinos were also otherwise in perfectly good condition.

The following experiment substantiated Hitchins and Keep's theory. A black rhino calf was captured in Hluhluwe at one year old and was sent at one and a half to a paddock situated 100 miles from the nearest population of black rhinos. By the age of five and a half, this rhino had not shown any sign of skin lesions, while every rhino in the Hluhluwe Game Reserve showed skin lesions by that age. It was concluded that there were no insects carrying the *S. dinniki* parasite in the area of the paddock, and therefore the animal was not infected and no lesions developed.

One further, fascinating note on the subject of skin lesions: A. T. A. Ritchie reports that "these sores appear to exercise a strong element of fetishism" during courtship.

As a very important part of his work, Goddard carried out extremely detailed studies of feeding behavior in Ngorongoro, Olduvai, and Tsavo. He set out to discover what rhinos eat, in what quantities, the availability of these plants, and, particularly in Tsavo, whether or not rhinos were in serious competition with elephants. Goddard watched individual rhinos feeding for an hour at a time, noting what they ate and what they rejected in a semicircle in front of their heads. He often made these observations on foot from only 10 yards away. Altogether he spent 377 hours watching feeding rhinos.

It was already known that the rhino is a browser, and Goddard confirmed that grass makes up only a very small proportion of its diet. In Ngorongoro and Olduvai the rhinos ate 191 species of plants from 49 botanical families. In Tsavo they ate 102 species from 32 botanical families. They showed a preference for herbs and shrubs, particularly legumes, which make up 60 percent of their diet in both the wet and dry seasons. Rhinos are highly selective, eating only certain specimens of a species. Goddard thought that they were able to detect by smell which specimens have nutritional value. They invariably reject dry and sterile plants.

It is interesting to watch a feeding rhino. With its prehensile upper lip it grasps vegetation, maneuvers it into its mouth, and cuts off what it wants with its teeth. The rhino moves from bush to bush or herb to herb, sniffing and selecting. It eats different parts of different plants, sometimes just the leaves, sometimes just the stems or tips of shoots, and sometimes just the bark. Much of the food it prefers are small ground plants interspersed among the grass; rhinos are often seen feeding out on a grassy plain with no shrubs in sight and have been mistakenly thought to be grazing. They do eat some grass, usually in the wet season, but only a very small amount.

One of the weirder facts to emerge about the rhino is that it is coprophagous — dung-eating. The Klingels were the first to report on this very unusual habit. Over a period of several days they watched four rhinos eating wildebeest droppings. "The rhinos selected fresh or superficially dried dung. They picked a whole heap of dung from the ground and chewed it, losing parts of it in the process, but swallowing most of it. Whilst engaged in this activity, they did not feed on any plant, but walked determinedly from one dung heap to the next. The reason for this extraordinary behaviour is not known, but possibly a mineral or other deficiency is balanced in this manner." Goddard saw rhinos eating dung on eight occasions, always in September or October, when it is dry and there are few legumes available. He also thought it might be a way of supplementing the diet with minerals found in the dung.

A discussion of the rhinoceros would not be complete without mentioning its temperament. Is the rhino really such a vicious, stupid brute? Goddard always stood up for the rhino, but then each scientist usually takes the side of the animal he is studying. Actually, what happens is that the scientist gets to know his animal so well that he knows how to approach it, how close he can get, and generally what to expect of it. In many cases he knows individuals' particular dispositions. In an excellent M-G-M–TV documentary on Goddard and his work called *Kifaru — the Black Rhinoceros,* Goddard revealed his feelings about the rhino: "The deeper you get into the study of one animal, the more you realize how very little you really know about it; and as time progresses, you find your attitude changes. At first it's just a very large, ugly, prehistoric-looking animal. But as you get deeper and deeper into the study and know these animals individually, you realize rapidly that these animals do have temperaments, moods, and, to be quite unscientific, personality." Goddard made a plea for the rhinoceros, saying it is "a shortsighted, harmless old beast that deserves, I think, the greatest degree of sympathy that you can give it."

Goddard felt that one of the reasons the rhino has such a bad name is its characteristic reaction to alarm. When the oxpeckers shriek and fly off, the rhino gets up. If he cannot detect anything on the wind, then he races forward, sometimes at an alarming speed, to investigate the cause of the oxpeckers' excitement. People mistake this investigating for a charge. Whatever the case might be, the rhino is a singularly terrifying animal met at close range, and when, puffing and snorting, it bears down on one like a runaway locomotive, one scarcely wants to contemplate the fine distinction between investigating and charging.

However, one cannot really conclude, as Goddard did, that the rhino is harmless. Goddard's knowledge of the rhinos in his study area certainly helped him, but a dangerous situation can sometimes arise. Rudolf Schenkel was charged and chased by a bull rhino that he had approached on foot. He was in an open area, outlined against the sky, so the rhino was able to see him, and immediately charged. Schenkel ran forward shouting at it, but it still came at him. When Schenkel swerved past the rhino and ran for a small fallen tree, the rhino turned and came after him, even though he had now caught the human scent, which would normally make a rhino turn away. The man and the rhino ran around the tree a number of times, and as Schenkel was trying to climb the tree, the rhino caught and tossed him. Schenkel landed on the rhino's shoulders and then fell to the ground. He crawled under the tree, but the rhino even pushed his way in there to get him. Schenkel lay with one foot in the air, and the rhino came to a stop with his nose against it. He pushed against the foot once and then suddenly turned and trotted off, leaving Schenkel bruised but intact.

Iain Douglas-Hamilton was not so lucky. He was walking in thick bush looking for an elephant migration route out of Lake Manyara National Park when he suddenly came on two rhinos, a mother and an almost full-grown calf. They came for him immediately; he turned and ran, dodging and swerving between bushes, but they followed his every twist and turn. (A rhino can reach speeds of 35 miles an hour and despite its bulk is amazingly agile and can turn on a dime.) Then his sandal broke and he fell. The female came charging over him and went her way. He was left with a crushed vertebra that halted his work for more than a month.

However, in both Tsavo and Manyara rhinos have long been hunted and have every excuse for feeling aggressive toward man. In places where they have been hunted with poison arrows they are particularly truculent. Dispositions vary from one area to another. In Maasailand and other pastoral areas the rhinos tend to be more placid because they have largely been left in peace. In any population there are differences among individuals, so that, as A. T. A. Ritchie remarked, "some are moderately even-tempered, and some irritable; some brave and some timid; some volatile and some phlegmatic." Basically the reaction of an individual rhino depends on the amount of harassment and hunting that goes on in the area where it lives and the particular conditions under which that animal is met.

Where rhinos are left in peace they may live well into old age. There are no records of maximum life spans for rhinos living in the wild, but there are records from zoos. In the Chicago Zoo there was a rhino who was thirty-six years old at the time of Goddard's study. The record is forty-nine years old, but this was for an Indian one-horned rhino (*Rhinoceros unicornis*). For wild black rhinos, Goddard estimated a maximum longevity of forty years.

Goddard arrived at his estimate of longevity by taking the zoo records and combining them with examinations of the teeth of living and dead rhinos. The rhino has four premolars and three permanent molars on both sides of the lower and upper jaws. By old age the rhino has lost its premolars and the larger permanent molars have worn down. Goddard devised a technique for determining the age at death of the skulls that were collected throughout his study areas. He immobilized forty rhinos in order to take measurements of their bodies, skulls, and teeth, and to measure the eruption and wear of the teeth. Once the rhino was immobilized with drugs fired from a dart gun, he pried the animal's mouth open and, with the aid of a flashlight, examined the teeth. Goddard stated quite nonchalantly that "with the rhinoceros under heavy anaesthesia this is a relatively simple procedure."

More than five hundred skulls of dead rhinos were collected in Tsavo, and by measuring these skulls and teeth and comparing them to the data from the living rhinos, Goddard worked out twenty age classes and was able to give an approximate chronological age to each skull and thus work out the life expectancy at any given age. His results showed that mortality was highest in the first and second years of life and then rose again after the age of twenty-five. He concluded that, assuming a stable population, the mean expectation of life at birth for a rhino is 8.4 years, rising to 10.2 years at four years of age, and then falling.

Man is the greatest single cause of death for the rhino and probably has been for the last one hundred years. Predation by large carnivores such as lions and hyenas is rare. Young calves are protected by their mothers. Goddard saw five incidents in which hyenas unsuccessfully tried to pull down rhino calves. If an adult rhino survives the hazards of poaching, hunting, disease, accident, and drought and lives to an old age, then the most probable cause of death will be malnutrition due to the wearing down and loss of teeth. The rhino harbors diseases such as typhoid, pneumonia, trypanosomiasis (sleeping sickness), and others. When the rhino becomes debilitated because of an inadequate diet, these diseases tend to take over.

In 1969, at the end of his study, Goddard was able to say that the future of the rhinos looked good in Tsavo. The population was stable and nutritious vegetation was abundant. Ten years later that picture had changed beyond all recognition. The estimated seven thousand rhinos in Tsavo were decimated by poachers, and fewer than two hundred remained. No one could have predicted that from 1975 to 1979 the price of rhino horn would increase by 2000 percent from $32 per kilogram (2.2 pounds) to $675 per kilo wholesale and as much as $11,615 per kilo retail!

In 1979, Esmond Bradley Martin, a geographer who specializes in Indian Ocean trade, was commissioned by IUCN to investigate the world trade in rhino products. In that same year, Kes Hillman, who had been scientific deputy on the IUCN Elephant Survey, was appointed chairman of the IUCN/SSC African Rhino Group, and she set out to do a survey of rhinos throughout Africa to determine their status and make recommendations for their conservation. In addition, the World Wildlife Fund mounted an international fund-raising campaign to save the rhino.

These measures may or may not have come too late. The plight of the rhino is very serious indeed. Hillman estimates that in the past ten years, 90 percent of the rhinos in Kenya, Uganda, and northern Tanzania have been killed. Bradley Martin reported that on average 7870 kilograms of rhino horn was exported annually from Africa between 1972 and 1978. This figure represents 2580 rhinos killed each year. As Hillman now estimates that there are only 15,000 to 25,000 black rhinos left in the whole of Africa, an annual offtake of this magnitude would exterminate the remaining rhinos in the next five to ten years. In Kenya alone, where the rhino population was estimated at 18,000 in 1969, there are fewer than 1500 left today, and many of these are in tiny remnant populations which are no longer viable. In Amboseli National Park, an area famous for its long-horned rhinos, there were once 70 rhinos in the central area of the Park and now there are only 13. The Ngorongoro Crater rhinos, from which Goddard learned so much, have been reduced to fewer than 20, and they are still being shot.

The question was what was happening to all this rhino horn. Bradley Martin traveled to North Yemen, India, Mauritius, Singapore, Hong Kong, Macao, Taiwan, Thailand, and Sri Lanka and carried out interviews with more than one hundred wholesalers, retailers, importers, and pharmacists to obtain information on prices and trading of rhino products. One of the first things he discovered was that rhino horn is not used as an aphrodisiac in the Far East but as a popular traditional medicine to cure a variety of ailments from headache to purifying the blood, the most prevalent use being for fever reduction. It is widely and openly sold in all the Chinese medicine shops throughout the Far East. In parts of India, rhino horn is used as an aphrodisiac (it is made into a paste and applied to the male genitals), but by far the greatest proportion of rhino horn sold in the East is used as medicine.

Trade in rhino horn has been going on for centuries, and the demand for it in the Far East has remained fairly steady, so it was puzzling why the price should have risen so phenomenally. Bradley Martin tracked down the origin of the new demand to North Yemen. We all suffer in one way or another by living at a time when the world economy is dominated by the price of oil, but it comes as a shock to find out that oil is also the root cause of the deaths of thousands of rhinos. It turns out that in North Yemen every adult male wears a dagger or *jambia*. The prized jambias have handles carved out of rhino horn. Until the mid-seventies only a few wealthy sheiks could afford to own rhino-horn daggers. (They vary in price from $300 to $13,000.) When oil prices tripled in 1973–74, Saudi Arabia started a massive program of development projects for which they needed manual laborers. The young men of North Yemen flocked to Saudi Arabia; by 1978, out of a total population of 6 million, almost 1 million Yemenis were working in Saudi Arabia and bringing home $1.5 billion. The first thing the young men wanted to do with their new-found wealth was to buy the prestigious rhino-horn daggers. There was not enough rhino horn on the market to meet the demand, and consequently the price rose sharply in Sanaa, the capital of North Yemen. The dealers in Hong Kong and other trading centers in the East soon found that they had to pay higher and higher prices to get any rhino horn at all. And the price continues to rise as rhinos become more and more scarce.

Conservation organizations are once again rallying round the rhino. Over $1 million was raised by the World Wildlife Fund, and these funds have gone mainly to antipoaching projects in areas where the rhino is severely threatened. Both governments and conservation groups have made pleas to the government of North Yemen, but so far to no avail. On their own initiative, dealers in Hong Kong approached their government and instituted a ban on the import of rhino horn. It is hoped that China will soon ratify CITES (Convention on International Trade in Endangered Species of Flora and Fauna), which would mean that it would no longer import rhino horn. Public awareness of the plight of the rhino in African countries that still have rhinos is increasing, and many governments have committed themselves to protective measures.

But these developments are only a beginning — the rhino is by no means out of danger. An all out effort must be made to end the poaching and stop the trade if man is going to save this remarkable beast who has lived on this earth for the past 25 million years.

IV

Zebras

THE ZEBRA IS an improbable animal. No matter how many times one sees zebras in the wild, one is startled at those black and white striped animals actually trotting around out there on the plains — their coloring seems so totally *unnatural*. Surely an animal that looks like that belongs only on the last page of a child's alphabet book. But there they are, a very familiar part of the African scene, existing in large numbers, and always looking clean and fat.

One need only watch a group of zebras for a short while to realize that they would make a fascinating subject for a behavior study, for they are very social animals and constantly interact with each other. As we have seen, an animal such as the giraffe can be frustrating for the behaviorist because it rarely interacts with other giraffes even when in a herd, and the solitary rhino can be a bit dull at times because it is basically antisocial. Zebras, however, seem to be always in touch with one another, whether they are grooming each other, fighting, playing, or simply resting their heads on each other's backs. Even when feeding, they are aware of the other zebras around them and react to one another.

As with so many wild animals, these interactions were not clearly understood by the casual observer and were often misinterpreted; until recently, knowledge about the social structure of zebras was surprisingly sparse for such a conspicuous and abundant animal. In 1962, C. A. Spinage (in *The Animals of East Africa*), through no fault of his own, could write only the following about what was known of zebra behavior: "But where there is little or no struggle for food, safety in numbers probably binds the zebra herds rather than mutual affection. We know nothing about the composition of zebra herds throughout the year. During the breeding season successful stallions gather a group of mares together. But whether the young stallions are driven out or tolerated within the herd, or whether any lasting relationships are built up between mature animals seems to be unknown."

In the same year, Hans Klingel arrived in Tanzania to begin his pioneering study of the plains zebra of the Serengeti and the Ngorongoro Crater, and soon found that, far from the amorphous herds that appeared to exist, plains zebras have a complex social system unlike that of any other known animal, based on personal bonds among individuals.

There are three distinct species of zebras in Africa, ranging from the southern Sudan in the north to the Cape Province of South Africa. The most familiar is the plains zebra, often called the Burchell's zebra, which includes a number of subspecies — Boehm's, Selous', Chapman's, Damara — having coat patterns varying from pure black and white in the northern Boehm's to an almost buff and brown with distinct shadow stripes within the lighter color in the South African Chapman's zebra.[1] There are two types of mountain zebra — the Cape mountain zebra (*Equus zebra zebra*) found in the Cape Province of South Africa and Hartmann's zebra (*Equus zebra hartmannae*) found in South West Africa. They differ from the plains zebra in that they are smaller and have a gridiron pattern of stripes running along the top of the rump and a slight dewlap on the neck. The third species, the Grevy's zebra (*Equus grevyi*) found in northern Kenya, Ethiopia, and Somalia, is distinctly different from the others. It is taller, its

---

[1] There is a certain amount of controversy over the correct Latin name for the plains zebra, some preferring *Equus quagga*, others *Equus burchelli*. As the first plains zebra to be described was the quagga, *Equus quagga quagga* (now extinct), it is argued that this would be the correct specific name; however, some people claim that the quagga was a separate species and the first true plains zebra to be described was the Burchell's of South Africa, *Equus burchelli burchelli* (almost definitely extinct also). To avoid confusion it is simpler to call all the subspecies plains zebras.

stripes are narrow and very close together, and its ears are large and trumpet-shaped. Many claim it is the most beautiful of all the zebras.

Since 1962 Hans Klingel and his wife, Ute, have managed the remarkable feat of studying all three zebra species in detail. They have studied the plains zebras (Boehm's) in Tanzania, both mountain zebras in southern Africa, and the Grevy's zebra in northern Kenya. To top it off, they carried out a six-month study of the Somali wild ass in the Danakil Desert of Ethiopia. Considering that Hans Klingel was also teaching in a German university during much of this period, their achievement is all the more outstanding. But the Klingels are a remarkable couple: both are tough, dedicated, extremely hard-working; they work as a very efficient team; and they can live and work under the roughest conditions. They use their time in Africa to the fullest.

The Klingels are currently writing up their results on the Grevy's zebra and the wild ass. Their most comprehensive work has been on the plains zebra, and thus the bulk of this chapter will concentrate on that animal. But the fact that they themselves have studied and compared a number of different zebra populations makes the comparative data particularly interesting. The similarities they found among the three species are not surprising, but the differences, especially between the plains zebra and the Grevy's, are fascinating and thought-provoking in terms of the evolution of behavior.

The Plains Zebra

Having worked in Africa in the early sixties, Klingel is one of the grand old men of East African wildlife scientists. He arrived in the Serengeti National Park at a time when wildlife research in East Africa was in its infant stage. He was one of only three scientists there, but their work contributed to what was later to become a unique body of knowledge. Subsequently dozens more scientists were attracted to the unparalleled opportunities that the large, relatively untouched Serengeti ecosystem offered for research. With the creation and building of the Serengeti Research Institute in the late 1960s, all research was coordinated with the aim of understanding how the ecosystem worked, so that its conservation could be assured. Today it is generally agreed that the Serengeti is ecologically the best-known area of its size in the world.

The main purpose of Klingel's plains zebra study was to find out which zebras should be shot if a cropping scheme were to be implemented. The study area included both the Serengeti National Park and the Ngorongoro Conservation Area, a vast expanse of more than 10,000 square miles with a population then estimated at over 150,000 zebras. As Klingel is basically a behaviorist, he was interested in the social organization and behavior of the plains zebra and set about studying this aspect, knowing that he could also answer the cropping questions from the data collected.

After preliminary investigations Klingel decided to carry out his detailed behavior studies in the Ngorongoro Crater, where there is a population of about 5500 zebras, most of which are resident year round. His goal was to be able to recognize 10 percent of the population, which is considered a large enough proportion to get substantial data on social organization. To have tried to know 10 percent of the Serengeti population of 150,000 would have been futile, and the vast distances the herds move would have made this difficult. Klingel spent half of his time each month in Ngorongoro and the other half in Serengeti, continuing to study herd structure and movements there.

It seems an almost impossible task to set about learning to recognize 550 individual zebras. Simply watching a moving herd of zebras makes some people dizzy. Klingel could see that each zebra has an individual stripe pattern, but from a distance this was not helpful. The system he devised to overcome this problem was to immobilize and mark a number of individuals. Although drug immobilization has become a matter of course in wildlife studies today, in 1962 it was a new technique, and one still very much in the process of trial and error. Special guns and crossbows were being tested; the dart syringes were more often faulty than not, failing to fire on impact or falling short of the target. And the scientists barely knew which drugs and what amounts to give the animals. Some of the drugs were new and extremely lethal — one sniff of M99 powder is enough to kill a man. Zebras became agitated under some drugs that were supposed to put them to sleep, while other drugs had no antidote and so the animal would remain unconscious for hours at a time. Through all this, Klingel lost some zebras, but in the end he had a remarkably successful record and managed to mark 122 zebras, many of which were immobilized several times in order to check their tooth wear for aging criteria.

The marking consisted of branding each zebra with letters of the alphabet, cropping their manes and tails, and in some cases attaching eartags. The manes grew back in a few months, but the squared-off tail hair remained a good field characteristic for two years or more. The eartags were not so successful because some of them came out as a result of infections. The brands are permanent, although in a few cases they became faint on young animals that grew up. In a large concentration of zebras, the cropped tail or mane caught Klingel's eye from a distance. On closer inspection, or through binoculars, he could read the brand.

When Ute Klingel came out in April 1963, they began photographing the zebras associated with the marked ones, and it was soon strikingly apparent that the marked animals were almost always found in groups made up of the same individuals. Every time they found a marked zebra, they checked the photographs to see if the same animals were present and made new photographs if there were any new animals. They photographed both sides of each zebra, using the whole stripe pattern for recognition, then glued the photographs onto file cards and carried the cards with them. Eventually they knew and had on file more than six hundred individual zebras.

The Klingels were the first scientists in East Africa to recognize systematically a large number of individual animals by their natural markings, and it can be said that they pioneered this system in Africa. They showed that photographic recognition of animals was feasible, and almost every subsequent behavior study has incorporated this method.

Once individuals were known, the social organization began to emerge. The zebra turned out to be much more fascinating than anyone had expected. Those amorphous herds are actually made up of small stable groups in which there are strong bonds between individuals. Although the structure is different, the cohesion of a zebra group is much like that of an elephant family unit. There are two kinds of zebra groups — family groups and all-male bachelor groups — and in addition there are some solitary stallions. The family group consists of a stallion, one to six mares, and their foals; it can number from two to sixteen animals but usually averages about seven animals. The bachelor groups range from two to ten animals, averaging about three per group.

What the Klingels found interesting about the social organization was the stability of the groups. Far from being forced together by the stallion, the mares and foals are bound together by personal bonds among themselves and with the stallion. When a group loses its stallion, the mares do not split up but are taken over as a whole by a new stallion. When male and female foals reach a certain age, they leave the group, but the adult mares stay in the same family group for years and probably for the rest of their lives. In forty-one family groups that the Klingels watched for two years there were 129 fully adult mares, and of these, 122, or 95 percent, were still in the same groups after the two years. The 7 missing ones were thought to have died from natural causes. Although it is possible for a mare to change from one group to another, the Klingels suspected that this was very rare. In only one case was an adult mare adopted into one of their known groups. They did not know where she had come from but thought that she might have lost her own family completely.

Although the bachelor groups are not as stable as the family groups, they are also maintained by personal bonds. Some adult males do leave to start their own families. Within the groups there are obviously strong bonds between certain individuals. Unlike bachelor groups of other species, these groups show no hierarchy among the members; fights for rank order were never seen. There is, however, a leader in each group, and he is always an adult.

In the family groups, on the other hand, there is a very strict rank order among the members, which is most clearly seen in the marching order: the dominant, or alpha, mare always leads the group; the others follow in single file in order of their rank, the lowest-ranking mare coming last. When the group is ready to move, the lower-ranking females wait until all the higher-ranking ones have gone past. If they try to overtake a higher-ranking mare, they are threatened until they return to their own place in the line. Sometimes the mares even kick at lower-ranking ones with their hind legs, but ordinarily one threatening gesture with head lowered and ears laid back is enough to keep them in place. The foals usually follow behind their mothers according to age, the youngest immediately behind the mother, then the next youngest. The Klingels knew several mares who were followed by three foals of their own, of different ages. However, foals do not always stick to the marching order. Foals of the same age prefer walking with each other, and so two may follow behind the mother of one of them. An odd characteristic of the rank order is that the foals temporarily take on the rank order of their mothers when they are standing near them. A lower-ranking mare will respect the position of the foal of a higher-ranking mare and accord that foal the same respect that she accords the mother.

It was not clear to the Klingels how the hierarchy among the mares was determined. They did not fight among themselves. In some groups the rank order remained the same over the two-year period of observations; in other groups it changed every few months. Any new young mares who were brought into the family by the stallion were kept at a distance by the other mares and were immediately the lowest-ranking. Old or sick mares never led for long, but changes also occurred among apparently healthy animals. It was not discovered what elements were necessary for the changes. The Klingels thought it could possibly be related to pregnancy and estrus.

The stallion is the dominant member of the whole family group. Although the lead mare determines the direction of the group's movements and actually choses the pastures, drinking places, etc., ultimately the stallion has control. He does not have a definite place in the marching order. He sometimes marches at the end of the group or a bit to the side of it. If he wants to change the direction of the group, he comes up along the side and drives the lead mare in the direction he wants the group to take.

The personal bonds among the group members are strengthened by mutual grooming, which is carried out by all members in a group — even foals only a few days old. The strongest bonds are revealed by who grooms with whom. Adult mares rarely groom each other. Most frequent grooming occurs between mares and their youngest foals, then between mares and their next oldest foals, then between the stallion and mares, and between the stallion and foals. The stallion has favorite mares with whom he grooms. His preferences, however, do not seem to have any effect on the rank order, nor do they seem to be correlated with estrus in the female. He simply prefers some mares to others. Perhaps they have a more efficient or more pleasurable grooming technique. Members of bachelor groups also indulge in mutual grooming, but here no preferences were observed.

Aside from the social function, mutual grooming serves a utilitarian end, for it helps keep the skin and hair of the animals in good condition. In grooming, two animals stand facing each other and nibble each other's necks and backs. The nibbling action extracts loose hair. They also scratch against the grain of the hair with their upper incisors, cleaning the hair and skin. Each side of the animal is groomed in turn. When they are finished with one side, each takes a step backward, turns the head to the other side, and resumes grooming. Grooming lasts anywhere from a few minutes to half an hour.

The Klingels kept six tame zebras in the Serengeti. They

found that the best way to tame them was to groom them. At first this could only be accomplished by putting a brush on the end of a long stick that could reach to all corners of the small taming enclosure. Despite themselves, the zebras could not help liking the brushing, and the Klingels were gradually able to shorten the stick, until within a few days they were able to groom the zebras by hand. By then the zebras were tame. In fact, when Klingel plucked at their hair, imitating nibbling, the zebras tried to groom his arm or leg, which was not entirely pleasurable for him. The tame zebras would never allow any person they did not know to groom them, just as in the wild, strange zebras never groom each other.

Both family groups and bachelor groups congregate in large herds [2] on good grazing land and the groups also mingle at water holes, but even in these large conglomerations the group remains intact. However, sometimes one member of a family, usually a foal, gets lost, and then the real cohesion of the groups can be seen. Members of the group frantically rush around, looking for the lost animal; at the same time the lost one runs from one zebra group to another, calling and looking for its family. From his observations Klingel concluded that zebras recognize each other by sight, voice, and smell. When zebras are visible to each other, it is probably primarily the stripe pattern that is used. It is only at night, in dense concentrations or in thick bush, that they resort to calling. Individual smell is probably used only at short distances. This could be observed with young lost foals who went from group to group, going up to individuals and smelling noses. It was interesting that when the foal finally found its mother, it walked directly to her but did not then touch noses with her. Recognition by sight was also seen in zebras that had been immobilized. When the animal revived, it walked in a straight line to its group, if the group was within 100 yards.

Concern for lost members of a group is not reserved just for

[2] "Herd," in relation to zebras, is used to denote a loose aggregation of groups. In this case "herd" is not synonymous with "group"; the latter refers only to small family groups and bachelor groups.

foals. All members are searched for, but not necessarily by every member. Mares do not search for other mares or for their older male foals, who are only searched for by the stallion. When the lost animal is found, it is led back to the group. Young lost foals were often chased away from a strange family. The Klingels never saw lost foals, who cannot survive on their own, be adopted. Even a female who has just lost her foal will not adopt a strange foal if she finds one.

The contact call that zebras use when trying to find each other sounds something like the combination of a donkey braying and dog barking. Individual zebra voices vary tremendously and can be distinguished even by humans. The contact call is also used by stallions when they want to get in touch with other stallions in the area. One stallion calls and waits for an answer. Then the two stallions continue calling back and forth until they meet and greet. Aside from the contact call the zebra makes a number of other noises: 1) A two-syllable alarm call is made when danger — a predator or a man on foot — is approaching. All neighboring zebras react immediately to this call by standing still and looking intently in the direction of the danger. 2) A loud snort is made when zebras are about to move into a dangerous area — for instance, thick bush or a water hole. 3) A long, drawn-out snort is a sign of contentment. Klingel heard this when his tame zebras where brought into their stable at night. 4) A short, high-pitched squeal is uttered by a stallion when bitten or threatened in a fight. This is probably an expression of pain or fear. 5) A long, drawn-out wailing call is uttered by foals in distress. This call is highly disturbing to other members of the group. When Klingel captured sleeping foals in order to measure them, they made this wailing call, and both mares and stallions would come at him in a threatening manner, but fortunately they never carried out an attack.

The family group, with its cohesion and mutual concern among members, is an ideal nursery. Every foal is born within a group and is protected and nurtured from birth to maturity. Zebra foals are born throughout the year, although there is a peak foaling time that extends from October to March and appears to be dependent on the rainfall pattern.

In Ngorongoro the Klingels knew every member of fifty-two family groups and were able to observe the histories of these animals over a two-year period. In many cases they were able to follow the development of a foal from its birth to its departure from the family. In fact, we have finally come to an animal of which it is possible to say that births in the wild have been seen and even described and photographed by scientific observers. However, it is still not all that common to see a zebra birth in the wild; if the mare is disturbed in the initial stages of labor, she can delay birth for hours.

The Klingels observed five births during their study and described the following birth and its aftermath in detail. They found a mare lying flat on her side, with the head and forelegs of the foal already exposed but completely covered in the amnion, or fetal sac. "Two minutes later parturition was completed. The foal moved its head and legs and succeeded in getting the amnion off its mouth and nose. The mother at the time sat up on her brisket and remained quietly in that position licking her lips; this was a notable feature. Three minutes after parturition the foal unsuccessfully tried to stand up and subsequently succeeded in shaking its head free. During the next 10 minutes the foal tried another three times to get up; it once stood for about a half a minute. Thirteen minutes after parturition, the mare stood up, walked to the foal, sniffed at it and licked it superficially around the anus, then around its mouth and abdomen for about 1 minute. The foal again tried to stand up, thereby freeing itself further from the amnion. Fourteen minutes after parturition the foal stood up and then the umbilical cord severed. The mare licked the foal again and then licked and chewed at the amnion on the ground, but did not eat any of it. The foal then started walking slowly about and was again licked by the mare. The placenta was pulled out by the foal; it and the amnion were eaten by vultures, while the mare and foal walked slowly away and joined the rest of the family, consisting of three mares, a yearling, two young foals and the stallion, who did not seem to take any notice of the new-born foal." An hour after birth the foal found the teats and suckled. During the first four hours it suckled for a total of fourteen minutes. The mare began grazing about one and a half hours after the birth.

While the mare was giving birth, the stallion kept guard over her, never moving farther than 50 yards away and not coming closer than 10 yards. This guarding behavior was seen in the other births, too. In each case the other mares of the family continued grazing, apparently unconcerned.

Zebra foals are lovely creatures from the very beginning, unlike many newborn animals. They have beautifully formed heads, large lustrous eyes, and extremely long, delicate legs. The coat is long and furry and distinctly brown and white. The brown gradually turns to black as the foal gets older.

During the first few days of its life the mother keeps all other members of her family and any other zebras away from her foal. She does this by threatening and chasing the other animals, even the stallion, who is the dominant animal. Klingel explains that "this behaviour is obviously correlated with the critical period of imprinting of the mother's image on the foal. New-born foals follow any object near to them during the first days of life. The aggressive behaviour of the mare thus prevents the foal from accepting another animal as its mother. Several days later this behaviour of the mare ceases and all members of the group can contact the foal, which by then seems to recognize its mother by her stripe pattern, voice and scent."

The zebra foal stays close to its mother when it is still young, although, as was mentioned earlier, foals are attracted to other foals of their own age, so that one often sees the foals of a group standing and moving together. Foals begin feeding on grass at an early age, but this does not take up much of their time in the first months. Instead, they spend the day resting and playing. As with any young animal, play is an important factor in the development of the young zebra. Zebras play from the age of a few weeks to several years. Running games are most frequently played by foals under a year old. Then the foal may gallop by it-self, running around its family and racing up to 150 yards away. Foals may also play racing and chasing games with each other, and even with foals from neighboring groups. In eight cases the Klingels saw mares playing with their foals, and once even a stallion joined a game. In these cases the adults always took the role of the chaser.

Zebra foals also make other animals their unwilling play-mates. The Klingles often saw foals chasing gazelles and birds. One gazelle was chased for over 100 yards, and a terrified mon-goose was chased for 30 yards until it escaped down a hole.

The foal is weaned at about seven months but does not leave the group until it is at least a year old; until then, it maintains a close relationship with its mother and other members of the group. The young females leave the family under very abrupt and violent circumstances. When a young mare is thirteen to fif-teen months old, she comes into estrous for the first time, and adopts a typical posture that has the immediate effect of attracting every stallion in the vicinity. She stands with legs apart and tail lifted, and it is the optic effect of this position that is the key. The estrous secretions also play a part, but probably not until the stallion has been attracted by the stance. When Klingel im-mobilized zebras of both sexes, they often adopted the estrous posture under the influence of the drugs, and strange stallions, at-tracted to both mares and stallions, fought them and even tried to mount them.

When the young mare takes the estrous stance, the mature stallions in the area converge on the family group and try to ab-duct her. The family stallion reacts to this situation by desper-ately attempting to fight the stallions off. First he attacks one and chases it far away, then he races back to his group and chases another one away. If one of these stallions takes up the challenge, he may even fight with him. In the meantime the other stallions chase the group until they manage to separate the young mare and drive her away. In the end the family stallion has to give up from sheer exhaustion. In one case the Klingels saw eighteen stallions fighting over the possession of one mare; the numbers alone make it almost impossible for the family stallion to keep the young female.

Under certain circumstances a family stallion might be successful in defending and keeping his young mare. Of forty-four individually known young mares in the abducting age group in Ngorongoro, only one remained with her original family; she was still with the family of her father at two and three-quarters years old. Klingel thought that the family stallions are probably successful more often in areas of low density of zebras, where there are not always enough stallions to defeat the family stallion.

After all the fuss and fighting over the young mare, she does not even allow her abductor to mount her, and what is more, she does not even stay with him for long. The fight over her resumes, and as she is in estrus for a week, she may get abducted a number of times during that period. In fact, every time she comes into estrus she may be abducted again. Two marked young mares were followed up after their first abductions; one was seen with three different stallions in a period of six months and the other, four, until each finally stayed with one of her suitors. What happens is that as the young mare gets older, she gradually takes a less obvious stance when she comes into estrus, and as a result other stallions no longer take an interest in her. The older mares in a family group take the estrous stance only immediately before being mounted by the family stallion and thus do not attract strange stallions at all. Klingel concluded that the estrus behavior of the young mare is extremely important in preventing inbreeding and encouraging outbreeding. With such strong personal family bonds, the young mare would never leave her father's group were it not for this behavior mechanism, which attracts the other stallions.

The abducting stallions are either bachelors starting their own families or family stallions attempting to increase the number of their mares. When a family stallion tries to introduce a newly adopted young mare to his group, she is bitten and chased by the old mares and the young mare has to keep a distance of 30 to 50 yards from the others. The stallion usually stands between the new mare and the old ones, and thus keeps the others from attacking her.

Although a young mare may have her first estrus at thirteen to fifteen months, she is apparently unable to become pregnant for a long while yet. The youngest mares actually seen copulating were eighteen months old, and the youngest mares seen with foals were three and a half years old. With a gestation period of approximately one year, this means that they were not fertile until two and a half years old. By two and a half — and usually several months before that age — they would have become permanent members of a family. In this way mares are served only by fully mature family stallions. Other stallions have no way of getting into contact with mature mares until they are able to take over a group or begin their own families.

Once a mare becomes a permanent member of a group, mating behavior within the family is relatively simple. When one of the mares comes into estrus, the family stallion becomes interested in her dung and urine. He defecates on her dung and sprays urine on the spot where she has urinated. This behavior was once interpreted as a means of hiding the condition of the mare from other stallions; but Klingel found that other stallions show no great interest in the dung and urine of estrous mares from other families, even when it has not been covered up, nor do they show any special interest in the marking activity of the family stallion. Even the stallions in bachelor groups defecate and urinate on each other's dung and urine, sometimes making communal dung heaps. After defecating one after the other on the heap, they often perform parts of a greeting ceremony. Klingel feels that the marking may be a carryover from an older system or may even be the beginnings of a gradual change to a new system, but in the present social system the marking does not have any obvious significance that he can find.

After the stallion determines that the mare is in estrus, he begins to pursue her, and from an anthropomorphic point of view the older mares appear to be taken for granted. Courtship behavior of any duration occurs only between the stallion and his young, newly adopted mares. The stallion is very attentive to the young mare when she comes into estrus, first grooming her on the neck, shoulders, flank, and rump before trying to mount her. For the first few days of estrus she keeps moving away when he tries to mount, and he keeps following her, grooming her and trying again. At the height of estrus, on the third or fourth day, she allows copulation, which lasts from one to four minutes.

While estrus might last a week in a young mare, it lasts only for a few days in the older mares, and there is practically no courtship activity. The stallion immediately mounts the mare over and over again but without attaining coition. At the height of estrus he mates with her several times at intervals of one to three hours for about a whole day. In between copulations he mounts her without an erection.

When they are mounted — or even before they are mounted, in the case of young mares — both the young and older mares display a typical face, which in German has been termed *Rossigkeitsgesicht*, or "estrous face." In this expression, Klingel writes, "their ears are held back and downwards, the corners of their lips are drawn upwards, and they chew with slightly exposed teeth and open mouths."

Once the mare reaches full maturity and produces her first foal, she is then capable of producing a foal every year for the rest of her breeding life, which may be until she is eighteen to twenty years old. About a week after the birth of her foal she comes into estrus and can become pregnant again. The shortest foaling intervals that the Klingels recorded were 378 and 385 days. Of course, not all females become pregnant this quickly, and not all foals survive. From 1963 to 1965, 50 percent of the mares in Ngorongoro had a surviving foal each year. Whether the other 50 percent lost their foals shortly after birth, during pregnancy, or did not become pregnant could not be determined. After the first few days of life, the survival rate of foals seems to be good. Of 158 foals known by the Klingels, only 8 disappeared.

The young stallions leave the family group under different cir-

cumstances. The relationship between the family stallion and his
sons is unusual and surprising. One usually hears of males being
forcibly ejected at puberty from a group in which there are females dominated by one male. But this is not the case with
zebras. The father and his sons have a strong, "friendly" personal
relationship. Young stallions leave the group between the ages of
one and four years, but they are never forced to do so by their father and it has nothing to do with sexual maturity. A combination of three factors is responsible for their departure: 1) the
young stallion's mother may have a new foal and the bonds between them might no longer be as strong; 2) there may not be any
foals of the same age and sex in the group for the young male to
play with; and 3) there may be bachelor groups nearby where there
are such playmates. If all these factors are present, the young
stallion may leave at about a year old, but if his mother does not
have another foal or the new foal dies, or if he has other play-
mates, he may stay as long as three years and possibly even
longer.

In one of the Klingels' known groups there was a young stallion
whose history had been closely followed. He was still in his father's group at the age of four and a half, which is unusually old.
The Klingels were particularly interested to see what would happen to this stallion; so they decided to immobilize and mark him.
If and when he left the family group, they would be able to follow his movements and associations. When they immobilized
him, he died. This is one of the more discouraging setbacks that
can happen to a wildlife scientist. Here was an animal they had
followed and watched and knew very well. He was an interesting
anomaly in their data, and they particularly wanted to see what his
future would be. But more than this, scientists do not just coldly
collect data in their wild animal studies; they get involved with
their animals, and for them it is truly heartbreaking to lose a
well-known individual.

The death of this young stallion showed most clearly and poig-
nantly the extremely strong personal bonds between father and
son, even with an animal as old as four and a half. The father

came back to the dead stallion several times in an attempt to rouse him and lead him back to the family. Later he left his family and went from group to group, calling for his son, searching for him for at least six hours.

A further indication of the allegiance between father and son is seen when the family stallion dies or leaves the group because of sickness or old age and the group is then taken over by a new stallion. The young stallions in the family are unable to transfer their allegiance to the stepfather, and any over the age of one year leave the group almost immediately. In one family where the family stallion was sick and had to leave the group, his 1½-year-old son also left the group and joined him, and three months later another 1-year-old son left and joined his father and brother. (This is obviously one of the ways in which bachelor groups are formed.) In another case the family stallion was immobilized and under the influence of drugs for over two hours. During that time another stallion became interested in his group and began to take it over. A 2-year-old stallion in the family left immediately, even though no sign of aggression was shown toward him by the new stallion. He waited a few hundred yards away, watching the group, and as soon as the family stallion recovered from the drug and rejoined his group, the 2-year-old returned.

In the normal course of events, young stallions leave their family groups between the ages of one and three to join bachelor groups. It is interesting that certain bachelor groups consist of mostly adult animals and new additions to these are also adult, while other groups consist mainly of younger animals, joined by other young animals. The animals in the bachelor groups, especially in those made up of young animals, are very high-spirited and playful. Their running games turn into races, with the whole group of them galloping across the plains at full speed. They indulge in mock fights and playful greeting ceremonies. In the play fights, all the elements of true fights are present but are not carried out with the same intensity. They neck wrestle, wheel around, bite at each other from standing and sitting positions, rear up on their hind legs, and chase each other. The play fights do not become serious, although they sometimes appear to be quite intense. When they are over, the partners often rest with heads on each other's backs in a friendly manner.

In zoos young stallions are reported to be sexually mature at three years old, although one case was reported in which a stallion mated at eighteen and a half months. In the wild, however, Klingel found that the youngest family stallions were five to six years old. He concluded that stallions are neither physically nor psychologically ready to fight for young mares until they are about five years old. The possession of young mares is a serious business among zebras, and to be in competition at all demands full strength and self-confidence. It is only when there is a young female in estrus that serious fighting occurs. Often a chase without any close contact is enough to decide an altercation, but if the challenge is taken up, a true fight will ensue.

Fighting is carried out in a ritualized manner only insofar as the opponents fight in the same way. They are at the same time both on the offensive and defensive. There are different phases in the fight; these follow each other in various order and include circling, neck wrestling, biting at each other from standing and sitting positions, striking at each other while rearing up on the hind legs, and kicking out with both hind legs while running.

The fight usually begins with the opponents in the reverse parallel position, with each animal circling around, trying to bite at the other's legs. In order to defend themselves, they go down into a sitting position and continue to circle around on their carpal joints. In this way their legs are protected under their bodies.

Neck wrestling also follows circling. In this type of fighting one animal puts its neck over the neck of the other, presses down with all his strength, so hard that his front legs might dangle off the ground, while the other animal strains upward with all his strength. In order to extricate himself, the one below may suddenly drop his neck, move back, and quickly get his head up over the neck of the other.

The most serious fighting is that in which both animals stand on their hind legs in a bipedal position and hit downward at each

other. At the same time each bites at the neck, ears, and mane of
the other, sometimes getting a good hold with the teeth. Zebras
can inflict vicious-looking wounds, but as their teeth are relatively
blunt and their skin is extremely tough, usually the wounds are
not serious. They also get badly bruised from kicking and striking blows, but zebras are very strong, resilient animals and apparently recover quickly.

Zebras do not fight to the death. As soon as one of them
decides he has had enough, he can turn and run away, and if the
other chases him, he can kick out with his hind legs. Klingel
never saw any gestures of submission after a fight, or at any time
during a fight. Klingel felt that gestures of submission were un-
necessary, as one animal can retreat by running, does not have to
fight again, and, in fact, is in a strong position by being able to
kick at his pursuer.

One of the striking things about zebra social life is the amicable
relationships among the adult stallions. Except for these fights for
young mares, which do not occur all that often, interactions
among the stallions are remarkably peaceful. Unlike other animals that are organized into groups led by a single male, the zebra
family stallion is not constantly threatened by other males of his
species trying to take his females away from him. Only old and
sick stallions lose their families to other stallions, and this probably happens without a fight. Out of forty-one families observed
by the Klingels, only five stallions were replaced in two years;
three of these died and two joined bachelor groups.

While the mares do not communicate with and are openly antagonistic toward mares from other family groups, the stallions actively seek each other out. On meeting, they perform a special
greeting ceremony. In one day a family stallion will greet all the
stallions in the vicinity; in a typical day in Ngorongoro a stallion
might greet thirty other stallions.

The greeting ceremony is most clearly and rigidly performed
by family stallions greeting each other. (The stallions in the bachelor groups also greet each other, but it is done in a "nonserious"
way — the various elements of the ceremony are there but are

repeated and varied in a playful manner.) When two family stallions are going to greet, they walk toward each other in a deliberate way, or one waits until the other has reached him. On meeting, they stop, stretch their heads forward, and smell noses. Then, either still facing each other or standing parallel, they show a facial expression called the "greeting face," in which they put their ears forward and chew with slightly open mouth and retracted lips. Then they move into the reverse parallel position, and each pushes his head into the flank of the other and rubs vigorously downward. Next, they smell each other's genital regions, either from the side or through the hind legs. Finally, they smell noses again and then jump up on their hind legs and part, in what is called the "farewell jump." The jump is rarely carried out completely; usually just one foreleg is kicked out or the head is thrown back.

Sometimes when stallions of unequal rank — for instance, a young stallion and an adult stallion — greet, the young stallion will adopt an expression of submission, using the same facial expression as an estrous mare — the Rossigkeitsgesicht. Then the greeting will not go beyond the nose-smelling phase. Once the adult stallion sees the expression of submission, he loses interest in the young stallion and pays no further attention to him. As Klingel says, "it looks as though the young stallion dared to do something it was not supposed to, and then felt that he could not cope with the greeting ceremony."

One really begins to appreciate the integrity of the zebra group when one sees how sick and old members are treated and how the group reacts to predators. It is so often assumed that among wild animals the weak, old, and slow are ruthlessly culled by predators while the other members of the species are busy looking out for themselves. This is certainly the impression one receives when witnessing a kill in the midst of a large herd of plains animals, and it is basically the system in effect for many of the species, but with the zebra there is a difference. There is a mutual concern for members within a group, and at times there is actual assistance. We have seen this with elephants, who also have stable family groups, but in a way it is surprising to find it with zebras also, because the zebra is a favorite prey species of the larger predators and as such is constantly in jeopardy. One would think that it would not be of value to the group as a whole to help old and slow animals, but this is exactly what the other members of the group do, and of course countless individuals are saved — at least temporarily — from predators because of this system.

The Klingels time and again saw wounded, sick, or old animals being taken into consideration by the other members of its group. If there is such an animal in the group, the others will wait for it and slow down their marching pace so that the speed of the whole group becomes that of its slowest member. The Klingels never saw any antagonism shown toward the weak animals, and sick mares and foals were never seen on their own. On the other hand, old and sick stallions were found on their own. When a family stallion becomes old or sick, he might leave his group and live on his own. In one case a known family stallion became weak because of an infected wound and left his group, which was then taken over by another stallion. The sick stallion remained on his own for two months, until the wound healed, and then joined a bachelor group.

Mares and foals remain with the group when they are sick and within it are often able to recover from what appear to be incurable wounds and injuries. The following is one of Klingel's examples: "A mare with a two-month-old foal had, on the first identification of the group in February 1964, a fresh, gaping wound 8–10 cm. [3 to 4 inches] deep, 40 cm. [about 16 inches] long on her right hip. The wound later became infected and purulent. She remained in the family and none of the group members seemed to react to the injury. The foal suckled from both sides. When migrating the group walked more slowly than usual and waited from time to time for the badly limping mare. Three months later the wound had healed completely and the scar could only be seen by a slight displacement in the stripe pattern."

If this mare and her young foal had been expelled from her group because of her injury, they would almost certainly have been killed by predators. This same kind of allegiance was also shown toward animals that Klingel immobilized. Other members of the drugged animal's group would come up to it, smell its nose and genital area, then walk past it again and again in an effort to get it to follow them. In this way the dazed and partially blinded animal would be led back to its group. In a few cases in which mares died during immobilization, the family stallion came up to them and pushed and nudged them with his muzzle, in the same way that a mother zebra nudges her foal to wake it up. On four occasions the stallions even bit the drugged mares to try to revive them. In one unusual case Klingel saw a family stallion show the assisting behavior toward a drugged stallion with whom he had had friendly relations. On three occasions Klingel saw direct assistance: the family stallion came up to a drugged mare from his group, took hold of her on the neck with his teeth, and dragged her back to the group.

The reaction of zebras to danger is mutually beneficial to the group and to other zebras in the vicinity. Their natural enemies are mainly lions and, to a lesser degree, hyenas, wild dogs, leopards, and cheetahs. When one of these enemies is spotted, the zebras react in a characteristic manner. They form a semicircle, facing the predator, and watch it intently, heads raised and ears alertly pointed forward. The semicircle and the posture of the zebras attract the attention of the other zebras in the area (and other animals as well), who are then also aware that there is a predator nearby. Zebras will sometimes walk closer to the predator when it is discovered, then watch it, occasionally grazing, but always keeping it in sight. If the predator moves in closer, the zebras move away, keeping a distance of about 100 yards, which is their flight distance from predators. Closer than this, the predator may be able to surprise them and run them down.

If zebras are forced to flee when the predators chase them or get too close, the stallion of the group remains behind, acting as a rear guard. He turns and threatens the pursuers, biting and striking at them, and is often successful in warding them off, allowing the mares and foals to get away first.

Female rhino and calf in Ngorongoro Crater.

John Goddard with a partially immobilized rhino. The dart is still in the rhino's hip.

Head-on identification photo of a female and nearly full-grown calf. (Note the difference in the snout wrinkles.)

A male and female engaging in courtship horn tussling before mating.

Their activity attracts two more rhinos — a female (left), accompanied by two tick birds, and her half-grown calf.

Plains zebras mating: the *Rossigkeitsgesicht* or estrous face is clearly seen in the first photograph; in the fourth, the mare rejects a further advance.

Mare and foal grooming.

A newborn foal not yet free of the fetal sac.

Stallions fighting: each tries to bite the other's front legs.

A Grevy's stallion on his territory with a mixed group of males and females behind him.

Hartman's mountain zebras in S.W. Africa: the dewlap and gridiron patterns on the rump distinguish them from the plains zebra.

Grevy's mares with foals.

Hans and Ute Klingel measuring the teeth for aging of an immobilized Grevy's zebra: a game warden and Samburu moran assist.

However, their alertness and group cooperation is not enough to keep zebras immune from predators, who are extremely adept in their own way; large numbers of zebras, foals and adults alike, are taken by predators every year. In the Serengeti the zebra is the most important prey species for the lion in terms of pounds of meat consumed; in Ngorongoro it is second only to the wildebeest as the most popular prey for both lions and hyenas.

For the lion, surprise is the key in killing a zebra. The lion has to be able to stalk close enough without being detected by the zebras, then rush in and take the nearest or slowest zebra. Wild dogs and hyenas will chase a herd until one animal drops back; then they converge on it and bring it down, disemboweling it while it is still alive.

Hugo van Lawick, the well-known photographer and naturalist, witnessed an attempt by wild dogs to kill a zebra foal and gave an excellent account of the hunting technique and the zebras' way of counteracting it. A pack of wild dogs that he was studying in the Serengeti managed to get within 20 yards of a group of about twenty zebras, which included a mare and a small foal. The zebras, who had been walking, turned and ran, and the dogs began the chase. Other zebra groups joined in, making about fifty zebras in all. Van Lawick noted that they did not run very fast, and thought that they were keeping to the speed of the slowest foal.

When the lead dog drew close to the mare and foal, one of the stallions turned and attacked. As the first dog swerved away from the stallion, another dog took the lead. This happened a number of times until the mare and foal and a yearling, probably the mare's older foal, somehow got separated from the herd in the confusion. The dogs immediately surrounded the three animals, and the rest of the herd disappeared over a rise. The dogs tried to bite at the foal, but the mother attacked them, and while she attacked one, the yearling lunged and bit at another. The little foal stayed glued to its mother's side and the dogs could not get at it.

Finally the dogs got more and more aggressive; one made a leap and tried to grab the mare's upper lip. If a dog can succeed in getting hold of the lip, the pack is usually able to bring down the zebra, as it becomes almost immobilized when held in this way. The dog missed on the first try, but van Lawick saw that the dogs were frantic and getting bolder. "The end seemed inevitable — and the end is always much worse to watch when the prey has bravely defended itself or its young one. But suddenly I felt the ground vibrating and, looking around, I saw, to my amazement, ten zebras fast approaching. A moment later this herd closed its ranks around the mother and her two offspring and then, wheeling around, the whole closely packed group galloped off in the direction from which the ten had come. The dogs chased them for 50 yards or so but were unable to penetrate the herd and soon gave up."

This type of assistance and cooperation within the group is obviously one of the main factors contributing to the success of the plains zebra as a species, and they are very successful in terms of numbers and area covered. As we have seen, the organization within the small groups is complex, and each member clearly has its own place. It is interesting that the Klingels could not find any higher level of social organization than the bachelor groups and the family groups. (The solitary stallions, being rare, do not serve any special function and probably are solitary by choice.) Although large herds of zebras are formed, as many as fifteen hundred in Ngorongoro and tens of thousands in the Serengeti, these are temporary and seem to depend only on grazing conditions. In the Serengeti the concentrations are particularly notable during the migrations, but eventually these always break up into the same small stable groups.

Each group has a large home range that overlaps with that of other groups and is utilized according to the availability of good grazing. The plains zebra is not territorial. In Ngorongoro some home ranges were only 30 square miles while others extended over 100 square miles. In the Serengeti the home ranges are huge: in the rainy season an individual home range might be 100 to 150 square miles on the plains; in the dry season it might be an additional 150 to 250 square miles in the woodlands. The migration routes alone are 60 to 100 miles each way. Altogether, the range of a Serengeti group is at least 400 square miles. Whether each group uses the same range every year is not known.

Since the home ranges in Ngorongoro Crater are relatively small, the Klingels were able to follow their known zebras' daily and seasonal movements and could also observe their daily activity patterns. In the crater individual family groups form into herds of several hundred animals, and although there is no definite organization and the herds are unstable, the groups making up a herd share certain sleeping and feeding grounds. At the end of the dry season there were seven herds using seven different sleeping grounds in the crater and in the daytime moving out to feeding grounds that might overlap. Neither the sleeping grounds nor the feeding grounds remained constant all year round. Sometimes there were only three sleeping grounds; in the wet season there were four sleeping grounds in the crater and two outside, where a portion of the population had migrated. In all cases the sleeping grounds are dry, open places on short grass.

The feeding grounds, of course, depend on the availability of good grazing. They may be as far as 8 miles away from the sleeping grounds. The movements back and forth between the two follow a fairly set pattern. Shortly after sunrise the groups set off from the sleeping area, each group moving in single file, with the top-ranking mare leading. They may stop and feed briefly on the way, but generally they move in a direct course to the feeding ground. Once there, the individual groups fan out to feed, each one remaining a cohesive unit.

Sometime during the day they walk to water, and they also stop feeding for grooming, wallowing, and resting periods. The rest period is usually in the middle of the day; the foals lie down to sleep, the adults stand around. On the open plains zebras cannot seek shade but they apparently are well adapted to standing out in the hot sun. These activities within a group — grooming, resting, feeding etc. — seem to be infectious, so that all the animals within the group are doing the same thing at the same time.

Zebras may change their daily routine on cold, cloudy days;

Klingel noted that on such days the zebras did not leave the sleeping grounds until two or three hours later than usual and then did not travel to their normal feeding grounds but just fed in a nearby area, returning to their sleeping grounds earlier than usual.

The Klingels were able to watch zebras on moonlight nights and note their activities. On these nights the zebras rested in three different periods — from about 8 to 9 P.M., 1 to 2 A.M., and 4:45 to 6:15 A.M. — and in between they grazed. In the resting periods it was interesting to see the system of sentinels at work. At night, it is only for a few minutes at most that all the animals of a group will be lying down. There is almost always one animal standing and apparently keeping watch, and individual adults seem to take turns off and on during the night.

In the Serengeti the seasonal movements of the plains animals are vast and spectacular, perhaps more so than in any other area of Africa. The Serengeti basically includes three different vegetation zones — the short grass plains, the long grass plains, and the woodland — and these areas are utilized at different times of the year, depending on rainfall. No two years are alike. The animals tend to mass on the short grass plains in the wet season, from about December to May, when the grass is green and growing and there is surface water available. When the grass and water dry up, usually in May or June, the animals, especially the zebras and wildebeests, gather, often in spectacular numbers, and begin to migrate to the long grass plains. They gradually move through the long grass plains and eventually end up in the woodlands to the northwest, where the grass is the longest and there is permanent water. At the onset of the rains, in October or November, they begin to move back toward the short grass plains.

What is particularly fascinating about these movements is the system of grazing succession that is in effect. Richard Bell, who worked on the topic, explains why it is not accidental that zebras lead the migration, wildebeests follow, and Thomson's gazelles come last. Each of these species utilizes a different level of the herb layer, according to its own needs and particular way of attaining protein.

The zebra eats the coarsest part of the grass, which is low in protein and has a high proportion of cell wall, but the zebra is best able to break down the cell wall and use the protein in that part of the plant; at the same time the zebra can get the large quantity of fodder necessary for a digestive system with a fast turnover. By coming first, the zebra eats down the top layer of vegetation, leaving the lower section of the grass — the leaves and stems — for the next animal in the succession, the wildebeest, which needs the higher protein content and easier digestibility of this part of the plant. The wildebeest in turn crops the vegetation down further, and the Thomson's gazelle eats the very lowest part of the herb layer — the growing shoots and herbs. These, although not available in the quantity of the higher levels, have a very high protein content, which is exactly what a small, selective feeder like the Thomson's gazelle needs.

The Serengeti Research Institute is attempting to compile data on this type of ecological interaction in order to make recommendations concerning the management of the Park. By monitoring the whole Serengeti ecosystem, the Institute is trying to understand the changes and trends in vegetation, animal numbers and distribution, and their interrelationships. Klingel's valuable data on the social organization of the plains zebra have made it possible for the Institute to fit one more important piece into the puzzle.

The Mountain Zebra

In 1965, after they had finished their study of the plains zebra in Tanzania, the Klingels went to South West Africa and South Africa for three months to do comparative studies of the mountain zebra. They were mainly interested in seeing what the mountain zebra's social organization was and in what ways, if any, it differed from that of the plains zebra. On that trip they concentrated on the Hartmann's zebra in the Etosha Pan Reserve in South West Africa.

There are between three and eight thousand Hartmann's zebras left in South West Africa, and only a few of these are protected in reserves. As a result of heavy poaching, they are very nervous, shy animals, and the Klingels encountered numerous difficulties in studying them. They could not photograph them, immobilize them, or move among them in the normal way; instead, they had to build a "hide" at a water hole that the zebras frequented and from there observe the structure of the groups that came.

In all, they observed 485 zebras at the water hole — 82 family groups, 72 stallions in bachelor groups, and 16 solitary stallions. The family groups were smaller than those of the plains zebra, averaging 4.7 members per group and consisting of a stallion, 1 to 4 mares, and their foals. The bachelor groups, on the other hand, were larger, ranging from 2 to 7 animals and averaging 3.2. Although the Klingels could only re-recognize a few individuals, they were able to conclude provisionally that the groups were stable. The groups mixed at the water hole but always re-emerged with the same composition.

The Cape mountain zebras in South Africa were much easier to study. In 1965 there were only fifty-five in a small park in the Cape Province of South Africa. These were very tame and could even be observed on foot. In the short time they were there, the Klingels photographed every individual and photographed the groups in order to have the composition on record. In 1967 Klingel returned, rephotographed the groups (there were then sixty-nine zebras), and was able to get some valuable data in this way.

In 1965 there were 9 families, consisting of 49 animals, and 1 bachelor group. The family groups, like the Hartmann's, included a stallion, 1 to 4 mares, and their foals. The groups ranged from 2 to 8 animals and averaged 5.5. The bachelor group consisted of 6 stallions, only 1 of which was adult. This bachelor group often joined the smallest family group, which consisted of a stallion and his young mare. It was thought that this family stallion had recently come from the bachelor group and still maintained friendly relations with it. A young stallion in another family group, who was about two years old, kept changing back and forth between his mother's group and the bachelor group, and was obviously in the process of joining it.

In 1967, on revisiting the Park, Klingel found nine families, consisting of fifty-seven animals, and two bachelor groups of eight and four animals each. There were also some other changes. Three adult stallions had been captured and sent to zoos, two from family groups and one from a bachelor group; another family stallion had died. The three orphaned families were taken over as entities by other stallions; two of these new stallions came from bachelor groups and the third had been a young stallion in a family group. All the adult mares were together in the same compositions in the same families. Of the young animals, seven young mares had left their families and joined other families, and five young stallions had left their families. Four of the males went to bachelor groups and the other was the one who had taken over a family.

This shows in microcosm exactly what happens in the plains zebra, and so it can be said that the social organization of the mountain and plains zebras are virtually the same. Although individuals were not known, all indications show that the social organization of the Hartmann's zebra is also the same. A few differences in behavior between the three populations were evident, however.

In the Hartmann's zebra the stallion almost always leads, especially when approaching a dangerous place; thus, the family stallion leads the way while approaching the water hole, but usually the highest-ranking mare leads upon leaving the water hole, when presumably there is less danger. In the Cape mountain zebra the stallion and the alpha mare take turns leading, with the result that each leads about half the time.

The groups of both types of mountain zebra were as cohesive as those of the plains zebra, but it was surprising to find that there was no mutual grooming among the members. At the same time, all members perform greeting ceremonies with one another, which is not the case with the plains zebra. All the stallions greet each other at meeting places, such as water holes; sometimes a stallion will walk or even trot more than 100 yards from his family to greet another stallion. The mountain zebra greeting ceremony ends with extremely vigorous rubbing against the flank and rump of the partner, and Klingel feels that this could be considered a kind of social grooming. When a stallion greets his mares, the rubbing also occurs but not with the same vehemence.

One somewhat amusing difference discovered was that mountain zebra adults are unable to roll over completely on their backs, while all plains zebras can. The Cape mountain zebra and Hartmann's zebra must first wallow on one side, then stand up and lie down again to do the other side. Klingel notes that they seem to try to roll over but are unable to do so.

While Klingel never heard Cape mountain zebras make any sounds, he heard the Hartmann's zebra make some sounds not heard among plains zebras. The Hartmann's zebra's contact call is a high-pitched whistle ending with a grunting noise, to which other zebras reply. They also make a short, hoarse barking sound that is probably an alarm. Another alarm call is similar to that of the plains zebra — a two-syllable call, "i-ho." They can also be heard squealing when greeting or playing; this may be an expression of pain or submission.

Mountain zebra stallions were interested in the dung and urine of other mountain zebras. The stallions defecated on fresh and even old, dried-up dung of other mountain zebras, but never on the dung of plains zebras, with whom their range overlapped. Family stallions urinate on the urinating places of their mares, sometimes scraping their feet on the places first. Several times Klingel saw two or three stallions congregate around a dung heap and then turn and mark it. As with the plains zebra, the function of the marking is not clear.

Where the ranges of the Hartmann's zebra and the plains zebra overlapped in South West Africa, it was clear that they did not take up contact with each other. They often met at watering places but did not pay any attention to each other. Often Klingel would see a Hartmann's zebra stallion pass within a few feet of a plains zebra stallion on the way to greeting another Hartmann's stallion. The stallion would simply pass, hardly acknowledging the other's presence. Since their behavior is similar in so many ways, it is puzzling that there is no interbreeding, but there are obviously subtle but important factors involved that keep the two species from mixing.

The Hartmann's zebra plays an important ecological role in digging water holes in dry sand. Both Hartmann's mares and stallions dig holes with their front feet, wait while the water filters up, and then drink. Once a hole is dug, the zebra in possession vehemently defends the hole against any usurper — members of its own group, other zebras, and other animals. Eventually, others do get a turn. When the zebras leave, the holes are used by giraffes, greater kudus, oryxes, hyenas, elephants, springbucks, and plains zebras. In the arid areas of South West Africa, these water holes are essential to some of the other animals.

The Grevy's Zebra

When the Klingels returned to Germany in 1965, they began writing up their results on the plains zebra, and at the same time Hans Klingel started teaching ecology and behavior at the University of Braunschweig. In 1967 he was able to get a sabbatical, and he and his wife returned to Africa to begin their study of the Grevy's zebra in northern Kenya.

They worked mainly in the Il Bonyeki plains near Wamba but also traveled in other parts of northern Kenya to make comparative observations. In their main study area they immobilized 25 Grevy's and marked them by branding, cropping the manes and tails, and fitting yellow collars around the animal's neck or girth.

They also photographed individuals and eventually knew 250 out of a population of about 600 Grevy's. Recognition of individual Grevy's is extremely difficult, as the stripes are so numerous, narrow, and close together. The Klingels found that the simplest and most time-saving method was to photograph all individuals they encountered in their study areas and then to analyze the photographs later. This way they could see whether the groups were of constant composition. What they discovered is that the Grevy's zebra has a strikingly different way of life from that of the plains and mountain zebras.

This was not altogether unexpected, since the species live in different environments, but that the differences should be so extreme was surprising. The Grevy's zebra's range covers an area that is dry and harsh, with very low rainfall — a distinct contrast from the lush green of the Ngorongoro Crater. In the semiarid conditions the large, donkeylike Grevy's zebras have evolved a way of life that is in such contrast to that of the plains zebra, it hardly seems they could be related. The Grevy's zebras have territorial stallions and mixed, unstable groups of males and females with no permanent bonds among members; there is no cohesion, no concern and assistance for each other, and practically no mutual grooming.

In the Klingels' study area all the available pasture was found to be clearly divided into large territories, each held by a territorial stallion. The territory is marked by dung heaps along the borders, by voice, and by the presence of the owner. The stallion in possession tolerates the presence of other stallions in his territory, but all of these males are subordinate to him. He is on a par only with his neighboring territorial stallions. They respect each other's territories and only fight when an estrous mare is in the boundary area. Then each tries to drive the mare into the center of his own territory. If one succeeds, the other does not pursue the mare into the other's territory but respects the boundaries.

The other animals — mares, foals, and nonterritorial stallions — move about freely, according to grazing conditions. The Grevy's, like the plains zebra, is exclusively a grazing animal. It is found in groups, and both mares and stallions are also found singly. The groups are sometimes all one sex, sometimes mixed, and they are unstable; mares and stallions move from one group to another during the course of a day, sometimes staying on their own for hours before joining another group. Some of the groups are distinctly homogeneous; there are, for instance, groups comprised of almost all mares with foals, or mares with no foals, or a very small percentage of foals, or all stallions. Groups range from two to fifty animals and somtimes congregate, forming herds of two hundred or more. The large herds are short-lived, and the homogeneous groups usually remain intact within the larger herd.

However, even the homogeneous groups are not stable; animals come and go at will. The Grevy's foal is thus born into a situation very different from that of the plains zebra. It will more than likely be born in a nursery crèche, a type of homogeneous group that includes mares with young foals, some mares with older foals, and heavily pregnant mares; nonterritorial stallions may also join these groups at times. The nursery herds are no more stable than any of the others. In fact, Klingel is not sure why they are formed; as he explains, "it would be easy to say that all mares with foals join up, but it could well be that mares with foals are slower and thus, the others walk away. Also, and this makes it more complicated, there are odd foalless mares in such groups."

An interesting facet of the nursery herds is that the foals are sometimes left behind, which is in some ways similar to the giraffe kindergarten system. The Grevy's foal usually stays close to its mother, but Klingel found that under certain conditions they do separate. At the end of the dry season in 1968, most of the zebras returned to the study area, but there was still no surface water available. In order to get water, the mothers had to travel long distances to drink. They often left early in the morning, leaving their foals behind, and would sometimes not return until after dark. Thus Klingel found that "a number of 'lost' foals, up to eight at a time, were recorded daily. Occasionally they stood near adult zebras, but there was no close relationship and the 'nurse' (either male or female) often walked away leaving the foals behind."

Grevy's foals, both males and females, stay with their mothers longer than plains zebra foals do. The females reach puberty later — not until they are about two or three years old. They also adopt an estrous stance and are then pursued by stallions and separated from their mothers. Male Grevy's foals stay with their mothers for even longer, until they are at least three years old, probably because there is no disruptive onset of puberty as in the female. Once the bonds between mother and foal are broken, both males and females take on the way of life of other Grevy's with no strong personal bonds.

Grevy's stallions are not fully mature until they are six years old; that is, they cannot become territorial stallions until at least that age. In a study carried out on reproduction in the zebra, John King found that the territorial stallions weigh more (up to 992 pounds, compared to 948 lbs. for the average stallion) and that they also have far heavier and larger genitals. Whether they become territorial stallions because they have larger genitals or develop large genitals once they acquire territories is not known.

The system of allowing nonterritorial stallions into the territories is necessitated by ecological conditions. As most of the available pasture is occupied by territory holders, it is to the advantage of the species to allow other stallions to use the territories for grazing; otherwise, there would be no reservoir for recruitment when a territorial stallion dies. The territories are unusually large compared to other herbivores; they range from 1 to 4 square miles and average 2.2 square miles. Klingel concluded that these territories mainly function as mating territories. In one case he saw nine stallions trying to mate with an estrous mare in an area where there was no territory holder because the resident stallion had just been shot by a hunter and the territory had not yet been occupied by a new stallion. The fighting over this mare was so fierce that none of the stallions succeeded in mating with her. When she moved into another territory, the stallions did not follow, and the territorial stallion immediately mated with her. Within a territory, stallions do not disturb the territorial stallion when he is with an estrous mare. If a nonterritorial stallion tries to contact an estrous mare, the territory holder will chase him away, but Klingel has never seen a fight occur in this type of situation.

At times the density of zebras on the territories is sixteen animals per square mile with as many as fifteen stallions to a territory. If the stallion had to fight for his territory constantly, he could not possibly maintain it. The perimeters alone of two measured territories were 4 miles and over 6 miles. (Klingel was able to measure the territories accurately by driving estrous mares toward the boundary with his car. The stallion would always follow, and when he met the neighboring stallion at the border, there would be a fight. Klingel could drive the mare to as many points as he needed and thus pinpoint spots along the border wherever fights occurred. He marked these places by putting white chalk on trees, anthills, and rocks, and was later able to plot the territories on a map.) The reason for the large size of the territories is not known. Klingel postulated that at one time during the evolution of the Grevy's they may have been feeding territories for a stallion and his mare or mares, but that that system has been superseded.

In the present system the mares, foals, and nonterritorial stallions migrate to other areas outside of the territorial system. The territorial stallion leaves his territory only for two or three hours every day or every other day for water, and he keeps his territory throughout the year, even when the other animals leave. In one particularly dry period in August and September 1968, a few of the territorial stallions also migrated, but they returned after a few weeks, even before the rains broke. Interestingly, the other Grevy's also came back to the territories before the rains came, but it is not clear why.

In parts of northern Kenya the ranges of the Grevy's and the plains zebras overlap, and in this area the two types of zebra actually form mixed herds. These herds act as coordinated units while fleeing predators or moving to and from water, but it is conspicuous that there is no interbreeding, as all animals are either distinctly plains zebras or Grevy's, with no intergrades. Stallions show no interest at all in estrous mares of the other species. In captivity it is possible to get different species of zebras to breed, but the offspring is sterile, just as in other equid crosses (for instance, a horse and donkey cross produces a sterile mule). It is obvious in the wild that the behavior mechanisms of the Grevy's and plains zebra are so divergent that they do not trigger any response from each other and thus the two species have remained separate and distinct.

What is interesting to contemplate is why the Grevy's has such a different way of life from that of the other two zebra species. Certainly the harsh conditions of its habitat must be a factor, although the Hartmann's zebra also lives in a semiarid habitat.

Klingel was fascinated to find that the wild ass, which lives in an even harsher habitat than the Grevy's, has the same social system as the Grevy's. Klingel has concluded that the territorial system of the wild ass and Grevy's is close to the original type of social organization for the equids. The nonterritorial system of the plains and mountain zebras evolved from the territorial one and became more successful. Without the territory the groups can remain stable and still migrate, the combination of the two making for a very successful species in terms of numbers and area occupied. The Grevy's and wild ass occupy relatively small ranges and have gradually been decreasing in numbers; of course, man's interference has also been an important factor here.

It would not be fair to conclude this chapter without discussing the one thing that comes to mind above all others when one thinks of the zebra: Why does it have those black and white stripes? Usually when an animal is marked so vividly, it is either a warning mechanism (as with brightly colored insects, for example) or a means of sexual attraction (for instance, the vivid coloration of male birds). Certainly the zebra's markings do not warn off the large African predators, and as all zebras — males, females, and foals — are striped in the same way, it is not a sex-specific attracting device.

There has been much speculation as to what function the coloring does then serve. Klingel has suggested one possible answer to the question: zebras probably recognize each other by their individual stripe patterns. This is, of course, more important for the plains and mountain zebras; with a social organization that depends on personal bonds, it is essential that they be able to recognize each other instantly. The Grevy's zebras may or may not recognize each other by sight. With the Grevy's zebras' narrow and numerous stripes, individual recognition was certainly difficult for the Klingels and may be just as difficult for the Grevy's themselves. The narrow stripes may have another function altogether.

One of the popular theories about the stripes is that they somehow help the zebra to withstand solar radiation. Zebras stand out in the hot, equatorial sun all day and apparently are well adapted to dealing with the incredible heat load. It has been suggested that the alternating black and white stripes somehow dissipate the heat, but physiologists who have worked on the problem have found that this is not the case. The black stripes, as would be expected, are hotter than the white stripes on the surface, but this has little effect on the amount of heat that hits the animal's skin surface. What actually keeps the zebra from getting too hot is its coat's thickness, which allows very little radiation to penetrate to the skin, and shininess; the coat reflects the surprising amount of 73 percent of the heat back into the atmosphere. Virginia Finch, who is working on the success of various coat colors, has concluded that the coat most efficient in combating heat is one that is light brown all over and very shiny. She does say that the almost gray appearance of the narrow stripes of the Grevy's would be advantageous to it in relation to solar radiation. It lives in a much hotter atmosphere than the plains zebra, and this may well be why it does have the narrow stripes.

One further theory is that the stripes are a type of camouflage called "disruptive coloration." The black and white stripes break up the outline of the body, making the actual shape of the zebra less conspicuous than that of an animal with a solid-colored coat. (Ships in the Second World War were painted with zebra stripes for the purpose of creating this very effect.) In a heat haze a herd of zebras can barely be made out from 300–400 yards away. When one comes across a mixed herd of zebras and wildebeests on a moonlit night, the wildebeests stand out clearly as dark shapes, while the zebras are indistinct forms. The zebra stripes are also said to confuse a predator's judgment as to its true distance from the zebra. It might be just that much more difficult for a lion to judge the exact distance and speed of a moving zebra as the lion rushes in for a kill, especially at dawn and dusk, when most attempts are made.

These, however, are only theories, and no one is yet sure exactly why the zebra has stripes, and we may never know all the permutations within its evolution that brought it to its present state. Thanks to the Klingels we do know a great deal more about its way of life now, and we can never again look at those "amorphous herds" of zebras and think, "Once you've seen one zebra, you've seen them all."

V

Antelopes

IF ANY ONE GROUP of animals is responsible for creating the "Pleistocene vision" of the African plains and savannahs of today, the
antelopes should be given the credit. They exist in such overwhelming abundance in some areas that the landscape sometimes
literally undulates with the movement of thousands upon thousands of hoofed animals; and the antelopes exist in such diversity
that one never ceases to be amazed at the variety of body shapes
and sizes, coat colors and patterns, and the many configurations of
their exquisite and sometimes bizarre horns.

Antelopes belong to the family Bovidae (the hollow-horned ruminants), which also includes the Cape buffalo. There are over
seventy species of antelope on the African continent. The
number fluctuates, because the classification of antelopes is still in
process; depending on whose classification one follows (there are
"lumpers" and "splitters"), there may be as many as ninety-three
species. Whatever number the taxonomists finally arrive at, there
will not be much fewer than seventy species, which in itself is remarkable for one group of mammals, when one considers that in
Africa there are only two species of hippopotamus, one species of
elephant, two species of rhinoceros, probably one species of
giraffe, and four species of equids (three zebras and one wild ass).
Even such a diverse family as the Old World monkeys is only
represented in Africa by about half as many species as the antelopes.

Needless to say, the antelopes have somehow proved to be

unusually successful, as they have radiated and diversified extensively. It is thought that the first antelopelike animals originated
in the forests of the Miocene epoch and that these animals had an
early form of the ruminant stomach, which was undoubtedly a
key to their success. The ruminant digestive system, with its
four-chambered stomach, is remarkably complex (it makes man's
seem simple) and very efficient. It provides a home for countless
microflora, which break down the cell walls of the ingested plants
and through a complex process make it possible for the host to obtain the plants' nutrients (protein, carbohydrates, etc.). This specialized digestive system is thought to have had advantages over
nonruminant systems, and as a result many nonruminants disappeared in the competition.

An equally important asset for the ruminant is the antipredator
benefits of its feeding style. A large amount of food can be eaten
without much chewing, in a relatively short space of time. The
food is swallowed and stored in the first compartment of the stomach, where some digestion takes place, but later the animal
regurgitates the vegetable matter, a mouthful at a time, rechews
it, and swallows it again; it is then sent along to the other
chambers for final digestion. An animal that can eat quickly in a
few hours and then stand with its head up, chewing the cud, will
be more alert to predators than an animal that must keep its
head down for most of the day.

The antelopes may have started to leave the forests even during
the Miocene, but certainly with the receding of the forests in the
Pliocene and Pleistocene, many of the species began to move into
the different niches that became available. Some moved to the
edges of the forest, others out into the bushland, and some right
out onto the plains. Others, of course, have remained in the
forests all along. All have adapted and changed throughout time,
but those that have left the forests have adapted more radically —
anatomically, physiologically, and behaviorally — to the environment to which they have moved and to the competitor and predator pressures imposed by the other animals with which they share
their habitat.

Today antelopes range over most of Africa, from the duikers living in the thick rain forests of Zaïre to the addaxes living in the Sahara. They vary in size from the tiny royal antelope, which weighs only 7 pounds and stands 10 inches at the shoulder, to the giant eland, which weighs nearly 2000 pounds and measures up to 6 feet at the shoulder. Although all antelopes are herbivores, some are browsers, eating only herbs, creepers, and the leaves of bushes and trees, others are grazers, eating only various species of grasses, and still others have a combined diet of both browse and grass, the proportion depending on the season. And finally, the social organization of the different antelope species is remarkably diverse, ranging from a single animal living on a small fixed territory to huge aggregations of thousands of animals roaming over hundreds of square miles. The antelopes, then, are spectacularly varied and so make a rich and rewarding field for comparative ecology and ethology studies.

It would take a whole book to deal with all of the antelope species, or even all of the East African species, so I have chosen six species that I feel are representative of the range of sizes, different habitats, varying feeding styles, and particularly the diversity of social systems. These six antelopes fit into the five categories (two fit into one class) set out by ecologist Peter Jarman in his clear and well-thought-out paper "The Social Organization of Antelopes in Relation to their Ecology." In this work Jarman divides the seventy-odd antelope species into five classes (A through E) based on the size of the animal, feeding style, group size, antipredator behavior, and social organization. Class A contains the small browsing antelopes such as duikers and dikdiks, which are territorial; at the other end of the range, Class E includes the eland and Cape buffalo, large, nonterritorial animals.

The six antelope species that will be dealt with in this chapter are the dikdik, the gerenuk, the impala, the Uganda kob, the wildebeest, and the eland. The way of life of each of these animals will be described in detail, and at the end of each section are listed the similar antelope species that Jarman has placed in the same class. It is hoped that these representatives will give some idea of the various ways in which antelopes have evolved, how they behave socially, use their living space, feed, avoid predators, and in general continue to be remarkably successful animals.

CLASS A

The Dikdik

Although one of the most common antelopes in East Africa, the dikdik is rarely seen for more than a few seconds at a time. Driving along, one sees dikdiks dash across the road and disappear into the bush; only rarely do these incredibly delicate, almost unreal-looking little creatures hesitate long enough for one to get a good look. The dikdik weighs only 10 pounds and stands a little over a foot at the shoulder, and even at that weight its slightly humped body looks too heavy for the slenderest twiglike legs imaginable. Most conspicuous about the dikdik are its large, dark eyes, accentuated by a white ring surrounding both the eye and a large black spot below the inside corner of each eye. These spots, called preorbital glands, produce a dark, sticky secretion that the dikdik uses for marking. Preorbital and anteorbital glands are common to many of the antelopes. The dikdik also has interdigital glands between its cloven hooves that are thought to be used for leaving a scent trail.

One of the most unusual things about the dikdik's appearance is its elongated nose, which looks like a miniature trunk. Although the nose is quite mobile, the dikdik does not use it for grasping vegetation as is sometimes mistakenly thought. Aside from its essential use in breathing, the dikdik's long nose is apparently an aid in smelling out palatable vegetation. When feeding, the dikdik extends its nose into bushes or fallen vegetation. The structure of the nose may also enable the dikdik to make its characteristic whistling noise when it is frightened or disturbed. This "zik-zik" sound gave the dikdik its common name.

Males can be distinguished from females by the presence of two tiny, spearlike horns, which are straight and ringed at the base. As is the case with some other small antelopes, the adult female is slightly larger than the adult male. Both males and females have a crest of hair running from the forehead up between the ears that is raised when the dikdik is alarmed.

Dikdiks occur in southwestern Africa and then not again until Tanzania, and from there they spread up into Kenya, Ethiopia, and Somalia. They are an animal of semiarid bush habitat and apparently prefer areas of low rainfall and hard, stony soil. It is thought that their feet are adapted to firm ground and that they do not do well on soils that tend to get muddy. The dikdik found in Tanzania and Kenya, Kirk's dikdik, is the same species as the one found in southwestern Africa, but the two populations have been separated for thousands of years, since the moist rain forest spread from central Africa down and across to Mozambique, cutting the Kirk's dikdik population in two.

The bush habitat in which dikdiks live, their size, and their shy, wary ways make them a difficult animal to study in the wild, but a few people have done some field work. A. M. Simonetta studied captive and wild dikdiks in Somalia, and K. L. Tinley studied the dikdik part-time in South West Africa while conducting an ecological survey. The most intensive study was carried out by Ursula and Hubert Hendrichs, a husband and wife team from the Max-Planck-Institut in Germany. They were based at the Serengeti Research Institute from February 1967 to May 1969 and during some of this time watched the dikdiks living in the kopjes (rocky outcrops) of the Seronera area. U. Hendrichs carried out most of the work while her husband studied elephants. The dikdiks in the Seronera area are accustomed to vehicles, because tourists frequently visit the kopjes looking for lions, leopards, and cheetahs. As the Hendrichses explained, the tourists ignore the dikdiks and the dikdiks ignore the tourists. At one of the kopjes the Hendrichses got to know the dikdiks individually, recognizing them by peculiarities of their horns and ears.

The results of the field studies carried out on dikdiks, together with observations made on captive animals, give us a fairly good picture of the dikdik's way of life, and it seems that the social organization is similar for the several dikdik species. Dikdiks live in pairs on a fixed territory. This type of social system is thought to be close to that of the forest-dwelling ancestors of today's antelopes, although some present-day forest duikers appear to live solitarily, each on a territory, with occasional meetings for breeding — a system probably even closer to the original. Scientists can only speculate as to what went on in the past from the existing social systems, for unfortunately, practically no information about an animal's social behavior is revealed in its fossil remains.

Compared to modern man, an antelope — or any wild animal, for that matter — requires only a few essential things out of life. An animal needs enough food, water, and space for itself, suitable terrain, not too many competitors, access to the opposite sex for breeding, and a relatively safe place in which to raise its young. For an antelope, there are various ways to secure these things, and each species has evolved a workable system according to its size, the habitat in which it lives, and the food it requires.

A tiny animal like the dikdik could conceivably have lived in large herds of twenty individuals or more, but it is highly unlikely. There are several excellent reasons why the dikdik instead lives in pairs on fixed territories. The dikdik is predominantly a browser, feeding on the leaves of bushes, trees, and shrubs, on herbs and creepers, and only infrequently on some grasses. It feeds by careful selection [1] among widely dispersed food items in a habitat that is by no means lush. It goes from bush to bush, picking one leaf here, a twig or bud there, getting a surprisingly nutritious diet in the process. But what is even more remarkable, the dikdik gets enough moisture from the vegetation it eats so that it does not have to drink water. The dikdik has very low water

---

[1] The term *selection* is used here with reservations, because, although feeding studies have shown that all antelopes are selective to some degree (that is, they do not eat everything within reach), certain plants are rejected, and only certain parts of other plants are eaten, the exact extent to which they are selecting for plant species and parts had not yet been adequately measured. Until proper measurements are carried out on availability and selection, we can only rely on qualitative assessments of how selectively an animal is feeding.

requirements because of physiological adaptations to its arid environment.

The dikdik's highly selective feeding style and the dispersion of its food require that it know its range intimately. If dikdiks lived in large groups, they would soon deplete the resources in one area and have to move on, or they would have to live in much larger areas than a pair does, and this would counteract the advantages of knowing a small area extremely well. Equally important, for a small animal like the dikdik the main antipredator device is to hide rather than to try to run or fight. Widely separated pairs of dikdiks have a better chance of not being detected than a herd of twenty, which would very likely attract predators. And again, intimate knowledge of their own small range is a tremendous aid for two dikdiks trying to elude predators. Thus it becomes clear that, for a small browsing animal like the dikdik, a social system that spaces out the dikdik population in an area is by far the most advantageous type of organization.

The dikdik has arrived at a system whereby the area in which it lives is held exclusively for one male, one female, and up to two of their offspring. Usually it is both a resource territory, with enough food and space for these animals throughout the year in both good and bad times, and a breeding territory, where the male has unhindered rights to breed with the female on the territory.

One of the most important elements in the system is the pair bond that is formed between the male and female. The process of bonding has not been followed closely in the wild, but it is thought to occur when both animals are young and have recently been chased out of their parents' territories. Whatever happens, the bond, once formed, is very strong. It lasts for years and perhaps, in some cases, for the life of the animal. The Hendrichses knew five pairs of dikdiks at one kopje and were able to follow their lives during the course of the two-year study. The individuals in four pairs remained the same, and in the fifth pair, the female disappeared, probably killed by a predator. After five months this male was still alone on his territory. It should not be difficult for a dikdik to find a new mate, as female offspring from neighboring territories mature and become independent, but for some reason this male did not form a new bond. In fact, the Hendrichses actually saw him chase a young female out of his territory one month after his mate had disappeared. (In another instance, an observer shot a female and seven months later the male was still on his own.)

The size of the territory occupied by a male and female varies from area to area. Around the kopjes in the Serengeti, territories range from 6 to 30 acres. In another habitat the average territory size was about 5 acres per pair. The male and female usually walk together in their territory, and both are apparently concerned with maintaining the integrity of the area, but the buck is more active in defending the territory. He carefully patrols and marks the borders, and attacks any other dikdik — male or female — that trespasses. However, there is little overt fighting. Marking seems to play a more important role in constantly reinforcing the message that a piece of ground is occupied by particular dikdiks.

The dikdik buck marks throughout the territory (females also do some marking), concentrating on the borders. Walking along the border, he places a small amount of secretion from the preorbital gland onto bushes and blades of grass at intervals of 2 to 50 yards. This is done very precisely, and although it looks as though the buck is going to poke out his eye, actually he carefully puts the opening of the gland over the end of a bare twig and allows the stick to go right into the orifice. This maneuver deposits a tiny amount of the black sticky secretion onto the twig in a little ball about the size of a pea. Presumably the droplet carries the individual odor of that dikdik. The glands in the dikdik's feet probably also leave a scent as he walks along, but the significance of these glands is not yet completely understood.

The most conspicuous way in which dikdiks mark their territory is with strategically placed dung middens. Walking through dikdik habitat in East Africa, one nearly always comes upon these dung middens — areas up to a yard in diameter covered with tiny little pellets of dung. The Hendrichses found that these dung piles are usually placed along the borders, particularly in areas where neighboring pairs are most likely to see each other. It seems that the dunging behavior of one pair stimulates the other, and in this way "dunging areas" get started. A dunging area on a border consists of two fresh middens, one used by each pair, and old piles that have been abandoned.

There is a well-known African folk tale that explains why the dikdik makes these dung middens. It seems that one day the king of the dikdiks was happily meandering through his kingdom when he tripped and fell over a large pile of elephant dung. He was so annoyed that he called a meeting of all his dikdik subjects, and they worked out a plan to get back at the elephant. Ever since that day, they have been trying to collect enough dikdik dung in one place to trip up a passing elephant.

What is particularly fascinating about the dung middens is the ceremony that is involved in the depositing of the dung. The male and female use the same dung piles in the territory and will usually go to a dung area together. The female almost always approaches first, steps onto the midden, and, without any preliminary movements, urinates in a hunched position and then defecates in an even more hunched-down position. (These conspicuous urination and defecation postures are common to many of the antelopes and, in the male especially, are thought to be a kind of optic marking — that is, the animal announces its presence and occupancy by a stance, posture, or movement that other members of the species will see and notice.) If there is a dikdik fawn accompanying the parents, it will also use the same dung midden, either before or after its mother, again with no ceremony. Finally the buck will move to the dung pile. He goes up to the dung of the female, smells it and scratches at it with his front feet, urinating on it as he scrapes it backward. Then he straightens up, makes a 180-degree turn, and urinates again. Next he makes a few more turns, somewhat like a dog getting ready to lie down, and then squats down to defecate. Then he makes one more 180-degree turn and finally squats again and finishes defecating. Afterward, the male and female both go to a nearby bush or stalk of grass and mark it with their preorbital glands. The bushes near the dung piles are sometimes heavily laden with little black peas.

There may be as many as twenty dung areas in one territory. The dikdiks visit the dung areas, but not necessarily all of them, several times a day. The two pairs of neighbors never use the dung area at the same time but will often do so one right after the other.

The two kinds of marking are indirect ways of defending the territory. The buck will also directly chase away any intruders. The doe, though alert and aware of other dikdiks, will not try to chase them away. If another dikdik approaches the territory, the doe will stand in a characteristic posture with head held high and her whole body stiff, and she may even approach a few steps. If the buck is in another part of the territory, nothing more will happen; the doe will either begin to feed again or, if the approaching dikdik comes nearer, she will run away. But if the buck is with her, which is more often the case, he will immediately notice her posture (if he hasn't seen the intruder himself) and will thus be alerted to the presence of the other animal. He will then stand with head high, in what the Hendrichses call the "show-off" posture. If the other dikdik actually reaches the borderline, the buck will race at it with tail held high, running in a high bouncing gait, which is apparently meant to threaten the stranger. If the intruder is a doe, the buck may butt her with his head when he reaches her. Usually she runs away first, but the Hendrichses occasionally saw a neighboring doe stand her ground, ignoring the buck despite the fact that he was hitting her so hard that he was raising dust from her coat.

On the other hand, if the intruding animal is a buck, it will almost invariably move away, as dikdik bucks seem to have a system that allows them to be aggressive but not actually dangerous to one another. The bucks have a way of fighting in which they never touch each other. The intruder may run away altogether, but usually he will stop at the border. Then an altercation may occur. The two bucks will stand 2 to 10 yards apart and then suddenly rush toward each other with tails held high. When they are about a yard apart, they abruptly bring their heads down hard in a nodding gesture, braking to a halt, and then reverse a few steps backward. They may then sweep their heads back and forth a few times, but usually they will turn around and walk away until they are again 2 to 10 yards apart, when they will again turn, rush toward each other and brake. This sequence may be repeated half a dozen times, usually with the intruder moving farther back each time until eventually he is back in his own territory. Then he in turn becomes more aggressive. The bucks usually get out of the situation by moving farther and farther apart after each rush until they stop altogether and begin to feed. Most often a dunging ceremony follows. The Hendrichses saw several of these "fights" and in none of them did the participants ever make contact. It is possible that more violent encounters do occur, but none has been recorded.

When not actively defending his territory or maintaining its boundaries, the buck spends his time resting, feeding, and chewing the cud. The male and female usually engage in these activities together. Of the five pairs of dikdiks that the Hendrichses knew well, in two pairs the male and female were never seen separated; in the other three pairs the male and female were usually, but not always, seen together.

In the normal course of a day the dikdiks feed in the early morning up until about nine o'clock, and then lie down and rest in the heat of the day. They start to stir again in the late afternoon and usually feed until just before midnight, when they take another rest. The Hendrichses found that dikdiks are most active at night. In all, they spend about 7½ hours feeding, 7 hours lying down doing nothing (a long period for an antelope), 6 hours chewing the cud, either lying or standing, and about 3½ hours standing up but not feeding.

The relatively high-quality diet that the dikdik manages to obtain throughout the year makes it possible for the female to be almost constantly pregnant and highly productive. The dikdik female produces two fawns each year. She no sooner gives birth than ten days later she becomes pregnant again. The gestation period is just under six months, and in the Serengeti dikdiks tend to give birth in June and again in December. What is particularly interesting about these peaks is that the fawn born in June arrives at the beginning of the long dry season and may not see rain until October or November, while the fawn born in December arrives during the rains and has only a short dry season and then the long rainy season ahead of it during its early growing months. The fact that the female can produce calves and then lactate while pregnant again, during such diverse seasons, shows how aseasonal the dikdiks' food supply is.

Dikdik births have not been recorded in the wild, but it is assumed that the female goes to a secluded place and may be accompanied by her mate. In captivity, a male that was kept with a female giving birth did not disturb or interfere with her in any way. At birth the fawn weighs about 1½ pounds, with male fawns weighing more than females (although adult females weigh slightly more than adult males). Like most newborn antelopes, the dikdik fawn spends a period "lying out" — that is, hiding in a clump of vegetation while its mother moves about her range, feeding and resting as usual. In this way predators are not as likely to find the helpless fawn as they would be if it followed its mother. The mother dikdik returns to her fawn four times a day and suckles it for one or two minutes, spending only about ten to fifteen minutes with it each time, or altogether about one hour in twenty-four. When it is time for the mother to suckle the fawn, she slowly feeds toward the place where the fawn is lying out. The buck and her older fawn, which is just over six months old, may follow her and rest nearby while she attends the fawn. When it is through suckling, the tiny fawn usually races around the doe and buck, darting under their bellies and jumping in the air. Then the mother leads it to the place where it is to lie down, leaves it, and goes off with the others.

After a few days the doe leads the fawn to a new place after each suckling period, probably as another antipredator device; this would keep the smell of the fawn from accumulating in one place. Soon the fawn actually chooses the lying-out places for itself, but in the case of danger the doe can somehow make the fawn lie down from over 20 yards away. (The dikdik's strange, whistling alarm calls may come into play here.)

When it is only a week old, the fawn begins to nibble on leaves and other vegetation and by three weeks old feeds regularly. At about six to eight weeks it stops suckling, and may even begin to move around the territory independently, but most often it will be seen with the buck and doe. When this youngster is six months old, its mother will have another fawn, and after that it may spend more time with its father. But since the young dikdik becomes sexually mature at this age, its time in the territory will soon have to come to an end.

The mother will actually chase away her mature daughter, approaching her in a high, threatening goose step. Eventually the daughter leaves. The buck will tolerate his son as long as the youngster makes submissive gestures, which involve stretching the chin forward, extending the neck, bending the legs, and then jumping toward the buck in a twisting movement. As soon as the youngster stops using these gestures and begins to show a sexual interest in his mother, the buck will chase him away. Often father and son run around in circles for hours with the buck never getting closer than about 3 yards, until finally they both stop, panting and exhausted. When the buck finally succeeds in chasing the youngster from the territory, the neighboring bucks will then take up the chase.

In fact, both male and female youngsters get chased from the territories they pass through until they finally arrive in an unoccupied area. By the time they leave their own territory, they are between seven and ten months old, and at one year they are fully grown. The fates of individually known young animals have not been followed closely, but it seems that once the young buck finds a place where he is not chased, he begins to gain confidence by learning just how far the nearest territorial bucks will chase him. He may begin to establish dung middens and mark along a border, until finally he is able to defend his own territory. The Hendrichses speculate that at some point in this process he meets a young doe and forms a pair bond with her.

However, in most areas where there are dikdiks, there is probably little, if any, suitable land that is not already occupied by dikdiks, and so the majority of the young leaving their parents' territories never establish new territories. A more likely fate for young dikdiks would be to replace adults who have been killed. A young male dikdik could remain in his own territory if his father has been killed or could find a territory occupied by a female whose mate has disappeared. The same could happen to a female whose mother has died or who chances upon a male who has lost his mate, but, as we have seen, the male is not always willing to take on a new mate and may chase the young female away.

Mating between dikdiks in the wild has not been described, but the Hendrichses did observe some precopulatory behavior. The male often tests the female's urine by putting his nose under her when she is on the dung heap and then performing Flehmen. Upon finding her in estrus, he begins to follow her intently, holding his trunklike nose straight out. When the doe stops, he comes up behind her and touches her backside; if she does not move on, he gently pushes his nose into a little fold of skin that opens up when the doe lifts her tail. He then pulls out his nose and performs Flehmen for up to sixty seconds, then closes his mouth, swallows, and wiggles his nose back and forth.

One of the more remarkable things about the dikdik pair is how well they avoid predators. At least twenty different species of carnivores are capable of preying on the small dikdik: eagles, mongooses, pythons, the smaller cats such as caracals and servals, and the larger predators — lions, leopards, cheetahs, hyenas, and wild dogs. At times there may be several of these predators in or near a dikdik pair's range, but dikdiks are very alert and are able to hide fairly easily, partly because of their size and coloring and partly because of their familiarity with their range. They watch and smell and listen for predators, and they respond to the alarm calls of other prey animals. Often the dikdiks will spot the predator well before it has spotted them, and they will react according to what type of predator it is.

A stalking predator like a leopard, which relies on surprise to make a kill, will be kept in sight, especially by the buck. He may even move closer to the leopard, making the peculiar whistling alarm noise characteristic of the dikdik. In this way the leopard is well aware that it has been seen and will most likely not try to make an approach. Sometimes, however, the leopard remains in the territory, resting under a bush or in a convenient tree. In this case the doe may start feeding again, but the buck remains alert, keeping his eyes on the leopard the whole time, which may be for hours. The Hendrichses saw bucks get visibly tired after long periods of whistling and trying to keep predators in sight.

On the other hand, if the dikdiks see a predator like a wild dog, which runs down its prey, they will drop to the ground and freeze, even allowing the predator to pass by within 30 yards. If the dikdiks are detected, they will not whistle but jump up and race away, darting in and around the bushes at a speed that bigger animals find hard to follow in such terrain. But the dikdik will not try to outrun the predator — it will run and then drop and hide again. This antipredator technique requires thorough knowledge of the range.

All in all, the dikdiks living on territories do not do badly, considering all the things that could kill them. The Hendrichses reckoned that 10 to 20 percent of the adults die each year, which means that, with a longevity of perhaps ten years, most dikdik pairs live together for several years. The youngsters do not fare so well — only 50 percent of those born are raised and leave the territories, and once out of the territories, many more of these young animals are killed. As relatively few adults are dying, there are not many territories for the young dikdiks to take over. The high rate of reproduction allows for a reserve; in the event of catastrophes such as droughts and floods, a dikdik population can recover quickly.

The dikdik is certainly a successful antelope, and one that will probably survive outside national parks and reserves for a long time to come, mainly because it is adapted to areas that are least suitable for human occupation. In some habitats there are as many as fifty-two dikdiks to the square mile; in harsher areas, perhaps thirteen. The vast tracks of semiarid land in East and Southwest Africa must carry many thousands of dikdiks, all fastidiously maintaining their territories with ritualized marking and dunging ceremonies, forming lifelong pair bonds, and fighting off intruders without receiving a scratch.

The other African antelopes that are similar to the dikdik and fit into Class A, the first of Peter Jarman's five classes of antelopes, are: probably all fourteen species of duikers (these and other forest antelopes have not yet been studied in detail), the royal antelope and Bates's pygmy antelope, the suni, steinbok, klipspringer, Sharpe's and Cape grysboks, the beira, and the other dikdiks (Guenther's, Salt's, and Phillip's). It must be emphasized that these antelopes are more or less alike; all, however, are small, live singly or in pairs, and are territorial.

CLASS B

The Gerenuk

The gerenuk is unmistakable. To my mind it is one of the most beautiful of the gazelles, although undeniably odd-looking. Its peculiar long neck has given it its name — *gerenuk* means "giraffe-necked" in Somali. It stands on long, graceful legs, measures about 35 to 40 inches at the shoulder, and weighs 80 to 115 pounds. The males are larger than the females and have lyre-shaped horns. The gerenuk has a small head with a pointed muzzle and relatively huge ears. Because the female has no horns, when she turns and faces one, her head appears to be all ears, with just a tiny nose in between.

Like the dikdik, the gerenuk is physiologically adapted to an arid habitat and does not need to drink water. It lives in particularly dry areas, ranging from northeastern Tanzania and eastern Kenya up through Somalia and part of Ethiopia. This is not a wide range compared to that of the impala or eland, and it may be that the gerenuk is able to exist only in arid bush country, where it can put its own peculiar adaptations to use. The most conspicuous of these adaptations is the way in which it feeds. Of all the antelopes the gerenuk is probably the most exclusive browser. It feeds primarily on small trees, bushes, and shrubs, and does so in a most unusual way. It often stands up on its strong back legs, resting its forelegs in the branches of the bush, and thus feeds at heights of up to 6 feet. The dikdik also stands on its hind legs from time to time in order to reach higher leaves, but the gerenuk feeds in this position almost as a matter of course and is seen in this position far more often than the dikdik is.

The gerenuk is a particularly difficult animal to study: it is shy and lives at relatively low densities in bush areas with poor visibility. Gerenuks are difficult to find, much less observe for any period, and they have few individual characteristics to distinguish them. Nonetheless, Walter Leuthold of the Tsavo Research Project set out to study the gerenuk and another browser, the lesser kudu, in November 1968. He is the only person to date to have studied the gerenuk (and lesser kudu) on a long-term basis in the wild. Others have made observations of gerenuk behavior in zoos and short-term observations in the wild. The main purpose of Leuthold's study was to try to determine what effect the destruction of woody vegetation by elephants was having on the other browsing animals in the Tsavo National Park. In the course of the feeding work, Leuthold also collected material on social organization and behavior. Much more work could be done on this fascinating animal.

As we look at the various antelopes in terms of their social organization, we can see that each system is adaptive for the particular size of the animal and the habitat in which it lives. However, the categories are not cut and dried but rather form a continuum. The gerenuk is still a small antelope feeding very selectively on browse in a semiarid to arid environment. Whereas each dikdik male holds enough area in his particular habitat for himself, his mate, and one to two offspring at a time, the gerenuk has arrived at a slightly different system, but why it should be better for the gerenuk is difficult to say.

According to data collected in Leuthold's Tsavo study area, each male gerenuk holds a territory of approximately 1½ to 3 square miles and in each of these areas live a few females, up to six, whose home range more or less coincides with that of the male. Whether the male forms any kind of bonds with the females in his range is unknown. The associations among the individuals living in the same range appear to be loose. Groups in the study area averaged about two or three individuals, and the greatest number seen together was twelve. (In some areas, particularly in the northern part of Kenya, groups appear to be larger.) The male may be found feeding with females or on his own; the females may feed together or separately. It is likely that the females living in one range are all related. Adult females are followed by their young, and although Leuthold could not be sure, it looked as though one of his known females, F_1, was at times followed by two calves of different ages, her young male calf and a subadult male that was probably her previous calf.

The question of territoriality is difficult with the gerenuk. The usual definition of territory is an area *defended* by an individual against other animals of its species, usually by males against males (although, as we have seen, a male dikdik will also chase females from his territory). As the gerenuk population is so sparse and the ranges relatively big, the chances of seeing two males from adjacent ranges in the same area is slight. In any case, Leuthold saw only one fight between males, and this was before he knew individuals; so he could not determine the circumstances surrounding the fight. However, from all other evidence he concludes that they are territorial.

First, adult males occur only singly, either alone or with female groups. Of the individually known adult males, each remained stationary in one area, and the ranges of these males did not overlap or, at the most, overlapped very slightly. (It was interesting that one male moved into the territory of his neighbor only after that male disappeared.) Although the gerenuk does not make dung heaps, it uses the conspicuous hunched posture for urinating and defecating that is thought to have a territorial advertising function in other antelope species. The gerenuk does mark extensively with its anteorbital gland, which is situated at the outer corner of each eye.

It appears then that each male holds an exclusive area that is both his territory and his whole home range. Like the dikdik's territory, it is both a resource and a breeding territory. The gerenuk holds enough area to feed himself and several females and their young throughout the year. He appears to have exclusive mating rights with the females in his range, and he does not have to herd them or try to make them stay in his territory (as, we will see, the male impala must). When he is with the females, the male gerenuk is dominant: if he approaches a female feeding on a bush, she will give way; he may even threaten her with a slight head shake. However, it is usually a female who leads the movement as they wander around their range.

In zoos gerenuks groom each other, nibbling at one another's heads and necks, but in the wild Leuthold found little physical contact. He did see gerenuks rubbing heads together, though. On these occasions one animal would put its forehead under the other's chin and push up. This occurred most often between two females.

Although Leuthold did not witness complete mating behavior in the wild, he did see some preliminary courtship behavior, which has also been described for gerenuks in captivity. The male gerenuk does several interesting things when courting the female. He frequently marks the female with the secretion from his anteorbital gland; this behavior is not common among antelopes, and its function is not altogether understood. The gerenuk also performs Flehmen, testing the female's urine, and often follows this with a fascinating behavior that is common to several of the antelopes, called *Laufschlag* (roughly, "leg beat" in German).

In this ritual the male approaches the female from behind (or sometimes the side) and lifts his leg between her hind legs, touching her underside. In many of the antelopes who use this action — for instance, Grant's and Thomson's gazelles — the movement is done rather violently, with a hard upward motion, which looks as though it would send any female running off. But with the gerenuk (and the Uganda kob, which will be discussed later), Laufschlag is performed slowly and gently. When the gerenuk lifts one long, delicate leg to the horizontal, gently tapping the female, it looks almost like a ballet movement. It is thought that Laufschlag helps prepare the female to accept further physical contact with the male. In a species that rarely touches, it is necessary for the male to get the female over her desire to keep her distance.

The gerenuk does not appear to have any particular breeding season. Young are seen throughout the year. The gestation period is six and a half to seven months, and the female often becomes pregnant again within a month, which would mean that generally the next fawn would be born at a different time of the year and probably in a different season from the previous one. It may be that with the high-quality, less seasonal diet of a browsing animal, it is not quite so important for the young to be born at a special time, or even for the mother to be pregnant and lactating at the optimal time. (We will see that seasonality has a much more profound effect on the reproduction of some of the grazing animals.)

The young gerenuk is born in a secluded spot and then lies out for a period of a month or more. The mother leaves the fawn in a protected place, usually under a bush, and goes about her usual activities; she may join other gerenuks in the area. In one observation made by Leuthold, a female was feeding with a male and two other females when she suddenly walked off in a "determined" manner, covering more than half a mile. She walked straight up to a young gerenuk several weeks old that emerged from a bush. They greeted by touching noses, and then the fawn suckled.

Eventually the young gerenuk begins to follow its mother, and joins other females and their offspring. If the youngster is a female, she will most likely stay on in the territory and mate with the resident male when she is mature. Whether she spends more time with her own mother or with other females in the area is unknown. The male youngster's future, however, is quite different.

Leuthold was able to follow part of the histories of two young males, called Max and Moritz, that were born in the territory of M_7 and were probably the sons of F_1. They were sometimes found in association with two other subadult males called Peter and Paul, but more often the four split into two pairs. As they grew older, M_7 began to try to chase them away, but not very effectively. When a young male is chased, he just keeps going around in circles until the adult finally tires. Eventually, however, Max and Moritz left the territory and appeared about 3 miles away at the edge of the territory of M_2, two territories over from their original home. They were seen only sporadically, and Leuthold speculates that they may have been "lying low" to avoid conflict with the territorial males. In the meantime M_7 disappeared and F_1 shifted her range to the west, into M_{11}'s territory (the territory between M_2's and M_7's); eventually Moritz turned up on this territory and M_{11} apparently disappeared. Moritz became the territory holder, associated with F_1, and possibly became both father and brother of her later offspring. Max, who was older, actually became a territory holder after Moritz; he appeared on M_2's territory, which had been temporarily taken over by M_{22}, who also disappeared. At the end of the study period Max and Moritz were both still on their territories.

So it seems that young males can survive outside of their natal territories in areas not held by adult males and there may act as a reserve in the event that a territorial male should die or give up his territory. It is interesting, though, that adult gerenuk males do not form bachelor herds as many other antelopes do. Groups of two to four subadult males were found in the territories, but outside of the territories there were no groups consisting of adult males that had not yet gained territories or had lost them. The males in the territories that Max and Moritz eventually occupied simply disappeared, and it may be that most adult males hold territories until they die or die soon after being dispossessed. We do not know whether Max and Moritz fought with these males or just walked in when they disappeared. The social behavior of these fascinating but elusive animals needs further investigation, particularly in higher-density areas, where interactions may be more frequent.

In avoiding predators, the gerenuk uses both concealment and flight. Being larger than a dikdik, it can not hide quite as well. Rather than dropping to the ground, the gerenuk will just freeze when it sees something disturbing; it will stand absolutely still and stare. If the situation necessitates it, the gerenuk will then run. The females usually run first, followed by the male. Often they begin to move off in a lovely, fluid trot on their long, graceful legs, but if very alarmed, they will break into a bouncing gallop. Again, as for the dikdik, knowledge of the home range is important in flight; gerenuks dart under and around bushes and trees, and most predators have a hard time following their maneuvers.

As we saw, a pair of dikdiks is probably less conspicuous than a group or herd. One might imagine that gerenuks would also be safer living in pairs in territories. Although one can only speculate, the fact that the gerenuk is bigger and cannot hide as well is possibly one of the reasons it forms small groups when feeding. Several animals together have a better chance of detecting a predator.

At the same time, the gerenuk's diet is made up of items that are widely dispersed. Obviously, large herds of gerenuks would have to move over much larger areas, which apparently would not be the most efficient or safest way to live in their particular environment. The gerenuk system spaces out small groups into areas that are held as both resource and breeding territories.

One never ceases to be amazed at how gerenuks live in the areas that they do. There seem to be endless numbers of gerenuks in Kenya's Northeastern Province; some are living in near-desert conditions. One wonders what they can possibly be eating, as the bushes appear to be completely dry, without a single leaf. There only appears to be a lack of food, though. By feeding from a wide range of plants at different growth stages, gerenuks are able to survive and apparently even thrive. Although the vegetation is usually consistent throughout their range (that is, their range does not usually cover more than one broad vegetation zone), their diet changes considerably according to the season. In the wet season they concentrate on certain plants — shrubs, creepers, and vines — that dry up completely in the dry season. As the dry season progresses, they turn more and more to evergreen plants such as *Salvadora persica*, which few other animals will eat. Certain acacias also maintain foliage throughout the dry season and these become important. Gerenuks are often associated with *Acacia mellifera* trees (named for their honeylike smell), which grow in arid areas. By choosing from a wide variety of plants (in Tsavo gerenuks have been recorded feeding on eighty-two different plant species) and by carefully selecting those parts that contain the greatest nutrition, the gerenuk is able to attain a relatively high-quality diet. It is interesting to watch a gerenuk select each individual bite as it goes along. It approaches a bush, often rises on its hind legs, and then sniffs around with its long, pointed muzzle before choosing a bite or moving on to another bush.

Leuthold investigated the feeding habits of gerenuks living in two different areas in Tsavo: one that was heavily damaged by elephants and one that had undergone less change. He found that the diets in the two areas differed considerably. In the altered area there were fewer species of plants from which to choose, but certain plants were preferred and these were selected. Leuthold concluded that "In view of this adaptability, and of the abundance of preferred food plants in the study areas, the vegetation changes in Tsavo National Park do not, at present, appear to endanger the continued existence of the gerenuk." What Leuthold strongly recommends is a continued effort to prevent fire, which can be more devastating to vegetation (particularly to the regeneration of woody species) than elephants alone. If the vegetation in

Tsavo is protected from any further drastic changes, then the gerenuk should be able to continue to exist there. In many other parts of its range, the gerenuk is in little danger, particularly in those areas where bush cover is increasing, apparently because of overgrazing by cattle. In these arid areas the gerenuk's special adaptations give it an advantage, and few other animals can compete with it. The beautiful *swala twiga* (Swahili for "giraffe gazelle") should be around for some time yet to surprise and delight us in its harsh and barren habitat.

Other Class B antelope species — that is, those that occur in groups of one to a dozen animals with adult males apparently holding individual territories — are the Bohor reedbuck, the southern reedbuck, the mountain reedbuck, the Vaal rhebuck, the oribi, the lesser kudu, and possibly the bushbuck and the sitatunga.

CLASS C

The Impala

In form alone the impala, for many people, represents the quintessential antelope. With its glistening red-orange coat, fantastic lyrate horns, velvet black eyes, and strategic black and white markings (which appear to have been placed where they are for purely aesthetic reasons but of course were not), the impala is one of the most visually satisfying animals in nature. This is purely a subjective feeling, but in many ways the impala's social organization and ecology could be considered representative of all antelopes, as it has arrived at a system midway between the precise territoriality of the dikdik and the nonterritorial system of the eland. Above all, the impala is highly adaptable and very flexible in both its social organization and the way in which it makes a living.

The impala is also a medium-sized antelope: it stands 33 to 37 inches at the shoulder and weighs from 100 to 180 pounds. It is a successful antelope in that it ranges from South Africa right up into northern Kenya. Throughout its range it generally lives in the "ecotones" — those areas that form the transitions from one kind of habitat to another (for instance, where grassland merges into woodland, or woodland into forest, or plains into riverine vegetation). With its mountains, valleys, rivers, lakes, escarpments, highlands, and lowlands, the southern and eastern parts of Africa contain constantly changing habitats; thus much of the area consists of ecotones. Generally impalas are found where there is some cover, not out in the open plains or in dense bush or forest.

Unlike the dikdik and gerenuk, the impala has been studied extensively by several researchers in different parts of its range, including South Africa and Rhodesia (where it was under particular consideration as a potential game-ranching animal). Rudolf Schenkel studied the impala in the Nairobi National Park part-time from 1963–64 and also watched impalas in other areas of East Africa. Walter Leuthold carried out a more intensive study of the impalas of Nairobi National Park in 1968 and came to some different conclusions from Schenkel's. Peter and Mattie Jarman have done the lengthiest and most comprehensive study of the impala. Peter Jarman has studied the impala throughout its range in Africa. He worked for three years in southern Africa and then carried out an additional three-year study of the ecology of the impala in the Serengeti National Park in Tanzania, while his wife, Mattie Jarman, studied the impala's social behavior.

For reasons best known to the early naturalists and explorers, it was generally assumed that antelope males had "harems" of females; that is, each male gathered together a group of females and by herding them and fighting off male challengers kept his females to himself. This was supposed to be the classic antelope social system, and yet, to date, there is no proof that any antelope actually lives like this. When Schenkel studied the Nairobi impala he found what, to him, appeared to be a harem system. There were breeding herds of females in groups of two to over a hundred, single dominant males, and bachelor herds of males. Through successive competition one male appeared to become the "owner" of a female herd. Schenkel concluded that impalas were not territorial.

After studying the Nairobi impalas for nine months, Walter Leuthold came to a different conclusion. He particularly wanted to investigate the question of territoriality and social organization, as two researchers in Rhodesia (R. F. Dasman and A. S. Mossman) had suggested that the impalas there were territorial, at least during the rutting season. In order to carry out his investigation, Leuthold had to identify individuals, and as in every other study mentioned, this was the key to understanding social organization. He photographed 109 individuals and resighted 94 of them at least once. He was then able to record where he saw individuals over a period of time and with whom they were associated. What he found was that solitary adult males each stayed in a particular area, whether there were females there or not, and what is more, the same females were not always associated with the same male. And finally, a new adult male would sometimes appear in an area, and the male that had been there previously would appear in a bachelor herd. Given these observations, it looked as though adult males held areas into which females wandered and the male was first and foremost attached to the area; he did not follow the females wherever they went. Leuthold had to cut his study short after only nine months, but he was able to conclude that there was "clear evidence for territoriality" in impalas.

Mattie Jarman began her study in the Serengeti in 1968 with the knowledge of Schenkel's and Leuthold's results. Like Leuthold, and initially with his help, she set out to know her animals individually. Male impalas are not too hard to recognize, as they have scars and individual horn shapes, but the females, having no horns and few scars, are far more difficult. In the end the Jarmans immobilized and marked some of the females. (They also devised a system of catching juveniles by hand in the glare of headlights in order to mark them.)

It was soon obvious to Mattie Jarman that certain males did stay in certain areas, whether or not there were females present. She too saw all the criteria for territoriality fulfilled, plus active defense, including the chasing off of bachelor males. Furthermore, she was able to observe the behavior and the territoriality system of the impala in far greater detail.

In the Serengeti, and apparently in most areas where there are seasonal changes in the habitat, impalas have a social system that allows them to adapt to the environmental conditions at the time. In the Serengeti the system is as follows: Single adult males defend and hold an area of approximately $1/10$ of a square mile. This is not held exclusively against other males; a male will allow bachelor males to pass through or feed in his territory as long as they ignore any females that might be there. Young males and adult males that are not holding territories form bachelor herds. Females live in loose breeding herds of ten to a hundred individuals. There do not appear to be any individual bonds between adult females. The females wander in a home range of 3 square miles or more, and within this area they may pass in and out of six to eight male territories.

When a herd of females comes into a male's territory, he tries to keep them there by various strategies, mainly herding. He also uses one amusing method in which he "pretends" that he has seen some danger over in the next territory and stands in an alarm posture in the hopes of persuading the females not to move on. He tests the females for estrus by sniffing the vulva or by collecting some urine and then performing Flehmen. If there is a female in estrus, the male will begin to herd her more intently. With the estrus female in his territory, the male does not have to worry about competition from other males. He will normally be left alone to mate with her, as he has complete dominance in his own territory.

The way in which a male impala gains and keeps his territory has been thoroughly investigated by Mattie Jarman; she was able to follow the life histories of several known males. Young males are driven out of the breeding herds by the territorial males when they are four to six months old. The young male stays around the periphery of the breeding herd for a while, trying from time to time to get back in. At this point the young males are particularly vulnerable to predation and by the age of three years there are far more females than males. Eventually the young male joins a bachelor herd, which consists of subadult males of various ages and fully adult males.

One of the most fascinating things about the bachelor herd is the hierarchical system within it. First, there is a hierarchy based on age: six-month-old youngsters are subordinate to one-year-old males, who in turn are subordinate to the nearly adult males; and all of these younger animals are subordinate to the adult males. Then, among the adult males there is a linear rank order based on dominance that is determined by frequent sparring. This is based not on age, but on strength, condition, weight, and also according to an interesting phenomenon in the impala that was discovered by the Jarmans. It seems that the males produce a secretion on their foreheads that accumulates in the thick hair above and between their eyes. This secretion is produced by sebaceous glands, and when a male is in a high-ranking position, he seems to produce more of it. The males test each other by sniffing one another's foreheads, presumably to see what state each male is in. Usually it is a subordinate male that will cautiously approach a dominant male and sniff his forehead. The dominant male stands stiffly and allows the approach; the subordinate male sniffs and then leaps away, and the tension is broken.

An adult male works his way up through the linear hierarchy until he is at the top and ready to challenge a male in possession of a territory. The challenge consists of a series of encounters and fights with a resident male until that male is defeated and leaves his territory to join a bachelor herd. Once in possession of a territory the male maintains it in several ways. He advertises his presence and possession by standing erect with head held high in what has been termed the "proud posture." He marks his territory with the secretion from the glands in his forehead, by rubbing his head on bushes and shrubs. He also marks with dung heaps, but not to quite the extent that the dikdik does. More directly, he chases off intruders, often roaring. The impala's roar sounds a little like the lion's but more like a strange bark of a dog.

Unlike the gerenuk and dikdik, the territorial male impala can- not maintain his territory for long periods of time. In the Serengeti males averaged eighty-two days on a territory before being replaced by challengers. Holding a territory is an exhaust- ing business. A male has to herd females, chase bachelors, fight with challengers, and mate with the females. M. Jarman watched one territorial male for two different twelve-hour periods: one period when there were females in his territory and one when there were none. When the females were around, he was far more active, devoted much less time to eating, and actually spent two of the twelve hours running! Not surprisingly, the condition of territorial males deteriorates fairly fast. Eventually a well- rested and well-fed bachelor will come along to challenge him.

The males fight head to head, each pushing and twisting to try to push the other off balance for a moment so that he can get at the head, neck, or shoulders with a rapier-sharp horn. Impalas can and do fight to the death, but usually they do not get badly injured because they are protected by a dermal shield — ex- tremely thick skin in the areas most likely to be hit. The main ad- vantage in a fight like this is not the size of the horns, but rather the thickness of the neck and the weight of the whole animal. As the territorial male loses condition, he becomes more and more at a disadvantage; eventually he is defeated and must join the bache- lor herd himself. When he first joins the herd, he is usually low down in the linear dominance order, but as he rests and regains condition, he works his way back up, until he is ready to chal- lenge again. Most often he will try to regain his former territory; there are indications that males have strong attachments to partic- ular areas.

We can see that the impala system is different from that of ei- ther the dikdik or gerenuk, which hold territories that provide year-round resources and a place for undisturbed mating. For the impala male, the territory is primarily a means to attain breeding rights. A successful male is one who passes on his genetic mate- rial through the most females, and for the impala, the best way to attain this goal seems to be to hold an area where he is completely dominant over any other male. While there is usually enough food in his territory for himself, there is not enough for females as well, so he must wait for the females to come to him. M. Jarman found that certain territorial males were with females more often than others were, and developed a theory about this situation. Their territories apparently had more to offer the females in the way of resources. Those males with larger and more diverse territories, which included more than one vegetation type and both wet-season and dry-season forage, seemed to be the most successful.

Ultimately, however, the impala social system is flexible, and in studying it throughout its range, P. Jarman has found that there are variations in different populations depending upon environmental conditions. He found that there is "a major watershed" in impala ecology and social behavior that runs approximately from just south of Lake Victoria to about Dar es Salaam. To the north of that line, impalas breed year round, and in many areas the territorial system is maintained throughout the year. To the south of the line, impalas are seasonal breeders, and full territoriality occurs only during the rut, with partial territoriality in the few months before and after the rut. The difference between the two areas depends on the predictability of rainfall: in the south rainfall is much more definitely seasonal than it is in the north.

The Serengeti population, which is near the line, proved to be adaptable from year to year. In 1969 the Serengeti had a particularly dry year, and the Jarmans were fortunate in being able to observe how the impalas reacted. In some years the territorial system was maintained throughout the year, but in 1969 it broke down altogether. An impala population usually stays within a definite home range, utilizing the resources throughout that range in both the wet and dry seasons. Peter Jarman has been able to show that the availability and dispersion of food has a profound effect on the social system. In the dry season, as food becomes less available and less nutritious, the females walk farther daily, move faster, and divide into smaller groups, and as a result move more frequently through the males' territories. The males are then faced with an increasing number of boundary receptions of females and more attempts to stop females leaving their territories, which prove to be both time- and energy-consuming. They find it nearly impossible both to herd these small groups of females and to get enough to eat for themselves.

By the end of the dry season in 1969 the females and bachelor males were mixing freely, and the territorial males were no longer using their energies to try to separate them. At one point the system broke down completely: all the impalas abandoned the study area and moved to an area several miles away, where there was a green flush. There males and females mixed together, and the dominant males did not try to set up territories. Nevertheless, the territorial males were the first to return to their home area, even before it was green again, and they went straight for their former territories. As soon as the rain came, the rest of the impalas returned, and fighting for territory (sometimes among two or three males who had each occupied the same territory), herding and courting of females, etc., were carried out with feverish intensity. Within three weeks things settled down to the normal wet-season social system with herds of breeding females, bachelor herds, and territorial males.

To appreciate the versatility of the impala it is necessary to look at its feeding style. Peter Jarman has shown that the impala is a very opportunistic feeder, adapting its diet to the conditions at the time. It is both a browser and a grazer, utilizing a wide variety of plant species. It grazes in the wet season, when fresh young blades of grass are growing and full of protein; when the grass dries out, the impala turns to herbs, shrubs, and bushes. The proportion of grass to browse in the impala's diet depends on the season and the habitat in which it lives. On the shores of Lake Kariba in Rhodesia, where P. Jarman worked, the impalas ate 4.6 percent grass and 95.4 percent browse; in the Tarangire National Park, where another ecologist, Hugh Lamprey, worked, impalas ate 92.5 percent grass and 7.5 percent browse; and in P. Jarman's study area in the Serengeti they ate 62 percent grass and 38 percent browse.

Impalas move throughout their range according to the season. An impala population's range usually covers a catena — the topographic sequence from a ridge (the highest part) to a sump (the lowest part). Typically the population is found on the upper part of the catena in the wet season and gradually moves down the catena as the dry season progresses. The lower levels of the landscape retain moisture, and the vegetation remains more nutritious for longer into the dry season. At the same time, by moving down the catena, the impalas get closer to water, which they need to drink in the dry season. In the wet season they may not have to drink at all, because they can usually obtain enough moisture from plants; in the dry season they may have to drink every day.

As a medium-sized antelope that can neither hide nor defend itself, nor in many cases outrun its pursuer, the impala cannot use the same antipredator devices as the dikdik and gerenuk. However, the impala does not live in as arid and harsh an environment as the latter do, where food items must be searched for and tend to be more dispersed. The impala's feeding style and habitat do not require the spacing out of individuals to the same extent — although impala group size does change with the seasons, to larger groups in the wet season and smaller in the dry. Still, impalas are able to group together, and this is perhaps their most important antipredator device. The clumping of individuals within a range reduces the chances of random meetings with predators, and many eyes and ears together aid in detecting danger. Also a mass of animals makes it difficult for the predator to pick out an individual, which for a hunter is a prerequisite. If the herd is surprised by an attack, rather than running away, the individuals leap explosively in different directions, while uttering a sharp, barklike alarm call. The sight of impalas leaping in this way — they can jump 10 feet high and span 30 feet — is a tremendous thrill; their power and grace are breathtaking. The effect of this device is to confuse the predator so that it can not concentrate on an individual.

The impala is also careful as it goes about its daily activities. It is mainly a diurnal animal, spending most of the night in a chosen resting place (usually out in the open), chewing the cud, and briefly sleeping. In the daytime the more dangerous activities such as drinking are done at midday when predators are least likely to be active. M. Jarman also found that the majority of births took place around midday.

In East Africa impalas are born throughout the year, but there are birth peaks in most areas, and these are more pronounced in areas where the seasonal changes are greater. In the Serengeti the birth peak varies, depending on conditions, but it usually occurs in October and November. M. Jarman is the first known scientist to observe and record births of impalas in the wild. She was able to detect a female's characteristic behavior before a birth. In all she witnessed five complete births and part of seventeen others.

Usually the female stopped feeding, her back became straight, she lifted her tail and appeared to strain. She left the other females and, despite the herding efforts of the territorial male, managed to get away to a secluded spot. In most cases the female lay down to give birth and jumped up as soon as the fawn was expelled. She then usually ate the afterbirth (although the expulsion of the placenta was variable — some did not produce it until hours later) and cleaned both herself and the fawn. The female impala does not generally leave the fawn lying out as so many other antelopes do. She and the fawn both stay in hiding for the first few days and then she introduces it to the herd. The members of the herd — especially other youngsters — show great interest in the new fawn, crowding around and sniffing at it. However, M. Jarman speculates that if there are no other youngsters in the herd, the mother may delay introducing the fawn, because as the only fawn, it would be conspicuous, and this is what a prey animal tries to avoid. If the delay is long, she may leave it in hiding and return to it from time to time to suckle it.

Eventually they will both join the herd, and within the herd the young fawn will immediately spend more time with other fawns than with its mother. The effect of the fawns' staying together is the formation of a crèche group that moves and acts together as a unit. The crèche may even be left behind when the females feed or travel to water. At the slightest alarm, however, the females rush to the crèche, calling; each identifies her own offspring by its smell. M. Jarman showed that the original isolation of the mother and young at the time of birth is important, not only as an antipredator device, but in allowing the mother and fawn to learn to recognize one another. When a fawn was born in the vicinity of the herd, the female was harassed by the territorial male, and by bachelors, females, and other youngsters, who immediately surrounded the newborn fawn and confused it. In these cases the fawn tried to suckle and follow animals other than its mother, and it was clear that it could easily "imprint" on the wrong animal.

The young impala suckles for five or six months and begins to nibble on food at less than a month old. The young female is mature at thirteen to fourteen months old and may produce her first fawn at twenty to twenty-four months, after a gestation period of six to seven months. The young male matures sexually at sixteen to eighteen months, and reaches physical maturity at about two and a half years, but he still has a long, hard struggle before he attains social maturity at three and a half years or more and can hope to sire any offspring.

The Uganda Kob

If the impala male's efforts to attain and maintain a territory seem difficult, one need only compare them to those of the Uganda (or Thomas') kob to gain perspective. The kob is similar to the impala in many ways, particularly in appearance, and it falls into the same class of social organization. It too is a medium-sized antelope with herds of breeding females, bachelor herds, and single adult males that hold territories. The Uganda kob's range is relatively small, however; it occurs mainly in Uganda, with only small extensions into the Sudan and Zaïre. (There are other subspecies of kob in the Sudan and Ethiopia and throughout much of West Africa.)

Although the impala represents the Class C antelopes quite adequately, I cannot resist including a section on the Uganda kob, mainly because it has a unique territorial system and probably the most fascinating sexual behavior of any antelope; what is more, it has been very well studied. Helmut Buechner began the pioneering work on the kob in 1957, making him one of the first scientists to study social behavior in the field in East Africa, and several students and associates of his have carried out subsequent behavior studies. These include Robert Schloeth (whose particular interest was mating behavior), Walter Leuthold (who later studied impalas and gerenuks), and J. A. Morrison.

Buechner and the others worked in the Toro Game Reserve in Uganda, where the kob population is extremely dense: in 1964 there were fifteen thousand kobs in only 150 square miles. It must be pointed out at the start that this density may account in part for the unusual social behavior found in this population. The Uganda kobs in the Toro Game Reserve have taken the territorial system to an extreme in terms of territory as mating ground.

The kob has a dual territorial system: there are both large individual territories spread out over the range and territorial breeding grounds where males congregate on a relatively small piece of ground only a few hundred yards in diameter. Virtually all mating occurs on these breeding grounds, and the function of the single large territories is not entirely understood, although they are thought to be the original form of territoriality and in some other populations of kobs are the only type of territories. In the Toro Game Reserve there are approximately fifteen breeding grounds (some of which have been in existence and continuous use for thirty years), and it appears that the kob population breaks down into units of about a thousand animals, each associated with one of the breeding grounds. The females in each of these units form herds of fifty to two hundred individuals.

On a breeding ground there are thirty to forty adult males that each occupy a tiny territory, which is approximately circular and measures 15 to 30 yards in diameter. Each individual territory consists of a bare piece of ground surrounded by slightly longer grass on the periphery. Some of the territories have common boundaries; others have neutral zones in between.

Neighboring males rarely fight; rather, they usually "display" toward one another, each walking toward the other with ears lowered until they meet at the boundary, where they may clash horns but not seriously; they then return to their other activities. If a female wanders out of one territory into another, the neighbors will respect each other's boundaries and will not pursue her.

Serious fights occur only when a bachelor male challenges a territorial male for his piece of ground. Then the fights are vicious and can lead to severe injuries and even death. Buechner has two records of males being killed in territorial disputes. The females seem to prefer the ten to fifteen territories in the central area of the breeding ground, and it is in these territories that most mating activity and fights occur. Here the competition is very stiff indeed. It is as if the system of the impala were encapsulated in both time and space. Instead of a male losing his territory after an average of eighty-two days, the male kob is likely to lose his territory after only two or three days — that is, if his is one of the central territories. The males on the peripheral territories may hold theirs for a year or more, and although their chances of mating with females appear to be much lower in the short term, it may be just as successful a strategy over a whole lifetime.

The activity in the central territories is intense; there are sometimes as many as ten females in three or four territories. These three or four males have to fight off challengers while courting and mating with the females. It sometimes looks like a three-ring circus, with males running in through the surrounding territories, fighting viciously with the possessor, and either running back out or winning and chasing the defeated male out. Males return again and again to fight for the territory they once held, and at times there are several males vying for the same territory.

The turnover rate is even more understandable when one takes into account that there is little or no food on the territory. In the daytime males will leave their territories for brief periods for food and water, but often the male cannot take the chance, and basically he has to live off his own reserves, which are soon depleted because of the tremendous amount of energy he expends. When a male finally gives in to a challenger, he will join a bachelor herd and, like the impala, there regain condition until he is ready to fight again. Almost invariably he will challenge the possessor for his former territory.

The kob is primarily a grazer, feeding almost exclusively on various grasses. Due to a combination of high rainfall and the periodic burning of old, dry grass, the kobs in the Toro Game Reserve are able to find grass at a fresh growing stage throughout most years. Although there are slight peaks of breeding activity in the two rainy seasons (April to May and October), the females breed throughout the year, being little restricted by seasonality. As might be expected, the territories are held year round, and at any given time, observers can watch the fascinating mating activity that takes place.

The courtship, mating, and postcoital behavior of the Uganda kob is the most complex of any antelope yet studied. When nearing or upon coming into estrus, the female leaves the herd of females she has been associating with and enters one of the territorial breeding grounds. As far as can be determined, she goes to the same one each year, and probably even goes to preferred territories within the ground. Most of the females seem to prefer the three or four most centrally located territories.

Upon entering a territory, the female is met by a highly excited male that is intensely interested in her. He usually approaches her in what Buechner has called the "prancing" display, holding his head high, revealing a white patch on the throat, and flashing the black bands on the front of his legs in a stiff, high-stepping gait. At the same time his tail is lifted and he has a full erection. When the female comes to a stop, he sniffs her vulva, she urinates, and he tests the urine, performing Flehmen. Next the male approaches the female from behind or from the side and, lifting a foreleg to a near-horizontal position, touches her underparts. This is the Laufschlag we saw in the gerenuk, and in the Uganda kob the action is also performed gently as compared to other antelopes. All the same, the kob female sometimes tries to avoid the touch and circles around, with the male following. She may even bite or butt his hindquarters. If she does not run out of the territory altogether (or lie down to avoid him), the male then

tries to mount. He usually mounts several times without copulating, and this series of mountings seems to be a necessary prepara-
tion before the male is fully stimulated. When coitus is finally
achieved, it is very brief. It lasts only one or two seconds and
consists, according to the observers, of one vigorous ejaculatory
thrust.

All the preliminary displays and actions may be carried out several times in different sequences; so prancing and mounting may
be interspersed with circling, Laufschlag, and Flehmen. Thus it
is all the more surprising to realize that the whole thing, from the
moment the female enters the territory to the completion of coitus, may take only two or three minutes. Sometimes, but not
often, there may be no displays at all: the male may just mount
and achieve coitus immediately. On the other hand, if the female
is in an early stage of estrus, there may be as many as twenty preliminary mountings before the male is successful. Then, too, if
the male is tired out from fighting and previous sexual activity, he
may take longer. Buechner and Schloeth also noted that virgin
females were very nervous and sensitive to the advances of the
male. "They entered new territories with hesitation, frequently
jumped abruptly and ran a few steps forward or turned at the
slightest touch of the male on the perineum, and often lay down
to avoid the male. Precoital displays over periods of 30 minutes
or more were common without ensuing coitus."

The most unusual thing about the kob's mating behavior is a
period of postcoital activity that may last up to five minutes. No
other antelope is known to perform behavior of this kind after
copulation. When the male dismounts, he almost invariably
stands quietly for a few seconds. Next comes a sequence of actions, the order of which can vary; parts may even be left out.
After standing still for a while, often the male will first whistle.
Other territorial males may answer the whistle, and they can be
heard whistling in turn across the territorial ground. Following
the whistle, the male usually licks his penis, first from one side
and then from the other. During this period the female is usually
standing quietly with her back arched, her tail raised, and her
hind legs spread apart.

Now begins the postcopulatory actions, which are most unusual. The male goes to the female and may briefly lick her
vulva. Then he pushes his head between her hind legs and nuz-
zles and licks the udders and the inguinal glands, little pouches
situated between the hind legs in both males and females, which
produce a waxy secretion with a strong odor. The function of
these glands is not fully understood, but they are thought to help
female and young recognize each other by smell.

After the licking and nuzzling, the male usually performs
Laufschlag from the side or between the hind legs, as in the precoital behavior. But now the male adds a further refinement: he
rests his chin on the back or rump of the female and very gently
holds her in a pincers grip, slowly squeezing her from above and
below. During any of these actions the female may react by
standing still, moving around in a circle, lying down, or running
out of the territory altogether. Several times Buechner and
Schloeth saw a female respond by butting the male, so it is not
necessarily something the female readily accepts. When the male
retracts his penis, it usually signifies the end of the copulatory behavior for the time being, and the partners may then lie down or
graze. It is possible for them to mate again after ten to fifteen
minutes, but often the male is distracted by another female or a
challenger; thus the interval is usually longer. The female is not
bonded to this one male. She will probably mate with several
males during the approximately twenty-four hours that she spends
on the breeding ground.

The complexity of the kob's mating behavior opens up many intriguing questions about function, some of which cannot be answered yet. Buechner and Schloeth theorize that the territorial
system of the kob has a profound effect on its sexual behavior.
Because of the small, clustered territories, the male must do his
utmost to keep a female on his territory; thus he must inhibit any
aggression that might be linked with mating. In most other antelopes the male herds the female with outstretched neck. The kob
male does the opposite — prancing toward the female, he holds
his head and neck high. This seems to attract the female, and
once in contact with her, the male performs the highly ritualized

precoital actions very gently. The rapid sequence of displays probably helps both partners get into synchrony with each other, a necessity when the female is in estrus for only one day and may be in the male's territory for only a short time.

The postcoital displays are more difficult to interpret. Beuchner and Schloeth speculate that the nuzzling, licking, and pincers grip may help to promote the transport of spermatozoa. In domestic cows, inguinal nuzzling and licking have been shown to increase uterine contractions, but if this is the case for kobs, then it is strange that it does not occur in other antelopes. Walter Leuthold suggests that the actions may have a behavioral function linked to making the territory more attractive to the female. The displays may also simply delay the female's departure to another territory and thus reduce, however slightly, the chances of her mating with other males.

The whole question of why there are territorial breeding grounds in some populations of kobs is also largely unanswered. Apparently the breeding grounds are in some way advantageous to reproduction, but in what way is unknown. The kob is the only antelope that has a breeding ground system and seems to be one of those animals that are endlessly rewarding to observe.

The other Class C antelopes with social systems incorporating bachelor herds, breeding herds, and territorial males are: the Defassa and the common waterbuck, the puku, the lechwe, the springbuck, Grant's and Thomson's gazelles, the greater kudu, and the nyala.

CLASS D

The Wildebeest

There is no way around it — the wildebeest is a singularly absurd-looking animal. Both males and females carry short horns that grow outward and then curve up on the ends, and with their long heads, with eyes placed high up and far apart, they tend to look either solemn or immensely surprised at the world around them. They have well-developed shoulders and necks, but the rest of the body slopes down to weak-looking hindquarters. This peculiar body sits upon remarkably thin little legs. Wildebeests are funny enough when they are standing still, but when they begin to move they are even more comical. They run in a peculiar jerky gait, and their spindly legs appear to be moving mechanically, so that the whole effect is that of a wind-up toy. When excited, they perform extraordinary cavorting actions that make them appear even more bizarre; these have earned them the description "the clowns of the veld."

There are two species of wildebeest in Africa today: the comparatively rare black wildebeest, or white-tailed gnu (*gnu* is thought to be the Hottentot name for the wildebeest), of South Africa; and the blue wildebeest, or brindled or white-bearded gnu, which ranges from parts of southern Africa up through southern Kenya. The last great concentrations of wildebeests can now be found only in northern Tanzania and southern Kenya, in the area including the Maasai Mara Game Reserve, Serengeti National Park, and the Ngorongoro Conservation Area.

With the wildebeest we have come to an animal that has moved about as far away from the forest habitat as an antelope can get: the wildebeest lives right out on the open plains, feeds exclusively on grasses, and is dependent upon water for drinking. At the same time, we are moving into the category of the large antelope: wildebeests stand 4 to 4½ feet at the shoulder; males weigh 400 to 500 pounds and females average about 100 pounds lighter.

The tiny dikdik and the small gerenuk, both mainly browsers that are water-independent, stay in a well-defined home range of a uniform vegetation type year round and survive by spacing out individuals with a territorial system and by feeding highly selectively. The medium-sized impala forms herds of females and herds of bachelors that move through a large home range including several vegetation types, which are utilized according to the season; males hold territories mainly for breeding purposes. Now what is a large, grazing antelope like the wildebeest going to do?

Wildebeests are gregarious animals and associate in huge herds sometimes numbering in the thousands. At first glance there seems to be no social organization at all. Males and females together roam over a huge area and seem to move according to whim or some atavistic drive that they are unaware of. They must have seemed strange creatures indeed to the early explorers, but to the scientists who have figured out what these antelopes are doing, wildebeests are infinitely fascinating.

Bernhard Grzimek and his son Michael began the work in the Serengeti — an ideal place to study the ecology of the wildebeest, with its vast herds moving over thousands of square miles. Using a small airplane, they attempted to count the wildebeests and other plains animals and plot their movements. Then in 1959 Lee and Martha Talbot started their three-year ecological study of the Serengeti wildebeest. They worked on the movements, feeding ecology, population dynamics, social structure, and behavior of the wildebeest. But it was not until Richard Estes' three-year ethological study of the Ngorongoro Crater wildebeest population was completed that we had a detailed picture of the wildebeest's social organization and behavior. Since then, several other studies have been carried out on the wildebeest in different areas, mainly concerning its ecology and population dynamics.

The Talbots' early work in the Serengeti was especially exciting because they brought out the first comprehensive information on the way in which wildebeests move. It had long been supposed that the wildebeests in the Serengeti area followed age-old migration routes each year, circling through an area that extended from the Ngorongoro Crater in the east to Lake Victoria in the west, and from Lake Lagarja in the south to the Maasai Mara Game Reserve across the border into Kenya in the north. The wildebeests do move over most of this huge area, which covers about 12,000 square miles, but the routes vary considerably from year to year. In fact no two year's movements are ever the same. The clue to this seemingly erratic movement is rainfall. Wildebeests, as the Talbots discovered, are constantly alert to where rain is falling and move accordingly. Thus they travel to where the grass will soon be green and growing, rather than waiting for the rains to come to them. How they detect the rainfall is difficult to say. The Talbots thought that it was probably by a combination of smell, sight, and sound, but it is remarkable that wildebeests are capable of moving in response to a rainfall 30 miles away.

It is possible, however, to plot a generalized movement pattern through the Serengeti over a year. In January the wildebeests are usually found out on the short grass plains in the east, where there is generally rainfall from around November through April. If conditions remain favorable, the wildebeests will usually stay out on the plains during January and February, when most of the calves are born. If rain continues to fall from time to time, they will stay out on the plains for another couple of months. By the end of May most of the grass on the short grass plains has dried up, and, just as important for the wildebeest, their sources of drinking water have disappeared. Then the wildebeests begin to move off the plains and into the woodlands to the west and north, where there are permanently flowing rivers. In some years, when the right conditions combine, the wildebeests mass together and move off the plains in a spectacular "migration" — thousands upon thousands of wildebeests move together in long columns across the plains. As the zebras and gazelles are also moving, there are sometimes over a million animals involved. There is nothing like this sight left in the world — this is what Theodore Roosevelt was talking about when he said he had had "a Pleistocene day."

It is incorrect to call the movement off the plains "*the* migration," as is often heard, because in effect wildebeests are moving

all year round; this is just the time most conspicuous. Once in
the woodlands, the wildebeests keep moving in response to rainfall or the depletion of grazing sources. In some years the mass
exodus is hardly noticeable. The wildebeests come off the plains
in dribs and drabs; sometimes part of the population will move
into the woodlands and then go back out onto the plains when
they detect a rainstorm there. Usually by June, however, as
there are no permanent sources of water on the plains, most of the
wildebeests have left. Generally they first move to the west, and
eventually they tend to the north, near or even into Kenya, where
they are often found at the height of the dry season in September
and October. This area in Kenya, the Maasai Mara Game Reserve, has the highest rainfall in the wildebeests' range and
frequent out-of-season rainstorms. In November and December,
when rain begins to fall on the plains again, the wildebeests head
south. The pull to the plains at this time is not fully understood,
because at that time there is also rain in the north and west, so it
is not rainfall alone that attracts them to the plains and causes the
movement. The routes they take over a year are very circuitous,
with much doubling back and circling around. When the Talbots
followed the migration route in 1960, they estimated that the wildebeests covered a minimum of 1093 miles.

The wildebeest's method of feeding is not as selective as those
of the animals we have looked at previously. Rather than carefully selecting from what is available in one area, the wildebeest
selects the area in which it will feed; that is, it selects a place
where the grass is at a growth stage that it prefers. Wildebeests
seem to prefer certain grasses over others, but basically what they
appear to look for is short, growing grass, which is easily digested
and full of nutrients. As the dry season progresses and they have
to turn to the older, longer grasses in the woodlands, wildebeests
apparently become more selective, choosing the leaf and sheath of
the plant, those parts that have the least fiber content.

Feeding in this style on contiguously distributed food items,
wildebeests do not need to be spaced out; in fact, they are usually
found clumped together in areas of favorable grazing conditions.
Thus wildebeests can group together in one area, feed until they

have depleted the resources there, and then move on to another area. (This method of feeding also keeps the grass short and growing for when they might return later.) They do not stick to a limited home range and carefully select each bite as dikdiks do. Since the wildebeests move in response to rain and favorable grazing conditions, it is not surprising to find them in large aggregations, but the attraction to a particular area is not the only thing that makes them come together. Wildebeests are naturally gregarious; they are one of the few antelopes that rub against each other and lie together with rumps or backs touching.

Aside from whatever social benefits wildebeests may derive from herding, the most obvious asset to moving in a large group is the antipredator effect. For an animal the size and color of a wildebeest, hiding would be nearly impossible, especially out on the plains. It can defend itself against some of the smaller predators, but its best strategy is to get into a large group in which it does not stand out as an individual. A wall of dark, gray wildebeests is not very inviting to a predator who wants to pick out one animal. A herd will even approach a predator, keeping watch on it all the time so that it does not have a chance to make a move undetected. The protection of the herd is particularly valuable for wildebeest calves, which, unlike most other antelope species, do not lie out as an antipredator mechanism.

So we can see that it makes sense for wildebeests to live in large herds, but what is difficult to discern, when one watches this mass of animals, is what is going on in the way of social organization. Once again, the Ngorongoro Crater proved an ideal place in which to observe social behavior. It was here that Richard Estes made his detailed observations on the wildebeest. In the crater there is a resident population of approximately fifteen thousand wildebeests, the majority of which migrate around the crater floor, acting almost as a microcosm of the Serengeti population. The rest of the population is far more sedentary and has a social organization similar to that of the impala; that is, there are small herds of females and calves, herds of bachelors, and territorial males. The migrating population forms into larger herds of females, from a hundred to a thousand; it also has larger bachelor herds; and some of the dominant adult males move with the aggregations, setting up temporary territories from time to time. Most of these males do not try to maintain their territories for long, but will move on when the females do; and as there is a definite period of rut for the wildebeest, some of these males may actively defend territories only during the mating season.

In Ngorongoro perhaps half of the dominant adult males are able to stake out territories and maintain them for most of the year. The females move around the crater floor and pass through the territories more or less freely, but intruding males are subject to challenging and chasing. At the time of the rut, usually in May, the females are often located in a particular part of the crater, and the males who have or can win territories there are the ones who will most likely sire the most young and thus be the most successful. These territories are so strategic that, rather than give them up at the time of little breeding activity, the males hold on to them year round so that they do not lose them. (It is easier to hold an established territory than to take one over from its owner.) A male may hold the same territory for several years; one wildebeest bull known by the warden in the Maasai Mara Game Reserve was seen on the same territory for thirteen years.

Under these more or less stable conditions in Ngorongoro, Estes was able to investigate the territoriality of wildebeests in detail, and his results show that they have one of the most complex repertoires of territorial behavior of any antelope. In Ngorongoro immature males and the 50 percent of the adult males without territories belong to bachelor herds comprising anywhere from half a dozen to more than five hundred individuals. The territory holders are intolerant of the bachelors, who consequently are forced to keep to what are thought to be the least favored parts of the range. Although a bachelor can sometimes mingle with female herds, he cannot participate in breeding until he holds a territory himself. The members of the bachelor herds are surprisingly placid; there does not seem to be a rank order or the same kind of sparring for position as there is in the impala. Estes suspects that the lack of aggression is linked with hormone levels, which may not rise until the male is actually in possession of a territory. As he says, "The gnu bachelor herd is thus a comparatively 'stodgy club.' It is as if bachelor wildebeests are marking time until they can become territorial. The essential sexual and aggressive forces appear to lie dormant pending the proper time and place for their expression."

The territorial male, on the other hand, is noted for his aggressiveness. A wildebeest bull's demeanor changes completely once he is in possession of a territory; the meek, gregarious bachelor turns into a solitary defender of his piece of property. The territorial bull is sometimes so antisocial that he will chase off females as well as males, and there is a limit to the number of females he will allow on his territory: if too large a group comes in, he will simply try to clear the area around him.

The male wildebeest is often seen racing around in circles, kicking up his heels, bucking and spinning in the most ridiculous postures. It might seem that he is just feeling frisky, like a young colt let out to pasture, but there is a method to his apparent madness. The bull is performing a display that both threatens any potential competitors and advertises the fact that he is in possession of that piece of ground.

Maintaining a territory takes up a considerable amount of a bull's time, although his territory may not be particularly large. The territories in the crater form a kind of mosaic. During the rut, when there are around two hundred territorial males per square mile in the best habitat, males are spaced out about 120 to 145 yards apart. At times of intense mating activity the males may be as little as 30 yards apart. In less active months the spacing may be 130 to 160 yards. It is difficult to determine the actual borders of a territory, if any exist. In what appears to be the center of the territory there is a bare patch of ground, called the "stamping ground," where the bull spends most of his time. As many as five neighbors may surround him, with a kind of no man's land between them rather than defined borders.

On the stamping ground, which is about the size of a table top, the bull urinates, defecates, paws, kneels, horns, marks, and rolls. Gnus have preorbital and interdigital glands, and they mark with both, by rubbing their faces on the ground and pawing at the earth. They often roll in their urine, dung, and marking secretion; afterward, they must give off quite an individual odor. As the wildebeest performs most of these motions vigorously and ostentatiously, it would appear that the performance also acts as visual advertisement.

But the simple presence of the wildebeest in his territory is probably as important as any other activity he may carry out. The territorial bull can easily be distinguished by his stance alone. Most gnus carry their heads on a level with their backs, but the territorial male stands and moves with his head held high. He may stand for long periods on his stamping ground, gazing off into the distance. While this vigilance may also serve as an antipredator device, its main purpose seems to be what is called "static-optic marking" — the animal is itself the territory marker. Estes visited the territories of twenty-one different bulls at all seasons and found them there 89 percent of the time. One bull that Estes immobilized and marked was absent from his territory overnight as a result; when the bull returned to his territory the next day, he found it occupied and had to fight hard to get it back. Thus, except for trips to water, it is advantageous for the bull to stay on his territory, even at a time of the year when there is little breeding activity. He cannot afford to lose his territory even then, because he would always be at a psychological disadvantage when trying to regain it later.

Besides advertising his presence in various ways, the gnu bull will actively defend his piece of ground. If other gnus come into his territory, he will go out to meet them with head held high, advancing at a characteristic rocking canter, swishing his tail. This posture and gait are unmistakable and will be seen only in a territorial bull. If the animals entering the territory are females, he will approach them in the canter, then usually stick his chin out and put his ears down in a sexual display. If the intruder is a male, he will react according to whether the male is a bachelor or a neighbor. Bachelors are actively chased out; neighbors are dealt with in a complex ceremony called the "challenge ritual."

The relationship between neighboring territory holders is one of the most fascinating aspects of wildebeest behavior. There are rarely any serious fights; rather, the neighbors seem to respect each other and to regard each other as "dear enemies" (a term devised by J. Fisher to describe the relationship among birds in a breeding ground, where they seem to need the stimulation of close neighbors). Even bulls spaced out half a mile apart will come together to perform the challenge ritual. In this way they can check each other out and in effect maintain the status quo. Estes found that a minimum of forty-five minutes a day was spent on challenges. The ritual lasts about seven minutes on average but may take anywhere from half a minute to half an hour. A bull meets and challenges each of his neighbors at least once a day. As he may have as many as five neighbors, one can see that he might be kept fairly busy.

It is difficult to describe a "typical" challenge ritual, because the encounter is very complex and never seems to be carried out in the same sequence. There are at least thirty different possible actions, which may be performed in almost any order. Sometimes steps may be left out altogether.

One of the interesting aspects of the challenge ritual is that it may take place anywhere on the territory, not necessarily or even usually on the border. Generally the ritual begins when one bull enters the territory of another and approaches, slowly grazing. The territory holder will usually stand sideways in front of the invader, in what is termed "lateral presentation." The two gnus may then move into a reverse parallel position and rub their heads on each other's rumps. This seems to be a kind of aggressive grooming; they may also be marking each other with their preorbital glands. Then the two bulls may perform an action that is rare among antelopes but also occurs in eland: one bull urinates, and the other samples it and performs Flehmen exactly as it would when testing a female. Estes thinks that the bulls are testing each other's hormone levels and thus their territorial status. Following this testing, the bulls usually circle one another, pretending to graze. Then suddenly one may feint an attack; both will drop to their knees in the typical combat position of the gnu, but in the challenge ritual they may not even touch heads. Instead, they often violently horn the earth or pluck grass in what looks like redirected aggression. Next they may both jump up and appear alarmed, looking off intently and snorting, but this is just another display — they need not actually see anything. At the same point in the ritual they may also cavort — "bucking, spinning, running sideways, shaking their heads and kicking up their heels." Even more amusing, one or both animals may sometimes appear to "forget" what he is doing and lie down and start ruminating right in the middle of the challenge ritual. Any and all of the steps may be repeated, but eventually the invader slowly moves off again in the "grazing attitude," which probably helps to avoid antagonizing the territory holder.

Although territories are often maintained throughout the year in Ngorongoro, territorial behavior increases tremendously in intensity during the rut. Then herding, courting, challenging, etc., go on at fever pitch. Bulls get so excited that they foam at the mouth, and both territory holders and bachelors sometimes make sudden pelvic thrusts and ejaculate. During the rut each territorial bull tries to round up and hold as many females as possible. The result of all this herding, chasing, and fighting is to fragment the large herds into small units, each defended by one bull, who will usually find no more than one female in estrus in a group. The actual courtship of the female is then very elementary, certainly as compared to that of the Uganda kob. The male follows and herds the female with his head held out, uttering a deep, croaking grunt. He keeps following until she finally stands for him, and then he mounts and copulates, all within a few seconds. If she will not stand, he may come around in front of her and, as described by Estes, "rear up before her with a full erection in a dramatic copulatory display." If the female will stand, she may be mounted several times in a few minutes by the same bull. If she moves on through the matrix of territories, she may mate with several bulls in a short space of time. Only territorial bulls have a chance to get a female alone and mate with her; so again we see that territory is a prerequisite for breeding.

The gnus of the Serengeti roam over a huge area and may be just about anywhere during the rut in May. Obviously it would be pointless for males to set up territories in a particular place and maintain them during the year. They too have to move around in search of good grazing, and in any case if they tried to stay put, they would probably be off the migratory route more years than not. Thus the majority of the males in the Serengeti move with the aggregations, which are still largely segregated by sex. What the dominant males do is set up temporary territories as they go along. During the rut the wildebeests are usually moving off the plains in huge aggregations, and the whole system seems to be in utter chaos.

The males move with the herds until they stop to feed; then the fully mature males immediately begin to stake out territories, advertising, displaying, and challenging other males just as the bulls in Ngorongoro do. These males also try to cut out a small group of females and keep them in their territory. There has been some controversy over the exact nature of these temporary territories. The Talbots thought that the males were defending not a piece of ground, but the small group of females they would herd as they moved along. The Talbots called this a "mobile territory." Subsequent research indicates that the bulls really are defending a piece of ground, because if the females move on, the bulls do not follow but stay on their territory. Sometimes they will even stay there for several days after the whole aggregation has left, but usually they will catch up with the herds and set up territories once more. Because of the nearly constant movement of the population and the necessity to start all over again each time the herds more or less come to a stop, the activity is frenetic. Everything seems to be happening at once: males are fighting and challenging other males, circling and herding the females, calling and courting and copulating. Wildebeests are particularly vocal for antelopes, and at this time the noise is almost overwhelming — the grunts are comparable to a chorus of thousands of frogs.

The antelope species we have looked at up to now have not been greatly restricted to breeding at a particular time of year (although some show breeding peaks). The wildebeests are far more obviously affected by the seasons. First, the rut occurs in a period of excellent conditions: it is after the rains, when all animals are in good shape. In good years more than 90 percent of the cows conceive. The gestation period is approximately eight months, which means that the calves are usually born in January or February. This is in another relatively good period, as it is during the rainy season on the plains. When the calves begin to eat solid food, they are able to find tender, growing shoots of grass. Thus, the basic calving peak is clearly affected by the seasons, but what is unusual is the intensity of the peak: a full 80 percent of all the calves are born during a three-week period! The remaining 20 percent are born mostly in the five-month period following the peak. This synchronization of births could be partly a result of the wildebeest's social system and the definite seasonal effects, but it is thought to be mainly an antipredator device for the calves, which do not lie out, possibly because they are usually born on the short grass plains where there are few places for a calf to hide. Thousands of baby wildebeests simply swamp the predators so that some calves have to survive. There is usually a 100-percent mortality for those born before the peak, when a single newborn calf is highly conspicuous. Those born after the peak have a slightly better chance of surviving, as there are already calves around. Those born in the peak have the best chances of avoiding predation.

The wildebeest female about to give birth does not, like many of the other antelopes, seek seclusion but gives birth in the midst of the herd. In Ngorongoro there seemed to be regular calving grounds where a dozen or more females would give birth in the course of the day, usually in the morning. Wildebeest births have been witnessed many times. Labor averages one and a quarter hours from the time the fetal sac first appears, but the female can forestall birth at will if disturbed. However, once the head emerges, the birth cannot be stopped. Usually the cow lies on her side for the birth; immediately afterward, she jumps up and turns to lick the newborn calf and remove the fetal sac. The calves become mobile remarkably soon. Generally within seven minutes and sometimes in as little as three minutes, the calf gets onto its wobbly legs and starts to look for the mother's teats. If the mother moves, the calf can follow and even run. The mothers of newborn calves group together and form nurseries, but the calves stay by their mothers' sides rather than forming a crèche as impala fawns do.

Although the nursery herd provides protection for the calves, there are also some disadvantages. A newborn calf will follow anything that moves and does not seem to "imprint" on its mother until it has suckled. In the large aggregations calves are often disturbed before they have imprinted, and if they become separated from their mothers, they may be lost forever. These lost calves are a pitiful sight; they walk around bleating and will follow anything, as many tourists and scientists discover when they find a newborn calf following their vehicle. An even worse sight is a tiny calf running hopefully toward a lion or hyena. The losing of calves, which are then taken by various carnivores, and predation by hyenas are the major causes of calf mortality. In Ngorongoro the hyenas take a huge toll of the calves, which stand out even within the herd because of their shaky gait. If they can survive the first few days, they are then able to run nearly as fast as the adults, and after two to two and a half months their light brown coats turn to charcoal gray and they are far less conspicuous.

The calves that survive stay with their mothers until the following year, when their mothers give birth again. Females may remain in some kind of association with their mothers, but this relationship has not yet been investigated in detail. There may prove to be small groups of related individuals within the female herds, especially in more sedentary populations. The young females come into estrus when they are sixteen months old, but not all of them get pregnant that first year. By the next rut, when they are two years and four months old, nearly all get pregnant, if conditions are normal. In periods of drought there may or may not be a rut; when there is a rut, the females often do not get pregnant or may conceive and then soon abort. Under good conditions the female will give birth each year for the rest of her life.

By the time the males are sixteen months old, they have usually

been cut out of the female herds and chased away by the territorial bulls. The youngsters then join bachelor herds and bide their
time until they are ready and able to take up the territorial existence. As Estes has shown, a young bull's chances of success in
attaining a territory depend a great deal on his persistence and on
the area in which he is living. In the general chaos of the rut in
the Serengeti, when the herds are on the move, a young male may
be able to gain a territory for a short while and succeed in mating
with some females. But becoming a resident territory holder is
another matter. In Ngorongoro a male can set up a territory
where there are no other males, but it would more than likely be
in an unfavorable area rarely visited by females. What the young
bull must do is go to an area in the territorial matrix and try to
squeeze himself in among the established territory holders.
Naturally, the other males challenge and chase the intruder. At
first he runs away, but every day he returns to the same spot over
and over again until he finally ceases to be quite such a disturbing
stimulus to the other males. Soon he begins herding females and
chasing bachelors, and gradually he gains enough confidence to
enter into a true challenge ritual with one of his neighbors. If he
can hold his own, to the extent of engaging in some fairly serious
fights, eventually the males accept him as a neighbor. The extent
to which newcomers move in among the existing territory holders
determines how the density and spacing change during the year.
Understandably, the density is highest and the spacing closest
during the rut.

We can see then that the wildebeest is quite a flexible animal.
It can adapt its social system to the residential situation in
Ngorongoro or to the nomadic situation in the Serengeti. Wildebeests living in other areas may fall anywhere in between these
two systems, incorporating parts of the sedentary system and
parts of the nomadic system. Above all, though, we can see how
ideally suited the wildebeest is to its plains existence. Given the
right situation, wildebeests can reach spectacular numbers, and at
this moment the Serengeti is the place to see them at their most
successful. After a decade of favorable conditions the Serengeti

ecosystem now carries more than a million wildebeests. As long as the Serengeti and the surrounding areas are protected, we will still be able to see the sight of thousands upon thousands of wildebeests forever on the move.

No other antelope is quite like the wildebeest, but there are other large plains antelopes that are grazers and have similar social systems and thus fall into Peter Jarman's Class D. They are the various hartebeests, the topi, and the tsessebe.

CLASS E

The Eland

The eland is something of an anomaly in the categorization of antelopes according to feeding style, group size, antipredator behavior, and social organization. It does not seem to fit anywhere. Certainly, it is the biggest antelope by far, measuring up to 6 feet at the shoulder and weighing up to 2000 pounds. It is sometimes found in large herds, sometimes in small groups, sometimes on its own. It is mainly a browser but occasionally feeds on grasses and, like a grazer, moves vast distances in response to rainfall and vegetation conditions.

Eland are big, sturdy animals, almost cowlike in appearance; both males and females carry lovely spiral horns, and to the untrained eye the sexes are difficult to distinguish. Man has always taken a great interest in the eland, as the many rock paintings of eland hunts attest. The eland possesses delicious, tender meat that is claimed to be as good as beef, and it is mainly this quality that has attracted man. It also has a reputation for being a gentle, docile animal. On one of Theodore Roosevelt's trips to East Africa he and some other men herded eland on horseback and claimed that they could be easily domesticated. Roosevelt heartily recommended that they be introduced in the United States to mix with or even take the place of cattle. Even the Maasai, who normally will not eat wild animals, sometimes hunt the eland, and if they find a young calf, they will raise it and run it with their own cattle. Eland milk is rich and has an excellent taste.

The idea of domesticating eland has been around for a long time. Lord Derby imported eland into England in 1842 and kept them in a "deer park." Later there were some unsuccessful attempts to crossbreed eland with cattle. In the 1890s the Russians imported several bulls and cows into the Ukraine, and bred them for their milk; the herd has grown and flourished ever since, despite the cold winters. In Africa itself there have been many experiments in cropping, ranching, and domesticating eland, with varying results. The South Africans and Rhodesians have taken a particular interest in the feasibility of ranching game animals and have had moderate success. Because of the eland's size, its excellent meat and milk, its ability to survive in semiarid environments, and its docility, it has been a main contender in domestication trials. In East Africa it has been hoped that the eland might be mixed with cattle in marginal areas in order to raise the productivity of protein-poor lands.

However, until recently, little work had been carried out on the wild, free-ranging eland. In 1971, J. C. Hillman began a three-year study of the eland in Nairobi National Park and the adjoining Athi-Kapiti plains. Hillman is only just completing his study, which will lead to a Ph.D. from the University of Nairobi, and has not yet analyzed his results, but he has very generously allowed me to use the material that he has available at present. Once his data are analyzed, much more information is expected to emerge. In the meantime, we have a better idea of the ecology and behavior of the eland, and some of Hillman's results reveal why the eland may not be suitable for domestication, as so many people have hoped.

Hillman's study area is huge, covering over 800 square miles. In this area there are approximately 1500 eland. That in itself is a revealing figure, because it suggests that eland live at very low densities, and counts in other areas reveal similar densities. Aside from being one point against the eland as a ranching animal, this also means that they are difficult to find and therefore very difficult to study. On top of that, they are extremely shy and have one of the longest flight distances of any antelope: most eland will run away when they see a vehicle at a distance of 400 yards. With patience and an excellent punch-card system for individual recognition, Hillman was able to overcome some of the problems. His system involved recording the various individual characteristics of each eland that he came across, such as stripes and dots on the coat, horn configurations, ear and tail peculiarities, body color, and for the males head color, state of the dewlap, neck size, and amount of mane. He recorded 160 different eland, and with the punch-card system, once the eland were on file, he could come across an eland, pick out the cards with the appropriate characteristics, and with a minimum of searching identify that eland. With animals that are difficult to tell apart, this system works better than a simple recognition file of photographs.

With his system Hillman was able to resight 60 to 70 percent of the recorded individuals at least once and saw sixty of his animals over ten times. One male, "Mr. MacGregor," was recently sighted for the sixtieth time. This may not sound impressive when compared to the resightings of known lions or elephants but is quite an achievement if one takes into account the difficulty in distinguishing one eland from another and the vast area over which they range.

Unlike the impala, whose social organization became clear once individuals were known, the eland remained perplexing for a long time, and certain facets of its social life are still puzzling. Hillman found four different kinds of eland groups, none of which seemed to be particularly stable. The size and membership of the groups can fluctuate from day to day. Basically these groups are: male, female, nursery, and juvenile. The male groups are the smallest, ranging from 1 to 13 individuals and averaging 3 or 4. Female groups range from 2 to 48 and average about 12; sometimes there are adult males associated with the female groups. Nursery groups consist of females with young calves, older calves, and subadults; there can also be adult males attached. The nursery groups are the largest found, ranging from 2 to 427 animals and averaging around 48. The juvenile groups, which form when the nursery herds break down, are small and short-lived; they consist entirely of young animals. Usually a juvenile group will soon attach itself to a female group or will later join a new nursery herd.

To understand these groupings, one must follow the eland through the seasons and through its reproductive cycle. One of the unusual things about the eland is that the females and males use their habitat in quite different ways, at least in Hillman's study area. The males behave much more like the eland's relatives, the bushbuck, bongo, and kudu. They tend to be sedentary, sticking to one area that provides food and water year round. As the eland males become older, they become more solitary and more sedentary until it becomes almost predictable where a given older male can be found. However, this behavior differs quite a bit from the system of most other antelopes, because there is no sign that the eland male is in any way territorial. He does not seem to mark or defend an area against other males. In fact he often shares it with several others.

The females, on the other hand, behave much more like plains animals, in some ways even like the wildebeest. They move over a very large area, at least 600 square miles, in response to seasonal changes in vegetation. Both males and females are basically browsers, and the eland is perhaps the most opportunistic antelope of all. Unlike the impala, who uses only three or four vegetation types in a limited home range, the eland may use a dozen or more. In Hillman's study area the altitude ranges from 4900 to 8000 feet, and the eland move through the various levels according to the seasons. Though they follow a general pattern, they are highly unpredictable animals; they can move long distances in one day, and it was not altogether unusual for Hillman to "lose" all his eland completely for a day or two. During the wet season in Hillman's study area, the majority of the eland population is generally found out on the plains, often feeding in large aggregations.

The plains are in the lowest part of the altitude range; to the west and northwest the land rises, first up the Rift Valley escarpment, then gradually on up to the Ngong Hills and Nairobi National Park. Except for some forest and bush found in the hills and in the Park, most of the area is made up of open plains interspersed with deep river gorges. As one moves up the altitude gradient, there is a corresponding rainfall gradient, with the higher land getting more rainfall. When the plains dry up, the eland begin to move up the altitude gradient. First they move into the river gorges, where there is permanent browse; then they finally move into the Park, up into the Ngong Hills, up on top of the escarpment to the west, or toward Amboseli in the southeast. In short, the eland using the study area disperse in the dry season, generally moving up in altitude, and aggregate on the plains again in the wet season.

The eland of the Athi-Kapiti and Nairobi area give birth to their calves over a period of approximately five months beginning in August, with peak calving around the short rains in November. At that time the cows are usually out on the plains. It is thought that the female about to give birth leaves the other females in the group she has been associating with (except during births, females are very rarely found completely on their own) and goes to a secluded spot. So far births have not been witnessed in the wild. There are indications that the female and calf stay on their own for several days, with the calf lying out while the mother feeds nearby. As with the impala, the amount of time spent lying out seems to depend on whether or not there are other young calves around. Usually the females with calves soon find each other and join up to form a nursery group. When there is a nursery group already in the vicinity, the mother and calf spend as little as twenty-four hours on their own before joining it. As soon as the calves get together, they form bonds with each other that are actually stronger than the mother-calf bonds. Calves form a unit within the nursery group and stand closer to each other than to their mothers. They often engage in mutual grooming, licking each other's coats. The eland is a singularly nontactile animal; so this type of touching is exceptional and is common only among the young. These calf-calf bonds are reminiscent of those formed between young giraffes.

The eland calf depends on its mother only for a fairly short period. Eland calves are weaned at about three months and begin to eat food much sooner. Gradually the bond with the mother becomes weaker; eventually she moves away from the nursery group altogether and joins with other adult females that are no longer attached to calves or have not yet had any. Toward the end of the breeding season and during the rains, when the animals are concentrated on the grasslands, the nursery groups can get very large. It seems that calves are very attracted to each other; when two nursery herds come into sight of one another, the calves immediately join up and the mothers just have to go along. With these amalgamations a nursery group may comprise more than four hundred individuals. Older calves stay on in the group after their mothers leave; juveniles and subadults up to two years old may also be attached to the group. There are almost always some adult females in the group, since the breeding is stretched over several months.

As the plains begin to dry up in January and February, however, the large groups begin to break up; the eland move into the river gorges and feed on more dispersed food items. Occasionally some juvenile groups form, with no females attached. They follow the same general movement as the females and will usually join the female groups after a short time. When the youngsters are about two years old, they leave the nursery groups: the females usually join other adult females; the males join groups composed mostly of males aged two years and older. Females may come into estrus as early as eighteen months old and, with an eight- to nine-month gestation period, have their first calves when they are about two and a quarter years old, but they usually do not get pregnant until they are about two years old. Captive male eland are known to reach sexual maturity at two years old, but whether they actually have access to females in the wild at this age is unknown; it seems unlikely, however, because fully adult males are nearly always present when there is a female in estrus.

With the other antelopes that have been discussed, we have seen how their social organization is related to their size, feeding style, and antipredator behavior. With the eland this connection is not quite so easy to perceive, but some of the eland's behavior does make sense when related to its ecology. What remains puzzling is why the males and females behave differently. The clue may lie in predation and reproductive demands. The eland is a very large antelope, and as we have seen, the larger the antelope, the more likely it is to form herds as a protective measure, since it is too large to use any kind of hiding technique. The nursery groups certainly act as an antipredator device. Within the group the calf is at once less conspicuous and protected by the many adult females, for eland females are formidable adversaries for most predators. Not only will they fight for their own calves but they will act in cooperation with each other to fight and chase off packs of hyenas and wild dogs; Hillman once saw a large group of cows attack a lioness — one predator few animals will stand up to.

Females still form groups when they do not have calves, and again this may be partly for the antipredator benefits. In these groups of adults there do not seem to be any stable associations. The bonds that are formed between youngsters apparently are not carried into adulthood. Here again, the eland behaves very much like the giraffe. Groups are very loose, with individuals coming and going from day to day. Hillman has found that the chance of a known female being seen with any other known female a second time is about one in a hundred. A male, on the other hand, is far more likely to be seen repeatedly with another male, probably because males are more sedentary than females.

Adult males form small groups that tend to stay in the bushier areas of the range — in and around the river gorges for instance — and do not move over nearly so large an area as female groups do. Here the males can find resources for themselves year round, and for an animal that may weigh close to a ton (males are quite a bit larger than females), the risk of predation is not great. Only several lions together can kill an adult eland bull, and large prides of lions are rare in these bushy areas. Hillman feels that the demands of reproduction and the protection of the calves necessitate that the females move in groups the way they do, seeking out a particular diet over a large area, and that these various factors influence the size and duration of the groups. The males too are concerned with reproduction, for a successful male is one who passes on his genes, but they require a different reproductive strategy.

In all of the antelope species we have dealt with so far, the prerequisite for mating was ownership of a territory where a single male had undisputed rights over any females that came on to his piece of ground or lived there with him. Since territory is so important to most male antelopes, one might well wonder how the eland gets along without it. Like elephants and giraffes, eland males bypass the territorial system by having a well-defined rank order. From the time the males enter the nursery groups as young calves, they frequently spar with each other, pushing and wrestling with their horns. In this way each male knows the relative strength of every other male and learns whom he can dominate and to whom he must be subordinate. (An odd turnabout in these sparring interactions is the tendency, after the horn tangling is finished, for the subdominant animal to mount the dominant one.) To a certain extent the hierarchy is based on age, but among the fully adult males, individual differences and condition come into play. It is important that the male keep in optimal shape so that when the time comes to mate, his weight and strength will put him at an advantage. Hillman speculates that this is probably one of the main reasons that males are more sedentary and stick to areas of high-quality browse. Fights over females in estrus are rare, as there is usually one male that is dominant over the others, and they will "politely" give way to him. The fights that do occur may arise when two males are close to each other in rank. In all Hillman has seen only three serious fights; generally there is little overt aggression among the adult males.

The male eland's status and dominance are accentuated in a number of unique ways. Perhaps of all the antelopes the male eland changes most dramatically as he gets older. Bulls continue to put on weight and muscle well past the age of five and most probably do not reach full stature until they are at least seven years old. As they get older, their coat color changes, from light rufous to tan, to gray, and finally to near black in very old age. The neck gets heavier; the mane and much of the hair on the neck gradually disappear; the dewlap hangs lower and looser and eventually loses its tuft of hair altogether. But most conspicuous of all is the change in the brush of hair that grows between the bull's eyes, from the forehead almost down to the nose. As the male gets older, the frontal brush gets longer, stands out farther from the face, and gets darker. The color also changes from rufous to black and back to rufous at different times of the year, but the significance of this change of color, which does not seem to be correlated with season, remains something of a mystery.

When the male is seen in profile with the frontal brush at its longest, darkest, and fullest, he is very impressive; the brush undoubtably has some visual signaling effect. The eland can also look rather ridiculous at times because one of his goals seems to be to get the brush as matted and mucky as possible. He does this by rubbing his forehead in mud mixed with urine, either his own or that of other male and female eland or other animals. The smell is reportedly very strong but would not seem to be particularly individual. The point may be just to have the smelliest frontal brush. Males also often sweep their horns aggressively through grass and bushes, which sometimes results in a great pile of vegetation on top of their heads. In the end they may look very comical to us, but for the eland this is probably another important display of dominance.

One of the most mysterious things about eland bulls is their "clicking" walk. Usually only adult males make the sound, and the older and larger they are, the louder it appears to be. There has been much speculation as to how the eland makes the noise and what purpose it serves; scientists are still not sure how it happens. Some say it is in the hooves or knees, but recent studies indicate that it may originate in the tendons of the front legs. As

the male moves along, a distinct click can be heard with each beat
of the front legs. This noise is much louder and clearer than the
clacking of the hooves, an irregular sound that many cloven-
hooved animals make. The eland click can be heard up to 1½
miles away in clear, still conditions.

It has also been suggested that the noise perhaps acts as a contact signal; it may help the animals find each other or follow each
other on a dark night. Hillman, however, thinks that the clicking
is connected with dominance and the eland's system of nonterri-
toriality, in which bulls frequently meet each other. The eland
bull does not usually begin to make the clicking sound until he is
well over five years old and a formidable animal, weighing more
than 1500 pounds, with a thick, strong neck, powerful shoulders,
and strong horns. The clicking may very well act as a signal,
telling other eland that there is a large dominant male around.
Depending on their sex and age, other eland may respond accordingly. Indeed, Hillman saw this system at work. One night,
while watching a young eland bull intently following a female in
estrus, he heard the clicking of a bull. At once the young male
moved off, leaving the female and walking in the opposite direction from the approaching male.

Eland matings have rarely been seen in the wild. In the precopulatory behavior witnessed, the male follows the female
closely, his head thrust forward, licking the air with his tongue —
a behavior that has been termed "empty licking." The male
frequently tests the female's urine, performing Flehmen. For one
pair of captive eland, the mating period lasted only one day, but
the male and female copulated dozens of times, until they both
looked exhausted. This does not appear to occur at such intensity
in the wild.

Eland reproduce readily under captive conditions. Females in
captivity may start giving birth as young as eighteen months and
will have a calf every year thereafter. Eland are thought to be
long-lived antelopes, with a life span of twenty to twenty-five
years; so in terms of reproduction they would appear to be an excellent animal to ranch.

However, Hillman's work on daily activity patterns provides a further clue as to why the eland may not be the best animal to domesticate. In his study area, where temperatures do not get very high, the eland feed on and off all day, usually spending two hours feeding and then two hours ruminating. They continue feeding at night until about 2:00 A.M.; then they usually take a rest until 6:00. In Tsavo National Park, which is a hot, arid area like the type of country proposed for game ranching, the eland seek shade in the daytime, using that period for their rest time, and then feed throughout the whole night, when they are not under heat stress and can get some moisture from the dew-laden plants. A group of captive eland has to be herded in the daytime and corralled at night, partly in order to protect them from predators and partly because it has been discovered that they are by no means easy animals to herd: they tend to wander and would be easily lost at night. Thus, in a captive situation the eland are expected to feed during the least desirable part of the day, when they are also unable to take in any extra moisture.

It is not known exactly how dependent the eland is on water under natural conditions. Hillman never saw his eland go out of their way to seek water: they would drink it when they came upon it but could go for weeks or even months without drinking. Eland are certainly not completely water-independent, like the dikdik and gerenuk; their needs probably vary from season to season, and certain animals, such as lactating females, may be more dependent on water than others. In one domestication trial carried out in an arid area, eland were found to need three-quarters as much water as cattle, and experiments carried out on eland by environmental physiologists have shown that they are well adapted to dealing with arid conditions. Eland normally sweat in order to keep their temperatures at a constant level, but under drought conditions with no access to water, they stop sweating in order to conserve water. During the day their body temperature actually rises several degrees as they store the heat in their bodies. Then at night, as the air temperature cools down, the heat is dissipated and their body temperatures return to normal. This way eland do not waste precious water in evaporative cooling. This adaptation is a great attraction for those considering ranching an animal in marginal areas.

All things considered, the eland is still a wild animal that has adapted to a particular way of life characterized by low density and a very large range. Most important, the eland moves about, seeking out a diet in a complex way and responding to subtle vegetation changes we do not yet fully understand. Unless a captive herd of eland can be herded in the same opportunistic way, they will not do well, and indeed may even compare unfavorably with cattle. It may be possible to use eland in a mixed ranching scheme in which a huge tract of land is taken over, the wild animals are left to roam about at will, and after careful study a certain number are cropped each year. But true domestication is another matter. The eland is an animal that lives in suberb harmony with its environment, *when* it is left to its own devices.

Peter Jarman had the greatest difficulty choosing the antelopes for his Class E. Not surprisingly, the further from the original size and the further from the forest habitat the antelope gets, the fewer animals there are. There are over twenty species of antelopes in Class A. In Class E, aside from the eland, Jarman includes: the Cape buffalo, which moves in large herds consisting of males, females, and young and is not territorial; and — tentatively — the oryx and the gemsbok, large antelopes that also live in mixed herds but have not as yet been studied in detail in the wild.

VI

Baboons

He is a born bully, a born criminal, a born candidate for the hangman's noose. As compared to the gorilla . . . the baboon represents nature's most lasting challenge to the police state. He is as submissive as a bulldozer, as gentle as a power-driven lawnmower. He has the yellow-to-amber eyes that one associates with a riverboat gambler. He has predatory inclinations, and in certain seasons he enjoys nothing better than killing and devouring the newborn fawns of the delicate gazelle. And he will steal anything.

— Robert Ardrey, *The Territorial Imperative*

By NOW MANY THOUSANDS of people have read about the aggressiveness of the brutal, domineering baboon, about the strict discipline and order maintained in the troop by a powerful elite or clique of adult males. Just about every popularizer of animal behavior studies — from Robert Ardrey and Desmond Morris to Lionel Tiger and Robin Fox — has theorized about man in relation to the baboon's way of life. According to these authors, it is the very magnetism of the ruling baboons that keeps the troop together; these males are constantly concerned with their position in the troop because status is everything for a baboon.

However, Ardrey and the others are going to have to do some rethinking. They have been basing their theories on a study that was conducted nearly fifteen years ago. The latest research on baboons reveals a quite different picture. A baboon troop is not held together by fear and attraction to despots, but by a complex matrix of family relationships and social bonds. The baboon social system described by the new research may not support the popular author's theories of male status and dominance, but it seems to be a logical, successful, and far less rigid way of life.

Before discussing baboon behavior it might be helpful to describe the various baboons and give a brief history of the major field studies that have been carried out. Of course, there is no general agreement on taxonomy. As usual there is the problem of what is a baboon and what is not, and then the question of which are species and which are races. The baboons belong to the genus *Papio*, of which there are five or seven species, depending on whether one includes the drill and mandrill of the West African forests.[1] The five others, the more typical baboons, are:

P. hamadryas — the sacred baboon of ancient Egypt, now most commonly seen in Ethiopia, but also found in the Sudan, Somalia, and across the Red Sea in southwest Arabia

P. papio — the guinea, or western baboon of West Africa

P. anubis — the olive baboon of western Kenya, Uganda, Ethiopia, and Tanzania

P. cynocephalus — the yellow baboon of eastern Kenya and Tanzania

P. ursinus — the chacma baboon of southern Africa.

Apart from the hamadryas baboon, which lives in harsh, semiarid areas and has a decidedly different social structure from that of the others,[2] the remaining four baboons are thought by some scientists to be merely races of one species of savannah baboon. There does seem to be some justification for this theory, for where there is overlap there are intergrades, and the social organization and behavior of the four are very similar.

The two baboons of East Africa — the olive and the yellow — are quite distinct in appearance where they do not converge. The olive is heavier and more squat-looking; the males have a thick

---

[1] The gelada "baboon" of Ethiopia has its own genus, *Theropithecus*, and is not considered a proper baboon, although some taxonomists would like to include it in the *Papio* genus.

[2] The hamadryas baboon has been thoroughly studied by Hans Kummer, but for reasons of space and for clarity, I have chosen to concentrate on the other baboons, particularly those studied in East Africa.

mantle or mane of hair on their heads, upper backs, and shoulders; the coat color is a grayish olive. The yellow baboon has longer legs and a slimmer body; the males have a much less conspicuous mantle; they are yellowish buff in color and have almost white underparts; the head has a more doglike appearance — hence its name: *cynocephalus*, or dog-headed. The West African guinea baboon is smaller, has a heavy mane, and is rufous-colored. The southern African chacma baboon is as large as the olive, but much more slender, has little mane, and is very dark olive in color.

The chacma baboon was actually the first of the baboons to be studied in the field in Africa. In 1953 N. Bolwig studied the behavior of wild baboons around the refuse pits in Kruger National Park in South Africa and supplemented these observations with some on captive chacma baboons. (It should be mentioned that this was only the first *systematic* study; we cannot dismiss *My Friends, the Baboons*, Eugene Marais's fascinating account of living with baboons in the early part of this century in South Africa.)

In 1958, K. R. L. Hall, a highly respected psychologist, began studying the chacma baboons of the Cape Peninsula of South Africa. This was really the first long-term study of baboons; however, Hall was able to observe his subjects for only one day a week during most of his one-year study.

The first intensive study of baboons was carried out by anthropologists Sherwood Washburn and Irven DeVore. They worked for ten months in 1959–60, concentrating on the olive baboons of Nairobi National Park, with additional observations of the yellow baboons of Amboseli Game Reserve.

Since these early studies, a number of other researchers have worked on baboons: in fact, of all the East African mammals, the baboon has probably been the most thoroughly studied, and yet we are only beginning to understand its way of life. The most notable of the subsequent East African studies are Stuart and Jeanne Altmann's in Amboseli, starting in 1963, and Thelma Rowell's in Uganda from 1963 to 1965. S. Altmann and Rowell are zoologists and brought the zoologist's approach and techniques to the study of baboons. They are mainly interested in how the baboon functions and behaves in relation to its environment, and once studies such as theirs were begun, it could no longer be said that primate researchers were interested in monkeys only as substitute humans.

The pioneering studies by Hall, DeVore and Washburn, the Altmanns, and Rowell are now being supplemented by several continuous long-term studies, the results of which are only just beginning to appear. At Jane Goodall's research station in Gombe National Park in Tanzania, the same baboon troop has been studied continuously since 1967 by a series of researchers — Timothy Ransom, Leanne Taylor Nash, and Nick Owens — with various students keeping up the observations in between. In Amboseli Stuart Altmann and his students have been keeping the baboons in their study area under observation for most of each year since 1971, with the main study being carried out by Glenn Hausfater. And finally, on a ranch in Gilgil in Kenya, four consecutive researchers — Robert Harding, William Malmi, Shirley Strum, and Neil Chalmers — have kept one troop under continuous observation since 1969, and a fifth observer, Lynda Muckenfuss, watched another baboon troop on the same ranch. These long-term studies have proved vital in understanding social organization and behavior.

In looking at all these studies and their results, it immediately becomes clear that baboons generate controversy. DeVore and Washburn's description of baboon social organization has for many years been considered definitive. Their results have been widely published in both scientific and popular form, and it was their description of baboon behavior that particularly appealed to Ardrey and the others. However, the more recent studies have arrived at different conclusions, which are not always in agreement with each other either. Trying to sort out the various descriptions is not an easy task, but it is still possible to present a picture of the savannah baboon's way of life.

What strikes one first about baboons is their ubiquity. They seem to be everywhere; in fact, they are the most successful ground-living primate next to man. They range from the tip of South Africa right up into Ethiopia and Sudan and across the Red Sea into Saudi Arabia, and they span the whole African continent from east to west. They can adapt to conditions as diverse as semiarid bush to tropical forest, and from sea level to the slopes of high mountains. The question asked, of course, is why are they so successful?

It is postulated that at one time baboons were primarily forest dwellers, living, eating, and sleeping in trees as many primates do today, but with climatic changes and the receding of the forests, the baboons opted for life on the savannah rather than remaining in the forest and competing for a diminishing resource. But the savannah, with its open pattern of grassland and bush and widely dispersed trees, presented a very different environment from that of the relatively lush and, at the same time, relatively safe forest. In the trees a primate has to worry only about a few predators — snakes, birds of prey — and has a ready and rich diet, but out on the savannah there are very large and very dangerous predators — lions, leopards, cheetahs, wild dogs, and hyenas — and there is not always a nearby tree to run to for safety. How, then, did the baboon survive its gradual shift away from the forest? The answer lies in the baboon's social organization and adaptability, and is one of the clearest illustrations of how social behavior relates to environment.

To exist in the open savannah, baboons live in troops averaging about fifty animals each and ranging from ten to two hundred. However, it is not numbers alone that make for success; it is the way in which the baboon troop works, the way the members relate with each other and together confront their world.

There are many variations in size and composition of groups, but a "typical" baboon group in East Africa might consist of the following: seven or eight adult males; a larger number of adult females, usually in the ratio of two females for every adult male — thus about fifteen; and about twenty-five subadults, juveniles, and infants.

Whatever its size, the baboon troop is a coordinated and fairly exclusive unit. The members travel, feed, and sleep together. All members know each other well and interact with baboons from other troops only infrequently. Within the troop a baboon is in the constant company of other baboons, and if for any reason it were to become permanently separated from its troop, it probably would not survive. A few cases of solitary baboons — usually males — have been recorded, but this is thought to be a rare and brief occurrence.

The females are the most stable element in the troop. With very rare exceptions, they stay in the troop they are born into for their whole lives. Subadult males appear to leave the troop on nearing maturity, and adult males switch troops from time to time. The frequency of adult male immigrations and emigrations seems to vary from area to area.

Within the baboon troop there are a number of complex relationships among the individuals that make for a viable and successful way of life. The "baboon controversy" lies in describing these relationships: some researchers have found relationships that others have not observed; others have awarded more importance to certain types of relationships, insisting that these are the key to success.

Hall and DeVore (in a joint paper on social behavior) concluded that "The baboon group is organized around the dominance hierarchy of adult males." In every baboon troop there is at least one fully adult male who is clearly dominant over the females, subadults, and juveniles. In most troops, especially larger ones, there is usually more than one adult male, and there may be up to a dozen. Any adult male can "displace" any nonadult male member of the troop at a resting place or at food or water sources; if the male approaches in a certain manner, the others will simply get up and move out of his way. (Displacing, or "supplanting," is a common interaction in primate groups.)

Adult males are formidable by any standards, and most observers agree that one of their most important roles is to defend the troop from predators. The males are twice the size of the females: they weigh 70–80 pounds, whereas the females weigh only about 35 pounds. The male's mantle of hair makes him look more impressive, actually giving his front half an almost lionlike appearance. But the crowning glory of every adult male is his awe-inspiring canine teeth, which he does not hesitate to display at the right moments. The canines are long, pointed, and decidedly dangerous. They are his weapons, and that is the message the baboon means to convey when he opens his mouth in a threatening "yawn." Predators are fully aware of these weapons; when several male baboons advance on a predator, it does not usually stick around.

What everyone does not agree on is the other roles that the adult males may or may not play and the males' relative positions in the troop. Because the males are bigger and are dominant, they attract more attention in a group of baboons under observation; thus, many researchers have tended to concentrate on adult male behavior. Certainly DeVore and Washburn were particularly interested in the adult males, and they were among the first to describe a system of dominance among the males.

During their study period in Nairobi, there were twelve troops of olive baboons present, and Washburn and DeVore knew all the members of two of these troops, recognizing individuals by scars and other distinguishing characteristics. What they found was not a simple hierarchical system among the males, with a so-called "alpha male" on top and the others ranked in linear order below him, but a system in which two or more males formed a coalition or "central hierarchy," which, as a unit, dominated all the other males and the other troop members as well. There was also an individual rank order that could be seen in fights whenever two males were isolated. For example, in one troop with six adult males there was a coalition of three males named Dano, Pua, and Kovu; the other males were called Kula, Mdoma, and Mark. Kula was actually the highest-ranking individual, but he did not have the other males' support. When he and Dano, the most dominant male in the central hierarchy, were isolated, Kula could dominate him, but at all other times Pua and Kovu would support Dano, and Kula would have to back down.

DeVore and Washburn felt that once the hierarchy is established among the adult males, it remains stable for long periods of time, and that because of this stable situation there are few fights and the males are able to fulfill their role in the troop. Troop organization revolves around these males: they are the leaders; they direct the movement of the troop, protect members from predators, interfere in and stop any fights in the troop, protect infants and juveniles from older animals, and mate with the females.

In the system that DeVore and Washburn describe, the females have an unstable hierarchy that gives rise to frequent quarreling and bickering. Females change status according to their current relationships with the dominant males. Thus a female in estrus or female with a newborn infant might rise in status because she is accorded special treatment by the males. Both females and youngsters are attracted to the males and seek out their company.

The relationships within the troop are reflected in the way the troop moves when it is traveling from one place to another. DeVore and Washburn described a distinct order of progression in the troops they watched. At the front of the troop march the lower-ranking adult males and subadult males, with females and older juveniles following; in the center are the mothers with infants, the younger juveniles, and the big, dominant males; at the rear of the troop there are again the subordinate males. This positioning assures that the mothers with infants and the juveniles are in the most protected places. Not only do they have the strongest and ablest males near them, but any predator would have to get through the various adults to the front and rear before reaching them. If an alarm call is sounded, the males investigate while the other members retreat. If the whole troop must run, then the big males keep to the rear, between the threat and the rest of the troop.

This general picture of baboon social organization has been accepted by the public for several years now, but within the field of primate research there have been murmurings and outright questioning. Subsequent observers have arrived at conclusions that conflict with DeVore and Washburn's. However, it would be hasty and unfair simply to say that they were wrong. They were the first to admit that the baboon was not a closed book. In an article in *Scientific American* in 1961, Washburn and DeVore wrote: "Our data offer little support for the theory that sexuality provided the primary bond of the primate troop. It is in the intensely social nature of the baboon, expressed in a diversity of interindividual relationships, that keeps the troop together. This conclusion calls for further observation and experimental investigation of the different social bonds. It is clear, however, that these bonds are essential to compact group living and that for a baboon life in the troop is the only life that is feasible."

There has been a great deal of new work done on baboons since Washburn and DeVore wrote this, and some of the studies have concentrated on social behavior, particularly the bonds to which they were referring. That the other researchers have come up with new conclusions is not altogether surprising. Subsequent research has been carried out in different areas, on different troops, and some variability is to be expected in different environments. But the main cause for the conflicting descriptions seems to lie in observer methods. Today, far more sophisticated and systematic methods for collecting data on behavior are being used. Researchers have worked out data sheets in which interactions can be recorded systematically and later quantified by computer analysis. In "focal sampling," the observer concentrates on the behavior of one individual for, say, an hour, recording onto special sheets everything that the animal does. After several hundred hours of focal sampling on the various individuals in a troop, one has substantial results with which to work. One can note, for instance, that out of thirty observed hours Male A spent ten hours within 3 feet of Female B and one hour with Female C. It is these quantitative results that are revealing the most telling new information on baboon behavior.

Glenn Hausfater's study in Amboseli is a good example of the kind of results that one can get with systematic sampling techniques. He was particularly interested in dominance relations in baboon troops. He concentrated on one troop and could recognize all its members individually. By carefully defining what he meant by "dominant" ("the dominant individual in a pair of animals is the one that consistently directed attack or threat behaviors towards the subordinate, who in turn consistently responded with behaviors of submission") and then recording the outcome of thousands of interactions between individuals, he came up with a quantitative description of dominance relations.

In the thirty-six-member troop that Hausfater was watching, the females proved to be the stable factor. During twenty-five hundred hours of observation over fifteen months, there were no changes in rank order among the thirteen females. In over thirteen hundred aggressive interactions among the adult females, there was only one reversal of expected outcome between two females, and after that one incident they returned to their respective positions. During the study, six females were observed going through forty-three sexual cycles, including estrus, when they were in "consort" (a temporary pair formation) with males, and at no time during their cycles did they change their dominance relations with any other individuals. Hausfater points out that although the rate of aggression changed (that is, females had more or fewer fights at certain times in their cycle) the outcome of the fights was always the same. Thus, in contrast to the impressions of DeVore and Washburn, Hausfater's findings showed the female hierarchy to be remarkably stable.

The dominance relationships among the adult males proved to be far less consistent. There were eight males in Hausfater's troop, thus twenty-eight possible "pairs" of males. Hausfater examined the dominance relations between the males in each of these pairs. The relationship between two males tended to remain consistent over a long period of time, but then they would have a series of fights that often would reverse their positions. Hausfater found that, far from having a consistent rank order over the fifteen-month period, at least one pair of males underwent a reversal of their dominance relationship on the average of every twenty-one days. For instance, from October 25 to November 9, 1971, Stubby consistently beat Ivan, B. J., and Peter, but then

B. J. defeated both Stubby and Ivan in a series of clashes, and for the next two hundred days, beginning November 16, B. J. consistently won his fights with the three others. During the next two months, Stubby, who had previously been on top, lost his fights with B. J. but continued to win his fights with Ivan and Peter. Then on January 2, 1972, Stubby began consistently to lose his fights with Ivan and Peter; this situation continued until May 2.

The above-mentioned males were the four top-ranking males in the troop, but at no time did Hausfater see anything resembling a coalition of mutually supporting males. Although two males would sometimes fight a single male, such fights made up less than 2 percent of all bouts, and participation in one of these so-called coalitions did not modify or change individual dominance but was based on it. Hausfater states, "One questions DeVore's repeated assertion that in a baboon group the adult male hierarchy is stable over long periods of time, or that male-male relationships are the most important for understanding the baboon social group."

If male dominance is not the basis for understanding troop organization and cohesion, then what is? DeVore and Washburn themselves recommended investigating the social bonds in a troop, and this particularly interested one of the researchers at Gilgil, Shirley Strum. Most of the recent researchers have concentrated on a single aspect of social behavior — mother-infant relations, play behavior, group fission, etc. — but Strum tried to get an overall picture of how relationships within a troop work, and because she has presented this broader description, I think it is worth concentrating on her results.

One element that Strum's work has revealed is not new, but hitherto little emphasis had been placed on it. Studies have concentrated on dominance, and aggressive behavior, when what may be even more important is not who can beat up whom, but who is related to whom and who is "friends" with whom. Strum's results do not simplify baboon behavior at all, however; when such intricate concepts as kinship and friendship are introduced, things get very complex indeed.

The ranch where Strum worked provided unique opportunities

for studying animal behavior, and she took full advantage of them. Her predecessors at Gilgil, Robert Harding and William Malmi, had watched the same troop and got them habituated to a car. When Strum arrived, she decided to try to follow the troop on foot. Although most baboon watchers have worked on foot, on Kekopey Ranch (a large cattle ranch that also supports an abundance of wildlife), Strum was particularly fortunate in being able to move about unrestricted by park regulations and the danger of large predators; her only worry was potential encounters with buffaloes.

When Strum first started getting out of the car, the baboons were afraid of her and would move away, but gradually they got accustomed to her presence; eventually she could move among them without disturbing them. However, while they were getting used to her, Strum had to overcome her fear of them. A big male baboon can be a terrifying animal. When there were disputes and fights, and the big males started running her way, Strum would turn and run. She realized, though, that she could not work properly under these conditions; so the next time she stood her ground and they simply avoided her. After that she could make her observations freely, walking or sitting among the baboons (sometimes as close as a foot away); they ignored her. Aside from the advantages of not having to maneuver a vehicle while keeping the animals in sight, this method, as Strum explains, allowed her "to observe baboons at baboon distance from other baboons."

Strum soon learned to recognize all the individuals in the sixty-six-member troop. She too used systematic sampling methods, and by the time she finished her sixteen-month study she had logged 1250 hours of observations, including more than 700 hours of focal animal sampling. From the material she collected on all kinds of interactions from avoidance and indifference to fighting, grooming, mating, and playing, a picture began to emerge: certain baboons spent more time with certain other baboons. In some cases the reasons for this were clear: the baboons in question were obviously related (for instance, a mother and her infant); or they were in the same age group and spent a great deal of time playing together. Other preferences were not so easily explained. Certain adult females spent considerably more time with each other and groomed each other rather than other adult females. But even more intriguing, an adult male spent more time with certain females rather than others, was groomed by them and groomed them in turn, whether they were in estrus or not.

Although the word "friend" has anthropomorphic connotations, Strum found that it best describes some of the preference relationships that she observed. Among the females, most of the affiliations are probably based on kinship ties — between a mother and adult daughter, sisters, even cousins. For the most part, the actual blood relationships were not known; however, some associations were known not to be based on close blood ties, and these could be called "friendships." Only long-term studies will show how friendships among females are made, but once formed, they appear to endure. During the sixteen months that Strum watched the Gilgil troop, none of the preference relationships among the adult females changed.

As the study progressed, it became clear that the social organization of the baboon troop involved two kinds of systems: that of the males, which is unstable, and that of the females, which is stable and long-lasting. Strum attempted to show how the two systems work and how they are integrated. It is possible to get a picture of baboon social organization by starting with the basic family unit within the troop and building up from there, like circles around circles, the largest circle being the troop itself.

The first circle is the family unit, which is the basic structure of the troop. A family unit consists of a mother and her offspring, which may number as many as three or four, ranging from a small infant to adults. As there are twenty mature females with offspring in the Gilgil troop, there are twenty basic family units and these in turn are related to each other.

The troop identity and cohesion is a result of the matrix of family relationships and friendships among the separate family units. Unlike the males, the females stay in the same troop all their lives;

there are very few records of a single female switching troops. When a troop splits up, some of the males, females, and young leave together to form an independent troop. Thus, during her lifetime a female is surrounded by baboons she is related to or knows well, and her relationships with these animals help to bind the troop together.

An adult female may have one to five female associates (who may or may not be related to her), and these can be ranked according to preference: the female will have a more intense relationship with one (at the most, two) of these associates and will spend more time with her than with the others. Two females who are close associates spend much of their time together—feeding, moving, resting, sitting together, and grooming each other. They support each other in disputes with other troop members and will even support each other's families.

Thus, a circle of kinship/friendship is formed, which may include two or three family units. Each of the females in the circle will probably have less intense friendships and family ties with other females that form other circles, and so the circles all have connecting links. The family and friendship bonds can be seen at work when there is a dispute; then a hierarchy of support is evident — the individual female will show her concern for other troop members in descending order. She will first and foremost support her youngest offspring against her older offspring, her associates, her associates' offspring, and nonassociates. Next, she will support her offspring against associates, associates' offspring, and nonassociates. She will then support her associates against nonassociates, and lastly her associates' families against nonassociates.

Among the twenty adult females in the Gilgil troop there was no easily discernible rank order. Certainly there were low-ranking and high-ranking females. The ones in the middle were not so easy to place, and with the complex system of family ties and friendships with mutual support, it is not always possible (nor may it be important) to tell who is dominant over whom. Strum prefers to call the high-ranking females "influential" rather than dominant; she feels that the dominance system is too simplistic a way of explaining the interactions and variables that go into determining a female's position. For example, the female Peggy could definitely displace any other female in the troop, but not only is Peggy influential, her large family is as well, and the family's influence may contribute to Peggy's rank and could also be a result of it. Peggy has one close female associate, Constance; if Constance or any of her family gets into a dispute, Peggy and her family will support them. (However, a female will not always interfere in disputes, even those involving her own offspring: it seems that the fight has to draw her attention in some way.) Constance is a high-ranking female also, but whether she would have been in her own right and/or whether her ties with Peggy are the important element is difficult to say.

These two families, Peggy's and Constance's, are both large: at the time of the study, Peggy had four offspring still maintaining close contact with her and Constance had three. With two high-ranking females and seven other family members, this circle of kinship/friendship provides certain advantages to its members. Any outsider that gets into a dispute with anyone in Peggy or Constance's families has to contend with all the offspring and is bound to lose the battle if the mothers intercede. Growing up within this circle would appear to have some effect on the youngster's personality. Peggy's oldest daughter, Thea, is already a powerful female in her own right; she can displace any adult female in the troop (other than her mother) even though she is still a subadult. Again, only long-term studies will reveal how a female arrives at her relative position in the troop once she is an adult.

There were seven adult males in the Gilgil troop during most of Strum's study, and their relationships with other troop members, particularly other adult males, proved to be relatively unstable compared to the females. First of all, since the males switch troops from time to time, a male must establish new relationships each time he enters a different troop. Strum was fortunate in that four males transferred into the Gilgil troop during her study and she was able to observe their integration into the troop.

Previously, it was thought that when a new male enters a troop he has to fight his way into the dominance hierarchy of the males in order to become a fully accepted troop member. Strum's data on the four males she observed suggests that integration is achieved in a more subtle way. Initially the new male spends his time on the periphery of the troop, and there he begins to interact with the females rather than the adult males. Once he has established a close relationship with one or two adult females, he gradually leaves the periphery and moves within the confines of the troop. However, his bonds with these females persist, and given the amount of time he spends with these females and the nature of their grooming interactions, it is possible and convenient to call their special relationship a friendship.

The way in which males "make friends" with females is one of the more fascinating aspects of baboon behavior. The initiator may be either the male or the female, and the approach may be in a sexual or a nonsexual context. Strum recorded five different examples of the way in which friendships begin.

In the nonsexual context the new male may consistently approach and try to interact with a particular female who is not in estrus. When Ray entered the troop, he remained on the periphery and there met Naomi, an influential female in troop movements, who also spends time on the periphery. At first she avoided Ray's advances, but then she allowed him to approach and gradually a relationship developed in which they spent considerable time together and groomed each other frequently.

In the sexual context, the new male may make friends with a female by becoming her consort while she is in estrus and then continuing the companionship afterward. When some females start cycling again after giving birth, the first two or three estrous periods do not seem to attract males, and the female does not usually form a consort with a male troop member. However, a new male may form a consort with this somehow less attractive female and a friendship may then result, as it occurred with Brutus and Zelda.

When the female is the initiator in the nonsexual context, she approaches and tries to groom the male. This happened with

Peggy and Strider. When Strider was a new arrival, Peggy (who was not in estrus) stopped her normal interactions with her other male friends and moved to the periphery of the troop to interact with Strider, and they became friends. Then, too, a female in estrus may solicit a new male, and they may eventually form a friendship as a result of their temporary sexual relationship.

Yet another way in which Strum observed friendships being formed was through the use of a black infant. Baby baboons are born with black coats that make them conspicuous; most troop members are attracted to them and inhibit their aggression toward them. When two males are fighting, one male, usually the one who is at a disadvantage, will sometimes take up a black infant and hold it to his stomach as the mother would do. The male gains an advantage by holding the black infant because the other male is inhibited, and usually the fight will stop at this point. The male who has picked up the infant is not necessarily the winner, but he has been able to get out of the fight "more gracefully." If a new male uses the infant of a particular female a number of times, this may lead to a friendship with her and her offspring, as happened with Ray and Debbie. At the same time, a friendship with a female who has a black infant may lead to the use of that infant in the male's disputes.

It is interesting that the friendship between males and females also includes the female's offspring of various ages. One often sees youngsters playing around an adult male; a black infant may even crawl on a big male and sit on his lap. The nearest adult female may be 200 yards away, but the infant seems relaxed. In the Gilgil troop these youngsters turned out to be the offspring of the male's female friends.

By the time the new male is fully integrated into the troop, he will probably have two to four female friends, and oddly enough these females may not be friends of each other's. For example, Carl, who is a long-standing member of the troop (he has been a member for at least three years), is friendly with Anne, Constance, Zelda, and Vicki, none of whom is a friend of another.

A male will come to the aid of his female friends — and occasionally their offspring — in certain fights (like the mothers, males intercede only in the fights that somehow draw their attention), but the females will not come to his aid in disputes with other males. If a male viciously attacks a female, a group of females — including his friends — may mob him; so ultimately the females will support each other.

Once the male has established his friendships with certain females, his relationships with them seem to run in cycles; that is, he may have an intense relationship with one female for a period of time and then ease off with her, while developing a more intense relationship with one of his other friends, but he seems to go back to the same friends and not to new ones. The period of intense friendship between a male and female may range from three to ten months. Several situations appear to influence the friendship. If a female has a new infant, she may be nervous and seek out her male friend's company. If a male is going through a tense period with other adult males, he may spend more time with a female friend who has a black infant because he is using the black infant in his fights, or he may seek the company of his most influential female friend.

What is particularly fascinating about these male-female friendships is that the female's status is apparently of some importance to the male. Peggy, the most influential female in the troop, has more male friends than any other female in the troop, whereas the least influential members in the troop, Beth and Willabea, have no male friends at all. But what is more, the formation of a bond with Peggy appears to be a turning point in a new male's integration into the troop. Once a new male becomes friends with Peggy, he is soon a fully integrated member of the troop and no longer moves on the periphery. So it appears that the social status of the females is important to the males, rather than simply the reverse, as was always thought to be the case.

In the Gilgil troop new males did not start interacting seriously with the other adult males until after they had established bonds with the females. Male-male relationships are quite different from female-female relationships in the troop. Strum did not find a stable hierarchy among the males. At any one time it was apparent only what the dominance relation was between two males, but all the males could not be ranked in a traditional linear order in relation to more than one variable. For example, the seven males could be ranked according to priority at the garbage pit, but this rank did not correlate with a rank determined by consumption at kills or by the number of female friends or number of consortships. And each male's position in relation to each of these factors changed from time to time as a result of fights.

When I visited Gilgil, Big Sam and Ray had just switched positions. Ray had been dominant for a while; then he had a series of fights with Big Sam, who appeared to have won that round, as he became dominant. Their relationship with the other males in the troop did not change at that time. This type of reversal is thus similar to that found among the males in Amboseli. In Gilgil, however, although fights are not frequent there are more interactions involving several males, and temporary alliances are sometimes formed (there are no friendships between males). For instance, at the time of my visit, Big Sam could rely on the support of two other males, but such a situation usually does not last for long, contrary to the situation described by Washburn and DeVore.

In Strum's description of baboon social organization, one of the basic working differences between the male system and the female system is that among the males, special events (fights, etc.) actually change the nature of relationships, whereas among the females, special relationships seem to influence the outcome of events. In other words, a fight, or a series of fights, between two males can completely change their relationship, but fights among females do not change the basic family and friendship relationships; in fact, the existence of a family tie or friendship can and does affect the outcome of the fights.

Thus, we find that the long-term studies reveal baboons as amazingly complex animals with an intricate social organization that we are only beginning to understand. These studies are being conducted in various types of habitat on troops of different sizes and with different sex ratios and age structures. The "controversy" itself is partly a reflection of the flexibility of the baboon's social structure and behavior under various conditions. Rowell has pointed out that baboons living in lush forest, who can fill their stomachs in a couple of hours and then spend much of the day socializing, are bound to have different patterns of social behavior from baboons living in an arid area where they have to feed all day. Then, too, baboons living in a troop with sixty or more members may show different patterns from those living in a troop with only twenty members. Rowell has suggested that there may be no such thing as a "normal social structure" for baboons. This in itself makes the study of baboons all the more fascinating and rewarding.

Life in a baboon troop, no matter where it is and whatever its size, must be far from simple; it is therefore interesting to follow the development of the baboon from birth to maturity, to see how it learns to function in its highly complex world.

The baby baboon is born after a gestation period of about six months. None of the scientists has recorded a birth in the wild, but apparently most births take place at night, very likely in the vicinity of the troop. There are no indications that the female goes off on her own to give birth.

As was mentioned earlier, the baby baboon is born with a black coat and seems to be irresistibly attractive to other troop members, particularly females. Seeing an infant, other baboons approach the mother, uttering a characteristic grunting noise that denotes interest and friendliness. They may try to take the baby or touch it but most often must be content with grooming the mother, which allows them to be near the baby. Some mothers are more nervous than others and constantly try to avoid the advances of other troop members. The baby's attractiveness may be partly a result of its appearance: the black coat with contrasting pink face and ears is definitely conspicuous against the olive or yellowish coat of its mother.

From the day it is born, the baby has a strong instinct to cling; it grasps the fur of its mother's sides and chest in order to hang on. The mother carries it against her underside, sometimes supporting it with one hand as she moves along, and when she sits, it lies in the curve of her leg. In the first month, the baby spends most of its time eating and sleeping, but when it is awake, it finds the world full of other baboons already trying to interact with it.

In the next few months the baby becomes more coordinated and begins to take a few steps away from its mother; it may also begin to play with its older brothers and sisters and other infants. At about five weeks, it begins to ride on its mother's back, hanging on with all fours. Eventually it will be able to sit up and ride jockey style. While still only a few months old, it becomes interested in the food its mother eats. It touches plants and puts bits of vegetation to its mouth without eating, much like the baby elephant playing with vegetation with its trunk.

Sometime in the fourth to sixth month the young baboon goes through a color change; its black coat gradually turns a uniform light brown, while its pink face and ears darken. From this age on, it begins to spend less time with its mother and more time with other youngsters. This is the age when exploration and intense interactions with peers begin. Not everyone finds adult baboons attractive, but it is difficult not to like the youngsters. Their faces are short and appealing, with serious, rather worried expressions, caused by wrinkles that will later stretch out with growth. Young baboons are full of energy and mischief, and are infinitely amusing to watch in their games.

The youngsters seem to play most of day, but with more intensity in the morning and evening. They may play in groups or on their own. When they play together, they are extremely noisy and there is much running, chasing, and wrestling — all activities that develop muscles and reflexes and provide practice for situations that will arise in adulthood. Even when a young baboon is on his own, he will find a game — a stick or stone, for example, to be examined and handled. They also seem to find falling out of trees a great pastime. One will climb up a tree, go out to the end of a branch, slip down until he is dangling off by one hand, and then finally let himself fall. He picks himself up, goes back up the tree, and falls again, repeating the game over and over. When more than one youngster is playing this game, several get on the end of the branch and try to push each other off.

General roughhouse seems to be the most common kind of play, with much wrestling and chasing, and if one gets very close (as is possible at Gilgil), one can hear them "chortling" — a delightful noise that sounds like repressed laughter. Of course, these games can get serious, and sometimes an animal gets hurt. Hitherto, it was thought that the males in the troop acted as a kind of police force, disciplining the youngsters and keeping them in line. In the Gilgil troop, however, what "policing" is done is usually carried out by a female and then only in support of her own family and close associates' families. A male might interfere in a fight if it is very close to him and will usually settle the dispute in favor of his friends, but he may also pick up a friend and punish it with a bite — mainly a symbolic gesture, for he will rarely draw blood. However, this kind of punishment, from an adult male or female, produces terrified screeches from youngsters; one would think they were being murdered on the spot. Perhaps they overreact so because they are still immature and do not know quite what to expect.

For the most part, though, the youngsters do not need disciplining, because they learn to restrain themselves. The youngsters in the troop range in age from newborn to subadult, and they all love to play. If a large, nearly subadult animal wants to play with a small one-year-old, then it must restrain itself in its play or else it will hurt the other; if the younger one does get hurt, it will not be willing to play with the older one again. Each animal learns restraint in its interactions with others, and the resulting inhibitions are important to the troop. If there was no restraint in the aggressive interactions among baboons, individuals would frequently be badly injured or killed (a baboon is equipped with highly effective weapons). Play is one way in which the animals develop inhibitions and, at the same time, learn the relative strength of individuals.

From about six months on, the young baboon begins to eat

solid food; now its experience in watching and smelling what its mother eats comes into play. By the time it is ten months old, it may suckle only rarely but will still spend a good deal of time with its mother while the troop is foraging. Between the ages of eleven and fifteen months the youngster is weaned: the mother becomes less and less tolerant of the juvenile until finally she no longer allows it to suckle or ride on her back. The reactions of the mothers may vary greatly; some mothers go on letting their offspring suckle for nearly two years, although they may be getting little milk.

Throughout the baboon's development, it learns the gestures, vocalizations, and rituals that it needs in order to function in the group. As one might expect, in a primate group these are extensive. Although most of the basic gestures and noises appear to be instinctive, some have to be learned and developed in relation to the social context.

What is popularly called "body language" is obviously at work in the baboon troop. It is fascinating to watch the animals communicate with each other through subtle postures without uttering a sound. Hall and DeVore interpreted thirty-two body gestures, from grins, yawns, and lip smacking to shoulder shrugging, ear flattening, and eyebrow raising. They also listed fourteen distinct vocalizations. By the time a baboon reaches maturity, it has a full repertoire of behavior to use in the various situations that arise. If, for some reason, it wants to intimidate a subordinate animal, it has a whole range of threatening gestures and noises that it can use, but at the same time, it recognizes the submissive gestures of the subordinate animal and will respect them as such. If the same animal should meet a threatening, more dominant animal, it will know how to avoid attack and how best to appease the more influential baboon.

Thus, the youngster grows up surrounded by family and friends, and by the time it reaches maturity, it is ready to participate in the world of the adult baboon. Females reach social and sexual maturity much earlier than do males. Sometime in her third or fourth year, the young female has her first estrous cycle.

Estrus is a highly conspicuous state in the baboon. At its onset the skin around the anus and vulva, called the "sexual skin," changes to a pinkish hue and begins to swell. As estrus progresses, the pink gets brighter and brighter and the swelling gets more and more pronounced, until the whole area is a swollen mass of red flesh — a most unattractive sight by human standards, but obviously not considered so by the baboon.

When the female is in estrus, she "presents" to adult males, which is her way of soliciting their sexual attention. She approaches a male, turns her backside to him, and lifts her tail, turning it to one side. He may or may not respond by copulating; he may just put his nose to her rump or groom her.

The female is not monogamous. In the early stages of estrus she will mate with any of the juvenile males, and it is incongruous to see a little one-year-old, less than a quarter the size of the female, climb up on her and copulate. However, during the period of maximum swelling, which may last three to eight days, the adult males usually monopolize the female. During that period she may form a consort with one or two of the adult males in the troop or all of them, one after the other. It has been suggested that the female will mate with the highest-ranking male in the troop at the time when she is most likely to be ovulating, but this is not necessarily the case; the relationship between dominance and mating success is still not clear.

Hausfater's study revealed that the two highest-ranking males in the Amboseli troop, B.J. and Stubby, clearly showed favoritism toward certain females. While Stubby was the first-ranking male, he consorted only with the females Oval and Judy, even though other females were in estrus. While B.J. was first-ranking, he consorted with Lulu and Judy and once with Oval, and also ignored other females that came into estrus, even though one of them might be the only female in estrus at the time. The lower-ranking males copulated and formed consorts with these other females. Overall, the second-ranking male carried out the highest proportion of copulations. As no one male held any one rank for very long, it was difficult to determine over a long period which males were most likely to father offspring.

A consort pair is usually found on the periphery of the troop, moving to the front, side, or rear of the main group. They can be seen to copulate from time to time throughout the day. Mating is a relatively quick affair — the male mounts the female from behind, holding on to her sides by her fur or placing his hands on her back and grabbing her back legs above the ankle with his hind feet, so that he is lifted off the ground; he gives a few quick thrusts (usually about six) and then dismounts. The whole act takes place in eight to ten seconds.

After a period of maximum turgescence the female begins to deflate, and the adult males and finally the younger males lose interest in her. She then returns to her normal life in the troop. As was mentioned earlier, Hausfater's data show that at no time during estrus and consorting does the female change status in relation to the other females in the troop, contrary to what was suggested by earlier studies.

The female usually produces her first baby at about four and a half years old. Although she may suckle her offspring for a year or more, her estrous periods may begin again six to eight months after the infant's birth. However, it is most likely that she will not get pregnant again until her baby is at least a year old. Thus, with a six-month gestation period, the average birth interval would be approximately eighteen months, but the interval seems to vary from area to area and from female to female. At Gilgil the birth interval ranged from seventeen to over twenty-six months. A female's breeding life is thought to be about ten to twelve years; so she could produce seven or eight infants in her lifetime.

Whereas females reach sexual and physical maturity when they are around four years old, at that age the males still have a long way to go. The young male may be sexually mature at four years, in that he can probably produce viable sperm, but he is by no means physically or psychologically mature. By five years old, he is larger than the adult females and dominant over some of them, but next to a fully adult male he looks like a female, and in fact, untrained observers watching from a distance often mistake subadult males for females.

The male baboon grows until he is about eight years old. Muscles, even bones keep developing and growing, and the olive baboon does not get the impressive mantle of hair until about eight years; perhaps even more important, it is not until that age that the canines are fully grown. So the male baboon is classified as a "subadult" for nearly five years of his life. Observations at Gombe National Park have revealed that most subadult males leave the troop they were born in before they reach full adulthood, then switch to other troops. It would be interesting to try to examine the forces that cause a young male to leave or attract him to another troop.

In fact, the whole process from birth to adulthood would be fascinating to follow. The average life span of a baboon living in the wild may be only fifteen years; even so, that is many times longer than most wildlife studies last. The baboon is such a complex animal that one can only begin to describe its social life by watching one troop or even several troops for a couple of years. The long-term studies at Gilgil, Gombe, and Amboseli should continue to reveal new information on the development of individual personalities, the formation of social bonds, mother-offspring relations, group fission, intergroup relations, and other behavioral phenomena.

Baboons are supremely adaptable animals and the way they relate to their environment is equal in importance to the way they relate to each other; in fact, the two are inseparable. Up to this point the vital fact that baboons must "make a living" has barely been mentioned. All the field studies, but in particular those of the Altmanns, Rowell, DeVore, and Hall, have contributed to knowledge about baboon ecology. By following a day in the life of a baboon troop, we can better understand how the individual and the troop function in relation to the environment. We will take an average baboon troop living in fairly open terrain that is considered typical savannah and follow it through a day.

At dawn the baboon troop is still peacefully sleeping in the branches of tall trees (or, in some areas, on the sides of steep cliff faces). In the early light the baboons dotted throughout the branches look like dark overripe fruits about to drop off. Gradually, as the light increases, they begin to stir, but baboons are far from early risers. In East Africa the sun rises at around 6:15 A.M., but baboons often do not come down out of the trees until 8:00 or 8:30; this may be either a response to predators, many of which are most active in the early hours of the morning, or, during certain seasons, a reflection of food availability — the baboons may not have to go far for food that day.

The juveniles, about one to three or four years old, are usually the first down and begin to play on the ground below. The older juveniles spend little time with their mothers (in the daytime, at least), preferring to eat, move, and play with others their own age in what is commonly called a "play group." The play group seems to be in action all day long: one rarely finds the troop without at least a few youngsters playing, but morning seems to be one of the times when they are most active.

In the meantime, the other troop members are waking and coming down out of the trees: mothers with infants, estrous females, pregnant females, subadult males and females, and the big adult males. These animals will also probably stay under the trees for a while, and this is one of the best times to watch social interactions. As they sit about, they form into clusters, often with one or two adults at the center of each. A cluster might consist, for instance, of a family (a mother with her offspring), or two female friends with their families, or a male with one or two of his female friends, or a male with his juvenile friends; one very common cluster consists of a female with a black infant surrounded by interested onlookers.

In the morning, one or more of the animals in each cluster will most likely be grooming another animal. Grooming has been discussed in other chapters, but with primates it seems to be particularly conspicuous, and its role in social binding is of great importance. Anyone who has ever had a baby monkey of any kind for a pet knows that grooming it, by picking through its hair, will satisfy and relax it far more than feeding it. The all-important touching of one individual by another is essential in a primate community.

The development and reinforcement of bonds among individuals is one function of grooming; at the same time, grooming serves a very practical purpose — keeping the animal clean. Contrary to reports about "insanitary brutes," a freshly caught baboon (according to trappers) is one of the cleanest wild animals found. They are almost always free from ticks or other insects and dirt. The baboon's grooming technique is highly effective. The groomer uses both its teeth and hands to rake through the hair, picking out bits of dead skin, dirt, and any insects that it finds as it goes along. The skin and insects are popped into the groomer's mouth and eaten. The groomee sits or lies in a relaxed position with an expression that can only be described as blissful. From time to time the groomee may turn or lift an arm or roll over on its back so that the groomer can get at a new spot. The groomer may continue for five to ten minutes, and when he or she finishes, the other usually reciprocates. The whole session may take half an hour. Strum once saw two females groom each other for two hours, but this is unusual.

All animals in the troop get groomed at some point, but young babies in particular are groomed frequently. The grooming response begins very early, and even very young babies will try to groom their mothers in turn, even if only for a few seconds. Grooming occurs throughout the day but is more frequent during rest periods and in the early morning and evening.

By now the baboon troop is beginning to get restless and a few members are setting off, away from the "sleeping trees." DeVore and Washburn suggested that the dominant males in the troop somehow determine the direction the troop takes, even though they do not actually lead the movement. Troop leadership is very difficult to determine. The animals actually at the front of the troop may be responding to something that is happening at the center or even to the rear of the troop. When a baboon troop travels in order to get from one place to another (as opposed to moving over the ground in search of food), they move in what is called a "progression," or column. This is not necessarily a single file; more likely there are two or three abreast. Whereas

DeVore and Washburn described a distinct order of progression — apparently an antipredator mechanism — with animals taking up definite positions according to their rank or sex, none of the subsequent researchers has found this order.

Observing the baboons along the Ishasha River in Uganda, Rowell found that "Only two frequent placement patterns were detected: an adult male often sat, glancing back down the trail, until the whole troop was ahead of him before moving on; and the outlying animals, following the most divergent paths, were usually pregnant females." But contrary to the Nairobi findings, the males were usually the first to run if there was real danger. The animals that found themselves at the back of the fleeing troop, closest to the danger, were the mothers with heavier babies.

The Altmanns found no particular order of progression in the yellow baboon troops in Amboseli. The females with infants did not necessarily stay in the middle or near adult males; nor did the subordinate males take up front and rear positions. What the Altmanns did find was that in moving about their range the baboons preferred to use well-known passes and corridors. The baboons seemed to have what the Altmanns called a "mental map" of their range and were familiar with all the potentially dangerous areas. It was this intense familiarity with the habitat that in many cases protected them from hazards.

Even though recent observers have not found an order of progression that reflects an obvious system of protection against predators, the role of the adult males when predators are confronted must not be underrated. The males are still a very important factor for survival on the savannahs. Almost every researcher noted examples of males "intimidating" predators. Reactions to predators are variable: under direct attack, the whole troop will usually run, but the sighting of a predator in the immediate area of the troop will often elicit another response. All the animals in a baboon troop are alert to signs of danger, and if one of them sees or hears a predator, he or she will sound an alarm bark. The adult males are then likely to go into action. First they try to find out where the danger is coming from, by getting up on a tree, anthill, or stump and looking around. If it is a serious threat, such as a leopard, the males may group together and advance in a threatening manner, flashing their long canines, grunting, and screeching. This is usually enough to send the predator slinking away.

The only nonhuman predator the baboons will not face, but invariably flee, is the lion (although George Schaller says that lions have a healthy respect for baboons' weapons and will avoid them when other prey is available); cheetahs, leopards, wild dogs, hyenas and jackals can be chased away especially when they are on their own. These predators are usually successful only when they can creep up on the troop and take a member by surprise, but with fifty pairs of eyes watching for danger this is not easy, as anyone who has ever tried to approach a wild baboon troop knows.

The most serious predator for the baboon is man, and baboons are very wary indeed of him and his weapons. In most parts of Africa the baboon is hardly considered "wildlife" at all. Outside the national parks and reserves, baboons are classified as "vermin," and as a result of their crop-raiding habits, they are slaughtered in great numbers throughout Africa. Nevertheless, they are cunning creatures and not about to be exterminated. It is interesting that baboons will run for the safety of tall trees when a lion approaches and there bark and screech at it, but will avoid trees when they spot a human. Baboons have learned that they are not safe from rifles and shotguns in even the tallest trees. If they happen to be in trees when a human approaches on foot, they immediately and silently come down and try to disappear into the bush or tall grass. And the group memory must be long, because even in parks where baboons have been protected for years they still frantically descend from trees when a human approaches. Coming down from the trees is the opposite of what almost all other dangerous situations dictate; this behavior shows the baboon's adaptability and gives us some idea of how it has survived outside national parks and reserves.

Once the baboon troop has reached the area where it is going to forage, the progression breaks up and the animals spread out to feed, moving in more or less a broad front rather than a file. Baboons are selective feeders: they do not take everything that is within reach but carefully choose from what is available. Their diet is extremely varied, probably even more so than the elephant's. Much depends on the time of year. Baboons utilize what is available, according to the season and the different stages of the plant's growth.

In savannah areas, grass is the most important part of the baboon's diet, and various parts of the grass plant are used in different seasons. After the rains have begun, when the grass is green and growing, baboons eat the young grass shoots; later in the season they eat the flowering seed heads; and in the dry season, when the part of the grass plant that is still above the ground is dry and no longer nutritious, the baboons dig out the rhizome (the base and lateral root of the plant) and eat this. The rhizomes are still succulent and full of protein even late in the dry season and so provide a good source of nutrition that few grazing animals of the savannah exploit.

The second most important plant for the savannah baboon is the acacia tree; in Nairobi National Park and Amboseli Game Reserve, the baboons concentrate on the fever tree, *Acacia xanthophloea*, and the umbrella tree, *Acacia tortilis*. In Nairobi and Gilgil they also feed on the small whistling thorn, *Acacia drepanolobium*. When the acacia trees are in bloom with flowers and green seed pods, the baboons often concentrate on these trees throughout the day, eating huge quantities of blossoms and pods to the exclusion of all other plants. Parts of the leaves and the sap are also eaten, but less frequently. Later, when the pods dry out, they are also eaten, but not with the same relish as when they are green; even dry, however, they provide an important source of protein.

Other kinds of vegetation — shrubs, herbs, vines, and creepers, etc. — are eaten at various stages of their growth, some at only one stage, others at all stages, and some more intensively than others. Baboons are very fond of fruits, especially figs, and will go out of their way to visit a tree in fruit.

It is fairly widely known that baboons are not exclusively vegetarian in their diet, but their role as bloodthirsty killers has been somewhat exaggerated by certain writers. Actually, meat forms a very small proportion of the diet of most baboons, and meat eating seems to be more popular in some areas than others. All baboons will eat ants, termites, grasshoppers, and other insects, when available, but not all baboons eat meat; nor, in most cases, do they seem to hunt purposefully for animals. In most areas where kills have been observed, the baboon doing the killing has been an adult male, and usually he has caught the animal by a fortuitous set of circumstances, not by actively searching and hunting it.

What happens most often is that a baboon, while foraging, will startle an animal, such as a hare or fledgling bird, and catch it before it has a chance to run or fly. During the first few weeks of life, Thomson's gazelle fawns hide in clumps of grass, and sometimes baboons will come across them and kill and eat them. DeVore and Washburn described one capture of a young "Tommy" that they witnessed: "An adult male grabbed it, brought it above his head, and slammed it to the ground. He immediately tore into the stomach of the gazelle and began eating. Beginning with the most dominant males, five of the six adult males in the troop participated in eating this gazelle, and two hours later only skin, teeth and large bones remained. The viscera were eaten first, followed by the flesh, and finally the thin brain case was bitten open and the contents carefully scooped out with the fingers — bits of skull being pulled through the teeth and licked clean. The incisors, not the canines, were used in biting and tearing the flesh."

In this case there was no systematic searching for or stalking of the prey — the baboon just happened upon the animal and took advantage of the situation. Taking into account the few kills seen during their many hours of observation, DeVore and Washburn reckoned that even with insects, eggs, fledglings, and small mammals, the Nairobi baboons still had a diet consisting of 98 percent vegetation.

Although still eating proportionately far more vegetable matter than meat, the baboons in Gilgil seem to be well on their way to becoming steady meat eaters. While Robert Harding watched the Gilgil troop in 1970–71, he saw forty-seven cases of predation by baboons in 1032 hours of observation; in all but three cases, adult males made the kills, and in all but one case, adult males consumed the kills. (The baboons killed and ate hares, various kinds of birds, and the young of the Thomson's gazelle, dikdik, steinbok, and impala.) During her study Strum observed a hundred cases of predation by baboons in 1200 hours of observation, and the sexes and ages of the animals that participated in the kills and in the consumption of meat showed a marked change.

Animals change habits or acquire new habits for a number of reasons. In the long term they acquire behavioral traits that are advantageous in their particular environment. Some changes in habits, such as learning a new habit from other group members, may be due to social modifications. When a habit is taken over by the group as a whole and transmitted to the younger generation, it might be called a "tradition." In this sense, a tradition seems to have formed in the Gilgil baboon troop in respect to killing and meat eating.

In early 1973, at the beginning of Strum's study, a few of the females were eating meat at the kills and one or two were making kills. As the study progressed, more females and then juveniles (who either came along with their mothers or came together in a group to investigate the activity) began eating meat or trying to get meat at most of the kills. What is fascinating is that once a juvenile had tasted meat it attended every kill thereafter. Toward the end of the study, the older juveniles started chasing down and killing hares, birds, and even young Tommies.

In the first ten days of November 1973 there were seven kills, and by then both sexes of every age class were eating meat. This was a very fast acceptance of a tradition by any standards. What is more, not only did the pattern of meat eating change in the troop; so did the patterns of predation. Rather than fortuitously finding prey, the baboons, particularly the males, were truly hunting by the end of the study. The males actually left the

troop, traveled up to two miles away from the periphery of the
troop, and spent as long as two hours in hunting behavior. They
followed Tommy herds and, upon reaching a herd, would "test"
individuals by running at the herd, making the Tommies run, and
then stopping, apparently to see if there was an appropriate individual to chase. In an actual chase the baboons employed a relay
system, which, though accidental, was successful, and they
quickly adopted it as a standard strategy.

This rapid development of killing and meat-eating behavior in
the Gilgil troop may be correlated with the number of suitable
prey animals on the ranch. In 1956 there were reportedly only
forty-eight Thomson's gazelles on the Cole Ranch. By 1974 there
were several thousand wild animals — Thomson's gazelles, impalas, dikdiks, eland, warthogs, zebras, and others.

Nevertheless, in most areas, the baboons (even the majority of
the members of the Gilgil troop) spend most of their day seeking
out a herbivorous diet. The amount of time they spend feeding
depends a great deal on what is available. Rowell's forest baboons
could fill their stomachs in less than an hour and had to spend
only several short periods in a day feeding, but in Nairobi, Amboseli, and Gilgil, the baboons have to work harder (especially
during the dry season), and they spend the better part of the day
feeding, with occasional rest periods.

The difficulty in obtaining food is often reflected in the distance
traveled in one day, although the Altmanns have shown that baboons are ultimately restricted in their movements by how far
they can get in one day and still be able to return to safe sleeping
sites in the evening. A typical day's journey for Rowell's forest
baboons was only 1 to 1½ miles, whereas the savannah baboons in
Nairobi traveled an average of 3 miles a day. Baboons have been
recorded traveling as much as 12 miles in a day.

Baboons are conservative in their movements. They stick to a
definite home range, which in Nairobi National Park averaged
about 15 square miles. The ranges of neighboring baboon troops
usually overlap, but the troops tend to avoid each other whenever
possible. They rarely threaten or try to chase each other from an

area, although occasionally disagreements arise over possession of sleeping trees or cliffs in overlapping zones. Within the home range, a troop uses some areas more intensively than others. These "core areas," as they are called, have all the necessary resources — sleeping sites, water, and food — and consequently the troop tends to concentrate its activities in these places. Neither the home range nor the core areas are territorially defended; neighboring troops may even enter the core areas, but almost always at a time when the normally resident troop is not there.

The need for water is an important factor in a troop's range. In areas where there is a permanent, easily accessible source of water, as there is along the Athi River in Nairobi National Park and along the Ishasha River in Rowell's study area, the baboons usually drink every day. On the Gilgil ranch the baboons drank at least once a day at the cattle watering troughs. The Amboseli troop that the Altmanns watched did not necessarily drink every day; in one period of nineteen consecutive days that the main group was under close observation, the group had one drinking session on eleven days, two drinking sessions on five days, and did not drink at all on the other three days. Where there is heavy dew and succulent vegetation, baboons may drink infrequently. Hall rarely saw his baboons drinking at the Cape, although he did see them licking rainwater off their coats.

Drinking from rainpools scattered throughout the baboons' range is a relatively uneventful and simple matter, but drinking from rivers and permanent water holes, both of which are usually surrounded by vegetation, is another matter. The drinking session is then the single most dangerous event of the day. Baboons approach a water hole very cautiously, then sit and wait, looking around. They prefer water holes in large open areas with trees nearby and try to avoid thick vegetation in which predators may be hiding. If there are other animals — giraffes, impalas, zebras — drinking, the baboons feel more confident and a few of them will venture down to the water's edge. The whole troop never goes at once; first a few will drink, then a few more, until the whole troop has finished. They drink by bending over and sipping the water with their mouths — a highly vulnerable position.

On some occasions it is the baboons who inspire confidence in other animals. This is particularly seen with the bushbuck, that shy, elegant creature of the forest and thick bush. In Lake Manyara National Park I saw baboons drink nearly every day below the research station on the Ndala River. On many of these days, shortly after the baboons began to drink, a lone bushbuck would come down to the river and drink among the baboons. What was unusual was that the drinking would often be preceded or followed by what certainly looked like play — the bushbuck would scamper and frolic in the shallow water, either chasing or being chased by a baboon. This same kind of play behavior has also been observed between bushbucks and baboons in Gombe National Park.

Baboons also seem to have a special relationship with impalas — they are often found feeding together. When baboons are feeding in the branches of acacia trees, impalas will often be attracted to the trees, because the activity of the baboons' feeding knocks many pods to the ground, where the impalas can get at them. When the two species feed together, it is likely that their combined alertness makes for an effective antipredator strategy.

After drinking, if it is at midday, the baboon troop will probably stop and have a rest, but it should be pointed out that there is no fixed routine, with baboons feeding in the morning and resting during the heat of the day; if they have had a rest earlier in the morning, they may be quite active at midday. Weather is an influence (on clear, sunny days baboons usually seek shade under bushes and trees), but it is difficult to make generalizations about a daily activity pattern. All that can be said is that a troop feeds and moves throughout the day, pausing for rest periods (when the baboons usually groom each other and take naps) and socializing.

In the afternoon the baboons will gradually begin moving in the direction of the trees (or cliffs) in which they will sleep. They either circle back to where they slept the night before, or move to a new sleeping site. The Altmanns found that their troop usually used one sleeping grove for a number of nights running, utilizing the area within a day's walk of that grove, and would then move on to another. It was not clear what prompted the move.

Baboons are conscientious in their choice of sleeping sites. In East Africa the safest place is usually a tall tree, but when trees are not available, baboons sleep on cliff faces. On the Serengeti Plains, where there are neither trees nor cliffs, they sleep on top of the bigger kopjes. Apparently a popular sleeping site may be abandoned because of negative associations: in Amboseli one sleeping grove was abandoned after two baboons were killed there by a leopard.

By 6:00 to 6:30 P.M. the baboons will have arrived at their chosen sleeping site (it gets dark between 6:30 and 7:00 in East Africa). Rowell's baboons sometimes went into the trees as early as 5:00 P.M. on cloudy days. Occasionally they would arrive after dark, but this is something baboons try to avoid, for as they rely heavily on sight, they are extremely vulnerable on the ground after dark. If they arrive at the trees with time to spare, the baboons usually engage in another period of intense social activity, although the Altmanns noted that on some evenings the baboons seemed obviously "fatigued at that time of the day."

After socializing for a while, the baboons gradually begin to ascend the trees. The large males usually take the places closest to the trunk in the crooks between branch and trunk. It has been postulated that they are taking the most comfortable places; but they also thus protect the females and infants from any danger that might come up the tree. Whatever the case, the females and infants are lighter and so can get higher and farther out on the branches.

Baboons generally sleep sitting up. (Sometimes one will lie prone, straddling a horizontal branch, but this is not common.) They are able to sleep in a sitting position because they balance on flat, hard, insensitive pads of skin on their backsides, called "ischial callosities." Once settled in the trees, the baboons become quiet and soon fall asleep. It is thought that baboons sleep lightly and wake frequently to keep from falling.

And so we leave the baboon troop sleeping peacefully, each member surrounded by its family and friends, perhaps dreaming of eating a delicious fruit or being pleasantly groomed. It seems unlikely that any of them would be having a nightmare about a fellow baboon as Ardrey's "born bully" or "born criminal," much less as a "power-driven lawnmower."

VII

The Big Cats
Lion, Cheetah, Leopard

WITH THIS CHAPTER we come to a group of animals whose way of making a living is radically different from those of the other animals we have looked at so far, for the big cats are carnivores — they must eat meat, and generally that means they must hunt and kill in order to get their meal. Up to this point we have been looking at herbivores (baboons are still predominantly plant eaters), who fill the second level of the ecological pyramid, the first level being taken by the plants themselves, and the third level holding predators and scavengers.

The predators definitely stir man's imagination, perhaps because man, as a fellow predator, cannot help empathizing with the hunt. But the emotion they arouse in us seems to make it difficult for us to look at them objectively; we always risk attributing outstanding qualities to them, whether through human value judgments about their "bloodthirsty killing" or sentimental attitudes about their "noble lives." It is possible, however, to approach the cats in terms of the environment in which they live and their role in it, without detracting from their fascination or denying them their beauty and excitement.

In any ecosystem the basic materials keep circulating. With energy provided by the sun, plants utilize inorganic substances from the earth and convert them to organic material. Herbivores eat the plants and eventually die or are killed by predators. The dead animals' decomposing flesh and bones, plus the feces of predators and scavengers, enrich the soil, which, if provided with enough rainfall, produces more vegetation, which is then eaten by the herbivores, and so on.

Predators exist for the simple reason that there are herbivores, and so there is a niche for the carnivores to fill. From the evolutionary and ecological point of view there is no master plan in nature, but because of the way the relationship between predator and prey has evolved, the end result is probably beneficial to the prey populations as a whole.

If there were no predators, herbivores would die anyway, but the turnover might be more erratic; without the predators to weed out diseased and malformed animals, the herbivore populations would probably oscillate far more than they do. At the same time, the herbivores would almost certainly lose some of their vitality without the pressures of predation, because the effect of the relationship between predator and prey is slow but constant evolutionary change. The herbivores must devise new or improved ways of avoiding being killed and eaten, while the predators must evolve better methods of outmanuevering their prey's antipredator devices. As the herbivores become faster, more alert, with stronger or more complex defenses, the predators must become faster, stealthier, and more powerful. As one scientist put it, it is a race with no winner or finishing line.

However, throughout the history of conservation in Africa, predator-prey relations have been viewed with varying attitudes, and rarely without strong feelings. There have been policies designed to eradicate the predators in order to allow the "peaceful" ungulates to live and policies whereby starving lions, particularly cubs, have been fed by parks authorities. Many wardens shot wild dogs on sight because their methods of killing were considered "unethical." Until recently the administration of Kruger National Park in South Africa had a policy of killing predators; in just one disturbing example, they killed fifty-one cheetahs between 1954 and 1960 alone. The "lowly" hyenas have borne the brunt of this antipredator attitude — they have been poisoned, trapped, shot, and wiped out in some areas with virtually every conceivable method.

Fortunately, attitudes are now changing. With a little more knowledge about the role of the predators in the African ecosystem, parks administrators are tending toward noninterference; that is, they neither help nor hinder. Nevertheless, one of the first questions managers of national parks and reserves want answered is what effect the predators are having on the prey animals. Are they taking only the surplus animals and the sick, weak, and old? Or are the predators keeping the prey below a desirable level? The scientific studies that have been carried out on the predators have sought to answer these questions.

Then, too, there is the question of the future of the predators themselves. They are, of course, a major tourist attraction, and without them a national park would seem less natural and certainly less exciting. Any tourist, when asked what he wants to see, will immediately name the big cats. Just knowing that they are there, that at any moment a lion or cheetah might kill the Thomson's gazelle or impala one is watching adds a completeness and authenticity to experiencing the African wilderness.

Studies and surveys have tried to determine the status of the big cats, but this is a difficult task. Lions seem to be holding their own, and the leopard is still widespread despite heavy poaching, but the cheetah is scarce and scientists would like to know why.

But let us now look at the three big cats. Although alike in some ways, each species has a different kind of social life, and each makes its living in its own way. Thus even in areas where the lion, cheetah, and leopard overlap they are able to coexist because they each fill a different niche. They have not been so fortunate in trying to coexist with man, but let us hope that we can share part of this planet with these exquisite creatures for as long as possible.

*

The Lion

Lions are experiencing a swinging pendulum effect at the moment, although they are blissfully unaware of it. Public opinion on the lion is either positive or negative; rarely do feelings fall in between. Throughout history the lion has been the symbol of power and nobility, but an actual lion met face to face may elicit other emotions. The early hunters and settlers in Africa considered the lion vermin, without the dignity of a game animal. Lions were simply shot on sight. Their reputation deteriorated even further when they became famous for man eating, as described in J. H. Patterson's book *The Man-eaters of Tsavo* (1907). During the 1920s and 1930s their status was raised somewhat, as they became suitable ferocious prey to be stalked by intrepid white hunters.

The in 1960 the pendulum swung dizzily to the pro-lion side with the advent of Elsa, the pet lion made famous in Joy Adamson's books *Born Free, Living Free*, and *Forever Free* and the popular films based on them. The lion became the best-loved animal in America and Europe, and Elsa Clubs sprung up by the hundreds. The emphasis in the books was on the lion's intelligence, its happy family life in the wild, and, of course, the kindness and affection in the relationship between this lioness and her understanding owners.

For more than ten years hardly a word was spoken against the lion. Then the results of scientific studies began to appear, and journalists started characterizing lions as lazy, selfish, scavengers, murderers, bad mothers, rotten fathers, etc. Nevertheless, these reports have not really affected the average tourist, who still wants to see a lion more than any other wild animal. The scientist working in the parks on such animals as elephants and baboons finds the driver of every tourist bus asking, "Where are the lions?" while he (or she) is sitting there watching his animals behave in what he thinks is a far more fascinating way. But I don't think the tourist wants to see lions because they are noble, affectionate, or interesting. Their appeal lies in the very power of the animal: the potential killer of man, the predator epitomized, all lithe muscle, sinew, and grace. It may be an atavistic attraction to what was once a serious enemy.

Whatever the cause, the attraction is there and no doubt will be for a long time to come. What had to go were the myths, which had to be exploded before a realistic attitude toward the lion was possible, and probably the best man to do the exploding was George Schaller, a highly respected field scientist who produces not only scientific works on the animals he studies, but also popular, well-written accounts of his findings. His more personal accounts of his experiences with the animals he studies, *The Year of the Gorilla*, *Serengeti: A Kingdom of Predators*, and *Golden Shadows, Flying Hooves* can be read and enjoyed by nonscientists.

Lions seem to attract outstanding observers. Schaller himself is an amazing man — he seems to pack more into a three-year study than is physically possible. He is known to be one of the most relentless workers ever to be associated with the Serengeti Research Institute. He also feels very strongly about the animals he observes. From 1966 to 1969 he devoted his energies to understanding the ecology and behavior of the lions of the Serengeti. He concentrated on the lions around the Seronera area, in a block of about 250 square miles, and there he got to know them as individuals, following their births and deaths, matings, fights, hunts, and kills.

Just before Schaller left, another zoologist, Brian Bertram, arrived and took over the observations of the Seronera prides. Bertram kept track of these animals for another four and a half years, keeping continuous records on these prides for more than seven years. Bertram spent the major part of his time conducting a study of the woodland lions to the north. The woodland lions were more difficult to locate, and so Bertram relied a great deal on radio-tracking to follow the more elusive animals. Bertram is currently writing up his work, and some of his results are just beginning to appear. A third researcher, David Bygott, has recently arrived to continue the study of the Serengeti lions.

While Schaller and Bertram were working in the Serengeti, a remarkable woman was studying the lions in Nairobi National Park. Judith Rudnai is a determined lady. Ever since she was a small girl in Hungary, she wanted to live with lions in Africa — an unheard-of idea at that time. She never gave up her dream, although it was a long time before she fulfilled it. She married, moved to the United States, became a citizen, lived a suburban matron's life for several years, and finally, as a middle-aged woman, came to Africa on her own. She enrolled at the University of Nairobi, completed the whole undergraduate program in zoology, and at last, as a Master of Science degree candidate, began research on the lions in Nairobi National Park. That was in 1968; since then she has completed her thesis, received her master's degree, published a book on her work with lions, and carried out an additional two years of research on the Nairobi lions.

One more study that should be mentioned was also carried out by a unique individual — an African park guide in Lake Manyara National Park. Stephen Makacha was a relatively uneducated man who became deeply interested in the way of life of the animals in the Park. He decided to follow the lives of the lions he saw nearly every day as he took tourists around the Park. Makacha recognized the lions by scars and cuts and gave each a name. Part of his behavior data consisted of delightful drawings of lions hunting, resting in trees, or making kills. When Schaller heard about Makacha's work, he came to see him and began to supervise him, and with Makacha's daily observations and Schaller's scientific direction they were able to produce some excellent results.

Prior to these systematic studies, C. A. W. Guggisberg, the well-known East African naturalist, watched the lions of Nairobi National Park over several years and wrote a comprehensive book, called *Simba*, on knowledge of the lion up to 1961. This still remains the best source of information on the history, myths, legends, and man-eating habits of lions.

With all the excellent scientific material on lions now available, we can begin to understand how the lion fits into and makes a living in African ecosystems. For a carnivore, one might expect that the best system would be every lion for himself (or herself and her cubs), each one killing enough for its own needs. This is basically the system of the solitary predator, epitomized by the leopard, but the lion is an intriguing feline in that it lives in a group and is therefore a social animal. However, its very sociability is of a strange nature, for lions do not seem to be fully adjusted to the communal life, and it has been suggested that their present social system evolved only relatively recently.

Most lions live in prides consisting of males, females, and cubs, and each pride sticks to a fairly well-defined range; some lions — only a small percentage in most areas, however — live a nomadic life, roaming singly, in pairs, or in small groups, with no fixed territories.

The size of prides varies from area to area and even within one area. The Serengeti is known for its large prides; the largest recorded had thirty-seven members, the smallest four, with an average of fifteen. On the other hand, Nairobi and Manyara parks have much smaller prides, fifteen being the largest group seen in Manyara and twelve in Nairobi.

The pride does not act as a close-knit, coordinated unit in the way that the elephant family unit or the zebra family behaves. Sometimes the members are all together, but often the pride breaks down into groups, with members scattered over the pride area. For instance, in three years Schaller never saw all the members of the large "Seronera pride" together, but rather found them in groups averaging 3.6 animals. These groups may change composition from day to day, but once individuals are known, it is obvious that some animals within the pride spend more time with certain other members. A pride is made up of several adult females, cubs, subadult animals, and one to four adult males. The males are usually found together and are often separated from the other pride members. Cubs are most often found with their mothers, and certain females are found with other females. Schaller noted that females seemed to form companionships, but it was not always clear why or how; he speculates that "possibly some lionesses become friends, to use a somewhat anthropomorphic term, for no reason other than that they find each other's company congenial."

One might well ask why these separate groups should be considered as one pride. The answer is that all the lions making up these groups within a certain area behave toward each other in a friendly manner and, as a whole, form a closed social unit. Any strange lion or lioness who enters the pride area and is detected will be greeted with hostility and chased away. Pride males and females will chase both sexes, though ultimately a pride female may accept a strange male, and pride males may tolerate a nomadic lioness, especially if she is in estrus. Basically, however, strangers are not welcome.

To understand pride organization, one must first look at the lionesses, because they are the stable element. Adult males remain with the pride for a few years at a time, but fully adult lionesses remain with the pride for their whole lifetime, which may be over twenty years. Because the pride is a closed system, all the females within a pride are related to one another. The seven years of observations on the Serengeti prides have shown that the number of adult females in a pride remains fairly stable, no matter how many cubs are born or die or how many males are associated with the pride. In the "Maasai pride" the mean number of adult females over seven years changed from seven in 1966 to ten in 1972, while in the "Seronera pride" the mean number remained at about eight. Thus, as Bertram points out, the size of the pride is best measured in terms of the number of adult females, who, it seems, regulate this number themselves, by expelling subadult animals.

The females also seem to exercise the leadership in the pride. They are usually the first to get up and make a move, and they initiate and make 85 to 90 percent of all hunts and kills. Although there were usually one or two noticeably dominant females in the Serengeti prides, Schaller did not find a clear-cut hierarchy among the females. In one Nairobi pride, Rudnai found a tentative rank

A male dikdik with his
tiny, spearlike horns.

A female dikdik: the crest, white eye ring, and
dark preorbital gland are conspicuous.

Three gerenuks, a male (right)
and two females, feeding in
their characteristic standing
style.

A male gerenuk using
Laufschlag, or leg beat, in
his courtship of a female.

Peter and Mattie Jarman at the Serengeti Research Institute: wildlife research is not all glamorous field work; considerable time must be spent organizing and analyzing data.

Left: A territorial male impala marks a bush with secretions from the glands on his forehead. (Note how thin he is.)

Right: Two bachelor males: one is smelling the frontal brush of the other, presumably to determine his dominance status.

A male Uganda kob performs the "prancing display" for a female who has just entered his territory. Another female rests on his territory after mating. (Note how close the territory of the male in the background is.)

Portions of
the territorial
male wildebeests'
"Challenge Ritual":

Kneeling and horn-
ing of grass;

"Pretending" to
be alarmed;

Cavorting

A newborn
wildebeest.

Male eland sparring; the loser mounts the winner or another more dominant male.

A small nursery group of eland calves temporarily separated from their mothers. (Coke's hartebeest, or kongoni, in the background.)

An adult male olive baboon exhibiting his canine teeth in a threatening "yawn."

Shirley Strum observing and walking with the Gilgil troop.

A youngster rides "jockey style" on its mother's back.

Two black infants playing.

Family and "friends" surround a black infant.

A male eating a
Thomson's gazelle fawn
that he has killed.

Yellow baboons in Amboseli share the shade of an acacia tree with a bushbuck, an animal that frequently associates with baboons.

An adult female grooming
her male "friend."

order based on priority in feeding at kills and on who was most consistently on the receiving end of aggression. In this pride the youngest and smallest female was the lowest-ranking.

What Schaller found among the members of his well-known prides was a curious kind of dominance pattern. In most groups of social animals there is a fairly well defined rank order, in that each animal knows its dominance relation with every other animal in the group and usually responds accordingly. True to the ambivalent nature of their sociality, lions do not behave in quite this way.

On size alone there is a built-in dominance, with males weighing as much as 400 pounds or more, females 250 pounds, and cubs, of course, less. Lionesses know that lions are bigger and stronger than they are, subadults know that adults can hurt them, and cubs know that everyone else can beat them up, but none of them accepts the situation. Lions rarely make submissive gestures; instead, they fight back, and surprisingly this does not cause more fights but fewer. A cub will fight vigorously to defend a piece of meat at a kill, snarling and slapping at adults who try to take it away. As Schaller says, "It fights for its rights so to speak, and this too affects the interactions, for it often makes the stronger animal reluctant to attack. Each lion in a group knows and responds to the fighting potential of every other member. It is a system based on the amount of damage each animal can inflict on an aggressor; it is a system based on a balance of power, something not unknown in human affairs."

Antagonistic encounters sometimes occur during competition over food, particularly if times are difficult, but for the most part the lions within a pride are amicable toward one another and there are few squabbles and fights. In fact, the impression a group of lions gives is one of lazy good fellowship. Asleep, they sprawl in the shade of a tree, touching and leaning against one another, and when they are awake, they lick, groom, play, and greet one another. There is a lot of greeting among lions and it is a pleasant interaction to watch. They greet when they meet after having been separated or upon waking up after a day's rest. The greeting consists of rubbing heads together; the whole body may even be rubbed along the other's, often with a swivel in of the rump and a flick of the tail up and over the other animal. A cub greets its mother by rubbing the top of its head under her chin and then its whole body and tail. Most often the animal greeted will greet in return, but males usually greet only each other. In Nairobi, the adult male known as Scarface did not like being greeted and would sometimes growl at cubs who tried to approach or else lift his head so that they could not reach him. On the whole, greeting among pride members, which indicates peaceful intentions and integrates the group before communal activities, serves to strengthen social bonds.

As one might expect with social, tactile animals, lions also do a certain amount of social grooming. The most grooming is carried out by a mother and her cubs, but adult females also groom each other by licking the head, face, and neck — in other words, those parts that the lion cannot easily reach on its own body. Lions were rarely seen washing their own faces with a front paw in the way that is so common in domestic cats. In both Nairobi and Serengeti, males seldom groomed females, except as a sort of symbolic gesture during courtship; at the same time females did not often groom males. Males are often seen grooming themselves, and the area they give the most attention to is their prime visual sexual characteristic — their thick, flowing manes. The next area in order of attention is their front paws.

But what of these lordly, lazy males sitting around licking their paws? They have come in for a lot of criticism from the popular press for letting the ladies hunt and then stealing the kills. It is true that the females do almost all of the hunting and that the males eat their fill first, but the males play an essential and extremely important role in the success of pride life, and not just by mating with the females; they also make it possible for the females to raise their cubs by providing a safe place for rearing the young. The ultimate criterion for the success of any species is whether it can reproduce itself and raise its young to maturity. Without the pride males and the territorial system that they help to maintain, lions would find it very difficult to fulfill their reproductive potential.

The way in which males associate with prides varies from area to area. The prides in Schaller's study area each had two to four males who, for the most part, associated with only one pride at a time. In Nairobi and Manyara, which are both small parks with high densities of lions, the more common practice was for one or two males to share two or more prides. During most of Rudnai's study there was only one male, Scarface, in the whole of Nairobi National Park (an area of 44 square miles), and he associated with all four prides of females and cubs. In Manyara during Makacha's study, two males together spent about equal time between the Chemchem and Mahali pa Nyati prides, covering an area of about 15 square miles. The Serengeti pride areas were sometimes as large as 150 square miles; thus, it is not surprising that the males associated with only one pride, as they would not be able to maintain more than one area this size.

Males stay with a pride — or prides, as the case may be — for a period of a few months to a few years. In Nairobi National Park a pair of males held an area for six years, but there appears to be a faster turnover in the Serengeti. In the Seronera prides Bertram found that the males changed every two or three years on average. Of the twelve prides that Schaller knew, three kept the same males during the whole three years, but the others underwent changes. These changes occurred for various reasons. Some males simply left for no apparent reason, but most often they were expelled by new males taking over and a few times left to take over a neighboring pride of females. Whether the males stay for two or six years, whether they are associated with one or more prides, their main concern while resident is to maintain the territorial integrity of the pride area, and Schaller's observations have been particularly revealing in regard to this aspect of lion behavior.

The area held by a pride is difficult to classify because it is not an exclusively held, clear-cut territory within definite boundaries. All of it can be termed a home range, and most of it is probably

also a territory, in that strange animals are chased away, but certain areas are rarely visited or defended, while other areas, called
the "foci of activity" (like the core areas of baboons), are used far
more often and are defended more vigorously. For example, the
Maasai pride's focus of activity was 25 square miles, whereas its
whole range was 150 square miles. To avoid confusion, Schaller
prefers to call the whole area that the pride uses its "pride area"
rather than its territory. To a certain extent the size of the pride
area reflects the number of lions in the pride — larger prides
usually have larger ranges — but ultimately the size seems to depend on the amount of prey available throughout the year.

The pride area is held in a number of direct and indirect ways.
Directly, both males and females chase away any intruders;
usually males chase males and females chase females. Males also
patrol the pride area, presumably keeping an eye out for
strangers, and generally seem more alert to their surroundings
than females. Indirectly, males and females proclaim their presence in an area in two ways: by scent marking and by vocalizing.
Both males and females participate in marking and roaring, but
females do less marking in the way of spraying than do males.
Lions mark bushes, trees, and other vegetation by spraying urine
on them. The urine has a strong smell, even to the human nose.
Aside from telling strange lions that there are other lions around,
the marking may also communicate information to fellow pride
members. Roaring also has the dual purpose of communicating to
both pride members and strangers. Lions may roar at any time of
the day or night, but they appear to roar most often early in the
morning before dawn and in the early evening. A roaring lion
may be alone or with other lions, and may be standing, sitting,
walking, or lying down. A roar seems to take quite a bit of
energy — the lion puts its head forward, its sides contract, and it
almost looks as if it were trying to vomit. The sound — a deep
series of rolling grunts reaching a climax and then diminishing
gradually — is undoubtedly stirring and, although somehow not
what one would expect it to be (having watched the M-G-M lion
"roar" from the silver screen all through one's childhood), more

exciting and more penetrating. When heard on a dark, African night, it makes one's spine tingle.

To pride members separated into several groups over the pride area, the roar means: "Here I am; where are you?" Often when one lion in a group begins to roar, the others will join in, and they may be answered by lions a few miles away. It is said that the roar can carry for five miles. At the same time, a strange lion hearing the roar may try to maneuver to avoid the residents, because to the intruder the roar is saying, "This is my land." Neither Rudnai, Schaller, nor Bertram ever heard lions roar while hunting in order to drive animals into ambush, as they are widely believed to do.

The importance of keeping other lions out of the pride area is twofold. First, only so many lions can live in an area before competition over prey becomes too great; and second, strange lions will not hesitate to kill cubs that they come across, and so their presence jeopardizes the safety of the young. This second point is illustrated very well by a series of events that Schaller witnessed during his study.

When Schaller first got to know the prides around the Seronera area, there were two males with the Seronera pride and three males with the neighboring Maasai pride. For the first year of his study there was little, if any, contact between the members of these two prides; then in July 1967 the three males of the Maasai pride were seen in proximity to the Seronera lionesses. In September the Maasai males were again seen near three Seronera lionesses and one of the pride's males, all of whom were on a zebra kill. The next morning Schaller found the Seronera male mortally wounded, evidently from injuries he had received in a fight with the Maasai males, who were still nearby. The male died that morning, and the Seronera females began immediately to associate with the Maasai males; in fact, one of the females, who was in estrus (which may have helped to precipitate the fight), mated with one of these males.

Left without a companion, the second Seronera male soon lost his self-confidence; males from other neighboring prides now penetrated deep into the Seronera pride area, and this remaining male seemed unable to do anything about it. In November three cubs were killed by a strange lioness, probably a nomad, and in December the male was chased by lions from the neighboring Kamarishe pride and was never seen again. On the same day these Kamarishe males killed three small Seronera cubs.

After this incident both the Kamarishe males and the Maasai males returned to their usual ranges, and the Seronera lionesses were left without any males for several months. However, eventually the Maasai males began to spend more and more time with the Seronera females, and by August 1969 they had left their former pride completely. In all, it took these males two years — from their first friendly advances in September 1967 — to make the move from the Maasai pride and to be completely accepted by the Seronera females. Meanwhile, two other males took over the Maasai pride in much less time and with far less upheaval.

It was interesting that at no time during these changes did lionesses of the various prides show any signs of getting together. On the contrary, they remained antagonistic toward one another; Schaller even witnessed a brief fight between the lionesses of the Seronera and Maasai prides when they met one day by chance. Thus, the females maintain a very stable and exclusive grouping; even new males sometimes have difficulty being accepted.

One particularly noteworthy aspect of this series of events is that during the two years of upheaval the Seronera females showed a very poor record of cub rearing. The lionesses produced twenty-six cubs during the period but were able to raise only two, whereas a nearby pride with three males in residence raised twelve out of twenty cubs born. Schaller makes a very strong point when he explains, "It required two years after the death of the male for the pride to settle down to a normal social life. While this may have been an extreme case, hunters who shoot pride males on the assumption that this has no effect on the population might well consider the long-term disruption and lowered reproductive success their act might cause."

Aside from maintaining the integrity of the pride area, a male's main goal is to mate with the females.   Once a male has access to lionesses, he fulfills this role admirably.   In Nairobi National Park the single male, Scarface, had the responsibility of siring cubs all to himself, and he duly mated with the females in each of the four prides.   Dume Kubwa (Big Male) and Chongo (One-Eye) shared the females of two prides in Manyara, and in the Serengeti the pride males took turns with the females in their pride.   When more than one male is concerned, there is rarely any fighting over estrous females — possession seems to be nine tenths of the law. Once a male was in close consortship with a female, the other pride males would not interfere, although they might wait 100 yards or so away.   On two occasions Schaller immobilized a male in consort with a female.   In both cases there was another male waiting nearby, and as soon as his pride mate succumbed to the drug, the waiting male took over the mating of the female.   When the original possessor recovered, he did not try to get the female back but merely took up the waiting position.

However, patience is usually rewarded in these cases, because no one male can keep up the copulation rate that seems to be typical of lions for more than a few days.   One lion mated 157 times in fifty-five hours: in the first twenty-four hours he mated 86 times (74 times with one female and 12 with another); during the second twenty-four-hour period he mated 62 times; and in the remaining seven hours, 9 more times.   During this time he mated every 21 minutes on the average, with a breathing space of as little as 1 minute or as long as 110, and he did not eat.   Since a female may be in estrus for five or six days, it is no wonder that the waiting lion can expect to get his turn.

Typically, a courting pair of lions moves away from the pride, often to an area out in the open.   They then stay in a small area, moving about more or less in a circle.   They sit, or lie down, or walk close together, usually with the male closely following and watching the female.   The mating sequence, as Rudnai describes it, often begins with the lion simply turning his head toward the female and performing the mating grimace by curling back his lips, wrinkling his nose, and showing his teeth.   If the female takes no notice, he may have to come over and give her a few token licks or even lightly paw her to get her attention. Once she notices him, if she is responsive, she will crouch in a copulation posture. He then mounts her, thrusts a few times, and, presumably upon ejaculation, emits a long, drawn-out yowl, at the same time taking the lioness's head or neck between his jaws but not biting down. The lioness makes a growling sound during all this, and just as the male is about to dismount, she will often turn, snarl, and even slap at the male. He then hurriedly dismounts, and she walks a few steps and rolls sensuously on her back, or rolls immediately. The lioness is far from passive in courtship and will often initiate the sequence herself by getting up and walking in front of the male, or very typically curling herself around the male and rubbing against him.

Several factors seem to bring a female into estrus. In both the Serengeti and Nairobi areas, periods with abundant prey in the pride area will bring on estrus, particularly when they have no cubs or their cubs are approaching independence. When one females comes into estrus, this seems to stimulate others in the pride; as a result, several females in the pride often get pregnant around the same time, which facilitates the communal rearing of the young.

A successful fertilization results in a gestation period of 100 to 120 days. When she is about to give birth, the female leaves the pride and goes to a secluded place, in thick vegetation or amid rocks, that she probably chooses beforehand. There she gives birth and keeps her cubs hidden. It has often been claimed that an "auntie" accompanies the female to aid in the birth and help look after the cubs, but Schaller, Bertram, and Rudnai, none of whom has witnessed a birth, have seen no evidence of this.

The cubs, each weighing about 3 pounds, with a spotted, fuzzy coat, are born blind and completely helpless. As lionesses keep their newborn cubs well hidden, it is difficult to determine the size of the average litter in the wild. In zoos the normal range is one to six. Most often the scientist working in the field does not see the cubs until they are five or six weeks old, and by then some of them may have died. The average litter size when cubs were first seen was 2.3 in the Serengeti, 2.2 in Manyara, and 3 in Nairobi.

For the first six weeks the mother divides her time between the pride and her cubs. She hunts and feeds with the pride, then returns to her cubs in order to suckle and groom them. This is a crucial period for the cubs, because in the first few weeks they are always in danger of being taken by predators — leopards, hyenas, and other lions. While their mother is gone, they usually stay hidden and quiet, but they will sometimes play and move around when they become stronger. When the mother comes, usually she calls to them and they come out to greet her, but when she leaves, they return to their hiding place and do not try to follow her.

It is also during these critical early weeks that the cubs are in danger of being abandoned by their mothers. It is the frequent total abandonment of litters that has given rise to the allegations of bad motherhood in the lioness. The reasons for leaving cubs are not easily detectable, but environmental factors must play a role. Schaller thinks that in some cases the pull to the pride is stronger than the maternal instinct and the mother just stops going back to feed her cubs. As Schaller explains, "The response of a lioness to her cubs is so finely balanced between care and neglect, between her own desires and the needs of her offspring, that the survival of the young ones is threatened whenever conditions are not the optimum."

Rudnai speculated on a possible reason why cubs are abandoned. It seems that when a mother has lost all but one cub or has given birth to only one cub, she will almost invariably abandon the single cub if it is less than three months old. This happened several times in Nairobi National Park and has been reported in zoos. George Adamson's semiwild lionesses abandoned single cubs on three occasions, although they later successfully raised litters of several cubs. Refusing to raise a single cub makes sense in terms of reproductive efficiency. If a lioness abandons the one cub, she will come into estrus again almost immediately and will soon have another litter, with the chance of raising two or three cubs.

Once the cubs survive the first six weeks or so, they are introduced to the pride, which, because of the synchronization of estrus and births, often includes other cubs around the same age. From this time on, the cubs are raised communally — they can suckle from other females who are lactating, and should their own mother die, they still stand a chance of surviving. Generally one sees two or three litters of slightly different sizes together. For instance, in the big Seronera pride at one point there were five litters ranging from six weeks to four months. In this case no two of the five litters were more than three months apart in age, and this fact appears to be critical. Rudnai observed that if a lioness gets out of synchrony with the other lionesses in the pride, she may not introduce her cubs at all and will instead raise the cubs on her own. This happens when the cubs already with the pride are more than three months older than her own cubs at the time they should join the pride. Probably the main reason that she then splits off from the other lionesses is that, with cubs so much bigger, her own cubs would be at a tremendous disadvantage in the competition for milk and meat.

The rearing of the young is a lengthy process. Cubs suckle until they are at least seven or eight months old, and sometimes even longer. Several cubs in the Maasai pride were still suckling at twelve months, even though their mother's milk had dried up when they were seven months old; and Rudnai saw fifteen-month-old cubs suckling. Cubs may begin to eat meat at around five weeks old, but the mother does not regurgitate meat for them or bring them small bits of meat as might be expected, so they probably eat very little meat until they can follow their mother to a kill when they are six to eight weeks old.

There are few sights more pleasant to watch than a pride of sleek, well-fed, golden lions stretched out under an acacia tree — the females sleeping peacefully, the young cubs playing or suckling, the big males, a bit off to the side, looking regal and indolent. The life of young cubs growing up in a pride seems very congenial: they spend their time resting, eating, and playing. When they are playing, lion cubs are very appealing indeed, with their huge paws, chubby, ungainly bodies, and mischievous, slightly crossed eyes. They stalk, pounce upon and wrestle each other; attack, shake, and "kill" sticks and stones; ambush their mother and chew on her tail with impunity. Play seems to be an important element in the development of the young, and it also appears to have some importance in the social life of the adults, for lions never totally lose their playful natures. Adult females play with their cubs and with each other; I have seen an adult lioness hide behind a bush and then playfully rush out at another lioness as she walked by. Even adult males sometimes play with cubs.

Unfortunately, one does not always find such a happy scene, for in lean times it is the cubs who suffer first; many of them die of starvation. In this respect lionesses are not altruistic mothers, but here again we risk making a human value judgment. When there is adequate prey around, the females make their kills, leave the carcass (or eat part of it), and go to their cubs and lead them back to the kill; then all feed — not necessarily in peace, but everyone gets something.

In certain seasons in the Seronera area, when the migrating ungulates have moved out and relatively few resident animals remain, there is severe competition for food. Fluctuations in prey abundance are much more pronounced in the Serengeti than they are in parks such as Nairobi and Manyara, where there are adequate resident populations the year round. In the dry season, when the majority of the prey animals are in the north, the lions in the Seronera area rely to a great extent on Thomson's gazelles — small antelopes that barely fill one lion's stomach. It is under these conditions that the lionesses come in for criticism, for then the conviviality of social life breaks down and it is every lion for itself. If a lioness is hungry, she will always fill her own belly first, fighting off her own cubs to do so. There is no sharing if it can be helped — except, oddly enough, sometimes by the males. Schaller found that while the lionesses would not share food with their cubs at these times, the males frequently stole carcasses from the females and then allowed the cubs, but not the females, to share them. This behavioral trait sometimes meant the difference between starvation and survival for some of the cubs. All the same, 67 percent of the seventy-nine cubs born in the Seronera and Maasai prides during Schaller's study died: thirteen were killed by predators, fifteen died of starvation, and twenty-five from unknown causes. Even in other parts of the Serengeti and in other parks the survival rate is only 50 percent, or less, what with predation, starvation, and abandonment.

Once the cubs can begin to hunt for themselves, their chances of survival are increased, but their period of dependence and learning is lengthy. Cubs do not actually begin to participate in the hunt until they are roughly eleven months old. Then they tag after the females, stalk and watch, and sometimes help to bring prey down. It is interesting that by this age male and female cubs already begin to show differences in character and interests. The females display an interest in hunting much earlier; in Nairobi, Rudnai watched two one-year-old female cubs partici- pate in a hunt while their brother stayed behind with younger cubs from another litter. At the same time, male cubs begin to sit apart from the others and show the male characteristic of being more alert to their surroundings.

It is not until the age of fifteen to sixteen months that a cub can catch and kill an animal on its own, and even then it can kill only small prey such as Thomson's gazelles. For larger prey, such as wildebeests and zebras, the cubs still need the help of adults until they are at least two years old. Generally cubs maintain a close relationship with their mother until she has another litter, which usually occurs when they are about two years old. When she in- troduces the new cubs to the pride she may even become aggres- sive toward her older cubs and force them to rest several yards away from the main group.

Eventually the subadult males leave the prides completely: in Serengeti they leave between two and a half and three and a half years old, in Nairobi, much younger — between eighteen months and two years. Some subadult females also leave; whether they do so voluntarily or under force is not always clear. Of twelve female cubs in the Seronera pride whose histories Schaller followed, seven left the pride between two and two thirds and three and a half years, two stayed in the area and visited the pride from time to time, and three remained as full pride members. Further records made by Bertram showed that when the number of adult females in this pride was less than seven, some young females stayed on, but that when the number was seven or more, the subadult females were expelled, and in this way the pride size was regulated.

Both males and females who leave the pride areas become nomads, probably for the rest of their lives, although females are sometimes reaccepted in their prides if there have been losses of adult females, and males may have a chance of becoming residents again if they return to take over a pride area when they are older. The nomads, of which there are about 400, making up only one fifth of the Serengeti population of 2000 lions, include these young lions and lionesses who have left the prides, adult males who leave or have been evicted from prides by other males, and a small number of males and females who have been born and raised as nomads. These lions follow the migration of the wildebeests and zebras, living out on the short grass plains in the wet season and moving right into the woodlands in the dry. One male, No. 57 (Schaller immobilized and tagged 156 lions and was thus able to get valuable records of their movements), ranged over a minimum area of 1800 square miles. Unfortunately for the nomads, they often range right out of the park and frequently are shot.

In terms of social behavior, nomads are strikingly different from residents in their remarkable tolerance of one another. They do not form closed systems but come and go in casual groupings with no fixed composition. However, some companionships are formed that may last a lifetime. Schaller knew of two females who were always together during his whole study, and he watched No. 57 form a friendship with another male that lasted for nearly two years, until No. 57 was killed. Male No. 134 formed a friendship with a female, and they remained constant companions for the rest of the study. The majority of these companionships are composed of two males, who are usually the same age and either are brothers or grew up together in the same pride.

In the wet season, when prey is plentiful out on the plains (where there are no permanent resident lions), two or more nomads may try to set up a temporary territory, but when the migrating animals leave, the lions have to abandon the area. In the Serengeti all available land that is suitable for year-round pride areas is already occupied by lions; the nomad males act as a reserve to replace resident males who die or get old. There is little intrinsic population expansion among the nomads. Nomad lionesses probably get pregnant and give birth as often as resident females, but it is difficult for them to raise their cubs without the secure environment of a guarded territory and the advantages of communal care of the young. Schaller's findings on the difference in reproductive success of nomads and residents show again how important the territorial system is for the lion and provide information essential to any consideration of future plans for national parks and reserves.

When the subadult animals leave the prides in Nairobi National Park, they move out onto the Athi-Kapiti plains, where their fate is unknown. Rudnai has begun a study of the lions out on the plains, hoping to find out what their relationship to the Park's lions is — whether they live as nomads, acting as a reserve, or whether there are resident pride areas out there as well. Rudnai, having devised a highly reliable system of identification that lasts for the life of the lion, can positively identify any lion who has been in the Park since the beginning of her study in 1968. This system does not rely on cuts and scars, which can heal and fade: she recognizes each lion by the pattern of its whisker spots on each side of its face. Since she can identify any cub or adult who has left the Park and is now living out on the plains, she hopes to get some idea of the fate of these animals.

As for the young lionesses who stay with their prides, they

reach sexual maturity and begin to produce cubs at varying ages, depending on the area. The Nairobi lionesses seem particularly precocious: they have their first estrus at about two years old and have their first litters between the ages of two and three. This is even younger than zoo lions, who, being regularly fed, would be expected to grow and mature faster than wild ones. Rudnai has found that each generation of lionesses is maturing at a younger age, indicating that environmental conditions in Nairobi National Park must be particularly good for lions at this time.

In the Serengeti young lionesses have their first estrous periods at three and a half to four years old and generally begin to produce litters at about four years. In both Nairobi and Serengeti lionesses are then able to produce cubs every two years, but since many litters are lost or abandoned or the cubs later starve, lionesses do not actually fulfill their reproductive potential. A good example of this inability to raise as many cubs as might be expected was provided by a well-known lioness in Nairobi National Park called Blondie. She gave birth to seven litters in twelve years but managed to raise only two litters successfully — six cubs in all.

According to zoo records, lionesses sometimes stop breeding after fifteen years old, and Blondie, too, did not produce any more cubs in the last seven years of her life (she was believed to be at least seventeen years old when she died). These older, nonproducing lionesses are still very much a part of the pride and are never ostracized. Schaller, Bertram, and Rudnai all knew old lionesses with worn-down and missing teeth in the prides that they watched. These old females are able to live out their lives — twenty years or more — because others do the hunting and killing.

The life histories of males follow a different course. All young males must leave the security of the pride and develop as nomads. Males mature at about three and a half to four years old and at about the same age have a surge of growth in both body and mane. Males continue to grow until they are about six years old and at full size may weigh over 400 pounds. A full-maned adult lion is an impressive sight, and although some lions with skimpy manes do hold territories and breed, the mane seems to be an important asset. As a sexual characteristic, it functions in two ways: as a signal to females the lion is courting and as a warning to rival males who try to invade his territory. When a male courts a female, he literally struts sideways in front of her, giving her the best view of his hair style. The very distinct outline of a maned lion enables other lions to distinguish males from females at a great distance and thus to avoid unwanted encounters. If males should fight, the mane helps to protect them from scratches and bites.

However, one disadvantage of having a mane is its conspicuousness; as Schaller pointed out, males look like haystacks moving through the grass. A male trying to stalk prey is much more likely to be detected than the sleek, golden female. When the females set off to hunt, the males usually follow behind along with the younger cubs, and in this way, whether consciously or not, the males protect the cubs from other predators. One can only assume that the advantages of the mane to the male patrolling the territory, for example, far outweigh any disadvantage, or else the lion's mane would have disappeared long ago in the course of natural selection.

Once the nomad males reach their prime, or even before, their goal is to become resident pride males, for a successful male is one who passes on his genetic material, and in the lions' social system it is basically only pride females who successfully rear cubs. In order to gain access to these females, a male or group of males must either take over a pride that is without a male or oust the males in residence. In Nairobi a single male, Scarface, ousted the previous single male, but in the Serengeti the key to becoming a pride male lay in forming companionships with another male or males and attempting it as a pair or a group. No one male on its own was ever able to take over a territory in the Seronera area.

If the males are successful, they may be able to hold the territory and sire young for a period of two or three years before they, in turn, are forced to leave. If they cannot then gain another territory, they again take up the life of the nomad, which for an older male is by no means easy. Schaller reckons that fewer than

10 percent of the males reach old age, which would be over fourteen years. Three quarters of the males die violently — killed by poachers and hunters or in fights with other males.

We come now to that essential aspect of the lion that makes it different from the animals discussed before: the lion is a carnivore and must eat meat. Therefore, it must either hunt and kill for itself, find animals already dead from disease (actually few and far between), or steal from another predator. Lions use all of these methods, depending on the circumstances.

In areas with sparse prey or otherwise difficult conditions, a lion may have to spend several hours each day finding enough food for itself, but in most of the areas where lions have been studied, their daily activity patterns indicate that they are remarkably efficient at making a living. In the Serengeti, lions spend twenty out of every twenty-four hours resting. Lions are consummate resters; they stretch out in sometimes ridiculous positions, utterly relaxed and apparently without a worry in the world. This quality makes them a difficult animal to study in a way — the scientist is forever in danger of falling asleep with his subjects. At two o'clock in the afternoon, with everything still and warm, it is a tremendous struggle to stay awake; and at two in the morning, during night observations, Schaller admits that he would sometimes succumb to sleep — and, of course, this was always the time that the lions decided to get up and move.

Despite all the sleeping the lions do, there is a pattern to their "activities." Generally lions rest all day, sleeping, dozing, or just lying around. By late afternoon they begin to get up, stretching and yawning, and often greet each other as if they had been away all day. The cubs begin to play more vigorously, and the females start to get restless as they prepare to set off to hunt. Most hunting is done at night, although the lions in the Serengeti also hunted in the daytime. The lions in Nairobi National Park very rarely hunted during the day, probably partly because of the harassment from vehicles — in fact, they used one part of the Park for resting and another part for hunting, and so had completely different day- and nighttime ranges. Usually hunting, feeding, and drinking take only a few hours and then the lions are able to go back to sleep again. Lions do not necessarily drink every day and, in a place like the Kalahari Desert, may go for several days without drinking.

Although lions kill and eat a wide variety of animals (in the Serengeti, eighteen kinds of mammals and four birds; in Nairobi, fifteen mammals, two birds, and ostrich eggs), they prefer to prey on medium-sized ungulates, such as the wildebeest, zebra, kongoni, topi, and impala. These species make up by far the greatest percentage of lion kills in the Serengeti and Nairobi. Manyara lions seem to be an exception in that the animal upon which they prey most is the buffalo — in particular, large, solitary males weighing as much as a ton. The hunting of buffaloes has to be carried out by more than one lion, and even for a group, to kill a buffalo is no mean feat; lions have been killed in these attempts.

Another lion population that is an interesting exception in terms of food habits is found in the Kalahari in Botswana. These lions live under near-desert conditions and appear to survive mainly on small mammals. F. C. Eloff followed groups of Kalahari lions, using bushmen to track their footprints in the sand. He could trace the activities of a group of lions for miles, and the footprints were so clear that they showed everything the lions had done the night before. The smallest animal that a lion had caught and eaten could be detected and identified from bits of fur or the animal's own tracks. Eloof followed the movements of lions for ninety-one hunting nights and found that more than 50 percent of their kills were of small mammals and the juveniles of larger animals. It came as quite a surprise to find that porcupines made up 25.6 percent of their kills. These figures probably reflect the relative scarcity of larger prey and the particular conditions of the Kalahari, where there is little cover in which to stalk larger animals.

In most areas where there are an adequate number of medium-sized prey, the hunting of small animals is not worth the tremendous expenditure of energy of the hunt for the return of only a few pounds of meat. Depending on its size, an adult lion needs between 11 and 15 pounds of meat a day. In order to get this amount from small prey, it would have to kill several animals in the course of a night. This is not efficient by lion standards. It makes much more sense to hunt and kill one zebra weighing 350 pounds and fill half a dozen stomachs.

The large predators can be divided more or less into two categories: the stalkers and the coursers. The lion is basically a stalker, as it does not have enough speed or endurance to run down its preferred prey. Most of the medium-sized ungulates can easily outrun a lion, whose top speed is only about 35 miles per hour; and the lion cannot sustain this speed for long, as, for instance, the wild dog and hyena can do. The lion must use stealth and tactical maneuvering. The more one hears about the lion's hunting strategies, the more impressed one becomes. Lions are amazingly adept at taking in a situation and using the various elements to their advantage. They use several hunting methods, depending upon the conditions at the time — the positioning of the prey, amount of cover, distance, time of day, etc. They do not appear to use different strategies for different species of prey; the method depends more on the circumstances.

Schaller was fortunate in his choice of study area, because the lions of the Seronera area often hunt along the river courses in the daytime. With observations on both day- and nighttime hunting, he was able to get a good picture of the way in which lions hunt and kill. In the Serengeti lions basically hunt in eight different ways: 1) unexpected hunting, when a lion simply takes advantage of a situation — for example, coming upon a sleeping zebra foal; 2) running, when a lion sees an opportunity and races straight at the prey with no preliminaries; 3) digging animals out of their burrows; 4) grabbing prey that is swimming or has fallen into water; 5) ambushing prey at water holes or along well-used paths; 6) driving, when one or more lions walk or trot openly toward prey, which often, because of the terrain, scatter and run back toward the advancing lions; 7) stalking; and 8) communal hunting.

Stalking and communal hunting are the most common methods employed by lions, and communal hunting is perhaps the most fascinating. Both strategies show the skill of an animal that has evolved to hunt and kill. A stalking lioness is a beautiful thing to watch: she becomes a quintessential cat. Using any available cover — bushes, termite mounds, even a conveniently parked vehicle — she moves carefully through the grass in a crouched, silent walk, her tense muscles rippling under her golden coat. What strikes one is how acutely aware of the prey's reactions the lioness is. (Strangely, lions do not take into account wind direction, as was previously thought, even though they are more successful when they hunt upwind rather than downwind.) If the prey animal stops feeding and lifts its head, the lioness freezes, often with one paw held in midair. As soon as the prey starts to feed again or turns its back, the lioness goes forward, even running several yards if she is certain she will not be detected. If she does startle the prey, either by being seen or smelled, it is amusing to see her sit up and nonchalantly gaze around as if she had not been interested in it at all. If all goes well, however, she continues the stalk until she is close enough to the animal to make a rush. The approach may take half an hour or more, but is usually less. Her chances of success are improved if she can get within 10 to 20 yards of the prey before making the attempt. When she reaches this point, she crouches, often quivering, and waits for the best conditions under which to make her spring. Even George Schaller, who saw numerous kills, never ceased to be moved by this moment: "I found the fleeting hesitation between the end of the stalk and the final explosive rush a moment of almost unbearable tension, a drama in which it was impossible not to participate emotionally, knowing that the death of a being hung in the balance."

The balance, however, is often in favor of the prey. If conditions are just right, the lioness will burst forth, overtake her prey, knock it over or pull it down, and kill it. But far more often, conditions are not right; a lioness stalking by herself succeeds in only 17 percent of her hunting attempts. Many factors may be responsible for a failure. Wind direction may be against her, or she may not have been careful enough, and we have seen how highly cautious prey animals are, how they are wary at water holes and avoid thick vegetation, how different species will alert one another to the presence of a predator and some will actually form a semi-circle around or follow a lion. In an actual attack, some prey animals are amazingly quick to react and outmaneuver the cat; others, like the impala, may confuse the lioness by making tremendous, explosive leaps in the air; others, like wildebeests, may bunch up so that the lioness cannot pick out an individual. All things considered, the lioness has a lot working against her; so she must use every possible advantage, either by hunting at night under cover of darkness or in thick vegetation in the daytime, or by hunting with other lions.

Success is greatly increased — in fact, nearly doubled — by communal hunting, and the results of this behavior must be one of the main advantages of social living for lions. In the Serengeti more than 50 percent of all attempts are made by lions hunting in a group, and so it is the most important method to consider. In a communal hunt two or more lions spread out, forming a broad front, and advance on prey. Usually the lions on the edge of the front go forward more quickly and then circle around behind the prey, often driving it back toward the others. Schaller observed this kind of encircling action twenty-nine times and noted that "the other lions waited during the flanking movement as if in anticipation of prey fleeing in their direction." Having watched their maneuvering, Schaller is convinced that lions knowingly cooperate in this kind of hunting — "Hunts such as these fit the definition of cooperation in that lions orient towards a common goal and their actions are similar, with each animal patterning its behavior after that of the others even to the extent of obviously looking at a neighbor during the stalk."

One of the reasons why the success rate on communal hunts is greatly increased is that lions are sometimes able to kill more than one animal on the same hunt. When a group of prey animals is encircled or driven toward waiting hunters, often each of several lions manages to catch an animal. Schaller has recorded as many as five wildebeests being killed at one time in this way, and Bertram once saw seven killed. Several lions hunting together are also able to kill large prey such as the eland, giraffe, and buffalo.

Having dealt with the problem of catching prey, lions have little trouble killing; they are well endowed with sharp teeth and claws and have tremendous strength. Lions generally knock running prey over with a swipe of a paw or pull it down with both front paws, keeping their hind legs on the ground. Lions rarely leap on an animal, as was so often depicted in old prints; nor do they usually grab prey by the nose in order to bend the head back and break the neck. (Schaller examined several hundred lion kills and could not find a single broken neck.) A small animal such as a hare or a fawn is killed by a bite nearly anywhere on the body. Larger prey, such as a Thomson's gazelle, is knocked down and then bitten, most often in the back of the neck. Medium-sized and large prey are killed either by strangulation or suffocation. As soon as the prey is down, the lion either grasps its throat, biting down on the windpipe until the animal strangles, or grabs the muzzle, covering and closing the animal's mouth and nose until it dies of suffocation. Both methods take several minutes — the longest duration Schaller recorded was thirteen minutes. The whole process of killing is amazingly quiet, and there is very little struggle on the part of the prey animal, except in the case of large animals such as buffaloes.

Once the animal is dead, the lions will sometimes move it to a secluded place or a shady spot. Depending on how hungry the lions are, they may feed quietly or there may be a scene of total social anarchy, with each lion fending for itself and all snarling and slapping at one another. If there are many lions on a kill, they simply eat anything they can get hold of and begin to drag pieces away as soon as possible. When there is less competition, there is usually an order to the feeding: the lions open the carcass at the groin and eat the intestines and inner organs, then the hindquarters, followed by the forequarters and finally the head. An odd habit of lions is to carry away the stomach contents of the prey and try to bury them, usually by scraping grass onto them. The function of this behavior remains a mystery.

A lion can eat an unbelievable amount of meat in one sitting and may get so engorged that afterward it can only sit around panting and looking distinctly uncomfortable. Males can eat about one quarter of their body weight; Schaller saw two males eat an adult topi in twenty hours, each consuming about 95 pounds.

Taking into account the energy requirements for an animal the size of a lion, the amount of meat fed to lions in captivity, and the amount of prey killed and eaten in the wild, Schaller estimated that the 2000 to 2400 lions in the Serengeti ecological unit had to kill or scavenge eleven to thirteen million pounds of meat per year. That figure sounds huge, and one might immediately assume that the lions are having a profound effect on the populations of prey animals in the Serengeti, but what this actually means is that each lion (including cubs) must "kill" about 20 to 30 animals per year; or the total lion population kills 40,000 to 72,000 animals per year. This is actually a very small percentage of the nearly two million ungulates that are available. In fact, most of the lions' favored prey species have increased in number over the last decade, and it is quite obvious that the predators in the Serengeti are having little or no effect on these populations.

On the other hand, the lion population is increasing only very slowly, whereas one would expect that with the dramatic increase of prey such as wildebeests, lion numbers would also increase. But it turns out that the Serengeti lions are limited by the behavior of their prey. It is usually assumed that predators control prey populations, but it is the opposite in the Serengeti, because there, 62 percent of the lions' prey migrate, whereas most lions do not. Schaller concluded that the Serengeti could actually support three times as many lions if there were more prey animals in the pride areas all year round and if the lions that left the Park were allowed to set up territories rather than being shot by hunters and poachers.

Even in a park with as high a density of lions as Manyara has, the main prey species of the lion, the buffalo, seems to be directly limited, not by predation, but by the restricted habitat. Also, in Manyara the lions mostly kill old bulls, which has little effect on the buffalo population.

One of the main reasons that Judith Rudnai was asked to study the Nairobi lions was the authorities' concern over the fact that the lions were killing a disproportionate number of wildebeests and might eventually wipe them out altogether. Before the severe 1960 drought wildebeests were the most common ungulate in the Park and the lions' favorite prey. The drought greatly depleted the wildebeest population, but the lions kept preferentially preying on them out of all proportion to their numbers in the ungulate population as a whole. It was thought that the killing of wildebeests had become a "tradition" among the Nairobi lions.

In fact, there may well have been such a tradition, but it did not remain a hard and fast rule — in nature one must be adaptable, and lions are fairly flexible animals. The Nairobi lions began to kill the far more numerous kongonis, and although they still preferred wildebeests, by the end of Rudnai's study in 1972, wildebeest kills formed a more proportionate part of the lions' diet in relation to what was available; the wildebeest population actually increased between 1968 and 1972. As is so often the case, natural adaptations occurred and it was not necessary for man to step in in order to "manage" the lions.

The lion's popularity may still be swinging back and forth, but people are beginning to see the lion as a natural part of African ecosystems, not just as a ruthless killer of innocent antelopes, a stock raider, a man-eater, a trophy to be hung on a wall, or a superpet. The lion can be viewed as one of the great cats of Africa — a predator who has evolved to carry out a role and just happens to be beautiful, with liquid amber eyes that arouse our emotions.

The Cheetah

It can easily be argued that the cheetah is the most beautiful of the cats. Its long legs, graceful, slim body, and small, rounded head combine to make an aesthetically pleasing whole. Every movement of this cat is executed with a natural elegance that would be the envy of most fashion models. A cheetah never looks awkward or ungainly, and to tourists' delight it always appears to be posing for pictures. Like most of the big cats, it is usually found in repose, stretched out on its side in the shade of a bush or sitting on an anthill, aloofly watching the world go by. It is a rare treat to see a cheetah on the move, and to see one actually hunting is a unique pleasure, for one cannot help being stirred at the sight of that glory of the cheetah — its 70 miles per hour sprint.

As the fastest mammal on earth, the cheetah has long appealed to man's imagination: art work dating from the time of ancient Egypt depicts cheetahs being tamed for hunting. It was the Arabs and Indians, however, who were particularly keen on using cheetahs for hunting: in India cheetahs were trained to kill black-buck antelopes. An interesting aspect of this semidomestication was that the trainers could not get hand-reared cubs to hunt. Only cheetahs captured nearly full-grown showed any hunting ability. The trainers surmised that the young cheetah had to be trained by its mother, and recent studies of wild, free-ranging cheetahs have proved that they were correct. Cheetahs are not born with the knowledge of how to stalk, pull down, and kill prey, although they have the inherent ability to do so. They must go through a long training period, watching their mother, then going along with her, stalking and helping to kill, before they can hunt on their own.

The development of a young cheetah from a ½-pound ball of fluff to a sleek 120 pounds of efficient killing cat is a fascinating process to follow, and Ronald McLaughlin was fortunate in being able to do this in Nairobi National Park. His study period coincided with the birth and rearing of two litters of cheetah cubs, and he watched their growth and development as research for a Master of Science degree at the University of Nairobi.

During McLaughlin's study there were two resident females in the Park, each with a litter of cubs, and two adult male cheetahs who were companions. Other cheetahs came into the Park on a transient basis and were sighted from time to time. McLaughlin concentrated his observations on the two families and, to a lesser extent, on the two males. In all he watched cheetahs for 1600 hours; he points out that he spent at least another 350 hours just looking for them. (He named one of the females Patience — not because she was patient but because it took patience to find her.) McLaughlin recognized individual cheetahs by their spot patterns, particularly on their faces, and by the unique ring patterns on their tails. Gradually the females and their cubs grew more and more used to his presence until they became so familiar with his car that they began climbing up on it to play and to use it as an observation point. This sometimes made it a little difficult for McLaughlin to make his own observations.

Compared to the lion, the cheetah has been studied very little. Randall Eaton observed the Nairobi cheetahs from October 1966 to February 1967. Joy Adamson in 1964 took the now famous Pippa, a family pet, and successfully released her in Meru National Park. Adamson's observations have provided valuable data on age of maturity, the birth and development of the young, and mother-cub relations.

Two filmmakers, Shep Abbott and Tex Fuller, watched and filmed cheetahs in the Serengeti for more than a year beginning in June, 1970, and their observations — although, again, not scientific — have provided some new insights into cheetah life. Also, in the Serengeti George Schaller spent 130 hours observing cheetahs during his 1966–1969 lion study and his wife, Kay, and other observers watched cheetahs when they could. Their records of cheetah kills and killing behavior are particularly valuable.

In 1964–65 two investigators with the firm Wildlife Services surveyed the status of cheetahs at the instigation of the East African Wild Life Society, which was responding to a growing fear that the cheetah might be on the verge of extinction. They collected their data from 205 questionnaires answered by people thought to have knowledge about cheetahs — hunters, wardens, ranchers, etc. With this information they concluded that cheetahs were still widespread in East Africa but occur at extremely varying densities; for instance, in Nairobi National Park there is one cheetah per 3 square miles, whereas in Tarangire National Park in Tanzania there is one cheetah per 170 square miles. The report stated: "In East Africa today, cheetah are still seen over some 406,000 sq. miles of country. Much of this is shared with man and his domestic stock and the expansion of man's activities will steadily reduce this area." The investigators did not recommend that the cheetah be "rescued," but that more research be carried out on the general biology of the cheetah in order to insure its conservation in national parks.

A more recent survey, conducted by Norman Myers for the International Union for Conservation of Nature and Natural Resources (IUCN) and the World Wildlife Fund (WWF), on the status of spotted cats in Africa, produced far more disturbing results. Myers feels that the cheetah is genuinely threatened: according to his data, there may be only fourteen thousand cheetahs left in all of Africa and the population, which has proably declined by half since 1960, may decline by half again in the next ten years.

Obviously the study of cheetahs in national parks and reserves should receive high priority, but McLaughlin's work is the only full-time, intensive, scientific study on cheetahs that has been produced so far. At least it is a beginning, and by combining his results with the earlier observations, we can begin to understand the cheetah's way of life and perhaps get some insight as to why they are declining.

One often hears conflicting statements about the cheetah — that it is social, solitary, territorial, migratory, etc. McLaughlin's study and the observations made by Schaller, Adamson, and others have begun to clear up a few of the misconceptions.

The cheetah's social life does appear to be puzzling. Cheetahs are said to be "sort of social"; that is, their type of social organization falls somewhere between those of the lion and the leopard — the lion being a social, gregarious animal, the leopard being solitary. In the Wildlife Services survey there was a record of twelve cheetahs seen in a group together, all of them adults. More frequently there were reports of two, three, or four adults

together — sometimes all males or mixed sexes, but rarely all
females. Although the most frequent sightings of cheetahs are of
single individuals, the sighting of groups seems to indicate that
adult cheetahs may sometimes live in groups. Closer examination
of the cheetah's way of life will explain the nature of these groups.

Reports of the cheetah's sociality derive partly from its family
life. The mother cheetah raises her young until they are about
seventeen months old, but young cheetahs are indistinguishable
from adults by the time they are about fifteen months old. Thus,
when one sees a female with her nearly independent cubs of both
sexes, they all appear to be adults. After the mother and young
split up, the youngsters often stay together as a group for a while,
and these types of groups are also reported. But soon the young
females, upon reaching sexual maturity, split from their siblings;
they remain solitary thereafter. The males, however, often stay
together into adulthood and remain companions. There are even
indications that they may allow other males to join them, just as
one young male in Nairobi joined two older males (who were
probably brothers) when he became independent.

The cheetah's system of land tenure is not an easy one to figure
out. They seem to be basically residential in some areas and migratory in others, and some observers claim they are territorial.
George Schaller found that the cheetahs in the Serengeti were migratory. There they follow the movements of the Thomson's
gazelles, their preferred prey. He would see his known cheetahs
around the Seronera area for several months at a time, and then
they would suddenly disappear completely for several more
months. They would appear again with the ungulate migration,
often coming back to the same area where he had sighted them
earlier. Schaller speculated that these cheetahs had a very large
home range, in which they moved according to the availability of
prey. He saw no signs of territorial behavior.

In Nairobi National Park during McLaughlin's study there
were eleven resident cheetahs and twenty-two other individuals
who used the Park from time to time. The residents were not
confined to the Park but wandered out at various times, using a

total area of 50 to 60 square miles, but for the most part the two families (one female with three cubs and another with four) and the two males used the Park in a fairly predictable way. It was possible for McLaughlin to plot home ranges for all of them. These ranges overlapped to a great extent, but the groups avoided each other quite deliberately; so there was little interaction.

One of the reasons that cheetahs are thought to be territorial is that they definitely scent mark, particularly the males. They spray bushes and trees with urine and leave their droppings on elevated places such as fallen trees and termite hills. The question is whether these scents and droppings have a territorial purpose — that is, whether they are meant to influence other cheetahs to stay out of the area. It would appear that the markings do not function in this way. When a cheetah comes upon the scent marking of another cheetah, it usually shows some interest. But it does not change its course; it continues on in the direction it was heading. Thus, the cheetah does not appear to be particularly concerned about entering an area that may "belong" to someone else. (Another cat, the North American cougar, who is territorial, reacts in just the opposite way: a cougar coming across the scent of another will immediately turn around and leave.)

Also, behavior that might appear to be linked to territory has rarely been observed. McLaughlin did not observe males fighting with males or females fighting with females. He did see males fighting with family groups, but in these cases the male was not trying to chase the female and cubs away; he seemed to be trying to keep them from leaving him. Alan Root, the wildlife filmmaker, saw and filmed two male cheetahs attacking and eventually killing a third male in the Serengeti, but this is the only such case recorded and the circumstances surrounding the incident are unclear.

The aspects of cheetah behavior that are fairly well understood now are the birth and development of the young and the relationship between mother and cubs. These areas have been investigated by both McLaughlin and Adamson, and their observations have been fascinating. Adamson's tame, free-ranging cheetah

Pippa mated with wild males and produced four litters of cubs by the age of four and a half, when she died. In all cases, Pippa led Adamson to the cubs before they were two weeks old. There were three cubs in the first litter, and four in each of the following three. As very few cheetah cubs have been born in captivity, there are few records of average litter size, but the range appears to be one to six. There is one record of a cheetah having been seen with eight cubs, all the same size, who appeared to belong to her. Pippa had thirteen teats, the tame lioness Elsa had five, and a baby leopard in Adamson's care had four; so it seems possible that a cheetah might suckle eight cubs, but this must be highly unusual. In the wild the average litter size falls somewhere between three and four, which is higher than those of either lions or leopards.

Pippa chose as her birth lair very thick bushes, almost impossible for a human (or, probably, any other large predator) to get into or even see into. In Nairobi McLaughlin found that the females used a flattened area in high grass, and in the Serengeti Abbot and Fuller found newborn cubs hidden in thick vegetation on a tiny island of hard ground in a marsh. The mother cheetah apparently tries to find the safest place for her vulnerable cubs.

A cheetah cub is a very strange-looking little thing. Like most cats, it is born with its eyes closed and can move only just enough to get to its mother's teats and suckle. The cheetah has an unusual natal coat; the lower half of its body is dark, nearly black, and the upper half is covered with a highly conspicuous mantle of long blue-gray hair. This mantle remains on the cub for about three months; its function is unknown. (The young cheetah retains a short ruff on the nape of the neck until adulthood; this is often the only way of distinguishing large cubs from adults.) Shadings on animals usually go from a darker color on top to a lighter color on the bottom (as, for example, with many of the antelopes); so the cheetah cub's coloration is unusual. Perhaps the mantle acts as a camouflage when the young cheetah is lying down in the shade of a bush or amid long grass.

Cheetah cubs remain nearly immobile in their birth lair for at least a week and open their eyes on around the tenth day. By this age the mother may have moved them to another lair. In the first six weeks of the cubs' life, Pippa moved her second litter twenty-one times and her fourth litter fourteen times, usually to a new bush about 200 yards away. (Her first and third litters were taken by predators before they were six weeks old.) On the other hand, a cheetah mother in Nairobi moved her cubs only three times in six weeks. When the mother cheetah moves her cubs, she moves them one at a time, picking each one up more or less by its nape; she sometimes drops them a few times on the way, but they seem none the worse for wear. She may go back to the lair several times to check that she has not missed one; apparently she is unable to count. As the cubs are highly vulnerable to preda-tion, she is probably moving them to keep the smell of them and herself from accumulating.

The mother stays with the cubs during the night, suckling and grooming them, and hunts in the daytime. She usually leaves the cubs at dawn; they remain behind, sleeping, and only occasionally move about or make any noise. The mother may be away all day if she does not make a kill until the afternoon, but McLaughlin observed that as soon as she finishes eating, she immediately re-turns to her cubs. If she has had a large meal, she stays with them that night and the whole of the next day, and then sets out to hunt the following morning.

By the age of about six weeks, the cubs begin to follow the mother some of the time but still return to a lair. The com-munications between mother and cubs are fascinating. Like the lioness, the cheetah mother goes to the lair and calls to her cubs; she makes a "whickering" sound and they come out to greet her. The calls made by the mother and young — chirping noises that sound like high-pitched bird calls — seem very peculiar for a large cat. Cheetahs also have a range of growls, hisses, and spits similar to that of other cats; however, the cheetah is the only big cat that purrs with a continuous sound like a domestic cat.

By eight weeks old, the cubs begin to follow their mother all the time and no longer return to a specific hiding place; now they simply go where she goes and bed down for the night wherever they happen to be when evening comes. It is when they begin following the mother that they are most vulnerable to predation, as they are not yet fast or alert enough to get away from predators. One of Pippa's six-week-old cubs from the fourth litter was killed by lions when the cheetah family happened upon a pride. One lion bit the youngster in the nape, killing it instantly, and then just left it. Predators are not tolerant of one another. Schaller reckoned that one-third to one-half the cheetah cubs die between the ages of five to six weeks and about three to four months; after that, mortality is low. McLaughlin estimated an overall cheetah cub mortality of 43 percent, which is lower than that for lion cubs.

A female cheetah who loses a litter comes into estrus soon afterward. When Pippa lost her first litter, she conceived three weeks later, and when she lost her third litter, she came into estrus and conceived a week later. Thus, cheetahs can be highly productive in the wild; why it is so difficult to get them to breed in captivity remains a mystery.

If the cubs get through the difficult period when they first begin following their mother, then they gradually get stronger and more alert to danger and are soon able to watch out for themselves. By three months old they are beautiful little creatures, a bit awkward but not clumsy-looking like lion cubs. They are very playful, and the mother may also join in their games. McLaughlin found that most of their play could be related to hunting tactics rather than to fighting, but they also seem to play for the pure joy of releasing pent-up energy. They stalk and pounce, race around, climb trees, slide down termite hills, and play "king of the mountain" on any convenient mound.

Compared to the lion cub, the cheetah cub is weaned fairly early. Pippa's cubs began to eat meat that Adamson brought them at five weeks old and were weaned at ten to eleven weeks, although Pippa's milk did not dry up for twenty-four weeks. McLaughlin has some evidence that the female Patience regurgitated meat for her four-week-old cubs. This behavior has also been recorded in captive cheetahs. Once the cubs start following the mother, they begin feeding on kills almost immediately. Eight-week-old cubs were seen feeding on a fresh kill in Nairobi National Park.

Cheetah cubs show interest in the hunting behavior of their mother almost from the time they begin following her. However, they are more of a hindrance than anything else at that age. As the mother carefully approaches prey, the cubs often run out ahead, alerting the prey and spoiling the hunt. Soon they learn to follow quietly behind; then when the female catches the prey, they quickly run up and may begin to eat before she finishes killing it. As soon as the mother drops the prey, a cub even only a few months old will often grab its throat in a strangle hold and sometimes struggle with it as if it were still alive. During feeding, one cub at a time may stop eating in order to take up the strangle hold — a behavior that serves as useful practice for killing when they are older.

When a mother and her cubs feed on a kill, even when the prey is small, there is not the fierce competition over the carcass that one sees with lions. After making the kill, the mother cheetah usually sits down and rests, but also keeps watch for other predators while the cubs eat, showing little antagonism toward one another. A few growls may be heard and there might be a tug of war — rarely lasting more than a few seconds — over a single piece, but on the whole, feeding is carried out very peacefully. No female cheetah has ever been known to take a carcass away from her cubs and consume it herself, as a lioness is apt to do. On the other hand, Abbot and Fuller saw and filmed several instances of male cheetahs stealing carcasses from females and cubs.

One of the most striking aspects of the relationship between a mother cheetah and her cubs is the way in which she deliberately provides opportunities for the cubs to learn hunting skills. She may do this in several ways. Indirectly, she will not interfere in the cubs' efforts to catch and kill prey until they have botched several attempts. Directly, she will capture prey and, when the cubs arrive, release her strangle hold on the weakened but still living animal and let one of the cubs kill it. The cub's efforts may be nearly ineffectual, but, again, she will not interfere unless the prey gets up and starts to run away. Also, a cheetah mother will capture a small, juvenile animal, release it near her cubs, and then stand by while they try to catch and kill it. She may even catch it for them several times, bringing it back and releasing it repeatedly.

Cubs have been seen making a kill without their mother's help at the age of five months, but usually it is not until they are about fourteen months old that young cheetahs can successfully stalk and kill prey. McLaughlin found that even at fourteen months the young cheetah does not always remain properly concealed or watch the prey carefully. It may also stalk prey of an inappropriate size — adult zebras and waterbucks, for example; one cub was seen stalking a herd of buffaloes, who turned and chased it.

When the cubs are fifteen months old, they are as large as their mother; the male cubs may be even larger. By now they may take the lead in movements and may take the initiative in hunts, whereas when they were younger, the mother was always the obvious leader. Between fifteen and seventeen and a half months old they make a complete break with their mother. Both Schaller and McLaughlin witnessed this break — Schaller with one family and McLaughlin with two. The break is very strange indeed, because it is so abrupt and total. In all three cases the mother and cubs were seen together one day; then the next day they were apart, and they were never seen in proximity again. With many animals — certainly with lions and leopards — independence comes gradually, as the mother and offspring spend less and less time with each other, finally splitting up; or else some antagonism is shown, particularly toward young males, who may be harassed until they leave. But the cheetah families that Schaller and McLaughlin watched showed no behavior indicating that a break was about to occur.

On the other hand, a different situation occurred with Pippa's first surviving litter. From about eleven months the cubs began to spend more time away from Pippa, sometimes spending up to half a day on their own, but always within a mile of her. When the cub called Whitey was sixteen months old, she left her mother and two sisters for seventeen days, but it was not known what she was doing. Adamson speculated that she was with a male, as Pippa had gone off with a male at about the same age, although neither appeared to get pregnant at the time. When the cubs were seventeen and a half months old, they made a final and complete break with Pippa. This more gradual break between mother and cubs may not have been altogether natural, because Adamson still fed both Pippa and her cubs.

In both the breaks that McLaughlin witnessed, the cubs left the mother as a group at sixteen to seventeen months old and stayed together for a while afterward. The two female cubs that Schaller watched also stayed together, and although they shared the same range as their mother and saw her from a distance from time to time, they rarely met, and "at such times they haughtily ignored one another as if they were strangers." By the following year, when they returned to Schaller's study area, the sisters had also split up.

It is not known why cheetahs have not evolved a social life. They might be more successful if they did cooperate in hunting and raising young, but perhaps the niche they fill can only accommodate a solitary hunter. Whatever the case, they have obviously not evolved many interactions that would create strong social bonds. What strikes one most about cheetahs is their amazing aloofness. Most of the time they seem totally detached from their companions. Cheetahs groom each other, but usually only after a meal, when their faces have blood on them, or after a rainstorm, when their coats are wet. They also greet each other, but most often just by sniffing each other's faces or briefly touching cheeks. They do not rub against each other sensuously as lions do. As Schaller expressed it, "Their contacts seemed constrained; they lacked the intense and uninhibited desire to touch one another that is found in lions."

In fact, female cheetahs seem to be so intent on keeping their distance from other cheetahs that any contacts they have with males appear to be fraught with aggression. Some of the interactions that McLaughlin witnessed between the families and the two males in Nairobi were very puzzling indeed. Whenever he saw males and females together, the animals were all highly tense and nervous. Four out of the six times that he saw males and family groups together, they all fought vigorously — on one occasion for an hour and forty minutes! The males would attack both mother and cubs, trying to bite them on the flanks and hindquarters, while the female and cubs tried to defend themselves and strike back. Although these fights appeared very violent, the animals involved received only minor scratches and bites. As was mentioned earlier, these skirmishes did not seem to be territorial in nature: the males did not try to chase the female and cubs away; rather, they appeared to be trying to keep them from leaving. What they wanted to do with them is another question. McLaughlin thought the encounters might be of a sexual nature, although the female did not appear to be in estrus.

McLaughlin observed what appeared to be premating behavior several times, but on most of these occasions there was also a surprising amount of aggression. Whenever the male (or males) tried to get near the female, she either behaved defensively or actually attacked him. On the one occasion that McLaughlin saw a male and female together showing little aggression, she gave birth three months later; so presumably there was a successful mating, although McLaughlin did not witness it. This high level of aggression between males and females — combined with the other disturbing elements that captivity creates — may be one clue as to why cheetahs rarely breed in zoos. (Schaller speculates that females want to breed with strangers, not friends. In most zoos males and females are kept together; he suggests that they be kept separate except when the female is in estrus.)

In the wild, cheetah females first conceive at about twenty-two months old. As the gestation period is ninety to ninety-three days, the cheetah finds herself a mother at around two years old. She may already be pregnant again by the time her cubs become independent at sixteen to seventeen months; so she can produce a new litter again in less than two years — a relatively fast reproductive rate for a large cat that must raise and train its young to make a living.

The daily activities of cheetahs revolve around making a living — for the carnivore, that means the hunt. Of the big cats the cheetah is the only predominantly diurnal, or daytime, hunter. (It has also been reported making kills on moonlit nights.) Cheetahs are most active during the early morning hours, and it is then that they are most likely to make a kill. In the two family groups that McLaughlin watched, the activity pattern was as follows: between 5:30 and 6:00 A.M. the cheetahs began to stir, sitting up, stretching, and yawning. If they were hungry, they began moving immediately. They walked at a leisurely pace but searched for prey the whole time. If they did not make a kill, they continued walking until late morning, and then rested during the heat of the day. They usually became active again in the afternoon and continued moving either until they had killed or until 7:00 to 7:30 P.M., when they bedded down. (McLaughlin's study confirmed that cheetahs are basically diurnal. When he stayed with them throughout the night, they rarely moved, and when he did not stay, he could usually find them in the same spot or nearby at dawn the next morning.)

While the cheetah families were on the move, they were always alert, stopping often to look around. Even during the rest period in the middle of the day they sat up and looked around as often as ten times an hour. (They may have been interested in prey animals from time to time, but they were also probably keeping a lookout for larger predators.) In all, the family groups were active about five hours during a day and covered an average distance of about 2¾ miles, with a maximum of 7 miles.

Male cheetahs seem to have a slightly different activity pattern from family groups. When a mother and her cubs are on the move, it is almost always with the purpose of finding prey, but males move without searching for prey, wandering around their range inattentively, compared to the families. McLaughlin found that males moved 4½ miles on average during the day and apparently did quite a bit of traveling at night. In one twenty-four-hour period they walked nearly 9 miles — perhaps in the hopes of actually finding a "friendly" estrous female for a change!

For the female and her cubs, though, the hunt is obviously the prime mover in their daily activities, and in terms of day-to-day existence, it is the most important event. With excellent reports from McLaughlin, Schaller, and Eaton, we now have good descriptions of how cheetahs hunt and kill, what they kill, and how many prey animals they take.

Scientists attempting to classify the predators as stalkers and coursers sometimes call the cheetah a courser; this is one of the many reasons it is considered doglike, along with its nonretractable claws, its somewhat greyhoundlike shape, and its uncatlike habit of hunting in the daytime. Although it may not be of the standard shape, the cheetah is most definitely a felid; its diurnalness and nonretractable claws are not enough to make it a dog. Furthermore, the cheetah is not a true courser: it does not have the endurance to run down its prey as wild dogs and hyenas do; rather, it sprints over a short distance at a very high speed in order to catch its prey. Moreover, most of its chases are preceded by careful, stealthy stalking.

The cheetah is a glorious hunter — in that flash of spotted gold one sees an animal performing what it has evolved for thousands of years to do so well, and somehow in that moment it is in essence the logical conclusion of natural selection. The cheetah is a particularly successful hunter. Of the five big African predators, it is second only to the wild dog in success rate, judged by the percentage of the times it kills in the attempts it makes.

Nevertheless, a cheetah cannot just decide to chase any prey that it happens upon. It is limited by its own size, strength, and physical traits: it has relatively weak jaws and teeth, and those blunt, nonretractable claws. Cheetahs rarely hunt animals weighing more than 130 pounds — the top weight of cheetahs themselves. When two or more cheetahs — such as a family group with large cubs or, more often, two or more male companions —

hunt together, they can kill larger prey. The males in Nairobi National Park killed adult kongonis and zebras, but the majority of the cheetah kills in Nairobi ranged from 10 pounds (newborn impalas and Grant's gazelle fawns) to 130 pounds (Grant's gazelle bucks). The four main prey species in Nairobi, accounting for 85 percent of all kills during McLaughlin's study, were the impala, Grant's gazelle, Thomson's gazelle, and kongoni. Of the 183 cheetah kills examined, 53 percent were of juvenile animals, which clearly demonstrated selection, as juveniles made up only 19 percent of the Park's prey populations.

In the Serengeti the cheetahs showed a remarkably strong preference for one species: the Thomson's gazelle. Of the 261 cheetah kills that Schaller found, 91 percent were of Thomson's gazelles. Schaller estimated that about two thirds of the kills were of animals under one year old; so there, too, the cheetah selects juveniles. In both Nairobi and the Serengeti the animals killed seemed healthy and previously uninjured, but in choosing them the cheetah may have detected slight weaknesses.

When hunting, the cheetah sets out and searches for its preferred size and species of prey. The search is entirely by sight, not by smell, and the cheetah's eyesight is acute. Many times McLaughlin had to use his binoculars to see what a cheetah was watching intently. As the cheetah moves along, it frequently stops and looks around, and it may jump up on vantage points such as low trees, termite mounds, and rocks. When the cheetah sights an animal, it stops and tenses, often lowering its head and pricking up its ears. Then it may or may not make an approach; this seems to depend on the size of the prey, the time of the cheetah's last meal, and whether the prey has spotted the cheetah.

In all, McLaughlin saw 271 hunting attempts, which he defined as an approach and/or a chase. Cheetahs made approaches in one of the following three ways: running to within chase range of unsuspecting prey; walking openly toward alerted prey; and stalking. The first two techniques of approach are usually used in open terrain. However, the stalk was by far the most frequently used hunting method in Nairobi; in fact, nearly three quarters of all approaches were made by stalking. This contradicted the widely held assumption that cheetahs never stalk. Although the cheetah used the first two methods more frequently in the Serengeti, Schaller still saw cheetahs stalking prey quite often, and he emphasized the importance of this method of hunting to the cheetah. In the Serengeti, where cheetahs often hunt on short grass plains, the first two methods would be more appropriate, as there is little cover for stalking. In Nairobi National Park, however, which has an uneven terrain with areas of scattered bush and trees, and tall grass, the conditions are more suited for stalking and the cheetah takes full advantage of them.

If the cheetah sees prey and knows it cannot be seen, it may begin the stalk walking rapidly, with its head up, but as soon as it is close to the prey or the prey becomes wary, it crouches down in the more typical stalking posture, with the head held low and legs slightly bent. The cheetah will not make a direct approach if the prey is facing it but instead will circle around so that it can approach from the side or rear. (Like the lion, the cheetah apparently does not take wind direction into account.) A cheetah will use natural obstacles to hide behind in its stalks but will not deviate from its path to do so. The cheetah watches the prey intently, and if it turns or lifts its head, the cheetah will freeze; sometimes it actually drops to the ground to avoid being detected. As soon as the prey animal resumes feeding, the cheetah begins to stalk again. If it is approaching a whole herd, it will wait until all the animals are looking the other way or feeding. As it gets closer, it becomes more and more cautious. McLaughlin says, "In the final stages of the approach, the cheetah moves very slowly, deliberately placing each step. Just prior to the chase, it usually stops, watching the prey intently. At this time, very slight movements of the feet are common, often just a shifting of weight from one foot to another." The cheetah will usually try to get within 50 to 60 yards of the prey before beginning the chase; then when the prey is not watching it makes its move, often by trotting a few steps first, then breaking into a run and attaining the full speed of the sprint almost immediately. A cheetah has been timed accelerating from a standing start to a speed of 45 miles per hour in two seconds and covering 65 yards in that time. Within another few seconds it can be running at 70 miles per hour. (A greyhound's top speed is about 39 miles per hour and a race horse's, 47.5 — they seem stolid in comparison.) With a newborn fawn, the chase may cover only a few yards; with an adult gazelle, several hundred yards.

Success or failure depends a great deal on the size of the prey. For young fawns, the cheetah has a 100-percent success rate. In the Serengeti cheetahs were successful in 54 percent of their chases of older juveniles and adults; for adults and young combined, the success rate was 70 percent. In Nairobi the overall success rate was 37 percent. This lower rate may reflect less favorable hunting conditions, but it is still high when compared to that of lions, who, at their best, when hunting in a group, are only successful 30 percent of the time.

Cheetahs may fail in their attempts for a number of reasons. The cheetah's long straight legs make it difficult for it to turn fast, and often the prey gets away by making sharp zigzag turns that the cheetah cannot follow. One cheetah was seen to slip and fall as it tried to make a fast turn. Cheetahs may also fail because they have started a chase from too far away: Eaton noted that in successful chases the average distance between the cheetah and the prey at the start of the chase was 58 yards; in unsuccessful chases the distance averaged 217 yards. Also, erratic flight patterns may confuse the cheetah, and flight through dense vegetation or difficult terrain may impede its run. Some animals, such as adult kongonis and warthogs, may actually turn and attack, and this will usually discourage the cheetah, although Eaton observed that a group of four male cheetahs took advantage of this behavior in kongonis and specialized in killing them as they came forward threateningly.

In the successful chase the cheetah gains on the animal until, coming up behind it, the cheetah reaches out with one or both front paws and knocks it over. It is commonly thought that the blow of the cheetah's paw knocks the prey off its feet or that somehow the cheetah trips up its victim. But Randall Eaton has come up with a different explanation. He was able to do some interesting research on hunting techniques by filming captive cheetahs in a safari park in the United States. The cheetahs were in a large enclosure and were given live sheep and goats to kill. (Whether the behavior pattern holds true with the far faster wild prey has yet to be determined.) The slow-motion film showed what the cheetah actually does when it comes into contact with the prey: it reaches out with one or both paws and hooks the flank or rump with its dewclaw (the fifth claw on the inside of the leg above the foot and the only sharp claw the cheetah has), then throws its own weight backward to unbalance the prey and bring it down. (Also of interest in these films was the cheetah's use of its long tail, which acted as a counterbalancing rudder when the cheetah made fast turns.)

Once the animal is knocked down, the cheetah quickly comes around from behind the animal and grabs its throat. With this grip, the cheetah closes down on the trachea and strangles its prey. Once the animal is dead, the cheetah releases its hold and almost always rests before beginning to feed; usually, it is still panting from the struggle of the hunt. If there are cubs along, they will begin to feed immediately; sometimes the mother will break open the skin of the animal for them. As the cubs feed, the mother looks around nervously, for a cheetah must be alert to other predators once it has made its kills. Lions, leopards, wild dogs, and hyenas can all easily take a kill from a cheetah, who does not try to defend a carcass from these animals. Twice George Schaller saw a cheetah give up its kill to a solid front of approaching vultures, but usually the cheetah can keep vultures and jackals off.

Sometimes the cheetah will move a kill to a safer, less exposed place, but often it just feeds where it is, starting at the thigh of a hind leg. An adult cheetah can eat as much as 20 pounds of meat at one sitting, but often it is interrupted in its feeding and may have to leave before it has had its fill. Schaller reckoned that 12 percent of all cheetah kills end up in another animal's stomach.

Fortunately, the cheetah is a relatively adept hunter and has a good chance of making another kill that same day if it should lose its meal. Schaller, his wife, Kay, and other observers kept one cheetah female under observation during daylight hours for twenty-six days. During that time, she killed twenty-four Thomson's gazelles and one hare — almost one kill per day. On three days she did not kill at all, but on two days she killed twice. The cheetahs in Nairobi National Park killed approximately once every two days. This killing rate seems high compared to those of lions and leopards, but usually a cheetah must eat its fill as quickly as possible and then leave the carcass for fear of other predators. It cannot stay by its kill and feed from the carcass for a day or two, as lions can; nor does it store its food in trees the way the leopard does. Also, cheetahs rarely pick up a free meal by scavenging; apparently they shun carrion. McLaughlin even offered cheetahs fresh carcasses and they would not touch them.

One might suppose that cheetahs, being such successful predators, would take a fair toll of prey animals every year, and, understandably, parks administrators want to know what effect cheetah predation is having on the prey populations. Except for Nairobi, cheetahs live at such low densities that they barely have any effect at all. In the Serengeti there are probably only 200 to 250 cheetahs in the 12,000-square-mile ecosystem. Schaller estimated that these cheetahs kill 27,000 to 35,000 animals every year. As at least 60 percent of those killed are Thomson's gazelles, this species should elicit the most concern. Cheetahs take an estimated 16,000 to 21,000 gazelles each year, but there are over half a million Thomson's gazelles in the Serengeti; so cheetahs are killing only approximately 4 percent of the population, which, on its own, would not seriously affect the numbers of gazelles. It is possible that the combined effect of all the predators of Thomson's gazelle would keep their numbers in check.

In Nairobi National Park the picture is different. There the cheetahs prey heavily on juveniles, particularly young impalas and Grant's and Thomson's gazelles. McLaughlin reckons that the cheetahs kill about 640 prey animals a year, the majority of them young animals. He feels that the impala and gazelle populations (estimated at 547 impalas, 244 Thomson's gazelles, and 427 Grant's gazelles during his study in 1968 and 1969) would increase if there were no cheetahs but that the current situation is not necessarily bad. As no one has yet studied the population dynamics and ecology of the impala and gazelle populations in the Park, it is impossible to say, but it may be that the cheetahs are keeping the numbers of these animals at a level that is desirable given the particular capacity of the Park. In any case, the cheetahs are not causing a decline in their major prey species.

The important question, as far as the cheetah is concerned, is not what effect they have on prey populations, but what the future of the cheetah itself is. Norman Myers' report for the IUCN/WWF is very disturbing indeed. It looks very much as if the cheetah may be on its way to extinction, and we still do not really know why. Compared to lions and leopards, cheetahs have large litters; there is not excessive cub mortality; the young mature at an early age; and cheetahs are relatively successful hunters and are not limited to a fixed range in their pursuit of prey. They seem to have many factors in their favor, and yet they are scarce.

One can only speculate as to why they are declining. Several factors are probably responsible. First, but not necessarily foremost, the cheetah has been heavily poached in some areas for its spotted skin which, though not so highly prized as the leopard's, is a good status symbol all the same. When spotted skins were the fad in the United States in the sixties, fifteen hundred cheetah skins entered the country each year.

Second, it is thought that the cheetah may have evolved its present way of life and hunting style in open, semiarid habitats that, more and more, have been taken over by humans and their cattle. Cheetahs are nervous, shy animals and cannot tolerate the disturbance of living in close proximity with man; so they have retreated to other areas where the habitat may not be so well suited to them. Joy Adamson speculates that when cheetahs live in less favorable habitats they are more prone to injuries, since it may be necessary to hunt less appropriate prey and in rougher terrain. A cheetah with even a slight injury is badly handicapped, as its hunting depends so much on its speed. (Pippa died as the result of a broken leg; one of her cubs also broke a leg but recovered with the help of veterinary attention.)

Third, being low in the predator hierarchy, the cheetah is at a disadvantage in competition with the other carnivores. It is postulated that where there are many hyenas, cheetahs have a difficult time, because their kills are constantly being stolen and their cubs are often killed. It is interesting that there are few hyenas in Nairobi and Amboseli National parks, places with relatively high densities of cheetahs.

And fourth, wherever cheetahs are safe from poachers, have good open country for hunting and moderate competition from other predators — in other words, in national parks and reserves like Nairobi, Serengeti, and Amboseli — they are continually being harassed by tourists. As a diurnal, open plains hunter, the cheetah is easily spotted by tourist guides and pursued while it tries to make a kill. This almost invariably spoils the hunt. When trying to rest in the daytime, the cheetah is surrounded by vehicles with engines running, as each car tries to maneuver into a better position for that perfect picture. This kind of harassment is seen frequently, and although complaints are sometimes made, very little has been done about it. Tourists do not understand what is happening, and the drivers and guides are thinking only about their tips at the end of the game run.

The situation in Amboseli National Park is a good example. This area was always one of the best places for seeing cheetahs — in the dry season, when game concentrates in the area, at least one cheetah was seen nearly every day. But in the last year or so, it has been getting more and more difficult to find cheetahs, and it is feared that they may be dying out or moving out of the area. Wesley Henry, a research associate at the University of Nairobi who has been carrying out a study on tourist use and behavior in Amboseli, recently spent a three-week period concentrating on the effects of tourists on cheetahs. Out of the twelve days when he found cheetahs with tourists, at least half the time the cheetahs were so seriously disturbed that they ran away, and on one of the days the cheetah's hunt was ruined by tourist cars speeding up to the scene in a cloud of dust.

It would be very sad indeed if it turns out that the parks and reserves — the places that perhaps offer the cheetah its last hope — are actually contributing to and accelerating its extinction.

The Leopard

There are certain adjectives that affix themselves to a word or a name so that they almost become a part of the word itself. The word *leopard* is rarely heard or seen without the accompanying adjectives *solitary*, *secretive*, and, particularly, *elusive* — the phrase "the elusive leopard" appears in nearly every wildlife book. Unfortunately for the tourist or the wildlife scientist, this phrase is all too apt. The leopard is wary, shy, difficult to find, and, even when found, difficult to see. With the exception of Serengeti National Park, there are no other parks or reserves in Africa where the leopard can readily be seen without the aid of baits set out in artificial light. This does not mean that leopards do not exist in many of the parks; they do and in greater numbers than one might guess, only they are seldom seen. Leopards are apparently adept at organizing their lives so as to avoid encounters with man.

One result of the leopard's secretive ways is that it is extremely difficult to find out how many leopards there are in any given place, or in East Africa, or in Africa as a whole. For years now, the leopard has been considered an endangered species, and certainly any animal whose skin is worth so much on the international fur market should be considered potentially endangered, but despite all the poaching for skins, the leopard is still numerous and widespread.

Unlike the cheetah, the leopard is a consummately adaptable animal. Of the large predators, it is the only one that can live in proximity with man and not even be detected. There are occasional reports of leopards seen crossing the roads in one of Nairobi's residential suburbs. These leopards are probably surviving in the patches of natural forest that remain in the area, living on an occasional bushbuck or duiker, but mainly on the small mammals — monkeys and hyraxes — with which they share the forest. Leopards can maintain this kind of existence for years, as long as they do not develop one of their renowned habits — preying on domestic dogs. People are willing to have leopards in their backyards as long as they "behave themselves."

In the survey that Norman Myers carried out on leopards and cheetahs for the IUCN/WWF, he reports that leopards are still abundant in five of the forty-three countries south of the Sahara and holding their own in fifteen others, and he speculates that there could be more than a hundred thousand leopards in the whole of Africa. What is more, he concludes that their numbers are not being depleted as rapidly as the lion's or even the giraffe's. In some areas leopards have been heavily poached and their numbers have declined drastically, but in other areas, particularly the central rain forests, they have been largely untouched. However, this does not mean that restrictions on hunting leopards should be relaxed or that women should start wearing leopard-skin coats again. As human population increases, the leopard's range will have to get smaller and smaller. Although it may be the last large carnivore able to exist outside of protected areas, its final refuge will eventually be the national parks and reserves.

Conservationists want to know what the future is for leopards in national parks. This is a question that cannot be answered until baseline information on leopards is obtained. To date (1974), there has not been a single scientific paper published dealing exclusively with the ecology or behavior of the free-ranging leopard in Africa. A full-length book called *The Leopard,* by Peter Turnbull-Kemp, contains some interesting information but very little material on the behavior of wild leopards. The leopard is only just beginning to be studied, and the reason for this delay goes back to the problem of the "elusive leopard": how can one study an animal that one rarely sees? Although few data are available as yet, I think it is worthwhile to show what research has been attempted, how the workers went about it, the problems they met, and some of the results that have emerged.

A few scientists — most notably, George Schaller — watched leopards when they could during their studies of other animals, but a full-time study of free-ranging leopards became potentially rewarding only in the last few years with the improvement of radio-telemetry equipment. The A.V.M. Instrument Company, a U.S. firm that helped pioneer the radio-telemetry equipment used in American wildlife studies, devised a package containing radio, batteries, and aerial that was small enough to fit into a collar that could be put around a leopard's neck; the whole thing weighs only 1½ pounds. The range of the transmitters has been increased over the years, so that, depending on the terrain, an animal can be picked up from the ground several miles away and from the air up to 40 miles away. Perhaps even more important, the batteries now last for over a year; some are supposed to last for three years. This very much improved equipment (plus increasing experience in the use of immobilizing drugs on wild animals) has made the study of leopards a real possibility.

For a number of years the Kenya Game Department has had a policy of trapping stock-raiding leopards and moving them to national parks and reserves rather than killing them. However, the fate of these leopards once released was unknown (except in one case when a leopard taken to Nairobi National Park ended up in the lavatory of a biscuit factory in the industrial area of the city). In 1970 researchers fitted two trapped leopards with radio collars and released them in Tsavo (West) National Park with the intention of tracking them to find out what they would do. Within two months they had both left the Park, one going north and the other south; unfortunately, both headed toward areas occupied by humans, where they would probably become stock raiders again. This exercise showed that if the policy of trapping leopards rather than shooting them was to continue, then some very basic information was needed: how many square miles does a leopard need in a particular habitat, how many leopards are already there, are leopards territorial, would new leopards be able to coexist with residents or is the area already filled to capacity?

Patrick Hamilton, a graduate student at the University of Nairobi, was set the task of trying to answer some of these questions for Tsavo West. Obviously the only way that this could be done was with radio-tracking. But how does one get hold of a Tsavo leopard to put a collar on it? The answer: hire the best and most notorious leopard poacher in the vicinity. There was no doubt in anyone's mind who that was — the great and unique Elui Nthengi. Elui was arrested for "trespassing" in the early days of the Park but ended up working with the antipoaching force. He had since left the Park services but Hamilton was able to trace and hire him. A wiry, indomitable little man who can track anything, Elui proved invaluable: from one footprint he could tell the sex and approximate age of a leopard, how long ago it had been there, where it was going — he might even venture to say why it was going where it was. At that point he certainly knew more about leopards than any scientist.

Hamilton and Elui first walked the approximately 100-square-mile study area to try to get some idea of the distribution and density of leopards. Then the long, laborious task of trying to trap the leopards began. They devised a system of baits hung in strategic trees; once a leopard started feeding, they would move the bait into a large metal box trap. This was a crucial phase because sometimes civets, jackals, and hyenas would get to the baits first and get trapped instead. The hyenas were a particular nuisance — two of them bit right through the heavy steel wiring and burrowed out. But eventually Hamilton and Elui would catch a leopard, which was then transferred to a special wooden box designed so that the leopard could be injected with an immobilizing drug. This was a tricky maneuver: Hamilton found it best to try to catch the leopard's tail, draw it out of the box, and inject into it, rather than try to get the rump or shoulder. The leopard is immobilized within fifteen minutes and can then be pulled out of the box and worked on.

Ideally, one person carefully watches the leopard's condition, breathing, and pulse rate, and swabs it down if it gets too hot (the drugs interfere with the animal's natural thermo-regulation; another person takes measurements and photographs the leopard's spot patterns; and a third fits the radio collar — an ingenious device made of quick-hardening dental acrylic that can be adjusted to the leopard's size and sealed in the field. Hamilton got assistance whenever he could, but often there were no trained helpers available, and he would have to do the immobilizing, caring, measuring, photographing, and fitting with the help of only Elui and a ranger.

Once the process is completed, the leopard has to be watched over until it has recovered from the drug. The drugs that have proved best for leopards do not have antidotes (as does M99, which is used on elephants and many other animals); so the leopard may take several hours to recover and during this time someone must stand by to see that it is not disturbed or attacked by other animals. After it has revived and regained its coordination, the leopard is free to go, now bleeping out signals that can be picked up with a receiver.

Although it took a while to get the radio-tracking program going, once Hamilton had perfected his trapping and immobilizing methods, there was no stopping him. At one time he had seven leopards bleeping at once. Each transmitter is on a different frequency and is picked up on a different channel on the receiver; so the signals do not get confused. By taking bearings on each leopard's signal from two or more known points, Hamilton could triangulate the leopard's position and get a fairly accurate idea of where it was, although often he could not actually spot the animal.

Hamilton drove around his study area in a Land-Rover with an aerial projecting above the roof, and one of the unexpected consequences of his study was a letter from a disturbed German tourist to Kenya's president, Mzee Jomo Kenyatta. The tourist had spotted the Land-Rover and was convinced that poachers were at work in Tsavo West tracking down leopards with "radar." (Presumably he thought that leopards give off natural radar waves that could somehow be picked up by the poacher.) He even wrote down the license plate number and sent it so that the culprit could be apprehended!

Once the leopards were collared and bleeping, Hamilton was able to pick up their signals nearly every day and plot their positions and movements on a map. With the aid of the directional aerial he could drive and then walk to within several hundred yards of them, but since the leopards in Tsavo are very timid, he did not want to disturb them unduly, and he usually did not drive off the roads and most often had to be content to know that the leopard was in that thicket over there or somewhere in those rocks on the side of that hill.

One of the puzzling aspects of Hamilton's study was that out of the twelve different leopards that he trapped only one was a female. This gave a somewhat lopsided look to the leopard community in the study area. Hamilton does not think that there are that many more males than females; in fact, his other data suggest that the sex ratio is probably close to fifty-fifty. Apparently the females are just far more cautious than the males. There were definitely other females than the one he caught; he saw several uncollared females in the area. On the other hand, some of the males were caught in the trap two or three times, and one came five times! This was convenient for Hamilton because he could then replace collars that had broken and fallen off or had ceased to function and continue to get more data from the same animal.

However, because of the leopards' extreme shyness, Hamilton was not able to get much material on behavior; nor was he expected to. His 2½-year study did produce valuable data on the movements and ranges of the leopards in his study area. (His results will be published shortly.) In the meantime, toward the end of his study of the woodland lions in the Serengeti, Brian Bertram collared and radio-tracked three leopards (a young male whom he followed for four months, and an adult female and her

1½-year-old daughter whom he followed for five months) in the northern part of the Park. There the leopards were beginning to get used to vehicles and could be approached, so Bertram was able to observe their behavior and social interactions. Bertram has only recently completed his work, but some of his preliminary results are now appearing.[1]

It is now possible to piece together something about the life of the leopard, although many aspects must remain speculative. As was always thought, it appears that leopards are basically solitary animals. Except when a female has cubs or when a male and female are courting, leopards spend most of their time on their own. Each leopard lives in a fairly well defined home range, which may overlap with those of other leopards. In the Serengeti Schaller discovered considerable overlap of leopard ranges but found that "each animal tended to focus its activities in an area little used by others at the time." During one period three females and a subadult male hunted along the same three-mile stretch of river; yet they did not associate with each other. A male leopard in the Seronera area had a range that overlapped with those of several females, but not with that of another adult male. Schaller speculated that males may be territorial, whereas females are not. However, both males and females scent mark by spraying urine in much the same way as lions do.

Hamilton's work in Tsavo tends to support the theory that adult males are territorial in that they do not tolerate the presence of other adult males in their home range. The ranges of the male leopards in his study area formed a mosaic, with some overlapping. Hamilton's radio-tracking showed that the males normally avoided each other, but when they did meet (usually in a border area), there was evidence that there had been fights — collars were broken off, and fresh tooth and claw marks and dried blood were found on some of the recaptured leopards.

Over an eighteen-month period two collared males in the study

[1] An intensive, long-term study of the leopards of the Kruger National Park in South Africa is currently being carried out by Theodore N. Bailey of the University of Idaho. He is also using radio-tracking and at the last report had trapped and collared eight leopards.

area occupied the same home range. These males were the same size but different ages. They seemed to avoid each other for the most part, but there was evidence that they fought when they met. On at least two occasions the younger one left his home range immediately after fights. He would stay away for one to six weeks but would always return to the same range, despite the fact that the other male was still there.

Hamilton's other collared leopards each stayed in a home range of approximately 4 to 20 square miles, venturing out of their usual area only occasionally. The study area covered two ranges of hills — the Ndawe and the Ngulia — and the leopards were usually found in or near the hills. Although they did prefer certain areas within their home ranges, they used most of the range regularly and frequently, often covering it every few days. Bertram's male leopard in the Serengeti, however, used a much smaller area than the Tsavo leopards, always staying in an area of about 5 square miles.

Primarily a nocturnal animal, the leopard spends the day resting in places that offer shade, cover, and sometimes a vantage point from which it can survey the surrounding countryside. In Tsavo leopards often rest on hillsides under overhanging rocks or in the branches of a tree. In the Serengeti they often lie up in the kopjes, and along the Seronera River they are frequently seen in sausage trees and yellow-barked fever trees. Both Hamilton and Bertram, by radio-tracking, found that leopards also spend a good deal of time resting on the ground, in thickets, and under bushes and fallen trees.

In the late afternoon or evening the leopard generally becomes active, setting out to hunt or perhaps to drink or meet another leopard. When I visited Brian Bertram in the Serengeti, we stayed with his collared male, who was resting in a tree, until after dark. Just at dusk the leopard got down out of the tree, walked away, and shortly after dark began "calling." The leopard's call, or roar, is very strange: it is a sort of rasping cough with the rhythm and sound of someone sawing on a piece of wood. It is totally unlike any sound that the lion or cheetah utters. In the evening this leopard often met up with an older female, who was probably his mother, and the pair then hunted together; so it might be assumed that the call is used at least sometimes for getting in touch with other leopards. If the male is indeed territorial, then no doubt the call also serves to announce his occupancy to other males.

Little is known of the mating behavior of leopards. Schaller saw one brief copulation that resembled that of lions. Hamilton also got a brief glimpse of copulating leopards after tracking to within 25 yards of the pair. He was not able to see much without disturbing them, but what was remarkable was the sound that they were making. Hamilton reports that there was much snarling and caterwauling, like that made by domestic cats, only louder.

Zoo records show that the gestation period is 98 to 105 days and that litters are relatively small, ranging from one to three. One rarely sees a leopard female in the wild with more than two cubs; most often she will have only one. There is little information on mother-cub relations. The leopard's habitat affords many well-hidden places in which to give birth, and presumably the cubs stay in lairs for the first eight weeks or so. But even older cubs are seldom seen. In two and a half years of walking and driving in an area that is thought to have a high leopard density, Hamilton never set eyes on a cub.

The few observers who have been able to watch mother and young together have noted that they are quite tactile. The mother frequently grooms her cubs, and they greet by rubbing the face and often the whole body sinuously against the other's. It has been suggested that once the cubs start following the mother, she uses her tail in leading them. The leopard's tail is very long, and the underside is nearly pure white. As she moves in front of the cubs, she loops her tail up over her back, providing a very effective guide through the tall grass. Mother and cubs stay together for at least a year and remain associated for nearly two years. As soon as the young leopard can kill on its own, which may be as early as one year old, it begins to spend more and more time away from its mother.

George Schaller was able to follow the fates of a few of the leopard cubs in his study area and relates the following case: "A male cub, born in September, 1967, remained closely attached to his mother until December, 1968, when he was two-thirds her size. In the morning of December 15 they played together: he stalked her, rushed and straddled her, then bit her lightly in the nape; she in turned pounced on him and they wrestled lightly, clasped in each other's arms, until she growled and they broke apart. Early in 1969 the male was sometimes alone, sometimes with his mother, but in May, at the age of 20 months, he had become essentially independent. Yet he still hunted in the same area as his mother and the two met occasionally."

The young female that Bertram had collared was becoming independent during the time that he was following her and her mother. She was able to catch small prey, such as hares, small birds, and hyraxes, on her own but was still unable to catch larger prey. Her mother, on the other hand, hunted larger animals, usually impalas or Thomson's gazelles. After placing the kill in a tree, she would go find her daughter and take her to the kill. They would then feed on the kill for a day or two.

About six weeks after the females came under observation, the mother mated with a male, spending a few days with him; after that, she was never seen with her daughter again. Bertram was still able to follow both of the females and found that, though they used the same area, they did not meet. Bertram speculates that "with their frequent smelling and urine-marking of tree trunks, each animal presumably knew pretty well where the other was at any time." Soon after gaining her independence, the young female was seen with kills of larger animals.

As with other aspects of leopard behavior, few people have witnessed leopard kills, much less the preceding stalk, chase, and capture. In a joint paper by Hans Kruuk and Myles Turner (former deputy chief game warden of Serengeti National Park), several attempts and complete hunts by leopards are described. All the attempts were made near thick cover or in high grass. Twice they saw a leopard in a tree spot a reedbuck, then come down, stalk, and jump at the reedbuck: in one case the leopard missed; in the other it succeeded in capturing and killing the reedbuck. On another occasion they saw a leopard stalk the sound of Egyptian geese; it got within ten yards of the geese, pounced, and missed. They twice saw a leopard waiting in ambush in high grass; in one case the leopard made a bound at a Grant's gazelle and missed, but in the other case an impala came so close that the leopard lunged upward at the impala, grabbed it around the neck and shoulders, pulled it down, and bit its throat.

It appears then that stealth is of the utmost importance in the leopard's hunting technique. It stalks as close as it can and then pounces; chasing seems to be at a minimum and frequently is absent altogether. This kind of hunting is best suited for the thick vegetation and uneven terrain in which the leopard usually lives. It is sometimes assumed that all of the leopard's hunting is done at night, but it certainly hunts in the daytime as well. Schaller saw nine daytime hunting attempts made by leopards in the Serengeti, one of which was successful. In Lake Manyara National Park I saw a leopard kill an impala at 4:00 P.M. (It had apparently sneaked up in tall grass; all I saw was the pounce, while the other impalas flew through the air in spectacular leaps, barking in alarm. Within a minute the leopard raised its golden head and, with the red-brown impala in its mouth, moved off to the forest.) Another observer in Manyara saw a leopard kill a baboon at 1:00 P.M. And Bertram observed sixty-four daytime hunting attempts, of which only three were successful (he presumes that leopards do better at night); so the leopard is by no means exclusively a nocturnal hunter.

Of the big cats, the leopard has the most varied diet. It will hunt and eat just about anything that moves, from small birds to animals three times its weight, and it will also scavenge. The leopard is an opportunist — its diet varies with the habitat and the prey available in that area.

Small prey are usually eaten on the ground where they have been caught, although occasionally they are first moved to a more secluded spot. Larger prey animals are often stored in the branches of trees. It is fascinating to watch a leopard carry its prey up into a tree. Pound for pound, leopards are considered to be the strongest of the big cats; this is certainly the impression one gets when watching a leopard carry an animal that weighs over a hundred pounds straight up a tree trunk. (Leopards usually weigh only about 80 to 120 pounds themselves; the leopards that Hamilton trapped in Tsavo averaged 88 pounds.) Once up the tree, the leopard carefully wedges the carcass in the crook of a branch so that it will not fall out. The leopard can feed on the carcass for several days without being disturbed by other predators and scavengers. Vultures find it more difficult to spot a kill amid the branches of a tree, and if they do, the leopard's presence keeps them away. Lions sometimes smell the carcass, and they have been seen to stand under a tree with a carcass in it, gazing up into the branches somewhat perplexedly. Lions can climb trees, too, but it seems that leopards do not lose their kills to lions in this way very frequently.

Schaller found that leopards sometimes kill more prey than is immediately needed. He saw one leopard with a reedbuck and two gazelles stored in one tree; another leopard had three gazelles. Because of the leopard's habit of taking carcasses up into trees, these are the kills that are usually spotted by observers; thus one tends to get a biased view of the leopard's diet. The small kills that are eaten on the ground usually remain undetected. In Tsavo, the killing of large prey animals, and the storing of them in trees, was the exception. Hamilton's leopards appeared to live mainly on small mammals — dikdiks, hares, and hyraxes — and various game birds such as guinea fowls and francolins. The leopards ate these animals as soon as they were caught, and it was only by finding bits of hair or feathers or by analyzing leopard droppings that Hamilton was able to identify the prey. The Tsavo leopards also killed larger animals, such as impalas, but these too were usually eaten on the ground. The most common prey species for Bertram's leopards was the impala.

One belief about the leopard's diet that can be dispelled — at least in regard to Hamilton's and Bertram's study areas — is that its favorite prey is the baboon. In the Serengeti, Bertram found that "they virtually never chase or catch baboons"; in Tsavo leopards rarely kill baboons, and Hamilton noticed a distinct disinterest in baboon meat when it was hung in trees as bait.

On the other hand, the leopard's predilection for killing domestic dogs can be explained: it seems that some leopards have a taste for other carnivores, especially the small ones — servals, caracals, bat-eared foxes, and jackals. While Richard Estes was studying the wildebeest in Ngorongoro Crater, he built an observation platform in a tree next to his cabin. A female leopard took to using the platform as a resting place, and as a result Estes was able to watch her activities. During a two-week period she killed two Grant's gazelle bucks, which she carried to the camp but not up the tree. Each buck weighed about 160 pounds; so presumably she could not carry them up. Instead, she placed them near Estes' Land-Rover and returned to feed on them from time to time. "But," Estes relates, "this leopard's main prey appeared to be jackals, of which she brought back eleven in a matter of three weeks, carrying them up to the platform as a cat carries a mouse, and sometimes playing with them in the same fashion, before finally biting into the vital spot. The preponderance of jackals in the diet of this leopard is highly interesting in view of the species' notorious predation on domestic dogs, suggesting that jackals or other small canids, where abundant, may be preferred prey."

It seems though that the leopard's diet may vary tremendously from area to area, and even from individual to individual, with each one developing its own preferences based partly on what it learns from its mother and partly on what is available in its range. At this point it is difficult to make a generalization about the leopard's diet and even more difficult to say what effect leopard predation has on various species in a given area. The work on leopards is only just beginning, and we still know little about its way of life. What can be said is that the leopard is a tremendously adaptable and versatile animal and therefore has a good chance of surviving, both outside national parks, as long as there are still some wild areas left, and inside parks and reserves, where both the leopard and its prey are protected.

VIII

The Spotted Hyena

RECENT POPULAR ARTICLES and film sequences on the spotted hyena have shown this much maligned and despised animal in a new light — as a hunter rather than a scavenger. Among those who take an interest in wildlife and keep up with the latest findings, this revelation is now quite widely known and accepted. What is not so well known about the hyena and should be of particular interest to the women of the 1970s is that the hyena has taken women's, or, to be more accurate, female liberation to an unexpected conclusion. Somehow in its evolution the female hyena has developed external genitals that are exactly the same in appearance as the male hyena's: her elongated clitoris is the same shape and size as the male's penis, and she has a sham scrotum. It is virtually impossible to tell male and female hyena cubs apart without dissecting them. Even as adults, the only field characteristics that distinguish the sexes are the enlarged nipples of a female who has had a litter of cubs. Furthermore, the female hyena has carried liberation one step beyond equality: she is both larger and stronger than the males and dominant in the hyena social system.

All the studies we have looked at so far have revealed unexpected information about the animals involved, but without a doubt the hyena study is the most exciting in terms of discovering the true way of life of an animal that has been obscured by myths and beliefs and vastly misunderstood, not to mention being actively loathed by man. With its huge head and jaws, its sloping back, ungainly gait, and scruffy overall appearance, the hyena is not an easy animal to admire. Adding its rather revolting eating habits to its looks, one finds an animal that is easily despised. It must have been with mixed feelings that Hans Kruuk agreed to join the Serengeti Research Institute in 1964 to carry out a study of the spotted hyena (*Crocuta crocuta*),[1] but when, after two months, he was asked to switch his study to lions, he was already so intrigued by hyenas that he decided to stick with his unpopular subjects. He has never regretted his decision and actually states that he now "loves" hyenas.

It was by no means an easy task to study the hyena, and Kruuk found his job very frustrating in those early months. First of all, it is impossible to count hyenas in any straightforward way. They sleep down in holes or in tall grass most of the day, and therefore cannot be counted from a car or airplane. Secondly, they are active at night; so the most important observations have to be made after dark, which in itself is a huge problem. In the early days Kruuk would go out on the Serengeti plains at night, see hyenas racing past, and then hear the terrific din of their cackling laughter and loud, whooping calls, only to find them a half-hour later finishing off the last few bones of a wildebeest or a zebra, or, even more confusing, surrounding a pride of lions on a kill. What had actually happened was anybody's guess.

The answer to Kruuk's problem was to study the hyena population in the Ngorongoro Crater. Like so many animals in the crater, the hyenas are relatively tame. In other areas of East Africa hyenas are usually wary, elusive animals, skulking away with their tails between their legs as soon as they have been discovered. In the crater they are fairly oblivious to cars, hardly bothering to lift a groggy head when one drives up to them. This was a great help to Kruuk, who could follow them in his Land-Rover day and night as they went about their various activities. Under these conditions he could study their social and hunting behavior in detail. He also continued to observe the Serengeti hyenas, dividing

[1] There are two other hyenas: the brown hyena, *Hyena brunnea*, of southern Africa; and the striped hyena, *Hyena vulgaris*, which ranges across northern and parts of central Africa.

his time between the two areas, and this proved to be valuable, because he discovered some intriguing differences between the populations.

Kruuk had one other important source of hyena information, and that was Solomon, his tame hyena, who was captured as a tiny cub and raised by Kruuk and his wife, Jane. Solomon was an affectionate and delightful pet, full of personality and in no way unpleasant in appearance, smell, or habits. Kruuk was able to follow Solomon's development from the time he was a week-old cub until he became a full-grown hyena. As Kruuk put it, "There is no better way to get the 'feel' of the behavior of an animal than to have one constantly around the house."

In both the Serengeti and Ngorongoro the hyena is the most numerous carnivore; thus it is important to an understanding of the overall ecology of the areas to find out to what extent the hyenas are responsible for the mortality of the various herbivores. Do hyenas hunt for themselves? If so, how do they hunt, how do they select their prey, approximately how many animals are killed per year, what species are favored, and in what proportions? Do hyenas in any way regulate the numbers of any of the ungulates? (In other words, does their predation keep down the numbers of, say, wildebeests, oryxes, zebras?) On the other side of the question, how do the numbers and availability of the prey species affect the hyena populations?

The first task, and a difficult problem to solve, was to find out how many hyenas there were. Since Kruuk could not use ground or aerial counts he worked out a system incorporating what is known as the "Lincoln Index." He immobilized two hundred hyenas in the Serengeti and fifty-one hyenas in Ngorongoro. The drugged animals were marked by cutting notches in their ears in various combinations: for instance, left ear, two notches high and low; right ear, one notch in the middle. With three possible notches in one ear, six in all, Kruuk could get sixty-three individual combinations. The hyena has large ears, which it cocks forward when it hears a car approaching, and with binoculars the notches could easily be seen from up to ⅔ of a mile away. By calculating the number of resightings of the marked hyenas against the number of unmarked hyenas seen, it is possible to get the proportion of marked to unmarked hyena, and then theoretically it is possible to estimate the number of the whole population.

In order to see as many hyenas at random as possible, Kruuk used three methods: he drove around and encountered hyenas incidentally; he observed and noted every individual at kills; and he played tape recordings of hyena noises at a kill, which invariably attracted hyenas — and often lions and even vultures — to his Land-Rover. Eventually his system revealed that there were an estimated 385 adult hyenas in Ngorongoro and approximately 3000 adults in Serengeti. With cubs, the figure in Ngorongoro came to 430 hyenas altogether. With the vast distances and greater movements in the Serengeti, the figure for the Serengeti is less reliable, and it was much more difficult to estimate the number of cubs, but the system does give an approximate figure with which to work.

Ngorongoro Crater has a population of only about forty to sixty lions. From the beginning it seemed to Kruuk unfeasible that over four hundred hyenas could live off the leavings of these lions' kills and the few natural deaths that occurred. He felt sure that the hyenas had to be killing at least some animals for themselves. F. C. Eloff in Botswana had written an article stating that the spotted hyenas of the Kalahari Desert were true killers, hunting in large packs and bringing down adult animals. His report was based largely on circumstantial evidence — footprints in the sand around the carcasses — with few direct observations, and the Kalahari hyenas were generally thought to be an exception.

Soon after he arrived in Ngorongoro, Kruuk set out to see for himself whether or not the hyenas were hunting. He and his wife began following the hyenas on moonlit nights, and they discovered an almost Jekyll and Hyde transformation in the hyenas between day and night. At night hyenas become aggressive, successful killers of large animals — not just of the young, sick, and lame, but of healthy adults. They are able to kill both young and adult wildebeests, zebras, and Thomson's gazelles, and, less frequently, kill other animals such as eland, buffaloes, waterbucks, and kongonis. This is by no means to suggest that the hyena is not a scavenger. Given a lovely ripe carcass, any hyena will feed from it with great relish. The hyena is an opportunist above all, and if there are no carcasses to feed from, the hyena will not starve to death for lack of hunting skills.

The reason that the hyena was not known earlier as a hunter in East Africa is remarkably simple: hyenas were rarely, and certainly never systematically, observed at night. Time after time Kruuk would be out all night with his hyenas, watch them make a kill, and then see a pride of lions take over the carcass. By daybreak the scene would be as follows: three or four lions are slowly eating the remains of a zebra; hyenas are circling around keeping a discreet distance from the lions; a tourist bus drives up and someone says, "Look at those disgusting hyenas waiting to scavenge from those noble lions." In Ngorongoro, at least, lions rarely make any kills of their own, relying almost exclusively on the hyenas to provide their meals!

Besides leading to the discovery that the hyena is a hunter, Kruuk's persistence in following the hyenas at night was rewarding in other aspects as well. It was only by observations at night, when hyenas are active and interacting with each other, that their whole way of life could be understood. Since Kruuk was able to recognize the marked animals in Ngorongoro individually, he was able to collect data on their movements and associations.

The hyena population of Ngorongoro Crater is divided into eight "clans," each consisting of males, females, and cubs, and numbering anywhere from ten to a hundred individuals. Each clan occupies a range of approximately 8 square miles. The ranges of the clans cover most of the crater floor and border on each other, forming a kind of mosaic. The borders are defined in the hyenas' minds and not necessarily by natural boundaries, although the lake and swamp do form natural barriers. Most of the clan's activities are carried out within its own range, although members will cross into other ranges at times. However, hyenas cannot move freely from area to area, for the ranges are held in a strictly territorial way; that is, they are defended from intrusions by members of other clans.

If a stranger is detected within another clan's range, it will be viciously chased and even attacked. As soon as it is out of its own territory, a hyena's whole manner becomes defensive and wary, and, as a result, it is even more easily seen to be a stranger. The territorial system can also be seen at work during hunting. A pack of hyenas in the full heat of a chase will sometimes stop dead in their tracks when their quarry runs across the border into a neighboring clan's range. On other occasions they may not stop; then, if they make the kill on foreign territory, and the clan's owners are aware of it, a dispute over the carcass will invariably take place. If the kill takes place far into the other territory, then the invaders will almost always give way to the owners, even if the invaders outnumber the owners.

There are various ways in which the clans maintain their ranges and reinforce the boundaries. In fact, if they do not stay on their toes, they can lose parts of their territories. Boundaries are not constant but move as a result of battles. One of the more important maintaining activities involves border patrolling. This is carried out by a group of hyenas usually led by a dominant female. They may start off from a den site or from a specific place away from the den, which Kruuk called the "club" because it seemed to serve as a meeting place for hyenas who were eventually going to do something together as a group. The same place might be used as a club for weeks or even months at a time. There they meet and greet and move off together toward the border. Patrolling groups can be distinguished from hunting groups by their activities as they move along and by the fact that they completely ignore prey animals.

Once on the border area, they begin marking, which the hyena does in two ways, in different places: "pasting" and defecating. Pasting consists of rubbing the anal glands against a long stalk of grass that is pulled between the hind legs and secreting a white substance that has a very strong odor even to humans and must be particularly strong to hyenas with their keen sense of smell. The

Three members of one of the Nairobi lion prides: the individual whisker spot patterns make accurate identification possible.

Above: Lioness stalking. Below: Lioness carrying a warthog with the suffocating throat-hold.

Parts of the mating sequence:

The male grimaces to initiate the sequence; sometimes the female reacts aggressively.

Often the female initiates the sequence herself by circling around and rubbing herself against the male.

Mating:
the male bites
the female's nape.

Ron McLaughlin and his cheetah subjects, who took to using his vehicle as an observation point.

Cubs around eight weeks old grooming each other: they still have a distinctive mantle of long hair on their necks and backs.

Two newly independent young males: their thinness shows that they are having a hard time hunting for themselves.

Cheetah cubs playing "king of the mountain" on a dirt mound.

Young cubs chasing and catching a Thomson's gazelle fawn brought to them by their mother: she finally had to kill it for them, but it was all good practice for young predators who have to learn how to hunt and kill.

Patrick Hamilton with an immobilized leopard just fitted with a well-camouflaged radio collar.

A leopard getting up after spending the day resting in a tree: at dusk it will begin its social and hunting activities.

Hans Kruuk with his
pet hyena, Solomon.

A female hyena and her young cub.

Hyena greeting ceremony.

Hyenas on a den: at left
two cubs play with an adult.

Hyenas on a "border patrol" ousting an intruder (right) from their
territory. (Note their aggressive posture, with tails over their backs.)

Hyenas hunting at night: clan members attack a wildebeest bull.

A hyena with a newborn wildebeest calf in Ngorongoro Crater, where hyenas take about three quarters of the calves born each year.

secretion sticks to the grass and the smell persists, making the pasting areas obvious to other hyenas. The other kind of marking area — the latrine — also has an odor, but it is particularly obvious visually. The latrines are specific areas — sometimes as large as a quarter of an acre and often found near borders — where the hyenas go to defecate. (They will defecate wherever they happen to be as well.) Hyena droppings are conspicuous because they turn bright white a few hours after being produced. This is due to the high mineral content of the feces, which consist mostly of the undigestible parts of bones. The large, white feces make the latrine areas noticeable from quite a distance.

Some of the marking places near the borders are actually used by neighboring clans — never at the same time, however. If the border patrols from different clans should meet up, there may be a clash. Very little physical contact, if any, is involved, but there is usually a good deal of displaying with aggressive postures and loud whoopings and callings. Although Kruuk never saw any serious injuries result from border clashes, Jane Goodall and Hugo van Lawick, who also observed hyenas in the crater, did see one hyena so badly injured in a border war that they suspected he would die of his wounds that night. Other members of the two clans involved were wounded and limping when the fight was over. These clashes, or a series of them, can result in one clan losing some of its territory.

Battles over kills are much more common than border clashes. These are liable to occur whenever a clan makes a kill in a border area or in another clan's territory. As the prey does not conveniently stick to one range when being chased, and chases may run up to 3 miles, the kind of situation in which a battle might occur arises frequently. There is more physical contact in these fights, and they are truly remarkable to witness. The fight is accompanied by the most incredible noises on the part of the hyenas. Kruuk describes one incident in which the Mungi River clan killed a zebra in the border area adjoining the Scratching Rocks clan's range, in a section where the boundary was not well-defined. There were seventeen Mungi hyenas and twenty-six

Scratching Rocks hyenas. The Mungi clan started eating the zebra they had killed but were chased off the carcass by the aggressive, tightly packed Scratching Rocks clan. "Several of the Mungi Clan came back, though, and for a brief while there was a great turmoil of forty-three hyenas chasing each other. Within seconds the Mungi animals fled, and the Scratching Rocks hyenas ate. But their victory was short-lived; after they had eaten for about 1½ min., the Mungi pack was back again and the roles were reversed. Again a wild turmoil and chase followed, this time leaving the Mungi hyenas eating. In this way, the carcass changed owners twelve times in 25 min.; once the two opposing packs were even pulling at it from opposite ends at the same time."

In this particular clash there was actually little physical contact and what biting there was did not cause serious injury, but on other occasions Kruuk saw hyenas badly mauled and found others dead near kills. In another clash between the Mungi and Scratching Rocks clans a Mungi male was "literally pulled apart" and left to die. Kruuk put him out of his misery with a drug and went back the next morning to find that the other hyenas had begun to eat him!

It is ironic that many of these clashes result in the loss of the carcass altogether, for the incredible cacophony of noise produced by the battling hyenas attracts lions from all around, who are usually able to appropriate the carcass, especially if there is a big male among them.

Despite the fierce battles between clans and the violent reactions to strangers, there is a certain amount of fluidity in the system. Members of one clan do move in other ranges. This may occur in foraging or hunting, as we have seen, or it may just be wandering. Males seem more apt to wander than females, who tend to stick to their own ranges. Some males actually appear to seek out neighboring clans and try to join them. Both Kruuk and Jane Goodall witnessed this behavior, and both found it puzzling. In the case that Goodall documented, a four-year-old male from the Scratching Rocks clan persistently attempted to join and finally succeeded in being accepted as a member of the Lakeside clan as well. One male that Kruuk nicknamed "the Butcher" appeared to be a fully accepted member of two clans for the first six months he was under observation, actually feeding with one clan in the morning and the other in the evening, but after six months he stayed in the range where he had originally been marked.

Of the eight clans in the crater, one, the North, was not permanent, as it completely dispersed when its area was flooded. The animals making up this clan joined the other clans wherever they could. The Hippo clan, which expanded, received new members from clans all over the crater. Obviously, the new members were motivated in some way to leave their own clans, but this aspect of their behavior is not clearly understood. In any case, the territories are not absolutely restricted; changes can and do occur.

Interactions among the members of one clan are complex and fascinating, and Kruuk would like to see more work carried out on this subject. Since he was concentrating on the hyena's effect on prey populations, he could not devote a great deal of time to social behavior, although he has certainly provided a huge amount of information on the hyena's way of life, forming a firm foundation for any subsequent study. In fact Jane Goodall did study the Ngorongoro hyenas after Kruuk left. With Kruuk's basework on the clan system to take off from, she concentrated on one of the eight clans, the one Kruuk had named the Scratching Rocks clan. She eventually knew half of the sixty-odd clan members by sight and could recognize the other half with photographs. Her findings are presented in a popular book, written with Hugo van Lawick, called *Innocent Killers*, in which basically she corroborates most of Kruuk's findings.

Hyena social structure is unique in many ways, but its most outstanding feature is the female's dominance, a most unusual phenomenon among mammals. The females are actually larger in bone structure, weigh more, and, as a result, are stronger than the males. An adult female may weigh as much as 175 pounds, but this is exceptional; normally the larger females weigh about 130 pounds, and the largest males at least 10 pounds less.

In any clan some members are dominant over other members, but Kruuk does not think there is a strictly linear hierarchy in the sense that each hyena has its exact place in a "pecking order." Females, on the whole, are higher-ranking than males. Any fully adult female will hold sway over any male, adult or juvenile. Even young females, not fully grown, will sometimes be dominant over adult males larger than they. Therefore it is not just the females' size that makes them dominant, but their whole behavior and personality.

In studying the Scratching Rocks clan in detail, Jane Goodall discovered that two females, whom she called Bloody Mary and Lady Astor, were the highest-ranking members of the clan and that Bloody Mary was slightly dominant over Lady Astor. Goodall's impression is that there is a definite rank order among members of a clan, but unfortunately her scientific data on this aspect of social behavior are not yet available. She also noted a hierarchy among the males, with a male she named Wellington holding the highest rank.

The best place to watch hyenas interacting is at the den. Clan activity centers around a cluster of dens, usually situated on high ground in the central part of the territory. The dens consist of aboveground entrance holes connected to a series of underground tunnels, which may have originally been started by other animals but are dug out and enlarged by hyena cubs. Females give birth to their cubs underground. Each mother cares for and suckles only her own offspring. Around the den the females are completely dominant and are often aggressive to the males, not letting them near their young cubs, and with good reason, as hyenas show definite cannibalistic tendencies. When Solomon was still fairly young, Kruuk was awakened one night by his cries and ran outside to find him being carried off by an adult hyena. Kruuk managed to rescue the cub, who was seriously injured, with a broken jaw and punctured windpipe. Kruuk does not doubt that the hyena was taking Solomon to eat and he speculates that most likely it is this rather unpleasant ability of hyenas to eat each other that has caused the females to be dominant. Without their larger size and natural aggressiveness, they would be unable to protect cubs from their voracious fathers. In the evolution of the hyena the dominance trait in the female developed and persisted, allowing the species to survive.

The den, then, acts as a central place where the cubs are raised and clan members meet. Usually, hyenas sleep during the day, away from the den in tall grass or shallow holes, come to the den in the evening, stay there for a few hours, and then leave to forage or hunt, returning again before dawn. The clan is not a closely coordinated group always acting together; it is, however, a social group — members know each other and must cooperate with each other. There are a number of behavioral devices that appear to keep the clan together. The hyena is both a social animal and a solitary animal; that is, it carries out some activities on its own and finds it necessary to act in cooperation with other hyenas for others. For instance, it does a lot of foraging and hunting on its own and it may lie up in the daytime by itself. At other times, it may hunt in a pack or participate in a border patrol. Thus the situation is such that the members of the clan must constantly re-establish contact with each other after being apart. Unlike the close-knit zebra group or elephant family unit, hyena clan members are often separated by large blocks of time and distance. Yet when they are together, they must act as members of a social group. One of the mechanisms that comes into play in the re-grouping of the hyena clan is the rather elaborate meeting ceremony performed by all members, in all combinations of males, females, and cubs.

Most hyena actions seem to be characterized by a strange combination of fear and aggressiveness, and this is most clearly seen in greeting ceremonies. The ceremony is usally performed when hyenas meet at the den or "club" and sometimes after kills, or when a pair are just walking along together or accidentally meet in their wanderings. It is often performed after there has been a squabble. Both animals usually show indications of fear and nervousness; the lower-ranking one will show the most fear and in fact will usually initiate the greeting. When two animals are going to meet, often one will stop and turn its head away while the other approaches. When they meet, they sniff each other's mouths, necks, and heads. Sometimes this is all that happens, but more often the whole ceremony takes place. Then the two stand parallel to each other, head to tail; each lifts the hind leg that faces the other, and licks and smells the other's genitals. The genitals have become erect during the approach; the clitoris or penis is sometimes pointed forward, sometimes back, and sometimes straight down, almost touching the ground. Even when erect the penis and clitoris look exactly alike. After sniffing for ten to fifteen seconds, sometimes longer, they put their legs down and walk off, often, as Kruuk says, "without so much as a backward glance."

Meeting ceremonies seem to occur most frequently between cubs and adults, and it is striking that the cubs have extremely well developed genital organs, which are almost as large as the adults' in total size — and, in proportion to the cubs' size, are larger. From a very young age the cubs participate fully in the meeting ceremony. In the evening the clan tends to come together at the communal den. As each animal comes up, it greets the others already there, and the cubs are particularly keen to greet each new arrival. As the subdominant animal, the cub usually takes the initiative, walking up to the adult and lifting a leg in greeting or pushing its nose into the adult's groin. Even cubs less than a month old will greet and show complete penis or clitoris erection. One often sees a cub roll over on its back, exposing its genitals, when an adult approaches. Kruuk theorizes that it is advantageous for the cubs to get in touch with adults as much as possible, while showing a submissive attitude. By presenting the most vulnerable part of its body, the animal that takes the initiative in the meeting ceremony is showing its good intentions, so to speak. The dominant animal, which may have been feeling aggressive, is distracted by the presentation and responds with a meeting ceremony instead.

Another behavior mechanism that helps strengthen the social ties of the clan members is a phenomenon that Kruuk calls "social sniffing" and that he thinks serves the "sole function of doing something together." A group of hyenas may be walking together at a fast pace, and one will suddenly stop, apparently at random, and start to sniff the ground; the others then come running up in an excited manner and push and shove to sniff at the same piece of ground. After sniffing for less than a minute, they go off — they may sniff more than a dozen places in an hour. These parties of hyenas may also visit pasting places and latrine areas. The conspicuous part about the sniffing is the close contact and touching of the animals. Both males and females participate in social sniffing, but cubs below ten to twelve months old do not join in the sniffing parties.

Many of the hyena's actions can better be interpreted once their various postures are understood. Hyenas show their moods and intentions quite plainly. The different tail postures are particularly noticeable, but the attitudes of the ears, mouth, and whole body are also important. When the hyena is standing or walking along, undisturbed, the tail is normally carried straight down. However, when it is frightened — by another hyena, a lion, a man, or a vehicle, for instance — it tucks its tail between its legs, flat against its belly. When a hyena is aggressive and about to attack or is hunting, the tail is carried straight up. When a hyena is extremely excited in a social situation, the tail is held up and pointed forward, right over the back. A hyena will sometimes flick its tail. This is not wagging; the flick generally occurs when the hyena is slightly nervous, usually as it is approaching a dominant hyena.

When the ears are held flat against the head, this indicates that the hyena wants to flee; when the ears are pointed forward, it means the hyena might approach or attack. The frightened hyena with flattened ears sometimes also stretches back its lips, baring the teeth in what Jane Goodall calls a "submissive grin." She also noted that often the dominant animal in a meeting ceremony would yawn widely.

Along with their postures, the hyena's calls are also very important in the social context. The melancholy whooping call, an extremely evocative sound, is the most frequently heard. People who have lived in Africa are often more nostalgic about that sound than even a lion's roar at night. But the hyena has a far greater repertoire of calls than people realize. It is an extremely vocal animal and accompanies most of its actions with sounds. These sounds range widely but grade into one another so that it is difficult to distinguish them individually. Kruuk characterized the different vocalizations as follows: "whoop; fast whoop; grunt; groan; low giggle; yell; growl; soft grunt-laugh; loud grunt-laugh; whine; soft squeal." In order to interpret any sound one must also see the posture of the animal, and even then it is difficult to make generalizations. Kruuk had "the impression that usually the very high-pitched calls involve either a strong tendency to flee or have a strong submissive quality (e.g., during begging), whereas the loud, low-pitched calls accompany a high tendency to attack."

The familiar whoop, which is usually made by an animal walking alone, may be a contact call, although it is rarely answered by other hyenas. This is the sound one hears at night when camping in Africa, and although it may sound as if the hyena were right outside the tent, it is probably a good distance away, as the whoop can be heard for as far as 3 miles. Many of the other calls, combined with postures, appear to have the purpose of discouraging actual combat, for although there is a lot of displaying between clans and among clan members, physical contact in disputes is rare. An intruder or a fellow clan member is easily intimidated by what Kruuk has termed the "parallel walk" — two hyenas approach walking shoulder to shoulder, with tails erect and manes bristling. The mere approach is usually enough to reduce the third hyena to terrified giggles and send it racing away. Hyenas using this offensive (with more hyenas to back them up) can sometimes successfully chase even a single lioness or immature lions from a kill. Female hyenas are particularly good at intimidating male hyenas with such displays. Two or more females feeding on a small kill can keep several males at a distance.

Considering the unusual dominance by females, it is particularly intriguing to find out how mating takes place. In the normal course of events males are treated with some disdain and are often chased away from the den by the females and sometimes even by a group of cubs. How, then, does the timid male get up enough nerve to actually mount one of these formidable females? Like so many hyena activities, mating is literally shrouded in darkness and has rarely been observed. It was once widely believed that hyenas have riotous orgies at certain times of the year. L. Harrison Matthews, who made an expedition to the Serengeti in 1935 to study the reproduction of the spotted hyena, heard a particularly large group of hyenas around his camp one night when he had put baits out and wrote that "the noise they made was indescribably hideous. Shrill shrieks and yells, accompanied by deep emetic gurgling and groans, made a background for wild peals of maniacal laughter . . . It is highly probable that a saturnalian orgy was in progress." In actual fact, it was more likely rival clans having a dispute over the baits, for interclan warfare is a very noisy affair, whereas mating behavior seems to be relatively quiet, with few hyenas present.

Perhaps one of the strangest phenomena to occur between the sexes — and one that may or may not be connected with mating — is "female baiting." Normally a female is highly respected by any male, but on certain occasions a group of males, anywhere from three to nine, will literally "gang up" on a single female, even a very high-ranking one, and try to sniff and bite her while she tries to defend herself. Sometimes the female is actually bitten and receives wounds, but even if she is only sniffed, she will show all the signs of fear and submission throughout the baiting. The males, on the other hand, display aggression, coming toward the female with manes bristling, ears forward, and tails up. Then the whole episode may suddenly stop and the female will walk away as if nothing had happened. This aspect of "female baiting" makes Kruuk suspect that there may be an element of play involved.

Jane Goodall also witnessed female baiting, and her subsequent observations indicate that it could be some kind of preliminary behavior to courtship. She watched Lady Astor being

baited by a group of males on one day, and the very next day individuals began what appeared to be courtship. The male performed what Goodall calls a "bowing display," in which he approached Lady Astor making pawing motions on the ground and
lowering his head, repeating these motions as he moved closer.
But as soon as Lady Astor raised her head, he turned and fled,
only to approach again bowing and pawing. Each succeeding day
a higher-ranking male displayed to her, until on the fifth day the
highest-ranking male in the clan, Wellington, became her suitor.
The following day, with Wellington in avid pursuit, it finally
looked as though Lady Astor was going to accept his advances.
Goodall was unable to confirm her suspicion, however; as she
wrote, "I was convinced that, at long last, I was about to witness
the consummation of the bowing display. But Lady Astor got up
and, as she walked into the reeds, I could swear she cast a trium-
phant look at me over her shoulder!" Every bowing display she
witnessed, though, was directed at either a young female or a
female who was about to wean her cubs or had just weaned
them — in other words, a female who could have been in estrus.
But in only one case did the female have a litter of cubs after a
suitable length of time; so the whole phenomenon of baiting and
bowing still remains something of a mystery.

Kruuk observed definite sexual behavior on fourteen occasions
and witnessed several successful copulations. It was interesting
that in each of the matings he saw, the female maintained her
dominance throughout the procedure; in one case, the female actually pursued the male, who had become reluctant after mating
with her a few times. In that observation only the male and female
were present, and a series of mountings took place, with short intervals between, during which they rested. On other occasions
there was more than one male in attendance, but in each case only
one of them attempted to mount. This was not necessarily the
largest male present but the one who seemed best able to keep the
others away. The males did not fight but chased each other
around, making enough noise at one point to attract three lions.
Thus, hyenas do make noise on some sexual occasions, but this incident was still a far cry from an orgy.

On one remarkable occasion Kruuk, to his amazement, saw a male hyena repeatedly rape a cub every time he was repulsed by an adult female. This male, along with several other males, unsuccessfully tried to mount a female who was not cooperative and snapped at them whenever they got close. She eventually went to a den and suckled her ten-month-old cub and then retreated into the den with only her head showing. The male who had been closest to her obviously found this extremely frustrating, and as Kruuk described it, he "showed several 'displacement activities,' lying down, rolling in the sand, and pawing it very viciously — by this time he had a penis erection. After some 10 min. of this, he suddenly walked to the cub, which was lying about 6 m. away, mounted it without inserting, and ejaculated. Then he walked back to the female in her hole, looked at her for a few seconds, and then went back to the cub and mounted again, and so on. The cub struggled in the beginning to escape this rape, then ignored it completely as far as that was possible." This happened eight times; each time the male went over to the female after mounting, and while mounting the unfortunate cub, he would face the female.

Not all hyena sexual encounters are this frustrating, but it is interesting to examine how intromission is physically possible, given the genital structures of the male and female. The hyena's anatomy has given rise to a number of myths, the most persistent one being that the hyena is a hermaphrodite; it is also even thought to be able to change its sex at will. Every sexual position imaginable has been attributed to the hyena except for the normal one, which of course is the one used. It mounts in much the same way as a dog does. The female's urogenital tract opens at the end of the clitoris (which, as has been said, is the same shape and size as the male's penis), and the male must insert his penis into her clitoris. This may sound impossible but it is not. The clue lies in the fact that during copulation the male's penis is erect and the female's clitoris is not; in fact, when the female is in estrus, the opening at the end of the clitoris swells and widens and thus intromission becomes possible.

The fact that the clitoris becomes erect during the meeting ceremony but not during sexual activity is noteworthy. Kruuk says, "This suggests that the pattern of erections during the meeting ceremony is not motivated by sexual drives but has probably become divorced from sexual behavior during evolution." As we have seen, the genitals play an important role in the meeting ceremony, and it is probably in this social context that the female has developed genitals that appear to be the same as the males, rather than in the sexual context. Kruuk postulates that if the female were different from the male there might be a distraction; that is, if her femaleness were obvious in every encounter, the integrating effect of the meeting ceremony might not be as easily accomplished.

Despite the complicated sexual life of the hyena, conceptions do occur and cubs are born at all times of the year, although there may be a slight peak during the wet season. The gestation period is about 110 days, according to zoo records. Usually two cubs are born, occasionally one, and rarely three. The mother gives birth to the cubs in seclusion in a den or a hidden place away from the central den and keeps all other hyenas away from her offspring for about two weeks. Goodall was lucky to discover one of her known females carrying a newborn cub one day. Goodall followed the female to a den where she was keeping her two cubs and was then able to keep this den under observation for the next two and a half weeks while the cubs were there.

The hyena cub is born with its eyes open, has a very dark brown coat, weighs about 3 pounds, and can just pull itself along with its front paws. The mother spent the entire first day of observation down in the den with the cubs. On the next two days she lay outside the den and went down only to suckle the cubs. On the tenth day Goodall found the cubs outside the den, suckling from their mother. By then they could walk but were rather wobbly. In the following week they stayed outside for longer periods and became more and more playful and curious. By this time another female (a close companion of the mother) and her daughter had begun to spend time at the den. When the cubs were about two and a half weeks old, the mother moved them to a den already occupied by two other females with cubs. This seems to be the normal procedure. Once the cubs of one clan have reached the age of a few weeks, they are kept in a communal den or cluster of dens. There are often many cubs at a den; Kruuk says it was not unusual to see over a dozen cubs, even up to twenty. However, the mothers do not share in the care of the offspring; neither Kruuk nor Goodall ever saw a hyena suckle cubs that were not her own.

The females usually visit the den twice a day, in the early morning and evening, and, while their cubs are still small, at other times of the day and night as well. With young cubs, the female comes to the den and calls her cubs by putting her head down the entrance hole and making a soft groaning sound, which brings the cubs out. Older cubs are usually already outside and immediately begin following the mother until she lies down to suckle them. The latter can be a fairly long process — Kruuk once timed two cubs suckling for just over four hours.

Hyena cubs are very playful, and the best time to watch them is in the early evening. Their play consists mostly of running and chasing each other. Sometimes the one being chased will carry a bone or something in its mouth. They also pester the adults, climbing over them and biting them.

Occasionally a group of cubs will mob a low-ranking male, racing toward him as he approaches the den. If the male is unsure of himself, he may run away giggling, and then the cubs will pursue and try to bite him, but if he stops and faces them, they usually lose their aggressiveness and merely greet him.

As the cubs get older, they gradually begin following the mother when she leaves the den. First they follow her farther and farther from the den each time before turning back. Eventually they will follow along on foraging and hunting expeditions. The age at which they begin to do this seems to depend a great deal on the status of the mother within the clan. Jane Goodall notes that the offspring of the higher-ranking females seem to be at a great advantage in that their mothers are able to protect them while they feed at a carcass.

Generally a hyena will suckle her cubs for twelve to eighteen months, sometimes longer. It is not surprising that hyena cubs suckle until that age and for such long periods at a time, for this is usually all they get to eat. Cubs may begin to eat meat from kills made in the vicinity of the den from the time they are about five months old, but such kills may be rare, and cubs do not usually begin to follow the adults on a hunt until they are about a year old. Even then, they do not participate in the actual hunt but come up at the rear of the party; thus they are not guaranteed much of the spoils. Contrary to some reports, hyenas do not feed their cubs by regurgitating meat for them as wild dogs do, nor do they bring food home specifically for the cubs. They may bring a bone or piece of skin back to the den, and the cubs may chew on it, but only after the adult is finished; so the mother does not appear to bring it with the intention of feeding it to her cubs.

As might be expected under these circumstances, weaning is a difficult time for both mother and offspring. Goodall saw cubs go into what she called "weaning tantrums." She describes how a young female, Miss Hyena, reacted when prevented from suckling by her mother: "She first backed away squealing — a harsh, grating long drawn out sound which goes on and on and on. Then she rushed back to Lady Astor and, with her legs bent so that she was moving along with her belly scraping the ground, she rushed around and around her mother, squealing and grinning with her tail erect. Again she tried to nurse, again she was repulsed by a quick nip, and again she rushed off squealing. Lady Astor walked away, followed by a squealing daughter. Ten minutes later she permitted Miss Hyena to suckle. And so it went on, day after day, the tantrums getting worse and worse, and often mother and daughter biting each other."

Eventually the cub gives up, and at eighteen months, when it is weaned, it is fully grown, but it does not reach sexual maturity for a while longer. The males are mature at two years old, the females not until about three years. Female offspring may maintain a more or less permanent relationship with their mothers, but the males are forced to become more independent and must fend for themselves. It is at this time in its life that the hyena has a particularly hard time. It no longer gets milk from its mother and, being young, is low on the dominance scale; so it is not likely to get more than pickings at a kill. Members of this age group make up the majority of those that die of starvation in lean periods.

As an adult, the hyena's place in the clan may be determined by many factors, but its mother's status is certainly one of the most important elements. There is every indication that the offspring of dominant animals tend to become high-ranking themselves, with different allowances for sex, of course. It would be fascinating to follow up a number of generations of hyenas to see how the offspring fit into the dominance order and to determine what changes take place and how. Hyena social behavior is particularly intriguing and certainly deserves more study.

So far we have concentrated on the hyenas of Ngorongoro Crater. One of the aspects of Kruuk's study that is most important to take into account is the differences he found between the Ngorongoro hyenas and the Serengeti hyenas. So often in East Africa one hears comments such as "The wildebeest's been 'done' already," or "So-and-so 'did' the warthog, in such-and-such a park," as if that animal had been all wrapped up — packaged, as it were — and could now be dismissed. Certainly, some generalizations can be made about a species, but it is dangerous to assume that an animal studied in one place is going to behave the same way in another area. Kruuk was careful not to fall into this trap and approached the Serengeti hyenas in their own right.

A comparison of Kruuk's two study areas shows how ecological differences make for differences in social structure and behavior. In Ngorongoro there are year-round resident populations of wildebeests, zebras, and Thomson's gazelles — the hyena's preferred prey species. These animals are fairly well distributed over the whole crater floor, and so it is possible for the hyenas to remain resident in fixed territories that also serve as hunting ranges. This is not the case in the Serengeti. As has already been described in previous chapters, the plains game are constantly migrating all year round. They mass on the short grass plains during the wet season and move from there into the woodlands as soon as the grass and permanent water dry up on the plains. One might immediately assume that hyenas would then follow the game, as nomad lions do; some hyenas do, but strangely, many do not. The natural habitat of hyenas seems to be the open plains, and they apparently prefer this area for their den sites. Rather than move into the woodlands with the migration, the hyenas move their dens right up to the edge of the woodlands, remaining on the edge of the plains for the whole dry season. This situation presents some difficulties.

Most important, the hyenas are left with few sources of food. When the wildebeest and zebra concentrations move far off into the north, right up into Kenya, the hyenas are forced to go off on long hunting expeditions lasting many days. These hyenas, which Kruuk calls the "commuters," may travel as far as 25 to 30 miles from the den. One male seen at the den one day was found one and a half days later with the nearest wildebeest and zebra herds, 29 miles away. In another six days he was back at the edge of the plains.

Obviously, this kind of setup is not particularly conducive to a group territorial system. For much of the year there is not even anything to defend in the way of hunting territory. So in the Serengeti hyenas have had to adopt a more flexible social system. Something of the clan system still remains, but it is not nearly so rigid as in Ngorongoro. Although the Serengeti hyenas do move around a great deal, they tend to come back to particular areas, and while on the plains, they set up territories and act in much the same way as the Ngorongoro hyenas, chasing away intruders and fighting with neighboring clans over kills. These fights over kills, however, appear to happen less frequently in the Serengeti, where hyenas seem to adhere to the boundaries far less strictly. Border clashes are less common, and instead of marking along boundaries, Serengeti hyenas mark along their routes — either car tracks that they frequently use or their own paths. It is also interesting that in the Serengeti hunting hyenas do not stop their pursuit of prey at a boundary as they often do in Ngorongoro.

The difference in hyena densities between the two areas may also make for some social changes. In Ngorongoro there is an estimated density of 4.3 hyenas per square mile; in Serengeti the hyena density is one-fourteenth this figure, or fewer than 0.3 hyenas per square mile. Hyenas are seen in groups far more frequently in Ngorongoro, whereas in the Serengeti hyenas appear singly or in pairs more often than in large groups. Kruuk explains that "in the Serengeti the constantly changing composition of the hyena population in an area might prevent individual hyenas from getting to know each other well, which is probably a prerequisite for the formation of packs." Pack activities are noticeably less common in the Serengeti — hyenas do not, for example, hunt zebras as often as they do in Ngorongoro, nor is there much border patrolling.

The Serengeti hyenas' social system undergoes its greatest strain during the dry season, when the ungulates are in the woodlands. It is at this time that the hyena cubs suffer. In order to get food for herself, the mother must travel to the nearest herd, which may take three days or even longer. She has no choice but to leave her cubs behind, and during her absence they get nothing to eat at all. Often a female returns to the den with nipples so enlarged that they have been rubbed raw against the sides of her legs. It seemed odd to Kruuk that hyenas have not adopted a system whereby females could suckle cubs belonging to other females. It would also be highly advantageous if they regurgitated food for their cubs or brought food home to them. This type of behavior would obviously help the hyena cubs in the Serengeti, but it does not occur. Kruuk often saw cubs in a pitiful state; he once actually found three cubs who had starved to death. As most of the cubs die inside the dens, he had no idea how many die in this way each year.

The migratory way of life thus does not seem to be optimal for the spotted hyena. If cubs were born at the most favorable time of year and were not dependent on their mothers for so long, it might work, but this is not the case. According to the number of prey animals available, the Serengeti hyenas should be much greater in number than they are, but apparently they remain in such low densities because of cub mortality. The Ngorongoro hyenas, on the other hand, have probably reached the highest numbers possible. Kruuk says, "It is tempting, therefore, to describe the Serengeti system of hyena movements and residence and the conditions there as suboptimal. Hyenas seem much better adapted to conditions in the Ngorongoro Crater and many of their behavior patterns (i.e. border patrols, scent marking, direct aggression to intruders — all of which are shown by Serengeti hyenas and which often seem rather out of context) fit very well with existence in resident clans."

Now that we know something about the hyena's way of life, as far as its social system is concerned, we can move on to the hyena's role as a hunter and scavenger and what effect the hyena populations of Ngorongoro and Serengeti have on the ungulates in those areas.

By no stretch of the imagination does the hyena fit the picture of a stealthy hunter — a sleek, graceful killing machine like the lion, leopard, or cheetah — and yet the hyena is an impressive-looking animal when viewed in terms of function. Its physique is admirably suited for scavenging from any size carcass. With its massive head and jaws and special bone-crushing teeth, it can break all but the biggest elephant bones. Its strong forequarters enable it to carry away large portions of meat and bone. Its senses — excellent eyesight and sense of smell, acute hearing, and a completely eclectic taste — also aid in the scavenging life. It will eat just about anything, from the rankest carrion to aluminum pots and pans (as many horrified campers have discovered too late). Needless to say, the hyena has a rather remarkable digestive system. Every bit of organic matter in the bones, which are splintered, chewed, and swallowed, is digested; the only bone material passed in the feces is inorganic.

What is surprising about the hyena is that its cumbersome "scavenger's" body can also kill quite efficiently. It was thought that the hyena was a slow, clumsy animal that could easily be outpaced by adult herbivores and so chose only slow, sick, and old animals. After watching more than two hundred kills, Kruuk was able to show us just how wrong this assumption is. The hyena is a clever and adaptable hunter with the stamina to chase an animal for 3 miles, reaching speeds of up to 40 miles per hour.

Hyenas hunt regularly in the Serengeti and Ngorongoro; in both areas they hunt more than they scavenge, and in Ngorongoro they are almost exclusively hunters. Hyenas were observed on 622 carcasses in Serengeti, and of these, 68 percent had been killed by hyenas; of 297 carcasses in Ngorongoro, 93 percent had been killed by hyenas. These figures show that the hyena is as much a hunter as any of the other large carnivores, all of whom also scavenge to some extent (with the possible exception of the timid cheetah). The lions in Ngorongoro turn out to be of a far more scavenging nature than the hyenas there. Out of 61 observations in Ngorongoro in which both lions and hyenas fed from the same carcass, 84 percent of the animals had been killed or first found by hyenas and only 6 percent had been killed by lions (the remaining 10 percent being uncertain cases). Even in the Serengeti, out of 129 observations in which both lions and hyenas fed, 53 percent of the carcasses had been killed by hyenas and 33 percent by lions (with the remaining 14 percent uncertain). As lions are almost always able to appropriate a kill from hyenas, they are a serious competition to the hyenas, who must therefore kill more often. In Ngorongoro, where lions rarely kill for themselves, an unusual situation arises in which the hyenas are responsible for selecting prey for both their own diet and that of the lions.

The great majority of all the kills made by hyenas are of medium-sized ungulates, although they will kill and eat a wide range of animals — as Kruuk says, "any size between a termite and a buffalo." The diet list he has compiled includes porcupines, spring hares, puff adders, and hyenas. Other observers have reported hyenas eating fish, tortoises, humans, black rhinos, hippo calves, and young elephants. In both Ngorongoro and Serengeti the most common prey species for the hyena is the wildebeest, with the zebra second and the Thomson's gazelle third in Ngorongoro, and the Thomson's gazelle second and the zebra third in the Serengeti.

Since the wildebeest, zebra, and Thomson's gazelle form the

bulk of the hyena's diet, Kruuk concentrated on the hyena's methods of hunting these animals. It is fascinating to see how the hyena adjusts its hunting methods to the different antipredator devices used by its prey. One cannot help gaining a new respect for the hyena once one becomes aware of its ingenuity.

Adult wildebeests are usually hunted at night by a single hyena, or two or three hyenas at the most. The hyena heads for the wildebeests and often is able to approach to within 10 to 20 yards before they react by picking up their heads. The hyena then begins a series of testings, by either dashing into the midst of the herd or chasing one individual at random. Once the wildebeests begin to run, the hyena usually stops and simply watches the running animals. The hyena may move from group to group, chasing and watching, until a victim is finally selected and chased in earnest. It is difficult to determine the factors responsible for the selection. The animal chosen generally looks healthy and fit to the human observer, but the hyena probably detects some slight difference in the animal's behavior or appearance that may increase the hyena's chances of a successful hunt.

Once the hyena begins a chase, other hyenas often join in. At speeds averaging 25 to 30 miles per hour, chases usually run just over a mile but may be as long as 3 miles or as short as a few hundred yards. As the hyenas get closer to the wildebeest, they snap at its legs and loins; these bites should bring the animal to a halt. Once the wildebeest is stopped, it is invariably killed, even if there is only one hyena. The wildebeest makes a few half-hearted attempts to protect itself with its horns, which the hyenas largely ignore. There is no killing bite: the hyenas simply tear at the animal until it is disemboweled. The more hyenas involved, the more quickly the animal dies.

Wildebeest calves are hunted extensively at the time of peak calving in January and February. Hyenas often hunt in the daytime then, seeking out the newborn calves, which are made conspicuous by their light brown coats and wobbly gait. The calves are selected and chased by one or more hyenas, sometimes after a dash into a herd. If the calf is less than an hour old, there may be no chase; if older, the calf may cover up to 2½ miles, but usually the chase covers 300 to 400 yards. The older the calf, the more chance it has of outrunning the hyenas. The mother of the pursued calf will often attack the hyenas. Kruuk has seen hyenas bowled over and butted, but has never seen one seriously injured in this way; often they just get up and continue the chase. If only one hyena is involved, a persistent attack by the mother will save the calf, but if there are more, the calf is invariably killed if the mother attacks, because as she directs her attention to attacking one hyena, the others are able to get the calf.

Zebras are hunted by a different method. In order to overcome the particular problems of killing an animal living in a close-knit family group, hyenas form packs of up to thirty animals. One of the most interesting aspects of zebra hunting is that the hyenas deliberately set out to hunt for zebras to the exclusion of all other prey. Before a zebra hunt, clan members meet at the den or often at the "club" and perform what seem like an infinite number of greeting ceremonies. There are usually more males present than females, but one or two of the older females of the clan always lead the pack. The hyenas set off from the meeting place in a group and often visit a latrine area or indulge in some social sniffing and pasting — activities that probably help to synchronize the group. Once they have had enough socializing, the pack moves off in the alert posture, with tails up. There may be no zebras in sight, but the pack will walk along, ignoring even large herds of wildebeests, until a group of zebras is found.

Hyenas do not test zebras as they do wildebeests. Usually the hyenas move slowly from group to group, looking for something that attracts them, before they begin a chase. Even before the chase starts, the family stallion may threaten the hyenas, and this is often enough to deter the hyenas, who may then go on to another group.

The chase may be initiated by the zebras fleeing when the hyenas get too close or by the hyenas running at them. The zebras bunch up and move away at a slow pace, sometimes not even running. The stallion keeps between his group and the hyenas, who follow in a semicircle behind. Each hyena then acts independently, trying to get past the stallion, who lashes out at the hyenas with his front hooves and also tries to bite them. The stallion may pursue a hyena for over 100 yards. In a successful hunt, one or more hyenas will manage to outflank the stallion and reach the mares and foals. If one of the zebras is in poorer condition than the others or is slowed down by bites from the hyenas and drops back, then the whole pack immediately converges upon it. At that point the stallion does not try to defend the individual, although a mother will try to defend her foal. Like the wildebeest, the zebra does not try to defend itself; it is also killed by disembowelment. As the number of hyenas involved in the hunt of a zebra is large, its death is usually quick.

The third species favored by hyenas, the Thomson's gazelle, is usually hunted by one hyena. Tommy fawns, which from birth to about two weeks old, lie hidden and camouflaged in clumps of grass, are actively searched for by hyenas, who will wander from clump to clump. When one is found, the hyena grabs it and bites and shakes it. If there is more than one hyena present, the fawn is torn apart and consumed in a matter of seconds. Older fawns and adults are selected by sight and chased. Often the gazelle "stots" (moves in a stiff-legged, bounding gait, which is thought to act as an alarm signal and a distraction technique) when it is first chased; as the hyena gets closer, it breaks into a flat-out run. Juveniles also bleat while they are being chased, and this, plus the stotting, attracts the mother and other female gazelles, who try to distract the hyena by running back and forth directly in front of or just to the side of it. The hyena simply ignores the mother or other females and continues chasing the fawn. The chase of juveniles and adults, which usually goes in a circle, is very fast, with speeds of up to 40 miles per hour, and may cover up to 3 miles. When the hyena gets close, the gazelle makes a series of quick turns, so that the hyena overreaches and must swerve back. The gazelle can sometimes escape by using this device, but more often the hyena catches up with it, grabs it, and kills it, usually with a bite to the head or neck.

Other animals, such as kongonis, buffaloes, eland, topis, and warthogs, are also sometimes successfully hunted. After watching more than two hundred kills, Kruuk was most impressed with the hyena's adaptability as a hunter — "Hyenas deal with the aggressive zebra, with the wildebeest or rhinoceros mother defending her calf, with the fast adult gazelle and its well-camouflaged fawn, with a wildebeest jumping into water and a waterhog backing down a hole; they are obviously very versatile."

Once the prey is killed — and often even before it is dead — the hyenas begin to feed at an amazingly fast rate. (In one case thirty-eight hyenas finished off the carcass of an adult female zebra in fifteen minutes, leaving only the head.) Because of competition among clan members, each hyena must tear off and swallow pieces of meat as quickly as possible or run off with whatever it can get. There is seldom any serious fighting over a carcass and relatively few injuries are incurred. Nevertheless, one wonders how the hyenas come away unscathed, when thirty to forty pile on top of a carcass, all tearing and pulling at the body, and some hyenas are actually buried under others. It looks like total chaos, but the dominant animals have the advantage and get the largest share of the kill and the best part of the carcass by hyena standards.

A carcass is eaten in a certain sequence: the most delectable parts and the first to go are the testicles or udder. Then the hyenas tear open the belly and loins and eat the entrails and organs. Another favorite is the fetus of a pregnant female. Once the prized parts are eaten, the hyenas begin feeding on the abdominal and leg muscles and soon begin tearing off legs and carrying them away. The head is always the last to go, but in the end this too is taken away to be eaten in peace or stored.

The larger the carcass, the more peacefully the hyenas feed from it, and once they are full, they may even begin to play around the remains. Sometimes adults and cubs pick up bones and walk around the kill with their tails up, apparently inviting others to chase them, which the others readily do; then they all race around in a large circle.

Kruuk estimated that the 430 Ngorongoro hyenas kill what amounts to 690,580 pounds of meat per year altogether; thus — by working out the body weights of the various prey — they kill 2331 animals. The three thousand hyenas in the Serengeti kill approximately 7,227,000 pounds per year, killing 32,356 animals in the plains and 23,595 in the woodlands. (By necessity the Serengeti figures are a much cruder estimate, but they give some idea of the impact the hyenas have on the ungulate population.)

In Ngorongoro hyenas act as the main mortality factor for the adult wildebeest population, killing 11 percent, and as the wildebeest recruitment rate is also about 11 percent, the population is kept at approximately the same number. In the Serengeti hyenas — or, for that matter, carnivores as a whole — do not seem to have any regulatory effect on the wildebeest population. There are simply not enough carnivores to make any difference. Ungulate populations in the Serengeti are apparently regulated by food supply, which in turn is affected by rainfall. In just over a decade of favorable conditions the wildebeests have increased from approximately 250,000 to over one million.

Although less is known about the population dynamics of the zebra, their numbers remain about the same in Ngorongoro, and it can be assumed that hyenas are an important regulatory factor as they are responsible for almost all the zebra mortality. The Thomson's gazelle, on the other hand, is also preyed upon by other carnivores — jackals, wild dogs, cheetahs — so the hyenas are not the sole agents of mortality and it is difficult to estimate for what proportion they are responsible.

The hyena numbers themselves remain fairly stable in the two areas, but for different reasons. In the Serengeti, although there is an abundance of food and hyenas appear to live to a relatively old age, they are not able to increase greatly in numbers, because of high cub mortality, which seems to be the result of the migratory way of life of the hyenas' main prey species. In Ngorongoro the hyenas are close to their upper limit in numbers, and it is competition over food that prevents an increase in the population. The competition must be very stiff indeed, because the hyenas there do not live to anywhere near a ripe old age. In captivity hyenas have lived to twenty-five years; but the oldest hyena skulls that Kruuk found in the Serengeti were around sixteen years old, and in Ngorongoro, only twelve to thirteen years old. Also, most of the dead hyenas found had died violently as a direct result of food competition. Out of twenty-four hyenas found dead in Ngorongoro, thirteen had been killed by lions, four by other hyenas, two by humans, and five had died from starvation or disease.

The killing of hyenas in East Africa, even in national parks, has been a generally accepted occupation. Maybe the hyena is not the most endearing of animals, but it is certainly an interesting one and can be important to the overall ecology of an area. Unfortunately, few people see the hyena in this way. Because of shooting and indiscriminate poisoning, hyenas have been eradicated completely in many areas and are gradually diminishing in much of their former range.

Kruuk has shown that the killing of hyenas in the Serengeti would not influence the ungulate populations at all, and that if the hyenas were reduced in Ngorongoro Crater, it would cause an immediate increase in the wildebeest and zebra populations, which might have a profound effect on the ecology of the whole area, leading to greater fluctuations in ungulate numbers instead of the present fairly stable situation. Upon concluding his study, Kruuk recommended that "a policy of non-interference with the population of hyenas and other carnivores is ecologically sound."

But Kruuk makes another interesting suggestion about a surprising benefit hyenas may have for us — the study of hyenas might shed new light on some aspects of human behavior. Although perhaps most people would be thoroughly offended to be compared in any way with a hyena, there is much to be learned from looking at the hyena's social life. Man is usually compared with his more closely related relatives, the other primates, but the hyena, as a social carnivore with a system of group territoriality, may come closer to early man in its social structure than any of the monkeys or apes. Kruuk points out that there are "some remarkable parallels" between hyenas and man and lists some of them: "the organization in large groups, within which individuals may behave solitarily or very socially; the defense of a group territory with special 'boundary' patrols marking the boundary; the hunting groups specializing in large or difficult prey and the individuals on their solitary foraging expeditions; sharing of food among the group; food storing; the aggregation of females and juveniles in a center within a territory, in which each female looks after her own offspring; the very elaborate greeting ceremonies."

So the next time you see a hyena, don't be revolted. It may be more like you than you ever imagined.

List of Support
Picture Credits
Bibliography
Index

List of Support

THE GOVERNMENTS of Kenya, Tanzania, and Uganda must be commended for their continuous support of wildlife research in their countries. By providing hospitality, encouragement, and financial assistance, they have made every effort to cooperate in gaining knowledge of their precious wildlife heritage.

In addition, the following governments, organizations, and institutions have contributed financial support or facilities to the projects mentioned, and without their generous aid research on African wildlife would not have been possible:

African Wildlife Leadership Foundation
Canadian Federal Government
Caesar Kleburg Foundation
East African Wildlife Society
Elsa Wild Animal Appeal
Explorers Club
Fauna Preservation Society
Food and Agriculture Organization of the United Nations
Ford Foundation
Fritz Thyssen Foundation
International Union for Conservation of Nature and Natural Resources
  (IUCN)
Kenya Game Department
Kenya National Parks
Leverhulme Foundation

Makerere University
Max-Planck-Institut für Verhaltenphysiologie
Medical Research Council (U.K.)
National Academy of Sciences — National Research Council (U.S.)
National Geographic Society
National Institute of Mental Health (U.S.)
National Science Foundation (U.S.)
Natural Environment Research Council (U.K.)
Netherlands Foundation for the Advancement of Tropical Research
  (WOTRO)
New York Zoological Society
Ngorongoro Conservation Area
Nuffield Foundation
Nuffield Unit of Tropical Animal Ecology
Overseas Development Administration of the British Government
Rockefeller University
Royal Society of London
Serengeti Research Institute
Smithsonian Institution
Smuts Memorial Fund
Swiss National Park, Federal Commission
Tanzania Game Division
Tanzania National Parks
Texas A & M University
Tsavo Research Project
Uganda Game Department
Uganda National Parks
University of Dar es Salaam
University of Nairobi
World Wildlife Fund

Picture Credits

following page 46

Identification photos.
Iain Douglas-Hamilton.
Douglas-Hamilton with Virgo.
Oria Douglas-Hamilton.
First-year calves playing.
Harvey Croze.
Calf playing. *Cynthia Moss.*
Family unit drinking.
Harvey Croze.
Ahmed. *Peter Jenkins.*
Newborn giraffe. *Marion Kaplan.*
Giraffe feeding. *L. J. Parker.*
Mejia with identification photo.
John Reader.

Calf taking vegetation.
Cynthia Moss.
Bull gouging baobab.
Cynthia Moss.
Young bulls sparring.
Harvey Croze.
Adults greeting. *Harvey Croze.*
Bull testing female.
Iain Douglas-Hamilton.
Giraffe drinking. *L. J. Parker.*
Male following female.
L. J. Parker.
Browse line. *Cynthia Moss.*

following page 110

Female rhino and calf.
Cynthia Moss.
John Goddard. *Hans Kruuk.*
Snout wrinkles. *David Western.*
Horn tussling. *L. J. Parker*
Courting couple and observers.
L. J. Parker.
Zebra mating sequence.
Audrey Ross.

Zebras grooming. *Cynthia Moss.*
Newborn foal. *Hans Klingel.*
Stallions fighting. *L. J. Parker.*
Grevy's stallion. *Hans Klingel.*
Mountain zebras. *Hans Klingel.*
Grevy's mares with foals.
Cynthia Moss.
Hans and Ute Klingel.
Hans Klingel.

following page 238

Male dikdik. *J. C. Hillman.*
Female dikdik. *L. J. Parker.*
Gerenuks feeding.
$\qquad$ *Walter Leuthold.*
"Laufschlag." Walter Leuthold.
Peter and Mattie Jarman.
$\qquad$ *John Reader.*
Impala marking. *Cynthia Moss.*
Bachelor males.
$\qquad$ *Mattie and Peter Jarman.*
"Prancing display."
$\qquad$ *Walter Leuthold.*
"Challenge ritual" sequence.
$\qquad$ *R. D. Estes.*
Newborn wildebeest. *R. D. Estes.*
Eland sparring. *J. C. Hillman.*
Loser mounts winner.
$\qquad$ *J. C. Hillman.*

Nursery group. *J. C. Hillman.*
Baboon "yawn."
$\qquad$ *Timothy W. Ransom.*
Shirley Strum.
$\qquad$ *Timothy W. Ransom.*
Riding "jockey style."
$\qquad$ *Cynthia Moss.*
Two infants. *Timothy W. Ransom.*
Family with black infant.
$\qquad$ *Timothy W. Ransom.*
Male eating kill.
$\qquad$ *Timothy W. Ransom.*
Yellow baboons and bushbuck.
$\qquad$ *Cynthia Moss.*
Baboon grooming sequence.
$\qquad$ *Cynthia Moss.*

following page 302

Three lions. *Cynthia Moss.*
Lioness stalking.
$\qquad$ *Judith A. Rudnai.*
Lioness carrying warthog.
$\qquad$ *L. J. Parker.*
Mating grimace.
$\qquad$ *Judith A. Rudnai.*
Aggressive female.
$\qquad$ *Marion Kaplan.*
Female circling male.
$\qquad$ *Judith A. Rudnai.*
Mating. *Judith A. Rudnai.*

Cubs with Thomson's gazelle
$\quad$ sequence. *L. J. Parker.*
Patrick Hamilton.
$\qquad$ *John King—AWLF.*
Leopard waking at dusk sequence.
$\qquad$ *L. J. Parker.*
Hans Kruuk with Solomon.
$\qquad$ *Hans Kruuk.*
Female hyena and cub.
$\qquad$ *Harvey Croze.*
Hyena greeting ceremony.
$\qquad$ *Hans Kruuk.*

Ronald McLaughlin.
Ronald McLaughlin.
Cheetah cubs grooming.
L. J. Parker.
Young cheetah males.
Harvey Croze.
"King of the mountain."
Marion Kaplan.

Hyenas on a den. *Hans Kruuk.*
"Border patrol." *Hans Kruuk.*
Night hunt. *Hans Kruuk.*
Hyena with wildebeest calf.
R. D. Estes.

Bibliography

CHAPTER I. THE AFRICAN ELEPHANT

Benedict, F. G., and R. C. Lee. 1938. Further observations on the physiology of the elephant. *J. Mamm.* 19(2):175–94.

Bere, R. 1966. *The African elephant.* New York: Golden Press.

Best, G. A., ed. 1969. *Rowland Ward's records of big game.* 13th ed. (Africa). London: Rowland Ward.

Blond, G. 1962. *The elephants.* London: Andre Deutsch.

Blunt, D. E. 1933. *Elephants.* London: East Africa.

Brooks, A. C., and I. O. Buss. 1962a. Past and present status of elephants in Uganda. *J. Wildl. Mgmt.* 26(1):38–50.

———. 1962b. Trend in tusk size of the Uganda elephant. *Extrait de Mammalia* 26(1):10–34.

Buechner, H. K., I. O. Buss, W. M. Longhurst, and A. C. Brooks. 1963. Numbers and migration of elephants in Murchison Falls National Park, Uganda. *J. Wildl. Mgmt.* 27(1):36–53.

Buechner, H. K., and H. C. Dawkins. 1961. Vegetation changes induced by elephants and fire in Murchison Falls National Park. *Ecology* 42(4):752–66.

Buss, I. O. 1961. Some observations on food habits and behavior of the African elephant. *J. Wildl. Mgmt.* 25(2):131–48.

———. 1962. The origin of certain sounds made by the elephant. *Wildlife and Sport* 3(1):33–35.

Buss, I. O., and O. W. Johnson. 1967. Relationship of Leydig cell characteristics and intratesticular testosterone levels to sexual activity in the African elephant. *Anat. Rec.* 157(2):191–96.

Buss, I. O., and J. M. Savidge. 1966. Change in population, number and reproductive rate of elephants in Uganda. *J. Wildl. Mgmt.* 30(4):791–809.

Buss, I. O., and N. S. Smith. 1966. Observations on reproduction and breeding behavior of the African elephant. *J. Wildl. Mgmt.* 30(2):375–88.

Corfield, T. F. 1973. Elephant mortality in Tsavo National Park, Kenya. *E. Afr. Wildl. J.* 11:339–68.

Croze, H. 1972. The trouble with elephants. *Wildlife News,* 7(2):2–6.

———. 1974a. The Seronera bull problem, I: The elephants. *E. Afr. Wildl. J.* 12:1–27.

———. 1974b. The Seronera bull problem, II: The trees. *E. Afr. Wildl. J.* 12:29–47.

Dougall, H. W., and D. L. W. Sheldrick. 1964. The chemical composition of a day's diet of an African elephant. *E. Afr. Wildl. J.* 2:51–59.

Douglas-Hamilton, I. 1972. On the ecology and behaviour of the African elephant. D. Phil. thesis, University of Oxford.

———. 1973. On the ecology and behaviour of the Lake Manyara elephants. *E. Afr. Wildl. J.* 11:401–3.

Douglas-Hamilton, I. and O. Douglas-Hamilton. 1975. *Among the elephants.* London: Collins.

1951. Elephant cemeteries. *African Wild Life* 5(2):111–16.

Field, C. R. 1971. Elephant ecology in the Queen Elizabeth National Park, Uganda. *E. Afr. Wildl. J.* 9:–123.

Flower, S. 1947. Further notes on the duration of life in mammals — V: The alleged and actual ages to which elephants live. *Proc. Zoo. Soc. Lond.* 117:680–88.

Glover, J. 1963. The elephant problem at Tsavo. *E. Afr. Wildl. J.* 1:30–39.

Hanks, J. 1969a. Growth in weight of the female African elephant in Zambia. *E. Afr. Wildl. J.* 7:7–10.

———. 1969b. Seasonal breeding of the African elephant in Zambia. *E. Afr. Wildl. J.* 7:167.

———. 1972. Growth of the African elephant (*Loxodonta africana*). *E. Afr. Wildl. J.* 10:251–72.

Hanks, J. and J. E. A. McIntosh. 1973. Population dynamics of the African elephant (*Loxodonta africana*). *J. Zool. Lond.* 169:29–38.

Harthoorn, A. M. 1970. *The flying syringe.* London: Geoffrey Bles.

Hendrichs, H. 1971. Freilandbeibachtungen zum Sozialsystem des Afrikanischen Elefanten, *Loxodonta africana* (*Blumenbach, 1797*). In *Dikdik und Elefanten.* Ethologische Studien. München: Verlag Piper.

Holman, D. 1967. *The elephant people.* London: John Murray.

Irwin, T. E. 1963. Elephants' stomach rumbles. *African Wild Life* 17(2):112.

Johnson, O. W., and I. O. Buss. 1965. Molariform teeth of the male elephant in relation to age, body dimensions and growth. *J. Mamm.* 46(3):373–83.

Kühme, W. 1962. Ethology of the African elephant (*Loxodonta africana* Blumenbach 1797) in captivity. *Int. Zoo Yrbook* 4:113–21.

Lamprey, H. F., P. E. Glover, M. I. M. Turner, and R. H. V. Bell. 1967. Invasion of the Serengeti National Park by elephants. *E. Afr. Wildl. J.* 5:151–66.

Lang, E. M. 1967. The birth of an African elephant (*Loxodonta africana*) at Basle Zoo. *Int. Zoo Yrbook* 7:154–57.

Laws, R. M. 1966. Age criteria for the African elephant, *Loxodonta a. africana.* *E. Afr. Wildl. J.* 4:1–37.

———. 1967. Occurrence of placental scars in the uterus of the African elephant (*Loxodonta africana*). *J. Reprod. Fert.* 14:445–49.

————. 1969a. Aspects of reproduction in the African elephant, *Loxodonta africana*. *J. Reprod. Fert.*, supp. 6, pp. 193–217.

————. 1969b. The Tsavo Research Project. *J. Reprod. Fert.* supp. 6, pp. 495–531.

————. 1974. Behaviour, dynamics and management of elephant populations. In *Symposium on the behaviour of ungulates and its relation to management*, vol. 2, paper no. 26, pp. 513–29. Alberta: University of Calgary.

Laws, R. M. and I. S. C. Parker. 1969. Recent studies on elephant populations in East Africa. *Symp. Zool. Soc. Lond.* 20:–59.

Laws, R. M., I. S. C. Parker, and R. C. B. Johnstone. 1970. Elephants and habitats in North Bunyoro, Uganda. *E. Afr. Wildl. J.* 8:163–80.

Leuthold, W. and J. B. Sale. 1973. Movements and patterns of habitat utilization in Tsavo National Park, Kenya. *E. Afr. Wildl. J.* 11:369–84.

Lydekker, R. 1926. *The game animals of Africa*. London: Rowland Ward.

McCullagh, K. G. 1969a. The growth and nutrition of the African elephant, I: Seasonal variations in the rate of growth and the urinary excretion of hydroxyproline. *E. Afr. Wildl. J.* 7:85–90.

————. 1969b. The growth and nutrition of the African elephant, II: The chemical nature of the diet. *E. Afr. Wildl. J.* 7:91–97.

————. 1973. Are African elephants deficient in essential fatty acids? *Nature* 242:267–68.

Morrison-Scott, T. C. S. 1947. A revision of our knowledge of African elephant's teeth, with notes on forest and "pygmy" elephants. *Proc. Zool. Soc. Lond.* 117:505–27.

Napier Bax, P. and D. L. W. Sheldrick. 1963. Some preliminary observations on the food of elephant in the Tsavo Royal National Park (East) in Kenya. *E. Afr. Wildl. J* 1:40–53.

Perry, J. S. 1952. The growth and reproduction of elephants in Uganda. *Uganda J.* 16:51–66.

————. 1953. The reproduction of the African elephant (*Loxodonta africana*). *Phil. Trans. R. Soc. Ser. B.* 643:93–149.

Poppleton, F. 1957. An elephant birth. *Afr. Wild Life* 2:106–8.

Short, R. V. 1966. Oestrous behaviour, ovulation and the formation of corpus luteum in the African elephant, *Loxodonta africana*. *E. Afr. Wildl. J.* 4:56–68.

Sikes, S. K. 1971. *The natural history of the African elephant*. London: Weidenfeld and Nicolson.

Spinage, C. A. 1973. A review of ivory exploitation and elephant population trends in Africa. *E. Afr. Wildl. J.* 11:281–89.

Temple-Perkins, E. A. 1955. *Kingdom of the elephant*. London: Andrew Melrose.

Ward, R., ed. 1953. *The elephant in East Central Africa*, a monograph by W. C. O. Hill, W. Barker, C. H. Stockley, C. R. S. Pitman, P. B. Offerman, G. G. Rushby, and W. Gowers. Nairobi: Rowland Ward.

Watson, R. M., and R. H. V. Bell. 1969. The distribution, abundance and status of elephant in the Serengeti region of Northern Tanzania. *J. Appl. Ecol.* 6:115–32.

Weir, J. 1972. Mineral content of elephant dung. *E. Afr. Wildl. J.* 10:229–30.

Williams, J. H. 1950. *Elephant Bill.* London: Hart Davis.

Wing, L. D., and I. O. Buss. 1970. *Elephants and forests.* Wildlife Monographs, No. 19. The Wildlife Society, Washington, D.C.

Winter, W. H. 1964. Elephant behaviour. *E. Afr. Wildl. J.* 2:163–64.

Woodford, M. H., and S. Trevor. 1970. Fostering a baby elephant. *E. Afr. Wildl. J.* 8:204–5.

CHAPTER II. THE GIRAFFE

Backhaus, D. 1961. *Beobachtungen an Giraffen in zoologischen Garten und freier Wildbalm.* Brussels: Institut des Parcs Nationaux du Congo et du Ruanda-Urundi.

Baker, Sir S. W. 1872. *The Nile tributaries of Abyssinia and the sword hunters of the Hamran Arabs.* London: Macmillan & Co.

Coe, M. J. 1967. "Necking" behaviour in the giraffe. *J. Zool.* 151:313–21.

Dagg, A. I. 1962. Giraffe movements and the neck. *Nat. Hist.* 71:44–51.

———. 1970. Tactile encounters in a herd of captive giraffe. *J. Mammal.* 51:279–87.

Dagg, A. I. and A. Taub. 1970. Flehmen. *Mammalia* 34(4):686–95.

Dinesen, I. 1937. *Out of Africa.* New York: Random House.

Foster, J. B. 1966. The giraffe of Nairobi National Park: home range, sex ratios, the herd, and food. *E. Afr. Wildl. J.* 4:139–48.

Foster, J. B., and A. I. Dagg. 1972. Notes on the biology of the giraffe. *E. Afr. Wildl. J.* 10:1–16.

Grzimek, B. 1970. *Among animals of Africa.* London: Collins.

Guggisberg, C. A. W. 1969. *Giraffes.* New York: Golden Press; London: Arthur Barker Limited.

Harrison, H. 1936. The Sinyanga game experiment: a few of the early observations. *J. of Animal Ecol.* 5:271–93.

Hediger, H. 1950. *Wild animals in captivity.* London: Butterworth Scientific Publications.

Innis, A. C. 1958. The behaviour of the giraffe, *Giraffa camelopardalis*, in eastern Transvaal. *Proc. Zool. Soc. Lond.* 131:245–78.

Leuthold, B. M. and W. Leuthold, 1972. Food habits of giraffe in Tsavo National Park, Kenya. *E. Afr. Wildl. J.* 10:129–41.

Nesbit Evans, E. M. 1970. The reaction of a group of Rothschild's giraffe to a new environment. *E. Afr. Wildl. J.* 8:53–62.

Spinage, C. A. 1968. *The book of the giraffe.* Boston: Houghton Mifflin Co.

Van Citters, R. L., W. S. Kemper, and D. L. Franklin. 1966. Blood pressure responses of wild giraffes studied by radio telemetry. *Science* 152:384–86.

Western, D. 1971. Giraffe chewing a Grant's gazelle carcass. *E. Afr. Wildl. J.* 9:156–57.

Wyatt, J. R. 1969. The feeding ecology of giraffe (*Giraffa camelopardalis* L.) in Nairobi National Park, and the effect of browsing on their main food plants. Master's thesis, University of East Africa, Nairobi.

———. 1971. Osteophagia in Masai giraffe. *E. Afr. Wildl. J.* 9:157.

CHAPTER III. THE BLACK RHINOCEROS

Fisher, J., N. Simon, and J. Vincent. 1969. *The Red Book, Wildlife in Danger*. London: Collins.

Foster, J. B. 1965. Mortality and ageing of black rhinoceros in East Tsavo Park, Kenya. *E. Afr. Wildl. J.* 3:118–19.

Frame, G. W., and J. Goddard. 1970. Black rhinoceros vocalizations. *E. Afr. Wildl. J.* 8:207.

Goddard, J. 1966. Mating and courtship of the black rhinoceros (*Diceros bicornis* L.). *E. Afr. Wildl. J.* 4:69–75.

———. 1967a. Home range, behaviour, and recruitment rates of two black rhinoceros populations. *E. Afr. Wildl. J.* 5:133–50.

———. 1967b. The validity of censusing black rhinoceros populations from the air. *E. Afr. Wildl. J.* 5:18–23.

———. 1968. Food preferences of two black rhinoceros populations. *E. Afr. Wildl. J.* 6:1–18.

———. 1969a. Aerial census of black rhinoceros using stratified random sampling. *E. Afr. Wildl. J.* 7:105–14.

———. 1969b. A note on the absence of pinnae in the black rhinoceros. *E. Afr. Wildl. J.* 7:178–80.

———. 1970a. Age criteria and vital statistics of a black rhinoceros population. *E. Afr. Wildl. J.* 8:105–21.

———. 1970b. Food preferences of black rhinoceros in the Tsavo National Park. *E. Afr. Wildl. J.* 8:145–61.

———. 1970c. A note on age at sexual maturity in the wild black rhinoceros. *E. Afr. Wildl. J.* 8:205.

Grzimek, B. 1964. *Rhinos belong to everybody*. London: Collins.

Guggisberg, C. A. W. 1966. *S.O.S. rhino*. London: Andre Deutsch.

Hamilton, P. H., and J. M. King. 1969. The fate of black rhinoceroses released in Nairobi National Park. *E. Afr. Wildl. J.* 7:73–84.

Hitchens, P. M. 1968. Some preliminary findings on the population structure and status of black rhinoceros (*Diceros bicornis* Linn.) in Hluhluwe Game Reserve, Zululand. *The Lammergeyer* 3(9):26–28.

———. 1970. Field criteria for ageing immature black rhinoceros. *The Lammergeyer* 3(12):48–55.

Hitchens, P. M. and M. E. Keep. 1970. Observations on skin lesions of the black rhinoceros (*Diceros bicornis* Linn.) in Hluhluwe Game Reserve, Zululand. *The Lammergeyer* 3(12):56–65.

Holman, D. 1969. *Inside safari hunting*. London: W. H. Allen.

King, J. M. 1969. The capture and translocation of the black rhinoceros. *E. Afr. Wildl. J.* 7:115–30.

Klingel, H. and U. Klingel. 1966. The rhinoceroses of Ngorongoro Crater. *Oryx* 8(5):302–6.

Mukinya, J. G. 1973. Density, distribution, population structure and social organization of the black rhinoceros in Masai Mara Game Reserve. *E. Afr. Wildl. J.* 11:385–400.

Parsons, B. T. and D. L. W. Sheldrick. 1964. Some observations on biting flies (*Diptera, Muscidae*, sub. fam. *Stomoxydinae*) associated with the black rhinoceros (*Diceros bicornis* L.). *E. Afr. Wildl. J.* 2:78–85.

Ritchie, A. T. A. 1963. The black rhinoceros (*Diceros bicornis* L.). *E. Afr. Wildl. J.* 1:54–62.

Schenkel, R. 1966. Zum Problem der Territorialitat und des Markierens be Säugern — am Beispiel des Schwarzen Nashorns and des Löwens. *Z. Tierpsychol.* 23(5):593–626.

Schenkel, R. and L. Schenkel-Hullinger. 1969. *Ecology and behaviour of the black rhinoceros* (Diceros bicornis L.), *a field study*. Hamburg: Verlag Paul Parey.

Western, D. and D. M. Sindiyo, 1972. The status of the Amboseli rhino population. *E. Afr. Wildl. J.* 10:43–57.

CHAPTER IV. ZEBRAS

Bell, R. H. V. 1971. A grazing ecosystem in the Serengeti. *Sci. Amer.* 225(1):86–93.

Keast, A. 1965. Interrelationship of two zebra species in an overlap zone. *J. Mammal.* 46:53–66.

King, J. M. 1965. A field guide to the reproduction of the Grant's zebra and Grevy's zebra. *E. Afr. Wildl. J.* 3:99–117.

Klingel, H. 1965a. Notes on the biology of the plains zebra, *Equus quagga boehmi* Matschie. *E. Afr. Wildl. J.* 3:86–88.

———. 1965b. Notes on tooth development and ageing criteria in the plains zebra *Equus quagga boehmi* Matschie. *E. Afr. Wildl. J.* 3:127–29.

———. 1967. Soziale Organisation und Verhalten freilebender Steppenzebras. *Z. Tierpsychol.* 24:580–624.

———. 1968a. Investigations on the social organization and population ecology of the plains zebra (*Equus quagga*). *Zool. Afr.* 4:249–63.

———. 1968b. Soziale Organisation und Verhaltensweisen von Hartmann- und Bergzebras (*Equus zebra hartmannae* und *Equus z. zebra*). *Z. Tierpsychol.* 25:76–88.

———. 1968c. Das Sozialleben der Steppenzebras. *Naturwissenschaft und Medizin* 24:10–21.

———. 1969a. Dauerhafte Sozialverbande beim Bergzebra. *Z. Tierpsychol.* 26:965–66.

———. 1969b. Grevy's zebra project. *Africana* 3(12):35–36.

———. 1969c. Reproduction in the plains zebra, *Equus burchelli* Boehmi: behaviour and ecological factors. *J. Reprod. Fert.*, Supp. 6. pp. 339–45.

———. 1969d. Zur Soziologie des Grevy-Zebras. *Zool. Anz.*, supp. 33, pp. 311–16.

———. 1971a. Notes and news. *Oryx*, 11(1):6.

———. 1971b. Notes and news. *Oryx*, 11(2–3):110.

———. 1972. Social behaviour of African equidae. *Zool. Afr.*, 7(1):175–85.

Klingel, H. and U. Klingel. 1966. Die Geburt eines Zebras (*Equus quagga böhmi* Matschie). *Z. Tierpsychol.* 23:72–76.

————. 1967. Tooth development and age determination in the plains zebra (*Equus quagga boehmi* Matschie). *Zool. Garten*, 33:34–54.

Spinage, C. A. 1962. *Animals of East Africa*. London: Collins.

CHAPTER V. ANTELOPES

Buechner, H. K. 1961. Territorial behavior in Uganda kob. *Science* 133:698–99.

————. 1963. Territoriality as a behavioral adaptation to environment in Uganda kob. *Proc. XVI Intern. Congr. Zoology* 3:59–63.

Buechner, H. K., J. A. Morrison, and W. Leuthold. 1966. Reproduction in Uganda kob with special reference to behaviour. *Symp. Zool. Soc. Lond.* 15:69–88.

Buechner, H. K. and R. Schloeth. 1965. Ceremonial mating behavior in Uganda kob (*Adenota kob thomasi* Neumann). *Z. Tierpsychol.* 22:209–25.

Dasman, R. F. and A. S. Mossman. 1962. Population studies of impala in Southern Rhodesia. *J. Mamm.* 43:375–95.

Dorst, J. and P. Dandelot. 1970. *A field guide to the larger mammals of Africa*. London: Collins.

Estes, R. D. 1966. Behaviour and life history of the wildebeest. *Nature* 212:900–1000.

————. 1969a. Behavioral study of East African ungulates, 1963–1965. In *National Geographic Society Research Reports, 1964 Projects*, pp. 45–57. Washington, D.C.: National Geographic Society.

————. 1969b. Territorial behavior of the wildebeest (*Connochaetes taurinus* Burchell, 1823). *Z. Tierpsychol.* 26:284–370.

————. 1972. Territory's invisible walls. In *The marvels of animal behavior*, pp. 230–245. Washington, D.C.: National Geographic Society.

————. 1974. Social organization of the African bovidae. In *Symposium on the behaviour of ungulates and its relation to management*, vol. 1, paper no. 8, pp. 166–205. Alberta: University of Calgary.

Grzimek, B. and M. Grzimek. 1960. *Serengeti shall not die*. London: Hamish Hamilton.

Grzimek, M. and B. Grzimek. 1960a. Census of plains animals in the Serengeti National Park, Tanganyika. *J. Wildl. Mgmt.* 24(1):27–37.

————. 1960b. A study of the game of the Serengeti plains. *Z. Saugetierk.* 25:1–61.

Hendrichs, H. and U. Hendrichs. 1971. Freilanduntersuchungen zur Ökologie und Ethologie der Zwerg-Antilope *Madoqua* (*Rhynchotrogus*) kirki (Gunther, 1880). In *Dikdik und Elefanten*. Ethologische Studien. München: Verlag Piper.

Hillman, J. C. 1974. Ecology and behavior of the wild eland. *Wildlife News* 9(3):6–9.

Hoffman, R. R. 1973. *The ruminant stomach*. East African Monographs in Biology, vol. 2. Nairobi: East African Literature Bureau.

Jarman, M. V. 1970. Attachment to home area in impala. *E. Afr. Wildl. J.* 8:198–200.

———. 1973. The quintessential antelope: a study of the behavior of the impala. *Wildlife News* 8(2):2–7.

Jarman, M. V., and P. J. Jarman. 1973. Daily activity of impala. *E. Afr. Wildl. J.* 11:75–92.

Jarman, P. J. 1974. The social organization of antelopes in relation to their ecology. *Behaviour* 48:215–67.

Jarman, P. J. and M. V. Jarman. 1973. Social behaviour, population structure, and reproductive potential in impala. *E. Afr. Wildl. J.* 11:329–38.

Leuthold, W. 1966a. Homing experiments with an African antelope. *Z. Saugetierk.* 31:351–55.

———. 1966b. Variations in territorial behaviour of Uganda kob, *Adenota kob thomasi* (Neumann, 1896). *Behaviour* 27:214–57.

———. 1967. Beobachtungen zum Jugendverhalten von Kob-Antilopen. *Z. Saugetierk.* 32:59–63.

———. 1970a. Observations on the social organization of impala (*Aepyceros melampus*). *Z. Tierpsychol.* 27:693–721.

———. 1970b. Preliminary observations on food habits of gerenuk in Tsavo National Park, Kenya. *E. Afr. Wildl. J.* 8:73–84.

———. 1971a. Freilandbeobachtungen an Giraffengazellen (*Litocranius walleri*) im Tsavo-Nationalpark, Kenia. *Z. Saugetierk.* 36:19–37.

———. 1971b. A note on the formation of food habits in young antelopes. *E. Afr. Wildl. J.* 9:154–156.

———. 1971c. Observations on the mother-young relationship in antelopes. *E. Afr. Wildl. J.* 9:152–154.

Schenkel, R. 1966. On sociology and behaviour in impala (*Aepyceros melampus*, Lichtenstein). *E. Afr. Wildl. J.*, 4:99–114.

Simonetta, A. M. 1966. Osservazioni etologiche ed ecologiche sui dik-dik (gen. *Madoqua*, Mammalia, Bovidae) in Somalia. *Monit. Zool. Ital.*, supp. 74, pp. 1–33.

Talbot, L. M. 1962. Food preferences of some East African wild ungulates. *E. A. Agr. and Forest J.* 27:131–38.

Talbot, L. M. and M. H. Talbot. 1963. *The wildebeest in Western Masailand, East Africa.* Wildlife Monographs, No. 12. The Wildlife Society, Washington, D.C.

Tinley, K. L. 1969. Dikdik *Madoqua kirki* in South West Africa: notes on distribution, ecology and behaviour. *Madoqua* 1:7–33.

Underwood, R. 1973. Social behaviour of the eland (*Taurotragus oryx*). Paper read at Southern African Wildlife Management Association Symposium on Wildlife Conservation and Utilization in Africa, June 1973, Pretoria.

Vesey-Fitzgerald, D. M. 1960. Grazing succession among East African game animals. *J. Mamm.* 41:161–72.

Von Richter, W. 1971. *The black wildebeest* (Connochaetes gnou). Nature Conservation Miscellaneous Publication, no. 2, pp. 1–30. Kroonstad: Orange Free State Provincial Administration.

Watson, R. M. 1967. Population ecology of the wildebeest (*Connochaetes taurinus albojubatus* Thomas) in the Serengeti. Ph.D. thesis, Cambridge University.

———. 1969. Reproduction of wildebeest, *Connochaetes taurinus albojubatus*

Thomas, in the Serengeti region, and its significance to conservation. *J. Reprod. Fert.*, supp. 6, pp. 287–310.

CHAPTER VI. BABOONS

Altmann, S. A., and J. Altmann. 1970. *Baboon ecology*. Bibliotheca Primatologica, No. 12. Chicago: University of Chicago Press; Basel: S. Karger.
Ardrey, R. 1966. *The territorial imperative*. New York: Atheneum.
Bolwig, N. 1959. A study of the behaviour of the chacma baboon *Papio ursinus*. *Behaviour* 14:136–63.
Crook, J. H. 1966. Gelada baboon herd structure and movement. *Symp. Zool. Soc. Lond.* 18:237–58.
Crook, J. H. and P. Aldrich-Blake. 1968. Ecological and behavioural contrasts between sympatric ground-dwelling primates in Ethiopia. *Folia Primat.* 8:180–91.
De Vore, I. 1965a. Changes in population structure in Nairobi Park baboons, 1959–1963, in *The baboon in medical research*, ed. H. Vagtborg, vol. 1, pp. 17–28. Austin: University of Texas Press.
———. 1965b. Male dominance and mating behavior in baboons, in *Sex and behavior*, ed. F. A. Beach. New York: John Wiley and Sons.
De Vore, I. and K. R. L. Hall. 1965. Baboon ecology, in *Primate behavior*, ed. I. DeVore, pp. 20–52. New York: Holt, Rinehart & Winston.
DeVore, I. and S. L. Washburn. 1963. Baboon ecology and human evolution, in *African ecology and human evolution*, eds. F. C. Howell and F. Bourlière, pp. 335–67. London: Methuen.
Eimerl, S. and I. De Vore. 1965. *The primates*. New York: Time-Life.
Hall, K. R. L. 1962a. Numerical data, maintenance activities, and locomotion of the wild chacma baboon (*Papio ursinus*). *Proc. Zool. Soc. Lond.* 139:181–220.
———. 1962b. The sexual, agonistic and derived social behaviour patterns of the wild chacma baboon (*Papio ursinus*). *Proc. Zool. Soc. Lond.* 139:283–328.
———. 1963. Variations in the ecology of the chacma baboon. *Symp. Zool. Soc. Lond.* 10:1–28.
Hall, K. R. L. and I. DeVore. 1965. Baboon social behavior, in *Primate behavior*, ed. I. DeVore, pp. 53–110. New York: Holt, Rinehart and Winston.
Hausfater, G. 1974. Dominance and reproduction in baboons (*Papio cynocephalus*): a quantitative analysis. Ph. D. dissertation, University of Chicago.
Jolly, A. 1972. *The evolution of primate behavior*. Macmillan Series in Physical Anthropology. New York: Macmillan.
Kingdom, J. 1971. *East African mammals: an atlas of evolution in Africa*, vol. 1, pp. 176–189. London: Academic Press.
Kummer, H. 1968a. *Social organization of hamadryas baboons*. Bibliotheca Primatologica, No. 6, Chicago: University of Chicago Press; Basel: S. Karger.
———. 1968b. Two variations in the social organization of baboons. In *Primates: studies in adaptation and variability*, ed. P. Jay, pp. 293–312. New York: Holt, Rinehart and Winston.

————. 1971. *Primate societies: group techniques of ecological adaptation.* Chicago: Aldine-Atherton.

Marais, E. 1947. *My friends, the baboons.* London: Methuen.

Morris, D. 1969. *Primate ethology.* Garden City, N.Y.: Doubleday & Co.

Rowell, T. E. 1964. The habits of baboons in Uganda. *Proc. E. Afr. Acad.* 2:12–127.

————. 1966a. Forest living baboons in Uganda. *J. Zool.* 149:344–64.

————. 1966b. Hierarchy in the organization of a captive baboon group. *Animal Behav.* 14:430–443.

————. 1967. A quantitative comparison of the behaviour of a wild and a caged baboon group. *Animal Behav.* 15:499–509.

————. 1968. Grooming by adult baboons in relation to reproductive cycles. *Animal Behav.* 16:585–88.

————. 1969a. Intra-sexual behaviour and female reproductive cycles of baboons (*Papio anubis*). *Animal Behav.* 17:159–67.

————. 1969b. Variability in social organization of primates, in *Primate ethology,* ed. D. Morris, pp. 283–305. Garden City, N.Y.: Doubleday & Co.

Saayman, G. S. 1968. Oestrogen, behaviour, and permeability of a troop of chacma baboons. *Nature* 220:1339–40.

————. 1971. Grooming behaviour in a troop of free-ranging chacma baboons (*Papio ursinus*). *Folia Primat.* 16:161–78.

————. 1972. Aggressive behaviour in free-ranging chacma baboons (*Papio ursinus*). *J. Behav. Sci.* 1(3):77–83.

Southwick, Charles H., ed. 1963. *Primate social behavior.* Princeton, N.J.: D. Van Nostrand.

Strum, S. C. 1975. Life with the Pumphouse Gang. *Natl. Geogr.* 147(5):672–691.

————. 1975. Primate predation: interim report on the development of a tradition in a troop of olive baboons. *Science,* 187:755–57.

Washburn, S. L. and I. DeVore. 1961. The social life of baboons. *Sci. Amer.* 204:62–71.

CHAPTER VII. THE BIG CATS

Abbott, S. and T. Fuller. 1971. A fresh look at the cheetah's private life. *Smithsonian* 2(3):34–42.

Adamson, G. 1964. Observations on lions in Serengeti National Park, Tanganyika. *E. Afr. Wildl. J.* 2:160–161.

————. 1968. *Bwana game.* London: Collins.

Adamson, J. 1960. *Born free.* London: Collins.

————. 1961. *Living free.* London: Collins.

————. 1962. *Forever free.* London: Collins.

————. 1969. *The spotted sphinx.* London: Collins.

————. 1972. *Pippa's challenge.* London: Collins.

Bertram, B. C. R. 1973. Lion population regulation. *E. Afr. Wildl. J.* 11:215–25.

———— 1974. Radio-tracking leopards in the Serengeti. *Wildlife News* 9(2):7–10.

Cowie, M. 1966. *The African lion.* New York: Golden Press.

Eaton, R. 1969a. The cheetah. *Africana* 3(10):19–23.

————. 1969b. Cooperative hunting by cheetahs and jackals and a theory of domestication of the dog. *Mammalia* 33(1):87–92.

———— 1970a. Group interactions, spacing and territoriality in cheetahs. *Z. Tierpsychol.* 27(4):481–91.

———— 1970b. Hunting behavior of the cheetah. *J. Wildl. Mgmt.* 34(1):56–67.

————. 1970c. Notes on the reproductive biology of the cheetah. *Intern. Zoo Yrbook* 10:86–89.

————. 1972. An experimental study of predatory and feeding behavior in the cheetah (*Acinonyx jubatus*). *Z. Tierpsychol.* 31:270–80.

Eloff, F. C. 1964. On the predatory habits of lions and hyenas. *Koedoe* 7:105–112.

————. 1973. Lion predation in the Kalahari Gemsbok National Park. Paper read at Southern African Wildlife Management Association Symposium on Wildlife Conservation and Utilization in Africa, June 1973, Pretoria.

Estes, R. D. 1966. Predators and scavengers. *Nat. Hist.* 76(2):20–29; 76(3):38–47.

Graham, A. 1965. East African Wild Life Society cheetah survey: extracts from the report by Wildlife Services. *E. Afr. Wildl. J.* 4:50–55.

Guggisberg, C. A. W. 1961. *Simba: the life of the lion.* Cape Town: Howard Timmins.

Hamilton, P. 1974. The Tsavo Leopard Project. *Wildlife News* 9(2):2–6.

Henry, W. R. 1974. Visitor use in Amboseli Game Reserve: a preliminary report. Mimeographed.

Kruuk, H. and M. Turner. 1967. Comparative notes on predation by lion, leopard, cheetah and wild dog in the Serengeti area, East Africa. *Mammalia* 31(1):1–27.

McLaughlin, R. T. 1970a. Aspects of the biology of cheetahs *Acinonyx jubatus* (Schreber) in Nairobi National Park. Master's thesis, University of Nairobi.

————. 1970b. Nairobi National Park census, 1968. *E. Afr. Wildl. J.* 8:203.

Makacha, S., and G. Schaller. 1969. Observations on lions in the Lake Manyara National Park, Tanzania. *E. Afr. Wildl. J.* 7:99–103.

Myers, N. 1974. Preliminary summary of a report on the status of leopards and cheetahs in Africa for the I.U.C.N./World Wildlife Fund. Mimeographed.

Patterson, J. H. 1907. *The man-eaters of Tsavo.* London: Macmillan & Co.

Pennycuick, C. J. and J. A. Rudnai. 1970. A method of identifying individual lions *Panthera leo* with an analysis of the reliability of identification. *J. Zool. Lond.* 160:497–508.

Rudnai, J. A. 1970. Social behaviour and feeding habits of lion (*Panthera leo massaica* Neumann) in Nairobi National Park. Master's thesis, University of Nairobi.

————. 1973a. Reproductive biology of lions (*Panthera leo massaica* Neumann) in Nairobi National Park. *E. Afr. Wildl. J.* 11:241–53.

———. 1973b. *The social life of the lion*. Lancaster, England: Medical and Technical Publishing Co.

———. 1974. The pattern of lion predation in Nairobi Park. *E. Afr. Wildl. J.* 12:213–22.

Schaller, G. 1968. Hunting behaviour of the cheetah in the Serengeti National Park, Tanzania. *E. Afr. Wildl. J.* 6:95–100.

———. 1969. Life with the king of beasts. *Natl. Geogr.* 135(4):494–519.

———. 1970. This gentle and elegant cat. *Nat. Hist.* 79(6):31–39.

———. 1972a. Predators of the Serengeti. *Nat. Hist.* 81(2):38–49; 81(3):60–69; 81(4):38–43.

———. 1972b. *The Serengeti lion: a study of predator-prey relations*. Chicago: University of Chicago Press.

———. 1973. *Serengeti: a kingdom of predators*. London: Collins.

———. 1974. *Golden shadows, flying hooves*. London: Collins.

Schaller, G. and G. Lowther. 1969. The relevance of carnivore behavior to the study of early hominids. *S. W. J. of Anthro.* 25(4):307–41.

Schenkel, R. 1966. Play, exploration and territoriality in the wild lion. *Symp. Zool. Soc. Lond.* 18:11–22.

Turnbull-Kemp, P. 1967. *The leopard*. Cape Town: Howard Timmins.

Willoughby, D. P. 1974. Running and jumping. *Nat. Hist.* 83(3):68–72.

Wright, B. 1960. Predation on big game in East Africa. *J. Wildl. Mgmt.* 24(1):1–15.

CHAPTER VIII. THE SPOTTED HYENA

Cullen, A. 1969. *Window onto wilderness*. Nairobi: East African Publishing House.

Deane, N. N. 1960. Hyena predation. *The Lammergeyer* 1(1):36.

———. 1962. The spotted hyaena *Crocuta crocuta crocuta*. *The Lammergeyer* 2(2):26–43.

Eloff, F. C. 1964. On the predatory habits of lions and hyenas. *Koedoe* 7:105–12.

Kambe, A. K. 1971. Hyaena mythology. *Uganda Journal* 35(2):209–11.

Kruuk, H. 1966a. Clan-system and feeding habits of spotted hyaenas. *Nature* 209:1257–58.

———. 1966b. A new view of the hyaena. *New Scientist* 33:849–51.

———. 1968. Hyaenas, the hunters nobody knows. *Natl. Geogr.* 134(1):44–57.

———. 1970. Interactions between populations of spotted hyaenas (*Crocuta crocuta* Erxleben) and their prey species. *Brit. Ecol. Soc. Symp.* 10:359–74.

———. 1972a. *The spotted hyena: a study of predation and social behavior*. Chicago: University of Chicago Press.

———. 1972b. Surplus killing by carnivores. *J. Zool.* 166(2):233–44.

Matthews, L. H. 1939a. The bionomics of the spotted hyaena, *Crocuta crocuta* Erxl. *Proc. Zool. Soc. Lond. Ser. A.* 109:237–60.

———. 1939b. Reproduction of the spotted hyaena, *Crocuta crocuta* (Erxleben). *Phil. Trans. Ser. B.* 230:1–78.

Parry, M. 1972. Safari notebook. *East African Standard*. June 30, 1972.

Van Lawick-Goodall, H. and J. van Lawick-Goodall. 1971. *Innocent killers*. Boston: Houghton Mifflin Co.

Watson, R. M. 1965. Observations on the behaviour of young spotted hyaena (*Crocuta crocuta*) in the burrow. *E. Afr. Wildl. J.* 3:122–23.

Supplement

Since this book was first published in 1975, many wildlife studies have been completed and published. Recent studies of elephants and rhinos have been mentioned in the revised chapters; recent studies of the other species are described briefly below. Again, as in the first edition, I have concentrated on research carried out in East Africa.

The Giraffe. Three studies of giraffes in East Africa have been completed in the last few years. Barbara and Walter Leuthold's work on the ecology and behavior of giraffes in Tsavo (East) National Park is now available, Bob Kakuyo's study of translocated Rothschild's giraffes has been completed as an M.Sc. thesis for the University of Nairobi, and Robin Pellew's extensive ecological work on the Serengeti giraffes is presently being written up.

Zebras. No major studies of the social behavior of zebras have been carried out since Klingel did his work, but Chris Gakahu has recently completed an extensive study of the feeding ecology of zebras in Amboseli National Park combined with feeding trials of captured, tame zebras.

Antelopes. Very little new work on social behavior has been done on the six antelopes covered in this book. A study of gerenuk in northern Kenya was completed recently by Willi Raeder, but the results are not yet available. Mattie Jarman's book on the social behavior of impalas has been published (1979). There is important information on the ecology of the wildebeest in Sinclair and Norton-Griffiths' edited volume on the Serengeti ecosystem (1979). Chris Hillman's Ph.D. thesis on the eland has been completed for the University of Nairobi.

Baboons. The emphasis in baboon research is on long-term studies of particular troops. There are major longitudinal studies underway in four study sites in East Africa. Three of these sites and the main workers involved have been discussed in the chapter. The fourth study in progress is in Mikumi National Park in Tanzania where R. J. Rhine and his students have been studying one baboon troop for several years.

The Big Cats. After Brian Bertram completed his work on the Serengeti lions, two husband and wife teams carried out further studies: David Bygott and Jeannette Hanby (1974–77) and Craig Packer and Anne Pusey (1977–81). With Schaller's work beginning in 1966 there are now fifteen years of continuous records on known individuals and prides.

In 1974 George and Lory Frame started a four-year study of cheetahs and wild dogs in the Serengeti. They have nearly completed writing up their research. In the Maasai Mara Reserve in Kenya, David Burney carried out a seventeen-month study on the effects of human activities (including tourism) on cheetahs. His work is available as an M.Sc. thesis from the University. Both he and the Frames have written several popular articles on cheetahs.

After completing his M.Sc. degree based on his work on the Tsavo leopards, Patrick Hamilton went on to study stock-raiding leopards that were being caught and translocated into Meru National Park in order to find out if this was a feasible conservation practice. Theodore Bailey completed his leopard study in South Africa and is currently writing up his results at the University of Idaho.

The Spotted Hyena. A major study of hyenas is underway in the Maasai Mara Reserve in Kenya. Laurence Frank's three-year study of the ecology and social behavior of the spotted hyena using radio tracking equipment should reveal some fascinating new information about these puzzling animals.

CHAPTER I. THE AFRICAN ELEPHANT

Allaway, J. 1981. The African elephant's drinking problem. *Nat. Hist.* 90(4): 30–35.
Barnes, R. F. W. 1979. Elephant ecology in Ruaha National Park, Tanzania. Ph.D. thesis, University of Cambridge.
Buss, I. O., L. E. Rasmussen, and G. L. Smuts. 1976. The role of stress and individual recognition in the function of the African elephant's temporal gland. *Mammalia* 40(3):437–51.
Caughley, G. 1976. The elephant problem — an alternative hypothesis. *E. Afr. Wildl. J.* 14(4): 265–83.
Cobb, S. 1980a. Tsavo: the first thirty years. *Swara* 3(4):12–17.
———. 1980b. Tsavo's next thirty years. *Swara* 3(4): 20–23.
Corfield, T. 1975. Elephant die-off in Tsavo's recent history. *Africana* 5(9):21.
Douglas-Hamilton, I. 1976. 80,000 elephant alive and well in the Selous. *Africana* 6(3):17–19.
———. 1977a. African elephant survey. *Oryx* 14(1):24.
———. 1977b. IUCN/WWF Elephant Project Report. *Africana* 6(5):21–22.
———. 1978. Where are all the elephants going? *Wildlife News* 13(1):8–12.
———. 1980a. African elephant population table. *Africana* 7(2):36.
———. 1980b. Elephant numbers are falling heavily. *IUCN Bulletin*, n.s. 2(1–2): 2–3.
———. 1980c. Elephants threatened by force of habitat: extracts from Final Report on the Elephant Ivory Trade Study and the African Elephant Action Plan. *Africana* 7(2):31–34.
———. 1980d. Uganda's elephants face extinction. *IUCN Bulletin*, n.s. 2(4):45.
Douglas-Hamilton, O. 1980. Africa's elephants — can they survive? *Natl. Geogr.* 158(5):568–603.
Eltringham, S. K. 1977. The numbers and distribution of elephant *Loxodonta africana* in Rwenzori National Park and Chambura Game Reserve, Uganda. *E. Afr. Wildl. J.* 15(1):19–40.
———. 1980. A quantitative assessment of range usage by large African mammals with particular reference to the effects of elephants on trees. *Afr. J. Ecol.* 18(1):53–71.

Eltringham, S. K., and R. C. Malpas. 1976. Elephant slaughter in Uganda. *Oryx* 13(4):334–35.

————. 1980. The decline in elephant numbers in Rwenzori and Kabalega Falls National Parks, Uganda. *Afr. J. Ecol.* 18(1):73–86.

Hanks, J. 1979. *The struggle for survival: the elephant problem.* New York: Mayflower Books.

Laws, R. M., I. S. C. Parker, and R. C. B. Johnstone. 1975. *Elephants and their habitats: the ecology of elephants in North Bunyoro, Uganda.* Oxford: Clarendon Press.

Leuthold, W. 1976a. Age structure of elephants in Tsavo National Park, Kenya. *J. Appl. Ecol.* 13(2):435–44.

————. 1976b. Group size in elephants in Tsavo National Park and possible factors influencing it. *J. Animal Ecol.* 45(2):425–39.

————. 1977. Spatial organization and strategy of habitat utilization of elephants in Tsavo National Park, Kenya. *Z. Saugetierk* 42(6):358–79.

Leuthold, W., and B. M. Leuthold. 1975. Parturition and related behaviour in the African elephant. *Z. Tierpsychol.* 39:75–84.

Malpas, R. C. 1977. Diet and the condition and growth of elephants in Uganda. *J. Appl. Ecol.* 14(2):489–504.

————. 1978. The ecology of the African elephant in Rwenzori and Kabalega Falls National Parks, Uganda. Ph.D. thesis, University of Cambridge.

Moss, C. J. 1977. The Amboseli elephants. *Wildlife News* 12(2):9–12.

————. 1978. A family saga. *Swara* 1(1):34–39.

————. 1980. The two and only. *Animal Kingdom* 83(6):25–27.

————. 1981. Social circles. *Wildlife News* 16(1):2–7.

Myers, N. 1976. Under the gun. *Int. Wildl.* 6(6):5–16.

Poole, J. H., and C. J. Moss. 1981. Musth in the African elephant *Loxodonta africana. Nature* 292:830–31.

Ricciuti, E. R. 1980. The ivory wars. *Animal Kingdom* 83(1):6–58.

Wilson, D., and P. Ayerst. 1976. *White gold, the story of African ivory.* New York: Taplinger.

CHAPTER II. THE GIRAFFE

Dagg, A. I., and J. B. Foster. 1976. *The giraffe — its biology, behaviour and ecology.* New York: Van Nostrand Reinhold.

Langman, V. A. 1977. Cow-calf relationship in giraffe (*Giraffa camelopardalis giraffa*). *Z. Tierpsychol.* 43:264–86.

Leuthold, B. M. 1979. Social organization and behaviour of giraffe in Tsavo East National Park. *Afr. J. Ecol.* 17(1):19–34.

Leuthold, B. M., and W. Leuthold. 1978a. Ecology of the giraffe in Tsavo East National Park, Kenya. *E. Afr. Wildl. J.* 16:1–20.

————. 1978b. Daytime activity patterns of gerenuk and giraffe in Tsavo National Park, Kenya. *E. Afr. Wildl. J.* 16:231–43.

Moore-Berger, E. 1974. Utilization of the habitat by the reticulated giraffe (*Giraffa camelopardalis reticulata* Linnaeus) in northern Kenya. M.Sc. thesis, University of Nairobi.

CHAPTER III. THE BLACK RHINOCEROS

Bradley Martin, E. 1979. The international trade in rhinoceros products. Gland: International Union for the Conservation of Nature and Natural Resources and World Wildlife Fund.

———. 1981a. The conspicuous consumption of rhinos, I. *Animal Kingdom* 84(1): 10–19.

———. 1981b. The conspicuous consumption of rhinos, II. *Animal Kingdom* 84(2): 20–29.

Frame, G. W. 1980. Black rhinoceros (*Diceros bicornis* L.) subpopulation on the Serengeti Plains, Tanzania. *Afr. J. Ecol.* 18(2–3):155–67.

Hillman, K. 1980. The status and conservation of Africa's rhinos. *Wildlife News* 15(2):2–5.

Hillman, K., and E. Bradley Martin. 1979a. The state of the game: death knell for the rhino. *Safari*, April/May, p. 5.

———. 1979b. Count-down for the rhino in Kenya. *Africana* 6(12):5–6.

———. 1979c. Will poaching exterminate Kenya's rhinos? *Oryx* 15(2):131–32.

Makacha, S., C. L. Mollel, and J. Rwezaura. 1979. The conservation status of the black rhinoceros (*Diceros bicornis* L.) in the Ngorongoro Crater, Tanzania. *Afr. J. Ecol.* 17(2):97–104.

Mukinya, J. G. 1976. An identification method for black rhinoceros (*Diceros bicornis* Linn. 1758). *E. Afr. Wildl. J.* 14(4):335–38.

———. 1977. Feeding and drinking habits of the black rhinoceros in Maasai Mara Game Reserve. *E. Afr. Wildl. J.* 15(2):125–38.

CHAPTER IV. ZEBRAS

Klingel, H. 1974. A comparison of the social behaviour of the equidae. In *The behaviour of ungulates and its relation to management*, ed. V. Geist and F. Walther, n.s. no. 24, pp. 124–32. Morges, Switzerland: IUCN.

———. 1975. Social organization of the equidae. *Verh. Deutsch. Zool. Ges.* 68:71–80.

CHAPTER V. ANTELOPES

Cobb, S. M. 1976. The distribution and abundance of the large herbivore community of Tsavo National Park, Kenya. D.Phil. thesis, University of Oxford.

Estes, R. D. 1976. The significance of breeding synchrony in the wildebeest. *E. Afr. Wildl. J.* 14(2):135–52.

Geist, V., and F. Walther. 1974. *The behaviour of ungulates and its relation to management*, n.s. no. 24. Morges, Switzerland: IUCN.

Hendrichs, H., and U. Hendrichs. 1975. Changes in a population of dikdik. *Madoqua* (*Rhynchotragus*) *kirki* (Gunther 1880). *Z. Tierpsychol.* 38:55–69.

Hillman, J. C. 1979. The biology of the eland (*Taurotragus oryx* Pallas) in the wild. Ph.D. thesis, University of Nairobi.

Inglis, J. M. 1976. Wet season movements of individual wildebeest of the Serengeti migratory herd. *E. Afr. Wildl. J.* 14:17–33.

Jarman, M. V. 1976. Impala social behaviour: birth behaviour. *E. Afr. Wildl. J.* 14(2):153–67.

———. 1979. *Impala social behaviour: territory, hierarchy, mating and the use of space,* no. 21. Berlin and Hamburg: Verlag Paul Parey.

Lewis, J. G. 1977. Game domestication for animal production in Kenya: activity patterns of eland, oryx, buffalo and zebu cattle. *J. Agric. Sci. Camb.* 89:551–63.

Leuthold, W. 1978a. Ecological separation among browsing ungulates in Tsavo East National Park, Kenya. *Oecologia* 35(2):241–52.

———. 1978b. On the ecology of the gerenuk (*Litocranius walleri*). *J. Anim. Ecol.* 47(2):561–80.

Leuthold, W., and B. M. Leuthold. 1975. Patterns of social grouping in ungulates in Tsavo National Park, Kenya. *J. Zool.* 175(3):405–20.

———. 1978. Daytime activity patterns of gerenuk and giraffe in Tsavo National Park, Kenya. *E. Afr. Wildl. J.* 16:1–20.

Pennycuick, L. 1975. Movements of the migratory wildebeest population in the Serengeti area between 1960 and 1973. *E. Afr. Wildl. J.* 13:65–87.

Sinclair, A. R. E., and M. Norton-Griffiths. 1979. *Serengeti: dynamics of an ecosystem.* Chicago: University of Chicago Press.

Underwood, R. 1975. Social behaviour of the eland (*Taurotragus oryx*) on Loskop Dam Nature Reserve. M.Sc. thesis, University of Pretoria.

CHAPTER VI. BABOONS

Altmann, J. 1978. Infant independence in yellow baboons. In *The development of behavior: comparative and evolutionary aspects,* ed. G. M. Burghardt and M. Bekoff. New York: Garland STPM Press.

———. 1979. Age cohorts as paternal sibships. *Behav. Ecol. Sociobiol.* 6:161–64.

———. 1980. *Baboon mothers and infants.* Cambridge, Mass.: Harvard University Press.

Altmann, J., S. A. Altmann, and G. Hausfater. 1978. Primate infant's effect on mother's future reproduction. *Science* 201:1028–30.

Altmann, J., S. A. Altmann, G. Hausfater, and S. A. McCuskey. 1977 Life history of yellow baboons: physical development, reproductive parameters and infant mortality. *Primates* 18:315–30.

Altmann, S. A. 1979. Baboon progressions: order or chaos? a study of one-dimensional group geometry. *Anim. Behav.* 27:46–80.

Altmann, S. A., and J. Altmann. 1979. Demographic constraints on behavior and social organization. In *Ecological influences on social organization,* ed. E. O. Smith and I. S. Bernstein. New York: Garland STPM Press.

Altmann, S. A., and S. S. Wagner. 1978. A general model of optimal diet. *Rec. Adv. Primatol.* 4:407–14.

Chalmers, N. R. 1978. A comparison of play and non-play activities in feral baboons (*Papio anubis*). In *Recent advances in primatology,* vol. 1, ed. D. J. Chivers and J. Herbert, pp. 13–133. London: Academic Press.

———. 1980a. Developmental relationships among social, manipulatory, postural and locomotor behaviours in olive baboons, *Papio anubis. Behaviour* 57:241–59.

———. 1980b. The ontogeny of play in feral olive baboons (*Papio anubis*). *Anim. Behav.* 28(2):570–85.

Harding, R. S. O. 1973. Predation by a troop of olive baboons (*Papio anubis*). *Am. J. Phys. Anthrop.* 38:587–91.

———. 1976. Ranging patterns of a troop of baboons (*Papio anubis*) in Kenya. *Folia Primatol.* 25:143–85.

Harding, R. S. O., and S. C. Strum. 1976. The predatory baboons of Kekopey. *Nat. Hist.* 85:46–53.

Hausfater, G. 1975a. *Dominance and reproduction in baboons: a quantitative analysis.* Contributions to Primatology, vol. 7. Basel: Karger.

———. 1975b. Knuckle walking by a baboon. *Am. J. Phys. Anthrop.* 43:303–5.

———. 1976. Predatory behaviour of yellow baboons. *Behaviour* 56:44–68.

Hausfater, G., and W. H. Bearce. 1976. Acacia tree exudates: their composition and use as a food source by baboons. *E. Afr. Wildl. J.* 14:241–43.

Lee, P. C., and J. I. Oliver. 1979. Competition, dominance and the acquisition of rank in juvenile yellow baboons (*Papio cynocephalus*). *Anim. Behav.* 27:576–85.

Owens, N. W. 1975. Social play behaviour in free-living baboons, *Papio anubis*. *Anim. Behav.* 23:387–408.

———. 1976. The development of sociosexual behaviour in free-living baboons, *Papio anubis*. *Behaviour* 57:241–59.

Packer, C. 1975. Male transfer in olive baboons. *Nature* 255:219–20.

———. 1977. Reciprocal altruism in *Papio anubis*. *Nature* 265:441–43.

———. 1979a. Male dominance and reproductive activity in *Papio anubis*. *Anim. Behav.* 27:40–45.

———. 1979b. Inter-troop transfer and inbreeding avoidance in *Papio anubis*. *Anim. Behav.* 27:1–39.

———. 1980. Male care and exploitation of infants in *Papio anubis*. *Anim. Behav.* 28(2):512–20.

Packer, C., and A. E. Pusey. 1979. Female aggression and male membership in troops of Japanese macaques and olive baboons. *Folia primatol.* 31:212–18.

Post, D. G. 1981. Activity patterns of yellow baboons (*Papio cynocephalus*) in Amboseli National Park, Kenya. *Anim. Behav.* 29(2):357–74.

Post, D. G., G. Hausfater, and S. A. McCuskey. 1980. Feeding behaviour of yellow baboons: relationship to age, gender and dominance rank. *Folia primatol.* 34:170–95.

Ransom, T. W. 1971. Ecology and social behavior of baboons in Gombe Stream National Park. Ph.D. thesis, University of California, Berkeley.

Ransom, T. W., and B. S. Ransom. 1971. Adult male–infant relations among baboons (*Papio anubis*). *Folia primatol.* 16:179–95.

Ransom, T. W., and T. E. Rowell. 1972. Early social development of feral baboons. In *Primate socialization*, ed. F. E. Poirier. New York: Random House.

Rasmussen, D. R. 1979. Correlates of patterns of range use of a troop of yellow baboons (*Papio cynocephalus*). I: Sleeping sites, impregnable females, births and male emigration and immigration. *Anim. Behav.* 27:1098–112.

Rhine, R. J., and B. J. Westlund. 1978. The nature of primary feeding habit in different age-sex classes of yellow baboons (*Papio cynocephalus*). *Folia primatol.* 30:64–79.

Rose, M. D. 1977. Positional behaviour of olive baboons (*Papio anubis*) and its relationship to maintenance and social activities. *Primates* 18:59–116.

Slatkin, M. 1975. A report on the feeding behavior of two East African baboon species. In *Contemporary primatology*, ed. S. Kondo. Basel: Karger.

Slatkin, M., and G. Hausfater. 1976. A note on the activity of a solitary male baboon. *Primates* 17:311–22.

Strum, S. C. 1976a. Predatory behavior of olive baboons (*Papio anubis*) at Gilgil, Kenya. Ph.D. thesis, University of California, Berkeley.

———. 1976b. Primate predation and bioenergetics: a reply. *Science* 19:314–17.

———. 1981. Processes and products of change: baboon predatory behavior at Gilgil, Kenya. In *Omnivorous primates: gathering and hunting in human evolution*, ed. R. S. O. Harding and G. Teleki. New York: Columbia University Press.

———. In press. Agonistic dominance in male baboons: an alternative view. *Int. J. Primatol.*

———. In press. Why males use infants. In *Primate paternalism*, ed. D. Taub. New York: Van Nostrand Reinhold.

Walters, J. 1980. Intervention and the development of dominance relationships in female baboons. *Folia primatol.* 34:61–89.

———. 1981. Inferring kinship from behaviour: maternity determination in yellow baboons. *Anim. Behav.* 29(1): 126–36.

CHAPTER VII. THE BIG CATS

Adamson, J. 1980. *Queen of Shaba: the story of an African leopard*. London: Collins.

Bertram, B. C. R. 1975a. Social factors influencing reproduction in wild lions. *J. Zool.* 177:463–82.

———. 1975b. The social system of lions. *Sci. Am.* 232:54–65.

———. 1976. Kin selection in lions and in evolution. In *Growing points in ethology*, ed. P. P. G. Bateson and R. A. Hinde, pp. 281–301. Cambridge: Cambridge University Press.

———. 1978. *Pride of lions*. London: J. M. Dent & Sons.

———. 1979. Serengeti predators and their social systems. In *Serengeti: dynamics of an ecosystem*, ed. A. R. E. Sinclair and M. Norton-Griffiths, pp. 221–48. Chicago: University of Chicago Press.

Bygott, J. D., B. C. R. Bertram, and J. P. Hanby. 1979. Male lions in large coalitions gain reproductive advantage. *Nature* 282:839–41.

Frame, G. W., and L. H. Frame. 1977. Serengeti cheetah. *Wildlife News* 12(3):1–6.

Grobler, J. H., and V. J. Wilson. 1972. Food of the leopard, *Panthera pardus* (Linn.), in the Rhodes Matopos National Park, Rhodesia, as determined by faecal analysis. *Arnoldia Rhod.* 5(35):1–9.

Hamilton, P. H. 1976. The movements of leopards in Tsavo National Park, Kenya, as determined by radio tracking. M.Sc. thesis, University of Nairobi.

———. 1979. Translocated leopards: where do they go? *Wildlife News* 14(3):2–6.

———. 1981. The leopard *Panthera pardus* and the cheetah *Acinonyx jubatus* in Kenya: ecology, status, conservation, management. Report for the U.S. Fish and Wildlife Service.

Hanby, J. P., and J. D. Bygott. 1979. Population changes in lions and other predators. In *Serengeti: dynamics of an ecosystem*, ed. A. R. E. Sinclair and M. Norton-Griffiths, pp. 249–62. Chicago: University of Chicago Press.

Henry, W. R. 1977. Tourist impact on Amboseli National Park. *Wildlife News* 12(2):4–8.

———. 1980. Relationships between visitor use and tourist capacity for Kenya's Amboseli National Park. Ph.D. thesis, Colorado State University.

Myers, N. 1975. The cheetah *Acinonyx jubatus* in Africa. Monograph no. 4. Morges, Switzerland: IUCN.

———. 1976. The leopard *Panthera pardus* in Africa. Monograph no. 5. Morges, Switzerland, IUCN.

Rudnai, J. 1979. Ecology of lions in Nairobi National Park and the adjoining Kitengela Conservation Unit in Kenya. *Afr. J. Ecol.* 17(2):85–95.

———. 1978. Conflict of interests: the Nairobi lions. *Wildlife News* 13(1):2–7.

Smith, R. M. 1977. Movement patterns and feeding behaviour of leopard in the Rhodes Matopos National Park, Rhodesia. *Arnoldia Rhod.* 8(13): 1–16.

CHAPTER VIII. THE SPOTTED HYENA

Bearder, S. K. 1977. Feeding habits of spotted hyaenas in a woodland habitat. *E. Afr. Wildl. J.* 15(4):263–80.

Gould, S. J. 1981. Hyena myths and realities. *Nat. Hist.* 90(2):16–24.

Hopkins, P. 1977. Interactions between the spotted hyaena and potential prey species in the Aberdare mountains in Kenya. *E. Afr. Wildl. J.* 15(2):165–66.

Kruuk, H. 1975a. *Hyaena*. Oxford: Oxford University Press.

———. 1975b. Functional aspects of social hunting in carnivores. In *Function and evolution of behaviour*, ed. G. Baerends, C. Beer, and A. Manning, pp. 119–41. Oxford: Clarendon Press.

———. 1976a. Carnivores and conservation. In *Proc. Symp. Endangered Wildl. in Southern Africa*, pp. 1–8. Pretoria: University of Pretoria.

———. 1976b. Feeding and social behaviour of the striped hyaena (*Hyaena vulgaris*). *E. Afr. Wildl. J.* 14:91–111.

Racey, P. A., and J. D. Skinner. 1979. Endocrine aspects of sexual mimicry in spotted hyenas, *Crocuta crocuta*. *J. Zool.* 187:315–26.

Index

Abbott, Shep, 264, 268, 271
Acacia drepanolobium, 55–56, 58, 223
Acacia mellifera, 149
Acacia tortilis, 12, 36, 223
Acacia xanthophloea, 37, 223
Adamson, George, 247
Adamson, Joy, 234, 264–268, 273, 282–283
African Wildlife Leadership Foundation, 331, 334
Allaway, James, 12
Altmann, Jeanne, vii, 195, 218, 221, 226–229
Altmann, Stuart, vii, 195, 196, 218, 221, 226–229
Amboseli Game Reserve: the rhinoceros, 65; the baboon, 195, 196, 201–203, 216–217, 218, 221, 223, 226, 227, 229
Amboseli National Park: the elephant, 31; the rhinoceros, 86; the cheetah, 283–284
Angola giraffe, the, 40
Animals of East Africa, The (Spinage), 88–89
Antelope, the, 127–192; Thomson's gazelle, 114–115, 146, 166, 224–226, 249, 260, 277, 281–282, 293, 300, 317, 321–322, 324, 326; Bates's pygmy, 142; the beira, 142; Cape grysbok, 142; duikers, 142; Guenther's dikdik, 142; the klipspringer, 142;

Antelope, the (*contd.*)
Phillip's dikdik, 142; royal, 142; Salt's dikdik, 142; Sharpe's grysbok, 142; the steinbok, 142, 225; the suni, 142; Grant's gazelle, 146, 166, 277, 281–282, 294, 296; Bohor reedbuck, 150; the giraffe gazelle, 150; the lesser kudu, 150; mountain reedbuck, 150; the oribi, 150; the sitatunga, 150; southern reedbuck, 150; Vaal rhebuck, 150; the bushbuck, 150, 184, 228; the Defassa waterbuck, 166; the greater kudu, 166; the lechwe, 166; the nyala, 166; the puku, 166; the springbuck, 166; the common waterbuck, 166, 301; the hartebeest, 181; the tsessebe, 181; the topi, 181, 256, 325; Cape buffalo, 192; the gemsbok, 192; the oryx, 192; *See also* Dikdik, the; Eland, the; Gerenuk, the; Impala, the; Uganda kob, the; Wildebeest, the
Arabia: the giraffe, 39; the baboon, 194, 197; the cheetah, 263
Ardrey, Robert, 193, 196, 230
Asia, the rhinoceros, 62
Askari wa kifaru, 79
Athi-Kapiti plains: the eland, 182, 185; the lion, 252
Australia, the giraffe, 60
Austria, the giraffe, 40
A.V.M. Instrument Company, 286

Baboon, the, 193–230; Egypt, 194; *Papio anubis*, 194; *Papio hamadryas*, 194; *Papio papio*, 194; *Papio ursinus*, 194; Somalia, 194; species of, 194; western, 194; hamadryas, 194, 194n; gelada, 194n; *Theropithecus*, 194n; *Papio cynocephalus*, 194, 195; Ethiopia, 194, 194n, 197; chacma, 194, 195; guinea, 194, 195; West Africa, 194, 195; savannah, 194, 196; Kenya, 194, 196, 203–211, 214–218, 223, 225–227; Tanzania, 194, 196, 218; Uganda, 194, 196, 221; social organization, 194, 196–212; Arabia, 194, 197; the Sudan, 194, 197; family units, 194, 205–207; yellow, 194–195; olive, 194–195, 218; Cape Peninsula, 195; Kruger National Park, 195; Amboseli Game Reserve, 195, 196, 201–203, 216–217, 218, 221, 223, 226, 227, 229; South Africa, 195, 197; Nairobi National Park, 195, 199–201, 221, 223, 224, 226, 227; Gombe National Park, 196, 218, 228; behavior, 196–203; antipredator behavior, 197, 198–199, 219, 221–222; feeding habits, 197, 212, 214–215, 222–226; troops of, 197–208, 218, 220–221; displacing among, 198; weight of, 198–199; males, 198–200, 202–203, 207–211, 217–218; hierarchy among, 198–203, 206, 211, 215; teeth of, 199; individual identification, 199, 202, 204; fighting among, 199, 202–203, 209, 210, 211, 214; sexual behavior, 200, 201, 202, 208, 209, 215–217; females, 200, 202, 205–210, 215–217; in estrus, 200, 202, 208, 209, 215–217; dominance relations, 201–203, 206–207; friendship among, 203–210; mutual grooming, 205, 206, 208–209, 219–220; mating habits, 208, 209, 215–217; birth of, 212; gestation period, 212; as mothers, 212–213; playing habits, 213–214, 219; chortling of, 214; restraint among, 214; body language, 215; birth interval, 217; life span, 218;

Baboon, the (*contd.*)
sleeping habits, 218–219, 228–229; daily activities, 218–230; hunting of, 222; the lion and, 222; diet of, 223–226; meat eating by, 224–226; the impala and, 225, 226, 228; hunting by, 225–226; home range, 226–227; drinking habits, 227–228; the bushbuck and, 228; Lake Manyara National Park, 228; resting habits, 228; Serengeti National Park, 229; the leopard and, 294, 295–296
Backhaus, Deiter, 41, 52
Bailey, Theodore N., 290n
Baker, Sir Samuel, 41
Baringo giraffe, 40
Barnes, Richard, 12
Basel Zoo, 13
Bates's pygmy antelope, 142
Beattie, Willa, viii
Beira, the, 142
Belgian Congo, see Zaïre
Bell, Richard, 114
Bere, Rennie, 16–17, 34
Bertram, Brian, vii, 235–236, 238, 241, 243, 246, 251, 253, 259, 289–295
Bibliography, 336–355
Big cats, the, 231–233; *See also* Cheetah, the; Leopard, the; Lion, the
Black rhinoceros, *see* Rhinoceros, black
Blixen, Karen, 61
Boehm's zebra, 89
Bohor reedbuck, 150
Bolwig, N., 195
Bongo, the, 184
Born Free (Adamson), 234
Bradley Martin, Esmond, 85, 86
Braunschweig, University of, 119
Brooks, A. C., 2–3, 13
Brown hyena (*Hyena brunnea*), 298n
Budongo Central Forest Reserve, 20
Buechner, Helmut K., 2–3, 161–166
Buffalo, the: Cape, 127, 192; the lion and, 256, 259, 261; the hyena and, 300, 325
Burchell's zebra, 89
Bushbuck, the, 150, 184; the baboon and, 228

Buss, I. O., 2–3, 6, 24, 28, 35
Bygott, David, 236

Caesar Kleburg Foundation, 331
Canadian Federal Government, 331
Cape buffalo, 127, 192
Cape giraffe, 40
Cape grysbok, 142
Cape Peninsula, the baboon, 195
Ceratotherium simum, 62n
Chacma baboon, the, 194, 195
Chalmers, Neil, 196
Chapman's zebra, 89
Cheetah, the, 232–233, 262–284;
Arabia, 263; Egypt, 263; India, 263;
semidomestication of, 263; weight at
birth, 263; hunting by, 263, 271–
272, 275–282; as a predator, 263, 271–
272, 275–282; weight of, 263, 276;
speed of, 263, 279; Nairobi National Park, 263–283; individual
identification, 264; Meru National
Park, 264; Tanzania, 264, 265, 268,
277, 278, 281, 283; Serengeti National Park, 264, 268, 277, 278, 279,
281, 283; population, 264–265, 281;
Tarangire National Park, 265; social
organization, 265–267; behavior,
265–284; family units, 266–273;
mother-cub relationship, 267–273;
females, 267–275; birth of, 268; litter
size, 268; natal coat, 268; mating
habits, 268, 270, 274; feeding habits,
268, 270–271; as mothers, 268–273;
sounds made by, 269; in estrus, 270;
mortality rates, 270; playing habits,
270; sexual behavior, 270, 274; greeting ceremony among, 273; mutual
grooming, 273; fighting among, 274;
gestation period, 274; as diurnal, 275;
resting habits, 275; daily activities,
275–276; males, 275–277; as a
courser, 276; the wild dog and, 276,
280; the impala and, 277; vision of,
277; the zebra and, 277; preferred
prey of, 277; as a stalker, 277–278;
killing process, 280; the leopard and,
280; the lion and, 280; the hyena and,
280, 283; poaching, 282; Amboseli
National Park, 283–284; tourist

Cheetah, the (*contd.*)
harassment, 283–284
Chicago Zoo, 84
China, the giraffe, 39–40
Cissus quadrangularis, 78
Cocuta crocuta, see Hyena, spotted
Controlling (shooting on control),
defined, 2n
Convention on International Trade in
Endangered Species of Flora and
Fauna (CITES), 38, 87
Corfield, Timothy, 12, 16
Crematogaster, 56
Cropping, defined, 2n
Croze, Harvey, vii, 12, 34, 37, 333, 334,
335
Croze, Nani, viii
Culling, defined, 2n

Dagg, Anne I., *see* Innis, Anne
Damara zebra, 89
Dar es Salaam, University of, 332
Dasman, R. F., 152
Dawkins, H. C., 2–3
Defassa waterbuck, the, 166
Derby, Lord, 182
DeVore, Irven, 195, 196, 198, 199–201,
202, 203, 215, 218, 220–221, 224
Dicerorhinus sumatrensis, 62n
Diceros bicornis, see Rhinoceros (black)
Dikdik, the, 130–142, 225, 226; height
of, 130; interdigital glands, 130; nose
of, 130; sense of smell, 130; weight of,
130; whistling sound of, 130; danger
reactions, 130, 131; feeding habits,
130, 132, 132n, 133, 137, 138, 139;
preorbital glands, 130, 134, 136;
Ethiopia, 131; females, 131; horns of,
131; individual identification, 131;
Kenya, 131; Kirk's, 131; males, 131;
Somalia, 131; South West Africa,
131; Serengeti National Park,
131–142; Tanzania, 131–142; social
organization, 132; pair bonds, 132,
133–134, 137, 140; as territorial, 132,
134–137, 139–140; drinking habits,
132–133; behavior, 132–141; home
range, 133, 134; antipredator behav-

Dikdik, the (*contd.*)
ior, 133, 138–139, 140–141; fighting
among, 134, 136–137; dung, 134–
136, 137, 139; urination, 135, 140;
chewing the cud, 137; daily activities, 137; resting habits, 137; fawning interval, 137–138; birth of, 138;
gestation period, 138; weight at birth,
138; as mothers, 138–139; alarm calls,
139; sexual behavior, 139, 140; in
estrus, 140; Flehmen, 140; mating
habits, 140; the leopard and, 140, 141;
the wild dog and, 140, 141; life span,
141; mortality rates, 141; Guenther's,
142; Phillip's, 142; population, 142;
Salt's, 142
Dogs, *see* Domestic dog; Wild dog
Domestic dog, the leopard and, 285, 296
Donne, John, 38
Douglas-Hamilton, Iain, vii, 3–20, 22,
26–27, 30, 36, 83, 333
Douglas-Hamilton, Oria, vii, 333
Duikers, 142
Duncan, Patrick, vii

East African Wildlife Society, 264, 331
Eaton, Randall, 264, 276, 280
Egypt: the giraffe, 40; the baboon, 194;
the cheetah, 263
Eland, the, 181–192, 226; height of,
181; drinking habits, 181, 184, 191;
feeding habits, 181, 184, 191; weight
of, 181, 187; horns of, 181, 189;
as food, 181–182; domesticating,
181–182, 191–192; behavior, 181–
192; cropping, 182; Great Britain, 182; hunting of, 182; milk
of, 182; population, 182; Rhodesia,
182; Russia, 182; South Africa, 182;
Athi-Kapiti plains, 182, 185; ranching of, 182, 190, 192; Nairobi National Park, 182–192; individual
identification, 183; females, 183,
184, 185–186, 187–188; juvenile
group, 183, 184, 186; males, 183,
184, 187–190; social organization,
183–184, 187; nursery group,

Eland, the (*contd.*)
183–187; birth of, 185; mutual grooming, 185; as mothers, 185–186; gestation period, 186; in estrus, 186, 188;
antipredator behavior, 187; the wild
dog and, 187; the lion and, 187, 259;
the hyena and, 187, 300, 325; fighting
among, 188; hierarchy among, 188;
mating habits, 188, 190; clicking
walk, 189–190; empty licking, 190;
Flehmen, 190; life span, 190; urination, 190; chewing the cud, 191; daily
activities, 191; Kenya, 191; resting
habits, 191; Tsavo National Park, 191
Elephant, African, 1–38; special aspect of, 1; intelligence of, 1, 18–19;
hunting of, 1, 21, 32, 33–34, 37;
ivory, 1, 37, 38; early naturalists'
observations, 1–2; population, 2, 4,
12, 35–38; environment and, 2, 12,
20–21, 35–36, 38; Uganda, 2, 17, 20,
28, 33, 34, 35; human population and,
2, 35, 38; hierarchy among, 3, 5–8, 9,
10, 28; the matriarch, 3, 5–8, 10;
family units, 3, 5–9, 10, 13–17;
females, 3, 5–9, 10, 13–17, 20, 21;
males, 3, 8–10, 20, 21, 22; Lake Manyara National Park, 3–12, 15, 16, 20–
21, 27, 28, 30, 32, 36; Tanzania,
3–12, 15, 16, 20–21, 27, 28, 30, 32,
36; social organization, 3–17; behavior, 3–37; ears of, 4; photographing, 4; tusks of, 4, 19, 32, 33; individual identification, 4–5; growling
contact noise, 6; sense of smell, 6;
trumpeting, 6, 8, 10–11; danger reactions, 6, 8, 19, 25; daily activities, 6,
26–31; home range, 7, 11, 27; feeding
habits, 7, 14, 18, 19, 27–28; kin
groups, 7–8; antipredator behavior,
8; competition among, 8; migrations,
8, 10, 11, 19; sexual behavior, 8–9,
10, 20–26, 34; in estrus, 8–9, 10,
21–25; mating habits, 8–9, 10, 21–25;
all-bull herds, 9, 10; fighting among,
9, 10; droughts and, 10, 16, 25, 34,
37; drinking habits, 10, 18, 27, 28;

Elephant, African (*contd.*)
communication among, 10–11; clan groups, 11; as territorial, 11; greeting ceremony among, 11, 19; Zambia, 12; Kenya, 12, 16, 20, 27, 28, 31–38, 87; Tsavo National Park, 12, 16, 20, 27, 28, 31–38, 87; Mkomasi Game Reserve, 12, 20; life span, 12, 31; Serengeti National Park, 12, 35, 37; destruction by, 12, 35–36, 63, 143, 149; birth of, 13; gestation period, 13; in labor, 13; orphaned, 13–14, 17–18; as mothers, 13–17; teats, 14; twinning, 14; weight at birth, 14; first month of life, 14–15; personalities of, 15; swimming by, 16; Ruwenzori National Park, 17; trunk of, 18; learning by, 18–19; mortality rates, 18–19; Kabalega Falls National Park, 19, 23, 35; Budongo Central Forest Reserve, 20; heat strokes, 20; puberty, 20–21; growth rate, 21; height of, 21; weight of, 21; musth gland, 21–22; courtship, 23, 24; calving interval, 24–25; menopause, 25; immobilized by drugs, 26; radio-tracking of, 26–27, 30–31; seasonal habits, 26–31; diet of, 27–28; intoxication of, 28; Kruger National Park, 28; bathing habits, 29; dusting habits, 29; mud-wallowing, 29; resting habits, 29–30; sleeping habits, 30; Zaïre, 30; Amboseli National Park, 22, 31; teeth of, 31–32; cropping, 33; poaching, 33, 37–38; death of, 33–35; culling, 36, 37; the rhinocerus and, 80–81
Eloff, F. C., 256, 300
Elsa Wild Animal Appeal, 331
Eltringham, Keith, 12
Equus burchelli, 89n
Equus burchelli burchelli, 89n
Equus grevyi, *see* Zebra, Grevy's
Equus quagga, 89n
Equus quagga quagga, 89n
Equus zebra hartmannae, *see* Zebra, Hartmann's
Equus zebra zebra, *see* Zebra, mountain

Estes, Richard D., vii, 168–176, 180, 296, 334, 335
Ethiopia: the giraffe, 39, 40; the zebra, 89, Somali wild ass, 90; the dikdik, 131; the gerenuk, 142; the Uganda kob, 160; the baboon, 194, 194n, 197
Etosha Pan Reserve, the zebra, 116
Explorers Club, 331

Fauna Preservation Society, 331
Filaria parasite, 79–80
Finch, Virginia, viii, 125
Fisher, J., 175
Food and Agriculture Organization of the United Nations, 331
Ford Foundation, 331
Forever Free (Adamson), 234
Foster, J. Bristol, vii, 41–45, 49–51, 53–60
Fox, Robin, 193
France, the giraffe, 39, 40
Frankfurt Zoo, 47, 71
Fritz Thyssen Foundation, 331
Fuller, Tex, 264, 268, 271

Garamba National Park, the giraffe, 41
Gazelle, the: Thomson's, 114–115, 146, 166, 224–226, 249, 260, 277, 281–282, 293, 300, 317, 321–322, 324, 326; Grant's, 146, 166, 277, 281–282, 294, 296; migrations, 169
Gelada baboon, 194n
Gemsbok, the, 192
Gerenuk, the, 142–150; drinking habits, 142; ears of, 142; Ethiopia, 142; height of, 142; horns of, 142; meaning of name, 142; Somalia, 142; Tanzania, 142; weight of, 142; feeding habits, 142, 143–144, 145, 146, 148, 149; Kenya, 142–150; Tsavo National Park, 142–150; social organization, 143–144; behavior, 143–149; fighting among, 144; as territorial, 144–145, 147–148; males, 144–148; anteorbital glands, 145; Flehmen, 145; mutual grooming, 145; urination, 145; home range, 145, 148; courtship, 145–146; Laufschlag (leg beat), 145–146; mat-

Gerenuk, the (*contd.*)
ing habits, 145–146; females, 145–147; birth of, 146; fawning interval, 146; gestation period, 146; as mothers, 146; antipredator behavior, 148

Giraffa camelopardalis, see Giraffe, the

Giraffa camelopardalis reticulata, 40

Giraffe, the (*Giraffa camelopardalis*), 39–61; Arabia, 39; Greece, 39; the Sudan, 39; Ethiopia, 39, 40; France, 39, 40; China, 39–40; historical background, 39–40; Angola, 40; Austria, 40; Baringo, 40; Cape, 40; Egypt, 40; *Giraffa camelopardalis reticulata,* 40; Great Britain, 40; Nubian, 40; Rothschild's, 40; Somalia, 40; subspecies, 40; Thornicroft's, 40; Uganda, 40; West African, 40; Zambia, 40; South Africa, 40, 41, 50, 60; Maasai, 40, 42; Kenya, 40, 42, 54, 55, 60–61; Tsavo National Park, 40, 42, 54, 55, 60–61; Garamba National Park, 41; markings on, 41, 42; vision of, 41, 43; height of, 41, 43, 54; Nairobi National Park, 41, 44, 49, 50–51, 53, 55–56, 59–60, 61; Zaïre, 41, 52; individual identification, 41–42; photographing, 42; feeding habits, 42, 44, 45, 51–56, 57, 58; social organization, 42–44; Serengeti National Park, 42–54, 57, 58, 59; Tanzania, 42–54, 57, 58, 59; behavior, 42–60; interactions among, 43; leadership, 43; radio-tracking of, 44; snorting by, 44; as territorial, 44; females, 44, 45, 49–54; males, 44, 45–47, 54; antipredator behavior, 44, 57, 59; home range, 44–45; threat behavior, 45; fighting among, 45, 46–47; in estrus, 45, 47–49, 54; hierarchy among, 45–46, 47; necking, 45–46, 47, 54; homosexuality, 46; horns of, 46–47; sexual behavior, 46–49, 54, 60; Kruger National Park, 47, 50; mating habits, 47–49, 60; Flehmen, 48; courtship, 48–49; gesta-

Giraffe, the (*contd.*)
tion period, 49; birth of, 49–50; as mothers, 50–52; first months of life, 50–53; nosing, 51–52; kindergarten, 52–53; mortality rates, 53, 59; calving interval, 54; growth rate, 54; ants and, 56; weight of, 56; chewing the cud, 56, 57; daily activities, 57; resting habits, 57; sleeping habits, 57; drinking habits, 57–58; voice of, 58; snorts of, 58–59; danger reactions, 59; the lion and, 59, 60, 259; life span, 59–60; Australia, 60; the hyena and, 60; poaching, 60; hunting of, 60–61

Giraffe gazelle, 150

Gnu, brindled, 167; white-bearded, 167; white-tailed, 167

Goddard, John, 62–86

Golden Shadows, Flying Hooves (Schaller), 235

Gombe National Park, the baboon, 196, 218, 228

Goodall, Jane, 196, 303–306, 309–316

Gordon, Marcia, viii

Gordon, Saul, viii

Gosnell, Mariana, viii

Grant's gazelle, 146, 166, 277, 281–282, 294, 296

Great Britain: the giraffe, 40; the eland, 182

Greater kudu, the, 166

Greece, the giraffe, 39

Grevy's zebra (*Equus grevyi*), 89–90, 119–124, 125

Grysbok, the: Cape, 142; Sharpe's, 142

Grzimek, Bernhard, 47, 168–170, 177

Grzimek, Michael, 168

Guenther's dikdik, 142

Guggisberg, C. A. W., 236

Guinea baboon, the, 194, 195

Hall, K. R. L., 195, 196, 198, 214, 218, 227

Hamadryas baboon, the, 194, 194n

Hamilton, Patrick, vii, 287–289, 290–292, 295, 296

Hanks, J., 12

Harding, Robert, 196, 204, 225
Hartebeest, the, 181
Hartmann's zebra (*Equus zebra hartmannae*), 89, 116–119
Hausfater, Glenn, vii, 196, 201–203, 216–217
Hediger, Professor, 30
Hendrichs, Hubert, 12, 131–141
Hendrichs, Ursula, 131–141
Henry, Wesley, 283–284
Hillman, J. C., vii, 182–192, 334
Hillman, Kes, 85–86
Hitchins, P. M., 79, 80
Hluhluwe Game Reserve, the rhinoceros, 80
Holz, William, vii
Hyena, spotted (*Crocuta crocuta*), 232–233, 297–328; the giraffe and, 60; the rhinoceros and, 85; the zebra and, 110, 111, 300, 317, 318, 321–324, 326, 327; the wildebeest and, 179, 300, 317, 318, 321–323, 326, 327; the eland and, 187, 300, 325; the cheetah and, 280, 283; external female genitals, 297; hunting by, 297, 300–301, 320–326; females, 297, 302, 305–307, 310–312; behavior, 297–328; brown (*Hyena brunnea*), 298n; striped (*Hyena vulgaris*), 298n; sounds of, 298, 300, 303, 304, 309–310, 311, 312; feeding habits, 298, 301, 306–307, 314–317, 319, 325–326; sleeping habits, 298, 307; Serengeti National Park, 298–299, 300, 311, 317–328; Ngorongoro Crater, 298–317, 319, 320, 321, 326, 327; Tanzania, 298–328; immobilized by drugs, 299; as a carnivore, 299, 301, 306–307, 317, 319, 325–326; population, 299–300, 319, 326–327; Kalahari Desert, 300; the buffalo and, 300, 325; the lion and, 301, 304, 321, 327; as a scavenger, 301, 320; home range, 301–303; social organization, 301–307; clans of, 301–309; female dominance, 302, 305–307, 312; hierarchy among, 302, 305–307, 312; sense of smell, 302, 320; pasting,

Hyena, spotted (*contd.*)
302–303, 323; as territorial, 302–305; dung, 303; latrines, 303, 323; fighting among, 303–304, 318, 327; males, 304–305, 313; individual identification, 305; weight of, 305; dens of, 306, 307; birth of, 306, 314; litter size, 306, 314; as mothers, 306; 314–317; greeting ceremony among, 307–314; ear postures, 309; tail postures, 309; social sniffing, 309, 323; parallel walk, 310; mating habits, 310–314; courtship, 311–312; female baiting, 311–312; bowing display, 312; in estrus, 313; gestation period, 314; weight at birth, 314; playing habits, 315; vision of, 320; speed of, 321; diet of, 321–322; killing of, 327; life span, 327
Hyena brunnea (brown), 298n
Hyena vulgaris (striped), 298n

Idaho, University of, 290n
Impala, the, 150–160; height of, 150; weight of, 150; as territorial, 150, 152–156; Kenya, 151; South Africa, 151; Rhodesia, 151, 157; Serengeti National Park, 151, 152–160; Tanzania, 151, 152–160; home range, 151, 156, 157–158; harem system, 151–152; mating habits, 151–152; Nairobi National Park, 151–152; males, 151–156; social organization, 151–156; behavior, 151–160; horns of, 152; individual identification, 152; photographing, 152; scars of, 152; females, 152, 153, 159–160; bachelor herds, 152, 154; in estrus, 153; Flehmen, 153; urination, 153; mating habits, 153, 155, 156; sexual behavior, 153, 155, 156, 160; dung, 154; hierarchy among, 154; the proud posture, 154; roaring sounds, 154; sebaceous glands, 154; fighting among, 154, 155; feeding habits, 156, 157, 158, 159, 160; courtship, 157;

Impala, the (*contd.*)
  Tarangire National Park, 157; alarm
  call, 158; chewing the cud, 158; daily
  activities, 158; resting habits, 158;
  drinking habits, 158, 159; antipredator behavior, 158, 160; birth of,
  159; as mothers, 159; sleeping habits,
  159; gestation period, 160; sense of
  smell, 160; the baboon and, 225, 226,
  228; the lion and, 256; the cheetah
  and, 277; the leopard and, 293, 294,
  295
India: the rhinoceros, 62; the cheetah,
  263
Innis, Anne, 41, 46–48, 50, 56, 57, 60
Innocent Killers (van Lawick-Goodall),
  305
International Union for Conservation of
  Nature and Natural Resources
  (IUCN), 38, 85, 265, 282, 285, 331

Jackals, leopards and, 296
Jarman, Mattie, vii, 151–156, 159, 160,
  334
Jarman, Peter, vii, 129, 142, 151–157,
  181, 192, 334
Java, the rhinoceros, 62
Jenkins, Peter, vii, 333

Kabalega Falls National Park, the
  elephant, 19, 23, 35
Kalahari Desert: the lion, 256; the
  hyena, 300
Kaplan, Marion, vii, 333, 335
Keep, M. E., 80
Kenya: the elephant, 12, 16, 20, 27, 28,
  31–38; the giraffe, 40, 42, 54, 55,
  60–61; the rhinoceros, 62–65, 76, 77,
  80–81, 83–86; the zebra, 89, 119–
  124; the dikdik, 131; the gerenuk,
  142–150; the impala, 151; the wildebeest, 167, 168, 170, 172; the
  eland, 191; the baboon, 194, 196,
  203–211, 214–218, 223, 225–227; the
  lion, 238, 242, 243, 244, 248, 250; the
  leopard, 286–289, 290–292, 295, 296;
  wildlife research, 331

Kenya Game Department, 286, 331
Kenya National Parks, 331
Kenyatta, Mzee Jomo, 288
Kifaru — the Black Rhinoceros (MGM–
  TV documentary), 82
King, John, vii, 122, 334
Kirk's dikdik, 131
Klingel, Hans and Ute, vii, 64, 66, 81,
  89–126, 334
Klipspringer, the, 142
Kongoni, the, 256, 277, 279, 301
Kruger National Park: the elephant, 28;
  the giraffe, 47, 50; the baboon, 195;
  the leopard, 290n
Kruuk, Hans, vii, 293, 298–328,
  333–335
Kruuk, Jane, 299, 300
Kudu, the, 143, 184; lesser, 150;
  greater, 166
Kummer, Hans, 194n

Lake Manyara National Park: the
  elephant, 3–12, 15, 16, 20–21, 27,
  28, 30, 32, 36; the rhinoceros, 83; the
  baboon, 228; the lion, 236, 237, 241,
  245, 247, 249, 256, 261; the leopard,
  294
Lamprey, Hugh, 157
Laws, R. M., 2–3, 9, 12, 14, 19–21, 23,
  25, 26, 31, 32
Leakey, Louis and Mary, 63
Lechwe, the, 166
Leopard, the, 233, 284–296; the dikdik
  and, 140, 141; the cheetah and, 280;
  poaching, 284, 285, 287; as solitary,
  284, 290; Serengeti National Park,
  284, 290, 291, 293, 294, 295; Tanzania, 284, 290, 291, 293, 295, 296;
  behavior, 284, 290–296; human population and, 285; hunting of, 285;
  population, 285; hunting by, 285,
  292, 293–294; as a carnivore, 285,
  294–296; feeding habits, 285,
  294–296; domestic dogs and, 285,
  296; Nairobi National Park, 286; immobilized by drugs, 286–288; Kenya,
  286–289, 290–292, 295–296; Tsavo

Leopard, the (*contd.*)
National Park, 286–292, 295–296;
radio-tracking of, 286–290; urination,
290; Kruger National Park, 290n;
South Africa, 290n; fighting among,
290, 291; home range, 290, 291; as
territorial, 290, 292; daily activities,
291; resting habits, 291; roaring by,
291–292; gestation period, 292; greeting ceremony among, 292; litter size,
292; mating habits, 292, 293; as
mothers, 292–293; playing habits,
293; the impala and, 293, 294, 295;
the reedbuck and, 293–294, 295; Lake
Manyara National Park, 294; the baboon and, 294, 295–296; the diet of,
294–296; the lion and, 295; weight of,
295; the jackal and, 296; Ngorongoro
Crater, 296
Leopard, The (Turnbull-Kemp), 285
Leopold, A. Starker, x
Lesser kudu, the, 150
Leuthold, Barbara, vii, viii, 42, 54
Leuthold, Walter, vii, 12, 31, 143–150,
151–152, 161, 166, 334
Leverhulme Foundation, 331
Lincoln Index, 299
Lion, the, 233, 234–262; the giraffe and,
59, 60, 259; the rhinoceros and, 72,
85; the zebra and, 110, 111, 126, 251,
256, 257; the wildebeest and, 111,
251, 256, 259, 262; the eland and,
187, 259; the baboon and, 222; public
opinion of, 234; as a predator, 234,
235, 237, 240, 243, 249–250,
254–262; as a carnivore, 234, 237,
239, 240, 243, 249–250, 254–262;
feeding habits, 234, 237, 239, 248,
249–250, 254–262; hunting of, 234,
244, 255, 261; prides, 235, 237–244,
248–249, 253, 254; social organization, 235, 237–244, 248–249, 253,
254; as territorial, 235, 237–244,
248–249, 253, 254; Serengeti National Park, 235–238, 240–259, 261;
Tanzania, 235–238, 240–259, 261;
Lake Manyara National Park, 236,

Lion, the (*contd.*)
237, 241, 245, 247, 249, 256, 261;
individual identification, 236, 252;
Nairobi National Park, 236–241,
245–247, 249, 256, 262; home range,
237, 241; males, 237, 241, 243–245,
250–251, 253–255; companionships,
237–238, 251–252, 254; females,
237–239, 240, 243–244, 247–253; behavior, 237–262; Kenya, 238, 242,
243, 244, 248, 250; Maasai Mara
Game Reserve, 238, 242, 243, 244,
248, 250; hierarchy among, 238–239;
fighting among, 239, 243, 244, 255;
weight of, 239, 253; sleeping habits,
239, 255, 256; greeting ceremony
among, 239–240; mutual grooming,
240; hunting by, 240, 243, 249–250,
254–262; scent marking, 242; urination, 242; roaring of, 242–243; killing
of cubs, 243, 244; in estrus, 243,
245–246, 247, 248, 253; sexual behavior, 243, 245–246, 247, 248, 253,
254; competition among, 243, 260;
copulation rate, 245; mating habits,
245–246, 253, 254; courtship,
245–246, 254; birth of, 246; gestation
period, 246; weight at birth, 246;
litter size, 246–247; abandonment of
litters, 247–248; as mothers, 247–249;
communal raising of, 248; playing
habits, 249; mortality rates, 250, 255;
immobilized by drugs, 251; nomadic,
251, 252, 253–254; population, 251,
261; Athi-Kapiti plains, 252; mane of,
253–254; antipredator behavior, 254;
resting habits, 255; daily activities,
255–256; poaching, 255, 261; drinking habits, 255–256; the impala and,
256; Kalahari Desert, 256; diet of,
256–257; the buffalo and, 256, 259,
261; as coursers, 257; as stalkers, 257,
258; communal hunting, 257–259; killing process, 260; the cheetah and,
280; the leopard and, 295; the hyena
and, 301, 304, 321, 327
Living Free (Adamson), 234

London Zoo, 31
Long, Carolyn, viii
Long, Jan, viii
Lorenz, Konrad, ix–x

M99, 26, 92, 288
Maasai giraffe, the, 40, 42
Maasailand, the rhinoceros, 83
Maasai Mara Game Reserve: the wildebeest, 167, 168, 170, 172; the lion, 238, 242, 243, 244, 248, 250
McLaughlin, Ronald, vii, 263–282, 335
Makacha, Stephen, 236, 241
Makerere University, 332
Malmi, William, 196, 204
Malpas, Robert, 12
Man-eaters of Tsavo, The (Patterson), 234
Map of East Africa, xii
Marais, Eugene, 195
Matthews, L. Harrison, 311
Max-Planck-Institut, 12, 42, 131, 332
Medical Research Council (U.K.), 332
Mejia, Carlos, vii, 42–54, 57, 58, 59
Meru National Park, the cheetah, 264
Mkomasi Game Reserve, the elephant, 12, 20
Morris, Desmond, 193
Morrison, J. A., 161
Moss, Cynthia, 333, 334
Moss, Martha, viii
Mossman, A. S., 152
Mountain reedbuck, 150
Mountain zebra, *see* Zebra, mountain
Murchison Falls, *see* Kabalega Falls National Park
My Friends, the Baboons (Marais), 195
Myers, Norman, 265, 282, 285

Nairobi, University of, 65, 236, 263, 283, 287, 332
Nairobi National Park: the giraffe, 41, 44, 49, 50–51, 53, 55–56, 59–60, 61; the impala, 151–152; the eland, 182–192; the baboon, 195, 199–201, 221, 223, 224, 226, 227; the lion, 236–241, 245–247, 249–256, 262; area of, 241; the cheetah, 263–283; the leopard, 286

Nash, Leanne Taylor, 196
Natal Parks, the rhinoceros, 79, 80
National Academy of Sciences — National Research Council (U.S.), 332
National Geographic Society, 332
National Institute of Mental Health (U.S.), 332
National Science Foundation (U.S.), 332
Natural Environment Research Council (U.K.), 332
Naylor, Penelope, viii
Netherlands Foundation for the Advancement of Tropical Research (WOTRO), 332
New York Zoological Society, 332
Ngorongoro Conservation Area, 332
Ngorongoro Crater: the rhinoceros, 62–67, 70, 76–81, 86; the zebra, 89, 91, 98, 101, 103, 107, 111, 112, 113; the wildebeest, 111, 167, 168, 171–176, 178, 179, 180; the leopard, 296; the hyena, 298–317, 319, 320, 321, 326, 327
Nthengi, Elui, 287–288
Nubian giraffe, the, 40
Nuffield Foundation, 332
Nuffield Unit of Tropical Animal Ecology, 332
Nyala, the, 166

Olive baboon, the, 194–195, 218
Oribi, the, 150
Oryx, the, 192
Out of Africa (Blixen), 61
Overseas Development Administration of the British Government, 332
Owens, Nick, 196
Oxpecker, the, 79, 80, 82; *askari wa kifaru*, 79

Papio anubis, 194
Papio cynocephalus, 194, 195
Papio hamadryas, 194
Papio papio, 194
Papio ursinus, 194

Parker, I. S. C., 3
Parker, Ian, 9, 23
Parker, L. J., vii, 333, 334
Paterson, J. H., 234
Perry, J. S., 2, 25
Phillip's dikdik, 142
Plains zebra, *see* Zebra, plains
Poole, Joyce, 22
Price, Sandra, viii
Puku, the, 166

Queen Elizabeth National Park, *see* Ruwenzori National Park

Ransom, Timothy W., vii, 196, 334
Reader, John, vii, 333, 334
Red-billed oxpecker, the, 79, 80, 82
Reedbuck, the: Bohor, 150; mountain, 150; southern, 150; the leopard and, 293–294, 295
Rhinoceros, black (*Diceros bicornis*), 62–87, 62n; Asia, 62; India, 62; Java, 62; Serengeti National Park, 62; Sumatra, 62; *Ceratotherium simum*, 62n; *Dicerorhinus sumatrensis*, 62n; *Rhinoceros sondaicus*, 62n; white, 62n; *Rhinoceros unicornis*, 62n, 84; population, 62, 63, 64–65, 76, 86; vision of, 62, 64, 69–70, 71, 82; hunting of, 62, 72, 83; Kenya, 62–65, 76, 77, 80–81, 83–86; Ngorongoro Crater, 62–67, 70, 76–81, 86; Tanzania, 62–67, 70, 76–81, 83; Olduvai Gorge, 63, 64, 66, 76, 78, 80–81; droughts and, 63; Tsavo National Park, 63–65, 76, 77, 80–81, 83–85; photographing, 64; snout wrinkles, 64; horns of, 64, 67, 75, 85–87; individual identification, 64–65; Amboseli Game Reserve, 65; Amboseli National Park, 86; social organization, 65–66; behavior, 65–84; as territorial, 66; males, 66, 68; females, 66, 68, 71–73; home range, 66, 70, 73, 75, 77, 78; feeding habits, 66, 71–72, 77, 78–79, 80–81; as mothers, 66, 71–72; fighting among, 67, 74, 75–76; greeting cere-

Rhinoceros, black (*contd.*)
mony among, 67–68; horning by, 68, 70, 74; mating habits, 68, 73–76; sexual behavior, 68, 73–76; in estrus, 68, 74–76; dung, 68–70, 81–82; sense of smell, 69–70; gestation period, 70; urination, 70, 74; birth of, 71; teats, 71; weight at birth, 71; antipredator behavior, 72; bellowing squeals, 72; mewing sounds, 72; the lion and, 72, 85; growth rate, 73; height of, 73; weight of, 73; courtship, 73–74, 80; Flehmen, 74; rutting periods, 74; aggressiveness of, 75–76; calving interval, 76; hierarchy among, 76; daily activities, 77; resting habits, 77; drinking habits, 77, 78; sleeping habits, 77, 78, 79; mud-wallowing, 77–78; Natal Parks, 79, 80; South Africa, 79, 80; the tick bird and, 79, 80, 82; skin lesions of, 79–80; Hluhluwe Game Reserve, 80; the elephant and, 80–81; the wildebeest and, 81; as coprophagous, 81–82; temperament of, 82–84; Lake Manyara National Park, 83; Maasailand, 83; teeth of, 84, 85; life span, 84–85; mortality rates, 84–85; the hyena and, 85; diseases, 86; poaching, 85–87
Rhinoceros sondaicus, 62n
Rhinoceros unicornis, 62n, 84
Rhodesia: the impala, 151, 152, 157; the eland, 182
Ritchie, A. T. A., 67, 80, 84
Rockefeller University, 332
Roosevelt, Theodore, 169, 181–182
Ross, Audrey, vii, 333
Rothschild's giraffe, 40
Rowell, Thelma, 195–196, 212, 226, 227, 229
Royal antelope, the, 142
Royal Society of London, 332
Rudnai, Judith A., vii, 236, 238–239, 241–253, 261–262, 334
Russell, Hugh, vii–viii
Russia, the eland, 182

Ruwenzori National Park, the elephant, 17

Sale, J. B., 12, 31
Salt's dikdik, 142
Salvadora persica, 149
Sansevieria ehrenbergii, 78
Savannah baboon, the, 194, 196
Schaller, George, vii; lion observations, 222, 235–261; cheetah observations, 264, 265, 270, 272–281; leopard observations, 286, 290, 292–293, 294, 295
Schaller, Kay, 265, 281
Schenkel, Rudolf, 65–71, 74, 77, 83, 151–152
Schenkel-Hullinger, Lotte, 65–71, 74, 77
Schloeth, Robert, 161, 164–166
Scientific American, 201
Selous' zebra, 89
Seneres, Gloria, viii
Seneres, John, viii
Serengeti: A Kingdom of Predators (Schaller), 235
Serengeti National Park: the elephant, 12, 35, 37; the giraffe, 42–54, 57, 58, 59; the rhinoceros, 62; the zebra, 89–115; the dikdik, 131–142; the impala, 151, 152–160; the wildebeest, 167–171, 176–177, 180–181; the baboon, 229; the lion, 235–238, 240–259, 261; the cheetah, 264, 268, 277, 278, 279, 281, 283; the leopard, 284, 290, 291, 293, 294, 295; the hyena, 298–299, 300, 311, 317–328
Serengeti Research Institute, 91, 115, 131, 235, 298, 332
Sharpe's grysbok, 142
Sheldrick, Daphne, 13–14
Sheldrick, David, 13–14
Sikes, S. K., 3
Simba (Guggisberg), 236
Simonetta, A. M., 131
Sitatunga, the, 150
Smith, N. S., 3, 24

Smithsonian Institution, 332
Smuts Memorial Fund, 332
"Social Organization of Antelopes in Relation to their Ecology, The" (Jarman), 129
Somali wild ass, Ethiopia, 90
Somalia: the giraffe, 40; the zebra, 89; the dikdik, 131; the gerenuk, 142; the baboon, 194
South Africa: the giraffe, 40, 41, 50, 60; the rhinoceros, 79, 80; the zebra, 89, 115, 116–118; the impala, 151; the wildebeest, 167; the eland, 182; the baboon, 195, 197; the leopard, 290
South Kabalega Falls National Park, *see* Kabalega Falls National Park
Southern reedbuck, 150
South West Africa: the zebra, 89, 115–116, 118–119; the dikdik, 131
Spinage, C. A., 88–89
Springbuck, the, 166
Stanley Price, Mark, vii
Steinbok, the, 142, 225
Stephanofilaria dinniki, 80
Striped hyena (*Hyena vulgaris*), 298n
Strum, Shirley, vii, 196, 203–211, 225
Sudan, the: the giraffe, 39; the Uganda kob, 160; the baboon, 194, 197
Sumatra, the rhinoceros, 62
Suni, the, 142
Swala twiga (Swahili for "giraffe gazelle"), 150
Swiss National Park, Federal Commission, 332

Talbot, Lee and Martha, 168–170, 177
Tanzania: the elephant, 3–12, 15, 16, 20–21, 27, 28, 30, 32, 36; the giraffe, 42–54, 57, 58, 59; the thinoceros, 62–67, 70, 76–81, 83; the zebra, 89–115; the dikdik, 131–142; the gerenuk, 142; the impala, 151, 152–160; the wildebeest, 167–181; the baboon, 194, 196, 218; the lion, 235–238, 240–259, 261; the cheetah, 264, 265, 268, 277, 278, 279, 281,

Tanzania (*contd.*)
283; the leopard, 284, 290, 291, 293, 294, 295, 296; the hyena, 298–328; wildlife research, 331
Tanzania Game Division, 332
Tanzania National Parks, 332
Tarangire National Park: the impala, 157; the cheetah, 265
Territorial Imperative, The (Ardrey), 193
Territory, defined, 144
Texas A & M University, 332
Theropithecus, 194n
Thomas' kob, *see* Uganda kob
Thomson's gazelle, 114–115, 146, 166, 224–226, 249, 260, 277, 281–282, 293, 311, 317, 321–322, 324, 326
Thornicroft's giraffe, 40
Tick birds, the rhinoceros and, 79, 80, 82
Tiger, Lionel, 193
Tinbergen, Nikolaas, x
Tinley, K. L., 131
Topi, the, 181, 256, 325
Toro Game Reserve, the Uganda kob, 161–166
Trevor, Simon, 10, 17
Tsavo National Park: the elephant, 12, 16, 20, 27, 28, 31–38; the giraffe, 40, 42, 54, 55, 60–61; the rhinoceros, 63–65, 76, 77, 80–81, 83–85; the gerenuk, 142–150; the eland, 191; the leopard, 286–292, 295–296
Tsavo Research Project, 143, 332
Tsessebe, the, 181
Turnbull-Kemp, Peter, 285
Turner, Myles, 293

Uganda: the elephant, 2, 17, 20, 28, 33, 34, 35; the giraffe, 40; the Uganda kob, 160–166; the baboon, 194, 196, 221; wildlife research, 331
Uganda Game Department, 2, 332
Uganda kob, 146, 160–166; Laufschlag, 146, 163, 164, 165; Ethiopia, 160; home range, 160; the Sudan, 160; Zaïre, 160; social organization, 160, 161–162; bachelor herds, 160, 162–

Uganda kob (*contd.*)
163; behavior, 160–166; Uganda, 160–166; population, 161; mating habits, 161, 163–166; sexual behavior, 161, 163–166; as territorial, 161–163, 165, 166; Toro Game Reserve, 161–166; fighting among, 162; courtship, 162, 163; feeding habits, 162, 163; prancing display, 163; urination, 163; Flehmen, 163, 164; in estrus, 163–164, 166; postcoital behavior, 163–166; circling, 164; whistling by, 164; sense of smell, 165
Uganda National Parks, 332

Vaal rhebuck, 150
Van Lawick, Hugo, 111–112, 303, 305

Warthog, the, 226, 279, 325
Washburn, Sherwood, 195, 196, 199–203, 220–221, 224
Waterbuck, the, 166, 301
Weil, Wendy, viii
West Africa, the baboon, 194, 195
West African giraffe, the, 40
Western, David, vii, 55
Western baboon, the, 194
White rhinoceros, 62n
Wild ass, the, 124; Somali, 90
Wild dog, the: the zebra and, 111–112; the dikdik and, 140, 141; the eland and, 187; killing of, 232; the cheetah and, 276, 280
Wildebeest, the, 126, 166–181; the rhinoceros and, 81; Ngorongoro Crater, 111, 167, 168, 171–176, 178, 179, 180; the lion and, 111, 251, 256, 259, 262; feeding habits, 114–115, 167, 170–171, 177, 178, 179; migrations, 114–115, 168–170, 171, 177; horns of, 166–167; black, 167; blue, 167; brindled gnu, 167; height of, 167; South Africa, 167; species of, 167; weight of, 167; white-bearded gnu, 167; white-tailed gnu, 167; Kenya, 167, 168, 170, 172; Maasai Mara Game Reserve, 167, 168, 170, 172; drinking

Wildebeest, the (*contd.*)
habits, 167, 168–170; Serengeti National Park, 167–171, 176–177, 180–181; behavior, 167–180; Tanzania, 167–181; social organization, 168, 171–174; herds, 168–171; birth of, 169, 178–179; bachelor herds, 171, 172, 180; antipredator behavior, 171, 174, 178; population, 171, 180–181, 262; as territorial, 171–177, 180; mating habits, 172–173, 174, 176–179; sexual behavior, 172–173, 174, 176–179; dung, 173; interdigital glands, 173; preorbital glands, 173; urination, 173; stamping grounds, 173–174; static-optic marking, 174; fighting among, 174, 176, 180; challenge ritual, 174–176; Flehmen, 175; chewing the cud, 176; courtship, 176; in estrus, 176, 179; gestation period, 178; in labor, 178; mortality rates, 178; as mothers, 178; droughts and, 179; the hyena and, 179, 300, 317, 318, 321–323, 326, 327
Williams, John, 23
Wing, L. D., 3
Woodford, Michael, 17
World Wildlife Fund (WWF), 85, 87, 265, 282, 285, 332
Wright, Tricia, viii

Year of the Gorilla, The (Schaller), 235
Yellow baboon, the, 194–195
Yellow-billed oxpecker, the, 79, 80, 82

Zaïre: the elephant, 30; the giraffe, 41, 52; the Uganda kob, 160
Zambia: the elephant, 12; the giraffe, 40
Zebra, the, 88–126, 226; interactions of, 88; stripes of, 88, 89–90, 91, 102, 124–126; feeding habits, 88, 113, 114–115, 120; social organization, 88–89, 91, 93–98, 108–112, 117, 125; behavior, 88–89, 91, 93–124; Boehm's, 89; Burchell's, 89; Chapman's, 89; Damara, 89; Ethiopia, 89: Selous', 89; Somalia, 89; subspe-

Zebra, the (*contd.*)
cies, 89; *Equus burchelli*, 89n; *Equus burchelli burchelli*, 89n; *Equus quagga*, 89n; *Equus quagga quagga*, 89n; plains, 89, 89n, 90–115; mountain (*Equus zebra zebra*), 89, 90, 115–119; Ngorongoro Crater, 89, 91, 98, 101, 103, 107, 111, 112, 113; personal bonds among, 89, 93–94, 95, 125; South Africa, 89, 115, 116–118; South West Africa, 89, 115–116, 118–119; Hartmann's (*Equus zebra hartmannae*), 89, 116–119; Kenya, 89, 119–124; species, 89–90; Grevy's (*Equus grevyi*), 89–90, 119–124, 125; Serengeti National Park, 89–115; Tanzania, 89–115; cropping, 91; population, 91, 112, 116, 120, 123; immobilized by drugs, 91–92, 104, 110, 119; individual identification, 91–93, 120; photographing, 92–93, 116, 120; family groups, 93, 94–98, 103–104, 112, 116–117; males, 93–94, 96, 103–107, 112, 116–117; stallion groups, 93–94, 96, 105–107, 112, 116–117; females, 93–100; hierarchy among, 94–95, 117; mutual grooming, 95, 117, 120; sense of smell, 96; herds, 96, 96n; lost member of a group, 96–97; snorts by, 97; wailing call, 97; danger reactions, 97, 110–112; alarm call, 97, 118; contact call, 97, 118; squeals by, 97, 118; birth of, 97–99, 121; in labor, 98; as mothers, 99; feeding habits, 99, 100; resting habits, 99, 114; playing habits, 99–100, 105–106, 118; abduction by, 100–101; fighting among, 100–101, 105–107, 120, 122–123; in estrus, 100–103, 106, 120, 122, 123; mating habits, 100–103, 106, 122–124; sexual behavior, 100–103, 106, 122–124; gestation period, 102; greeting ceremony among, 102, 105, 107–108, 118; urination, 102, 118; dung, 102, 118, 120; courtship, 102–103; foaling interval, 103; Ros-

Zebra, the (*contd.*)
sigkeitsgesicht (estrous face), 103, 108; father and son relationship, 104–105; neck wrestling, 105, 106; circling, 106; antipredator behavior, 108, 112; the lion and, 110, 111, 126, 251, 256, 257; the hyena and, 110, 111, 300, 317, 318, 321–324, 326, 327; the wild dog and, 111–112; home range, 112–113, 120; migrations,

Zebra, the (*contd.*)
112–115, 123, 169; sleeping habits, 113, 114; herds, 113, 121,123; daily activities, 113–114; Etosha Pan Reserve, 116; poaching, 116; digging water holes, 119; as territorial, 120, 122–123; weight of, 122; the cheetah and, 277
Zurich Zoo, 30